D0875234

DEC

HOW THE NAZIS

EPT

TRICKED THE LAST

ION

JEWS OF EUROPE

DEC
EPT
ION

HOW THE NAZIS
TRICKED THE LAST
JEWS OF EUROPE

CHRISTOPHER HALE

The
History
Press

For Alice, Felix and Jacob

First published 2019

The History Press
97 St George's Place, Cheltenham,
Gloucestershire, GL50 3QB
www.thehistorypress.co.uk

British Library Cataloguing in Publication Data.
A catalogue record for this book is available from the British Library.

ISBN 978 0 7509 8817 9

Typesetting and origination by The History Press
Printed and bound in Great Britain by TJ International Ltd.

'Over the years I learned which hooks to use to catch which fish.'

'Hungary really offered the Jews to us like sour beer, and Hungary was the only country where we could not work fast enough.'

'If we had killed 10.3 million Jews, then I would have been satisfied and would say, good, we annihilated an enemy. … I wasn't only issued orders, in this case I'd have been a moron, but I rather anticipated, I was an idealist.'

Adolf Eichmann, Sassen interviews, 1957

Kasztner: I've wondered many times whether, instead of the negotiations, it wouldn't have been better to call on the Zionist youth and rally the people to active resistance to entering the brickyards and the wagons.

SS officer Kurt Becher: You wouldn't have achieved anything this way.

Kasztner: Maybe, but at least we would have kept our honour. Our people went into the wagons like cattle because we trusted in the success of the negotiations and failed to tell them the terrible fate awaiting them.

Kasztner–Becher minutes, 15 July 1944

CONTENTS

A NOTE ON THE 'AUSCHWITZ' CONCENTRATION CAMP

'Auschwitz' is today the most notorious site in the memorial topography of the German genocide. The Second World War is now viewed through the lens of the Holocaust – and the memorialisation of this genocide is seen through the lens of Auschwitz. Historians now recognise that the murderous German onslaught on European Jewry was not initiated inside the KL (concentration camp) system. A huge proportion of the more than 5.5 million Jews murdered under the Nazi regime were killed in ditches, forests, fields and burial pits across Eastern Europe and only later in the specialised death camps such as Treblinka, Sobibór, Chełmno and Bełżec. In the aftermath of the Wannsee Conference convened in February 1942, Himmler issued an order: 'Jews into the KL.' From mid 1942 until the end of the war, the majority of Jews were deported to specialised camps to be worked to death if they were deemed 'fit', or murdered. A second important point is that 'Auschwitz' (the German word for the Polish town of Oświęcim) was an archipelago of camps that had many different functions in the KL system administered by the SS. The SS managers ordered the construction of facilities to carry out mass killings at Auschwitz II, which was originally built in 1941 on the cleared site of a village called Birkenau (Březinka).

Birkenau was not built to exterminate Jews but to incarcerate Soviet prisoners of war; however, in March 1942 the SS began to deport European Jews there and constructed gas chambers and crematoria to incinerate corpses. Inside the Auschwitz camp archipelago, Birkenau was transformed as a specialised extermination facility and entered its most lethal phase in the spring and summer of 1944. Between 1940 and 1945, approximately 1.3 million people were transported to the Auschwitz complex: 1.1 million perished. Nine-tenths of those killed ended up there because of their Jewish origin, and every third victim was a Hungarian citizen. The largest group of victims were Hungarian citizens. I have used 'Auschwitz' to refer to Auschwitz II–Birkenau.

PRELUDE: CAIRO, JUNE 1944

On 14 June 1944, in the early hours of the morning, the twice-weekly train from Haifa in the British-mandated territory of Palestine pulled into the main station at Bab el Hadid, the Iron Gate, in Cairo. As the big, sand-dusted locomotive exhaled a gasping wheeze of steam, a British military police officer emerged from the carriage behind the engine. He was quickly followed by a stocky, middle-aged man who sweated profusely in a crumpled brown suit that had seen better days. He was a Hungarian Jew called Joel Brand and he was to all intents and purposes a prisoner of the British. For a few moments, Brand hesitated, blinking in the harsh light that pierced the station roof and blinded by a torrent of perspiration, before he descended unsteadily to the platform.

Brand's journey to Cairo had begun six weeks earlier and more than 3,000 miles away in Budapest, and he had already endured many tribulations. Months earlier in March, Adolf Hitler had ordered German troops to occupy Hungary. His loyal henchman, Heinrich Himmler, the Chief of the SS, had despatched a 'Special Commando' led by SS Colonel Adolf Eichmann to liquidate the last intact Jewish community in Europe numbering some 800,000 souls. Brand had taken to referring to himself as the 'emissary of the doomed' and many who encountered him feared for his state of mind. His fragility is not difficult to understand for he had an astonishing tale to tell. He had been entrusted, he claimed, with a mission to barter the lives of a million Hungarian Jews for 10,000 military trucks.

This perplexing yet tantalising ransom offer had been put to Brand by Eichmann with the approval, Brand alleged, of Himmler himself.

What would soon become infamous as the 'Blood for Trucks' offer was already being dissected, pondered, disputed and quarrelled about in the corridors of power in Washington, London and Moscow. It would seem that the unprecedented offer to ransom lives was a tiresome inconvenience for the Allied warlords. At every waking moment in his long journey, the weight of these million lives, among them his wife and sons, weighed heavily on Joel Brand's soul. They haunted his nightmares. That day in Cairo, he was not aware that Eichmann and his Hungarian collaborators were herding tens of thousands of Hungarian Jews into cattle cars every day – and despatching them to the Auschwitz camp in occupied Poland. There, in the words of Paul Celan, the sky became their grave.

In Egypt, the summer heat was brutal even at this early hour. The British police officer firmly placed a hand on his prisoner's shoulder and guided him towards the swarming and cacophonous station entrance, lit by low beams of sunlight cutting through swirling clouds of dust stirred up by the great army of hawkers lured to the great station. A British army staff car stood parked, its engine muttering fitfully, in front of the main entrance. The policeman, who had accompanied Brand from Haifa, opened the back door with a tight smile. The elderly Egyptian driver waited impassively, then without so much as a glance behind, steered the car into the churning flow of heavily laden donkeys, camels, carts, trams and motor vehicles that eddied perpetually around the Iron Gate.

In the summer of 1944, Cairo, like Budapest, was an occupied city. Egypt was independent only in a nominal sense. For the British Prime Minister, Winston Churchill, the war with the Axis powers was as much about sustaining the tottering British Empire as defending the British Isles. 'I have not become the King's First Minister in order to preside over the liquidation of the British Empire. I am proud to be a member of that vast commonwealth …' he insisted. Britain still ruled the oceans of the world and the Empire still covered two-fifths of the globe. In Churchill's mind, British national identity was rooted in the multitude of colonies, protectorates and dominions that were either ruled or controlled from the Colonial Office in London and together made up the most far-reaching empire in world history. This was not just an emotional attachment. Britain depended on the peoples and raw materials sucked out of her imperial possessions to sustain a globalised war.

The Second World War was a battle for supremacy between rival empire builders and Nazi Germany's imperial ambitions, inspired by Churchill's cherished Indian Raj, posed a mortal threat to British strategic interests. The Middle East was the strategic hub of the Empire and the Suez Canal the gateway to India. This meant that GHQ Cairo was the epicentre of Britain's imperial struggle. To protect its Egyptian base, the British had for more than half a century ridden roughshod over the nationalist aspirations of countless Egyptians. A British army had seized the canal at the end of the nineteenth century and in 1922, after the collapse of the Ottoman Empire, Egypt was offered a severely restricted kind of independence. As they did in other regions of the Middle East, the British wielded power through a ruling dynasty, often corrupt, which in Egypt was descended from Mohammed Ali who had, at the turn of the nineteenth century, ousted the Turkish Mamluks and made himself master of the Nile Valley. A British consul had boasted that, 'We do not govern Egypt, we only govern the governors of Egypt.' Now King Fuad I, installed and cosseted in the sprawling Qubba Palace, repaid British investment in his despotic rule as the King of Egypt and Sudan, Sovereign of Nubia, Kordofan and Darfur by holding down, for now, simmering discontent and nationalist revolt. Dissent could not be permitted in such a vital imperial hub. The British insisted on what were called 'Reserved Points', which meant that they retained control of the Sudan and, most importantly, the defence of Egypt and the Suez Canal, the gateway to India.

When Italy invaded Ethiopia in 1936, Fuad was forced to seek closer British protection. But, in the aftermath of decades of tension and instability, the Anglo–Egyptian Treaty, signed that year, gave Egypt a status that bore a resemblance to sovereignty. The British High Commissioner, Sir Miles Lampson, was demoted to ambassador and Egypt joined the League of Nations. But in return, the British forced the Egyptian government to accept the stationing of 10,000 British troops to defend the Suez Canal. The treaty wrought other, unintended changes that would have far-reaching consequences. The Royal Military Academy, which had been dominated by Egypt's pampered young elites, threw open its doors to a broader section of this riven society. Among the new intake were Gamal Abdel Nasser and Anwar Sadat – bright, ambitious young men from poor families who would never have enjoyed such opportunities before 1936. That same year, as Nasser and Sadat took their first tentative steps out of poverty towards the road to power, King Fuad died and was succeeded by his corpulent playboy son Farouk, who secretly reached out to Hitler through Egypt's pro-Nazi consul in Istanbul and Haj Amin al-Husseini, the Grand Mufti of Jerusalem who had fled the Middle East to find refuge in Berlin.[1]

As Joel Brand was driven through the grand boulevards that led to the magnificent medieval citadel, the symbol of British power in Egypt, he was startled by subtle echoes of Budapest, the city he had left behind and to which he would never return, and which centuries before had been conquered by an Ottoman army. To be sure, the streets were crammed with a multitude of turbans and tarbushes that bobbed vigorously behind creaking carts and wheezing trucks loaded high with vegetables and raw hunks of fly-crusted meat. Through the half-open window, he was taken aback by Cairo's unique and inescapable odour that churned together acrid spices with exhaust fumes, manure, perfume and the sweat of starved and beaten cab horses and their whip-happy masters. Imperious Europeans in gleaming motor cars waged war with sputtering motorbikes, camels and mangy dogs. Buses and trams, overflowing with their human freight, rattled past festooned with blue beads to ward off the evil eye. Although the armies of the Axis powers had at last been driven out of North Africa, the British could not be avoided. Men and women in sweat-soaked uniforms rushed from office to café or bar, conveyed in a honking armada of petulantly driven British staff cars and military trucks. They turned their eyes from the multitudes of the sick, the misshapen and the poor who occupied their own pavement empires. A young sapper wrote in his diary: 'Beggars, in filthy robes, accosted all and sundry, wailing eternally for "Baksheesh, effendi" – for the love of Allah!' The British novelist Lawrence Durrell was a British military attaché in wartime Cairo: he came to hate the city. Durrell complained about the miasma of dirt, dust and flies, and the unavoidable sight of grinding poverty. Through his eyes, Egypt was a place of 'cripples, deformities, ophthalmia, goitre, amputations, lice, fleas … horses cut in half by careless drivers … obscene dead black men …'

This was the underworld of callous British imperialism that so deeply offended the American businessman Wendell C. Wilkie when he arrived in Cairo as President Franklin Roosevelt's emissary. Wilkie soon realised that Lampson, the loud, 6ft 5in British Ambassador, 'for all practical purposes' ruled Egypt. In the sanctimonious way of American critics of empire, Wilkie was disgusted by the British elites who 'exhibited Rudyard Kipling, untainted even with the liberalism of Cecil Rhodes. [sic] Those, executing policies made in London, had no idea that the world was changing …'[2] Just as Stain craved possession of Eastern Europe freed from Nazi rule, Roosevelt was intent on calling time on the British Empire.

Like Budapest, Cairo was a cosmopolitan city, a human patchwork of Copts, Muslims and Jews, who all had deep roots in the city's ancient fabric, as well as French, Italian and Greek expatriates. In every nook and cranny, the British bristled in their stiff uniforms or tumbled loud and red-faced out of backstreet bars, but in the city's tearooms and cafés, French was still the medium of gossip. French fashion and furniture were ubiquitous in the city's most affluent homes. While the Germans had swept through Jewish communities in a bloody swathe across Europe, in Cairo, the grand Jewish families – the 'Haute Juiverie' like the Rolos, the Hararis and the Menasces – still proudly played their parts as the financiers of Egypt, rubbing shoulders with Copt and Greek grandees at the Gezira Sporting Club. In the wealthy heart of Cairo, imposing buildings in Viennese, Italian, art nouveau and neo-Arab styles proclaimed the paradoxical pride of a city as pluralistic as Budapest that, in 1944, remained firmly under the British thumb. It had been a close-run affair.

The loss of Tobruk to the German Panzerarmee Afrika in June 1942 had been a stunning blow. The German and Italian forces under Field Marshall Erwin Rommel had pushed deep into Egypt, scattering the British 8th Army in a confused rout. In the wake of the Panzerarmee came a 'Special Unit' or Einsatzgruppe tasked to destroy the ancient Jewish communities of North Africa. At least 23,000 British soldiers deserted and hid out in the Delta; in Britain, national morale plummeted. At the end of this catastrophic month, Rommel's exhausted troops dug in close to El Alamein in the Qattara Depression, a mere 60 miles from Alexandria. The Empire itself was in peril. But it was in the bleak terrain of the Western Desert that the tide of war turned, at last, against the Axis. In October 1942, by means of a ruse masterminded by camouflage expert Jasper Maskelyne, the 8th Army massed its tanks and artillery, and on the evening of 23 October 1,000 British guns opened fire, smashing the German lines. Rommel was forced to fall back and on 12 November Tobruk was retaken. Church bells rang out all over Britain.

So it was that Joel Brand was brought to a city that clung to the swagger of imperial confidence. GHQ Cairo coordinated supplies and operations across the region. Hidden away inside the Rustum Buildings, a humdrum block of flats known to taxi drivers as 'The Secret Building', was the headquarters of the Special Operations Executive (SOE), which deployed a smokescreen of names such as MOI (SP), Force 133 or just 'The Firm' to conceal its identity. It was from inside the Rustum Buildings that SOE operatives Basil Davidson and Captain William Deakin launched missions to back Colonel Draža Mihailović's Cetnik resistance forces fighting the Germans in the Balkans. Mihailović was a devout royalist who spent as much time fighting a rival partisan army led by a Communist called Josip Broz, known as Tito, as the Germans. From another office, intelligence officer James Klugmann covertly channelled funds away from the quarrelsome Cetnik forces to Tito's partisans. Klugmann had won a Double First in Modern Languages at Cambridge and was an intimate friend of the yet to be exposed 'Cambridge Spies' Guy Burgess and Donald Maclean. Klugman made no secret of his beliefs and had met Mao Zedong in China. Despite his open commitment to the Communist cause, he was trusted by his SOE commanders and proved himself in all matters to do with the Balkans. Just months before Brand's arrival as a prisoner in Cairo, the SOE had despatched the 'Jewish Parachutists', including the Hungarian Zionist Hannah Szenes, who had been trained in mandate Palestine, to Yugoslavia. Brand knew little about the mission of the 'Parachutists' to occupied Hungary. But his friend and colleague, Rudolf Kasztner, who had remained in Budapest, would have a fateful encounter with these doomed young men and women.

The SOE was not the only intelligence organisation in Cairo. Brand was the prisoner of SIME, Security Intelligence in the Middle East. According to intelligence expert Roger Arditti, SIME was established in 1939 as a coordinating body, an inter-service organism, as he calls it, that would counter Axis penetration of the Middle East.[3] The role of SIME was to harmonise the work of MI5, responsible for security within the Empire, and MI6, which collected intelligence in foreign territories. At a meeting in Cairo in March 1942, Brigadier R.G. Maunsell and other SIME agents discussed how they could acquire and exploit decoded top secret communications sent by agents of German military intelligence, the Abwehr. As I will show, this goes a long way towards explaining why it was that SIME agents took charge of Brand, who had surprising connections with treacherous Abwehr agents in Budapest and Istanbul.

Brand was, it would seem, a rather privileged prisoner of the British intelligence service. In his bitter account of his mission he reveals that on arrival inside the sprawling British military base 'a friendly corporal led me to my cell, which in fact was a large and well-furnished room. He left the door open, but always remained near at hand. If someone passed by, he would temporarily lock me in …'[4] He was, he admits,

> treated as a person of importance. The food was excellent, and an Arab waiter laid the table with great attention and asked me what wine I would care to drink. He served me the choicest of foods, and far more than I was able to eat … No one entered the room without first knocking on the door.

Soon after his arrival in Cairo, Brand discovered that a second Hungarian was locked up in a neighbouring cell. This was Samu Springmann, a Budapest jeweller who, like Brand, had been involved with raising funds to rescue Jews in Europe. Springmann had spent time in Istanbul developing connections with the little group of Zionists who represented the Jewish Agency in Turkey but had been expelled by the Turkish authorities. He had travelled to Aleppo hoping to enter Palestine, but he had been arrested by British agents and brought to Cairo six weeks before Brand.

There was a third Hungarian incarcerated by British intelligence in Cairo and in much less salubrious conditions. His name was György or Andor ('Bandi') Grosz. Brand described him as a 'boastful, scheming fellow': 'ein Grosser Bluffer'. When Brand was taken to meet Grosz in his cell, he recalled 'he looked ill and weak, and I saw at once that he had been treated very differently from me … He was kept in an ordinary cell, poorly furnished and without a chair. He lay on a wooden pallet. I was almost ashamed …' Both men were interrogated separately by Lieutenant W.B. Savigny – a secret service officer who would later write German textbooks for secondary schools. Brand's mission had already provoked a flurry of memoranda between London and Washington, fretting about how to deal with the German ransom offer. Savigny did not inform Brand that days before his arrival in Cairo, the British Foreign Secretary Sir Anthony Eden had insisted to his American counterparts in Washington that he could not permit negotiations of any kind with the Germans. What becomes evident in the lengthy interrogation files and reports in the UK National Archives is that SIME now saw both Brand and his Hungarian companions not as 'emissaries' but sources of intelligence about the baffling interactions between rival Nazi organisations and the confusing circus of personalities involved.

In Cairo, Brand was not too proud to spurn the lavish hospitality offered by his British hosts. At a cocktail party in the garden of an institution Brand calls the British–Egyptian Club, by which he almost certainly means the Gezira Club, he claimed that he was introduced to Lord Moyne, Walter Guinness, the British Minister of State in Cairo and a close friend of the British Prime Minister. According to Brand, Lord Moyne enquired: 'Did you take this offer of Eichmann's really seriously?'

'Absolutely seriously,' replied Brand. 'I am completely convinced the mass murders will be stopped if Eichmann's offer is accepted.'

Brand's account continues:

Moyne: How many people will be in the advance party?
Brand: I've already told you, a hundred thousand people.
Moyne: And how many people will there be altogether?
Brand: Eichmann spoke of a million.
Moyne: What on earth are you thinking of Mr Brand? What do I do with those million Jews? Where shall I put them?

Brand's story of his encounter with Moyne at the Gezira Club is not corroborated in any other source, but such derogatory remarks may have had fatal consequences. For radical Zionists, Lord Moyne became the embodiment of callous British officialdom that refused to allow Jews to take refuge in Palestine and he paid with his life. On 6 November 1944, Eliyahu Bet-Zuri and Eliyahu Hakim, members of the Jewish terrorist group Lehi, known as the 'Stern Gang', ambushed Moyne and his driver Lance Corporal Arthur Fuller, and shot both men. Fuller bled out instantly; Moyne was rushed to hospital but died of massive injuries that evening. The decision to assassinate Moyne had been taken by Lehi leaders Israel Eldad and the future Prime Minister, Yitzhak Shamir. In an interview, decades later with the *Times of Israel* in 2012, Shamir was unrepentant:

Certainly, we had known about his hostile attitude towards Zionism, towards the idea of ingathering of the Jewish people here. He was against any Jewish Aliyah, any Jewish immigration. He didn't believe that there exists such a thing like a Jewish nation, or a Jewish people … and therefore, we decided to make this operation.[5]

For decades after Brand's flight from Budapest and incarceration in a British military prison, the story of Blood for Trucks and the stories told by this embittered 'emissary of the doomed' gathered ever deeper layers of myth. This encrustation has made it almost impossible to see through the dense patina shrouding the records of the perplexing encounters that took place between Hungarian Zionists, German SS officers, British colonial mandarins and a supporting cast of secret agents and mendacious double dealers in 1944. It is the ambition of this book to expose the remarkable historical narrative that lies beneath the murky waters of myth.

1

'BLUT GEGEN WAREN': A PUZZLE WRAPPED IN AN ENIGMA

It is one of the most notorious events of the Second World War – and yet one of the most mysterious. Seventy-five years ago, on 19 May 1944, an SS officer called Hermann Krumey drove two Hungarians from Budapest to an airport close to Vienna. Two months earlier, Hitler had ordered troops to occupy Hungary, which had been Nazi Germany's military ally since the invasion of the Soviet Union, to forestall any attempt by its government to abandon the Axis alliance. In the wake of the army divisions came a *Sonderkommando* led by SS Colonel Adolf Eichmann. His task was to liquidate the last surviving Jewish community in Nazi-occupied Europe. At the airport, the two men boarded a German aircraft and were flown to Istanbul in neutral Turkey. The names of the two men were Joel Brand and Andor 'Bandi' Grosz. The leaders of the Allied governments in London, Washington and Moscow soon discovered that Brand had been sent with an extraordinary mission. In a series of meetings with Eichmann and other SS officers, he had been offered the chance to barter Jewish lives for military trucks and other supplies.

Not long after they were flown out of Hungary to Istanbul, Brand and Grosz were arrested by British police in Aleppo and brought to Cairo for lengthy interrogations. At the highest levels of government in Washington and London, the offer to barter hundreds of thousands of Jewish lives provoked incredulity, confusion and dismay. On the eve of D-Day, the Allied invasion of Europe, the release of hundreds of thousands of Jewish refugees was unthinkable. How could they be cared for? It was assumed that many tens of thousands of Jews would try to reach the British mandate of Palestine. For the British such an influx was anathema. The mandate was already a tinderbox. In short, it was rapidly concluded that there could be no negotiations. When the story of the ransom offer was leaked, British and American newspapers denounced a German trick. Brand and his mysterious companion stayed under lock and key in Cairo. For the rest of his life, Brand blamed the British for abandoning the Jews of Hungary to a terrible fate.

There was very good reason to doubt the good faith of the ransom offer. Throughout the summer of 1944, between mid May and early July, Eichmann and his Hungarian collaborators deported hundreds of thousands of Jews from the Hungarian countryside to Auschwitz in occupied Poland. Three-quarters of the deported Jews perished in a paroxysm of slaughter.

As this tragedy unfolded, another remarkable story was unfolding in Budapest. Brand was a member of a Zionist Rescue Committee known as the 'Va'adat ha-Ezra ve-ha-Hatzala e-Budapest' or simply – the Va'ada. The most prominent member of the committee was a former journalist called Rezső, or Rudolf Kasztner. When Brand had been chosen to travel to Istanbul with the SS ransom offer, Kasztner had remained in Budapest and continued negotiating with Eichmann and another SS officer, Kurt Becher. Through Kasztner's efforts, the Germans permitted, in exchange for substantial payments, some 1,700 Hungarian Jews, most of them from Kasztner's home town of Kolozsvár, now the Romanian city of Cluj-Napoca, to leave Hungary on a special train. After a terrifying journey, the Germans held the Hungarians hostage for some months in a special compound known as the 'Ungarnlager' (Hungarian camp) at the Bergen-Belsen concentration camp. Between 18 August and December 1944, the majority of the passengers on the train arrived in the Swiss village of Caux. And yet the story of 'Kasztner's Train' remains mired in toxic argument to this day. A recent book is called *Kasztner's Crime*. Was the Jew who negotiated with Eichmann a *criminal*?

When Kasztner settled in Tel Aviv after the war, many Hungarian survivors of the Holocaust who had come to live in the new state were dismayed by his assiduously cultivated reputation as a rescuer of Jews and his increasingly cosy relations with Mapai, the ruling political party led by David Ben-Gurion. Many survivors alleged that Kasztner had failed to warn Hungarian Jews of what he knew about German plans for mass murder. For the leaders of Mapai, it was imperative to protect Kasztner's reputation and in 1953 the Attorney General sued one of his accusers for libel. The 'Kasztner Trial' had calamitous consequences. For many Israelis, he was no longer a rescuer of Jews but a despised collaborator. At the conclusion of the trial, the judge made biting use of a phrase from the Roman poet Virgil:

> *timeo Danaos et dona ferentes* (I fear the Greeks even when they bring gifts). By accepting this present [the rescue train] Kasztner had sold his soul to the devil ... The success of the rescue agreement depended until the last minute on the Nazi goodwill, and the last minute didn't arrive until long after the end of the extermination of the Jews in the provincial towns.

Just after midnight on 4 March 1957, a squad of right-wing Zionists waited for Kasztner to return to his apartment in Tel Aviv. He would not live to see his German tormentor Adolf Eichmann kidnapped by Mossad agents and brought to stand trial in Jerusalem. Even today, the embers of Kasztner's trial still smoulder.

These are the bare bones of the narrative this book will unfold. Telling it again requires some justification. The Blood for Trucks deal has been recounted, often at length, in most accounts of the Holocaust. This obsessive retelling was started by Brand himself, who published books about his story and confronted the shabby and diminished Eichmann across the Jerusalem courtroom. Brand was a man consumed by bitterness who believed until the end of his life that his mission had been coldheartedly betrayed by both the British and the wartime Zionist establishment. He could never forgive. After Brand's early death in 1964, many historians have reiterated and amplified Brand's recriminations. Just as the Allies refused to bomb the railway lines to Auschwitz, it is argued that they rebuffed the offer to ransom the lives of a million Hungarian Jews.

I first heard about the story from an old university friend who had fled Britain to become an American citizen and had cultivated some contempt for the land of his birth. Some years ago, he wrote to me about Joel Brand and the dastardly way his mission had been sabotaged. He quoted the notorious and perhaps apocryphal words of Lord Moyne (Walter Guinness), the British Minister of State in the Middle East: 'What can I do with a million Jews?'

It was a troubling story. Had the Allies betrayed the Jews of Hungary? Might the chronicle of the Holocaust have turned out differently if British and American officials acted with greater moral resolve? As I sifted through the many retellings of Brand's mission and its aftermaths, I became ever more puzzled. To begin with, Eichmann was insistent that the 'ten thousand trucks' would be deployed only on the Eastern Front against the Soviet Army. This was surely an outlandish condition. In the spring of 1944, Franklin Roosevelt and Winston Churchill feared putting at risk their bond with Joseph Stalin, and indeed competed obsequiously for the Russian dictator's favours. Blood for Trucks seemed to be more provocation than deal. I was surprised to discover that Eichmann had repeatedly insisted to Brand and the Rescue Committee that he could not permit any Jews to travel to Palestine. He explained that Hitler did not wish to offend Arab opinion. This implied that if the ransom offer was serious and the German conditions were met, hundreds of thousands of Hungarian Jews would need to be sent towards the West. Since an Allied invasion of Europe was expected at any moment, this was simply not a convincing proposal. The most chilling realisation was that at the very moment Brand set off for Istanbul, Eichmann and his Hungarian allies had already begun to deport Hungarian Jews to Auschwitz at a rate of up to 12,000 people a day. For weeks, Eichmann had been working closely with his friend, the camp commandant Rudolf Höß, to prepare for the arrival of daily transports from Hungary and the liquidation of anyone not deemed fit to work. Camp guards alluded to enjoying 'Hungarian salami' when the transports arrived. It would seem that Eichmann acted in the very worst of bad faith. What then was the purpose of his offer to trade lives?

I began to suspect that the story of Blood for Trucks, which has so often been told as a callous refusal to barter and save lives, concealed a very different narrative. But what was it? I was reminded of the legal axiom: *cui bono*? Who gains? I discovered that the SS officers who came to Budapest in the spring of 1944 had a very great deal to gain from playing a cynical and deadly game of deception and bluff. The German onslaught on European Jews was motivated not only by racial fanaticism but by a lust for profit. During the war, the SS had grown into a bloated and avaricious business empire. As he preached a message of German decency and probity, Himmler hatched a campaign of plunder that was itself founded on the mythologies that fuelled the mass killings of European Jews under German rule. In Nazi ideology, Jews were either murderous Bolsheviks or mercantile robber barons. It was the moral duty of the Nazi state to reclaim the vast and uncounted riches of the global Jewish clans. It is a newsroom cliché to urge reporters to 'follow the money' but mercenary plunder on a vast scale was integral to the Nazi Final Solution. Herding Jews into ghettoes and then deporting the majority to camps for labour or death was inextricably bound up with a systematic pilfering of assets. Inside the German camps, a finely tuned and ruthless apparatus of avaricious pillage harvested every remaining possession of the dead from the clothes on their backs to the gold in their speechless mouths. Mass murder took place hand-in-hand with the most ruthless profiteering. I began to suspect that it was these mercenary plans and desires that drove the deceitful actions of the SS men who enticed Brand and Kasztner with offers of rescue and salvation.

In the chapters that follow, I will try to follow the money to reveal the true story of the Blood for Trucks ransom offer. But, invariably, human action has many and contradictory motivations. Over time, these intents shift and alter in a kind of fractal psychic topology. When Eichmann was dispatched to Hungary in March 1945, he and his superiors were preoccupied by two strategic setbacks that had taken place the year before. On 19 April 1943, the eve of the Jewish Passover, German forces began the final liquidation of the Jewish ghetto in Warsaw. They were taken by surprise when a Jewish resistance group known as ZOB (Zydowska Organizacia Bojowa) fought back – with a fierce and passionate resolve. It took heavily armed SS forces, led by SS-Gruppenführer Jürgen Stroop, close to a month to crush the Jewish uprising. Even as Stroop set charges to destroy the Great Synagogue and rejoiced in the destruction of the ghetto, other Germans voiced disquiet. The liquidation had proved 'very difficult' reported one official: 'One noticed that armed Jewish women fought to the last …' Then in September, Hitler insisted that the semi-autonomous government of Denmark, occupied in 1940, 'solve its Jewish problem' and begin deporting Danish Jews. As I will explain in detail in a later chapter, the German plans were unexpectedly thwarted. Some 7,000 Jews were ferried to safety in neutral Sweden by Danish rescuers. The majority of Danish Jews survived the war. For the German master planners of the Final Solution, the Jewish ghetto revolt followed by the spectacular rescue of Danish Jews were troubling setbacks. Despatched to Budapest in the spring of 1944, Eichmann understood that his reputation as the master planner of deportation could not survive any more mishaps.

There is another puzzle. Why was Brand accompanied by 'Bandi' Grosz? The decision to send a second emissary to Istanbul was made by Eichmann or someone else on the German side and Brand, it seems, was taken by surprise. He was bewildered by the presence of someone he knew well both as unscrupulous smuggler and a devious informant who played off German and Allied intelligence agencies. Like Brand, Grosz ended up in a British military prison in Cairo, where he soon confounded his interrogators. He insisted that he, not Joel Brand, had been entrusted with the 'real mission'. The ransom plan, he claimed, was a smokescreen. According to Grosz, the SS Chief himself, Heinrich Himmler, had grasped that Germany could no longer win the war and was 'putting out feelers' to the British and Americans behind Hitler's back. The strategic purpose of the Brand/Grosz mission was not to end the war but to rupture the western alliance with the Soviets. A number of historians continue to argue that this was indeed Himmler's masterplan – and accept that 'the architect of the Final Solution' was willing as early as the summer of 1944 to spare hundreds of thousands of Jewish lives as a means to acquire military supplies and/or a strategic lever to split the Allies. For historians of the Second World War and the Holocaust this argument has very significant implications. Might the lethal momentum of the Final Solution have taken a different course in the final years of the war? How convincing, then, is the evidence?

In this book I hope to prove that the evidence for Himmler's ransom masterplan is flimsy and circumstantial. It is, in my view, a chimera. To begin with, Himmler was intent on mass murder until the very end of the war and remained the stubbornly loyal perpetrator of Hitler's racial obsessions 'to the final hour'. Neither Himmler nor his henchmen would have made any serious decision to deviate from that course. That is one aspect of my case. Another is that much of the evidence cited to explain Himmler's involvement in the Blood for Trucks mission is based on claims made by the enigmatic 'Bandi' Grosz when he was arrested by British intelligence agents. The records of these marathon interrogations can be found in the British National Archives – and close reading of these documents casts serious doubt on Grosz's credibility and motivations. The records show that Grosz was deeply involved with a network of spies, informers and couriers known after the code name of its founder as Dogwood. 'Dogwood' was a Czech Jew called Alfred Schwarz who had lived for many years in Istanbul. All his agents were named after flowers. Grosz was 'Trillium'.

During the Second World War, Turkey was a neutral power and the streets, cafés and hotel rooms of her second city resembled the cells in a noisy hive of conspiracies and secrets. Istanbul was a refuge for a number of shady Germans who occupied their time fantasising about plots to depose or assassinate the upstart corporal Adolf Hitler. The American OSS, the fledgling precursor to the CIA, eagerly forged links with 'Dogwood' and his agents such as 'Trillium', who boasted about running valuable 'assets' in Eastern European cities including Budapest. Schwarz also cultivated representatives of the Jewish Agency based in Istanbul, who used Dogwood to smuggle messages and money to Jewish rescuers inside German-occupied Europe. Until it was too late, the OSS and the Zionists stubbornly refused to take seriously a stream of evidence that the Dogwood network had been compromised of German and Hungarian intelligence agents. By the spring of 1944, Dogwood was a poisoned snare, the leakiest network in the history of wartime intelligence. The story of the 'Brand Mission' was closely woven together with the downfall of Dogwood.

The story of Blood for Trucks cast a long shadow across the tumultuous decades that followed the end of the war and the foundation of the state of Israel. Brand's desperate journey was undertaken inside a hall of shattered mirrors that has hidden its secret purpose to this day. After the violent birth of the new state of Israel, Brand struggled to make a living in his new homeland. He was embittered and forgotten. Brand appeared, reluctantly, as witness for the defence at the trial that shamed his old friend Rudolf Kasztner and devoted his time to writing a memoir about his wartime mission to save the Jews of Hungary. Then, on 20 May 1960, a team of Mossad agents abducted Adolf Eichmann as he returned to his shabby family home in Buenos Aires, Argentina. He was secretly flown, disguised in an air steward's uniform, to Israel to stand trial. Gideon Hausner, the Attorney General, signed a bill of indictment against Eichmann on fifteen counts, including crimes against the Jewish people and crimes against humanity. Now the arrogant SS man who had managed the destruction of so many lives stood before the world inside a bulletproof glass booth: an unkempt symbol, it was said, of the 'banality of evil'. It was in that courtroom that Joel Brand confronted Eichmann once again.

Finally, a few comments on the form of this book.

It is conventional, even obligatory, to shape non-fiction with the story of a single character, or protagonist. It became clear that this approach was neither feasible nor appropriate. The truth about the rescue negotiations in

Hungary in 1944, if it was possible to recover at all, could not be excavated from the experience of a single life. What follows is not 'the story of Joel Brand'. There are few heroes in this tale. It was necessary to probe events from multiple points of view. We must enter and take account of a political landscape in which power was distributed with extreme inequality. In German-occupied Europe, the exercise of power by a tyrannical state committed to violence compromised every individual drawn into its corrosive web. The narrative of this book must, then, find its way through this tangled and continuously evolving terrain. This Nazi state extinguished the lives of millions and destroyed the moral footing of those men and women who carried out its bidding. Hitler's malevolent exploitation of the loyalty of satraps like Himmler generated a treacherous landscape of competitive struggle. The violence of the state was mirrored by aggressive pursuit of power and favour among its elite. At the lower levels of the Nazi state, subalterns such as Eichmann and his SS colleagues engaged in a struggle for survival that stripped away the values they purported to defend. There is no single individual who, alone, illuminates such a world of power.

It became clear too that I could not hope to understand the tragic fate of hundreds of thousands of Hungarian Jews by confining the narrative to a single year, or even the entire Second World War. The experience of Hungarian Jewry was forged by the experience of Jews as citizens of the Austro-Hungarian Empire and its traumatic dissolution at the end of the First World War. Before 1914, the Emperor's Hungarian realms wove a network of alliances that connected, uneasily to be sure, Jews and Magyars. It was Jewish entrepreneurs, lawyers, doctors, writers and journalists and their gentile partners who powered the advent of a Hungarian modernity before the cataclysm of the Great War.

After 1918, the evisceration of Austro-Hungary by the Allied powers tore open festering wounds between the peoples of the defunct empire. The collapse of the German Empire infected the violent fantasies of Adolf Hitler and his followers with the same kind of poison. They believed that Imperial Germany had been 'stabbed in the back' on the threshold of victory by a conspiratorial cadre of disloyal Jewish profiteers and traitors. The Russian Revolution, they believed, had spawned a hostile new state that threatened the existential survival of the West. Other new nation states that sprang up in the aftermath of the Great War shared this detestation and terror of their Jewish minorities. Two decades later, the poison of ethnic hatred would infest the strategic bonds between Hitler's Germany State and the leaders of Romania and Hungary. As the fugitive Eichmann boasted: 'Hungary was the only country where we could not work fast enough.'

The Jewish philosopher Walter Benjamin did not live to experience the horror of Germany's war. But he foresaw what would take place:

This is how one pictures the angel of history. His face is turned toward the past. Where we perceive a chain of events, he sees one single catastrophe which keeps piling wreckage upon wreckage and hurls it in front of his feet. The angel would like to stay, awaken the dead, and make whole what has been smashed. But a storm is blowing from Paradise; it has got caught in his wings with such violence that the angel can no longer close them. The storm irresistibly propels him into the future to which his back is turned, while the pile of debris before him grows skyward …

2

GENEVA, APRIL 1945

The war was over. Adolf Hitler was dead. A petty, vindictive and self-pitying wreck of a man, he had ended his life in a foul-smelling concrete bunker beneath the ruined city of Berlin. Many millions of soldiers and civilians had died in a titanic struggle that the German Führer avowed would be a 'War of Annihilation' fought to protect the German people from the menace of Bolshevism and its supposedly Jewish leaders. It was a promise that he and his fanatical apparatchiks had amply fulfilled. Among the dead were more than 5.5 million European Jews who had been torn from their homes and murdered in the killing fields and camps that formed an archipelago of mass murder across the war-ravaged regions of Eastern Europe and the Soviet Union. Europe had been turned into a vast cemetery across which multitudes of desperate refugees stumbled towards uncertain destinations. Great cities as well as lives lay in ruins. In Hungary, Budapest was a smoking ruin of ash-blackened stone and brick that had been shattered by the monstrous struggle between the Soviet Army and the city's German occupiers and Hungarian collaborators. In the ghettoes of Pest, Jews who had somehow survived the Russian bombardment and murderous gangs of Hungarian fascists known as the Arrow Cross, struggled to identify the nameless dead who were piled high in the streets, squares and even the synagogues of the city. The freezing waters of the Danube were freighted with corpses.

In pristine Geneva, Rudolf Kasztner had taken refuge in the modest 'Sergei' pension with his wife Elizabeth (Bodiya).[1] According to his physician Max Weisberg, Kasztner was sick and severely depressed. He was, Weisberg diagnosed, a man who had been abruptly deprived of power.

There were no more meetings with the powerful; no more blustering telephone calls to colleagues. Kasztner was fixated with bolstering his reputation as a heroic rescuer of Jews on the one hand and fending off slurs about his compromising familiarity with certain German SS officers on the other. In their cramped room in the pension, he quarrelled frequently with Elizabeth. In more ebullient moods, Kasztner boasted of his exploits. By then, close to 1,700 Hungarian Jews who had been allowed to purchase their passages out of Hungary on the 'Kasztner Train' had at last reached Switzerland. For these privileged survivors, Kasztner was without any doubt a hero: he had saved their lives. Their praise was not enough. When he heard praise for other Jews who had organised rescue efforts, Kasztner often flew into jealous rages. 'The truth is that *we* organised that transport ...' he insisted again and again. He grumbled about being 'dispossessed of his work and sacrifice'.

Kasztner's insistence on tribute troubled even some of his most loyal friends. 'I found his behaviour repulsive ...' recalled one. Cooped up in his room, Kasztner poured out a stream of letters and telegrams lauding his exploits and denouncing a whispering campaign that, in his mind, was poisoning his reputation. Already, just months after the end of the war, he knew that a bitter thread of acrimony and innuendo was being woven around a single word: negotiations. A schism was beginning to open between the posthumous reputations of the heroic Jews who had led the Warsaw ghetto uprising in 1943 or fought with partisans and the compromised leaders of the Jewish Councils such as Chaim Rumkowski, who had, it was said, done the bidding of the Germans. Where did Kasztner fit? In the shattered Jewish world in 1945, opinion was divided. Moshe Schweiger, a respected member of a refugee support organisation, applauded Kasztner for extracting concessions from 'Nazi beasts' despite his own revulsion. The problem was that many others suspected that in Kasztner's case, such negotiations had shaded into fraternisation. It was rumoured that Kasztner had become inappropriately close to an SS officer called Kurt Becher. It was even implied that Kasztner and Becher had jointly profited from the destruction of Hungarian Jewry. For reasons that even today remain hard to explain, Kasztner went out of his way to exculpate Becher. In words that would, years later, condemn him to death by an assassin's bullets, Kasztner had boasted: 'Three months ago, I was invited to testify at the Nuremberg Trials. I took the opportunity to speak with Kurt Becher ... who served as a liaison officer between Himmler and me [*sic*] during the rescue operations, and has in the interim been released by the occupation authorities thanks to my personal intervention …'

The stomach-turning and delusional self-importance of Kasztner's boast that he helped to secure the release of an SS officer who had dedicated his career to a criminal organisation strongly implies that he persistently failed to recognize the razor-thin gap between negotiation and collaboration. This moral failure would contaminate his moral reputation for the rest of his life. From his youth, Kasztner had been a passionate Zionist. The irony is that the fulfilment of his dream of a Jewish national home would deepen the shadows that attached to his name. Was he rescuer or villain?

In December 1946, the revered veteran of the Zionist movement, Chaim Weizmann, opened the first Zionist Congress after the war in Basel. He recalled the harrowing experience of standing before the assembly to 'run one's eye along row after row of delegates' and discover that 'Polish Jewry was missing; Central and South-eastern Jewry was missing; German Jewry was missing.' For Kasztner, the Congress offered another platform to silence his critics. His obsessions focused on the former head of the Palestine Office in Budapest, Moshe (or Miklós) Krausz. In May 1944, Kasztner had revealed to his colleagues on the Rescue Committee the terms of his agreement with the SS to purchase the release of more than 1,000 Jews. When Krausz heard about the ransom plan he warned that Kasztner had fallen for 'empty talk' by the Germans. The deal was something to 'keep the Jews preoccupied'; Eichmann wanted to 'get the Jewish leaders into their hands as hostages'. As we will discover, Krausz's insight was remarkably prescient but Kasztner refused to listen to his warnings. He had too much invested in the negotiations. Krausz, for his part, was unforgiving of Kasztner's disastrous naivety. After the war ended, he encouraged the Hungarian journalist Eugen Jenö to write a report about the destruction of the Hungarian Jews and the activities of Kasztner and the Rescue Committee. I discovered an English language version of the report, entitled *The Black Book on the Martyrdom of Hungarian Jewry*, in the State Library in Berlin. It is journalism informed by anger, not an academic history, but no less powerful for that. The English version includes grisly photographs showing the executions of Hungarian collaborators. Jenö did not pull any punches when he turned his attention to Kasztner and the Rescue Committee. *The Black Book* was published in Hungarian a few months before the Zionist Congress opened.[2] As Krausz had intended, the revelations in the book were very damaging. Jenö characterised Kasztner as tyrannical, arrogant and jealous; he persistently ignored advice. In the margins of the Congress, Kasztner and Krausz waged a noisy war of words to assert their own version of events. Congress leaders were dismayed, fearing that such an ugly squabble would tarnish the Zionist cause. They promised to investigate the contested claims, but nothing was settled when delegates had to leave Bern to resume their interrupted lives. Kasztner returned to Geneva consumed by anger.

Joel Brand, too, was tormented by rage and frustration. The British had released him in at the beginning of October – and he took the night train to Jerusalem. He vented his anger not only at the British but against the Zionist establishment in Jerusalem, the Yishuv.[3] In *Satan and the Soul*, the book he wrote with his wife, Hansi, he raged against the duplicitous Zionist leaders who in his mind had betrayed his mission: 'Immediately after my release, I went from one office to the next in Tel Aviv and in Jerusalem, hoping to ascertain what was going on in Hungary … and if possible, return to Budapest … There was no one willing or able to help me. Everyone understood what I was saying, but probably found it difficult to understand what I was asking of them …' He must have been aware that Ben-Gurion and the Zionists were preoccupied preparing for a new war – to oust the British and confront the Arabs. The Jewish community in Palestine was increasingly militarised. Cooperation with the British ended after the German defeat at El Alamein. The Arab nationalist movement was compromised by the Grand Mufti's Nazi connections – and its tendency to factionalism. As Hitler's war entered its protracted final act, the Zionists had their eyes on the future. They had little time for an angry Hungarian obsessed with saving a few lives. He recalled:

> I was dealing with an impersonal organisation … All my efforts to return to Hungary, or at least to Europe, came to nothing, and all my activities at this time seemed to be regarded as those of an impractical visionary … The officials were tired of seeing me in their offices and regarded me as a monomaniac.[4]

In Palestine, Brand's torment was sharpened by the uncertain fate of Hansi and his two sons, who remained trapped in Budapest. During the terrible winter of 1944–45, Jews were in desperate peril as Arrow Cross gangs ran amok in the Pest ghetto. It was almost impossible for Brand to find out what was happening and whether his family had survived. Nor was he aware that following his departure for Istanbul in May, Hansi had embarked on an affair with Kasztner, his friend and colleague. Isolated, embittered, far away and living from hand to mouth, Brand refused to give up: 'Well-trained secretaries would tell me glibly that their bosses, whom I had asked to see, were out and no one knew exactly when they were due to return.' He demanded to be recognised as an official representative of Hungarian Jewry. Lives, he insisted, could still be saved. No one, he recalled, wanted to listen; he was treated as a pariah. Soon, he recalled, he was being warned to stop 'pestering people': 'Drop the matter, wipe everything from your mind otherwise you won't even be able to get a job cleaning streets in Tel Aviv.' In May 1945, with the war over, Brand set off on the long journey to Switzerland. He needed to talk to Kasztner – and hoped that Hansi and the boys would join him in Geneva.

It was an emotional encounter. At the Hauptbahnof, the two men embraced wordlessly. They strolled through the streets of the Old Town to the shores of the lake. From the Perle du Lac park, Kasztner pointed out the great pyramid of Mont Blanc. A sharp wind sent clouds scudding across the sky, their reflections skittering across the lake. The war had barely touched the brilliant surface of the Swiss city. A single bombing raid, made in error, had scandalised its citizens. Young men and women leapt into the freezing water from pontoons or discreetly embraced on the rocky shore. Prosperous citizens, whose lives had barely been touched by the war, promenaded along the Quai Wilson. The views and the spring weather did little to lift the spirits of the two exiled Hungarians, who sat together awkwardly in the little park. Brand recalled that his old friend could not disguise that he was in a depressed state of mind; his 'inner light seemed to have gone out.' He was 'grey not only in his features but also in his thoughts'. It did not take long for tensions to develop and for the rows to begin.

Brand had discovered that Kasztner had disparaged his efforts in Istanbul and his arrest. He boasted that if *he* had been sent to Istanbul, the Blood for Trucks mission might have been successful. Such innuendos were cruel and galling, and reminded Brand that Kasztner had always been a difficult colleague. He had been arrogant, self-centred, deaf to contrary opinions. And then there was the fraught matter of what had happened between Kasztner and Hansi after Joel's departure from Budapest. He had been informed by his niece that the pair were 'very friendly' and 'always seen together'. Matters worsened when Hansi arrived in Geneva with their sons. The journey had been arduous. During their first night together, Joel and Hansi began rowing. Hansi remonstrated with Joel that he had made a terrible mistake in falling into the hands of the British and not returning to Budapest. He retorted, feebly, that in wartime, 'many men are plucked from their families' arms'. When Joel turned his ire on Kasztner, she vehemently defended her former lover: 'If not for him we should all be among the dead.' Hansi insisted that she wished to stay in Europe with her sons, but Joel insisted the family return with him to Palestine. He won the argument. As soon as he was back in Tel Aviv, Joel Brand joined 'Lehi', an extremist Zionist organisation known as the 'Stern Gang' after its founder Avraham Stern. He had lost patience with the Zionist establishment.

In December 1947, Kasztner, Elizabeth and their daughter Zsuzsi left Geneva and followed the Brands to Palestine. They arrived in the port of Haifa penniless, with few resources. Kasztner had exhausted his savings travelling back and forth to Nuremberg as a witness for the International Military Tribunal and shoring up his battered reputation. He was now in his forties, in a fragile state of mind and forced to begin his life all over again. He was forced to borrow money from a relative and the Kasztner family moved from one cramped and sordid apartment in Tel Aviv to another.

By then, the struggle for the possession of Palestine had escalated – both on the ground and through international diplomacy. In October 1945, the armed wings of the Zionist movement Haganah and Irgun had launched an all-out rebellion against the British by sabotaging the railway system. The following year, in April, the Anglo–American Committee of Enquiry accepted the idea of a 'bi-national' state and called on the British to allow some 100,000 Jewish refugees to enter the mandate. The Committee, however, did not persuade the British and American governments, already at loggerheads in the Middle East, to agree a common policy – and the Haganah campaign intensified. Zionist militias destroyed bridges across the Jordan and the Irgun detonated explosives that had been smuggled inside milk churns into the basement of the King David Hotel in Jerusalem, the headquarters of the British civil and military administration. The blast killed ninety-one people, a third of them Jews – and marked a deadly turning point in the conflict.

In February 1947, the British, bankrupted by the war and heavily committed on other colonial front lines, threw in the towel and submitted the Palestine question to the raw, untested officials of a brand new global organisation, the United Nations. The UN set up a Special Committee on Palestine (UNSCOP) – and a ten-member committee was despatched to Palestine to wrench a solution from the toxic situation on the ground. As the campaign of Zionist terror continued to mount, the members of UNSCOP bickered over solutions. A minority argued for a federal state with Jerusalem as its capital. Seven out of the ten committee members recommended partition, with international status for Jerusalem. The British government racked up the stakes by threatening to leave Palestine within six months if there was no agreement. On 29 November 1947, the UN General Assembly, following aggressive lobbying by Zionists, voted to partition Palestine into Jewish and Arab states. Jerusalem would be governed as a *corpus separatum*. There could be little argument for UN Resolution 181 was backed by both the United States and the Soviet Union, the two powers that now dominated the new era. The agreement was bitterly opposed by the Palestinian leadership, such as it was, and all the Arab states. They saw partition not as a strategic compromise but as the fulfilment of Zionist ambitions: a 'line of blood and fire'. On the Jewish side, there was exultation. Standing on the balcony of the Jewish Agency just hours after the UN vote, Ben-Gurion proclaimed in a moment of profound historic significance: 'We are a free people!' It was said that there were 'few dry eyes and few steady voices'.

For the Palestinians, who had been rooted in the 'Holy Land' for thousands of years, 29 November was the opening act of a tragedy that came to be called the 'Nakba', the disaster – and for both peoples, the beginning of a war without end. In the aftermath of the passing of the UN Resolution, Palestine was engulfed by violence. Israel was born to the sound of machine guns and the detonation of high explosives. By the end of 1947, scores of thousands of Palestinian civilians had begun fleeing their homes in Jerusalem, Jaffa, Acre and Haifa. Historian Ilan Pappé has shown that the Zionist leadership was intent on a strategy of ethnic cleansing. Their militias attacked Arab villages and destroyed Arab houses. Haganah commanders used the Hebrew word *tihur*, meaning 'purifying', in their documents – and operations had code names such as Matateh (Broom) and Biur Chametz (Passover Cleaning). By the spring of 1948, on the eve of the British departure, Jewish fighters had won their first war. Big cities including Tiberias and Haifa had fallen to the Zionist armies. A 15-year-old Palestinian Salah Khalaf remembered the sight of a 'huge mass of men, women, old people and children, struggling under the weight of suitcases or bundles, making their way painfully down to the wharfs of Jaffa in a sinister tumult.'[5] On 15 May, the British finally evacuated – and in Tel Aviv, Ben-Gurion proclaimed the sovereign state of Israel. Within hours, the new state had been recognised by the two global superpowers, the US and the USSR. The war was over; the dragon's teeth of a new conflict had been sown.

In the new state, the Kasztners' lives had at last begun to improve. He had long supported the leftist Mapai Party, which had won the first elections, and was offered a position in the new government as a spokes-man for government minister Dov Joseph, a Canadian Jew who had been governor of Jerusalem during the War of Independence. Between 1949 and 1953, Kasztner was employed as director of public relations in the var-ious ministries that Joseph headed. He also found work as a night editor on the Hungarian daily *Új Kelet* and later produced Hungarian language broadcasts on the Voice of Israel. There was a big Hungarian community in the new state, but few had mastered Hebrew. Soon Kasztner's voice, speaking Hungarian, became a familiar part of their lives. His ubiquity would be his undoing. Many of the Hungarian survivors who made their homes in Israel had come with damaging information about Kasztner's activities during the German occupation. And it would not take long for these troubled and angry voices to be heard.

For the time being, Kasztner put the past behind him. He seemed to regain his animal spirits and began to look forward to achieving high office. A journalist who worked under Kasztner at *Új Kelet* left us a vivid pen portrait. Kasztner had a lot of charm, 'which had its effect on women in particular', he remembered, and a cynical sense of humour. He liked to recall a hoary old Hungarian joke about the sexually voracious Empress Maria Theresa, whose carriage driver kept a diary recording their trysts. When the calendar was accidentally erased, the driver complained, 'Damn, now I'll have to start all over again.' 'That's the situation I'm in!' com-plained Kasztner.

Although Kasztner's friendship with Brand was in a deep freeze, he fre-quently met with Hansi. She knew he had not shaken off the demons that had plagued him since the end of the war. In *Satan and the Soul*, the book she wrote with her husband, Hansi recalls that, 'All around Rezső, there was the sound of slander and gossip … Someone would say "Yes, but …" Once again we realised the truth of the saying – how hard it is for a man to be a survivor and to carry the burden of gratitude to his rescuers.' Then in July 1952, an elderly Austrian Jew called Malkiel Grünwald published a mimeographed newsletter that ferociously attacked Kasztner: 'The stench of a carcass is grating on my nostrils ... Dr Rudolf Kasztner must be annihilated.' The chain of events that led to Kasztner's murder five years later had been set in motion.

The war was over. The Nazi state had been crushed. Many of its leaders were dead by the hangman's noose or their own hand; others were locked away. But Hitler's war and the terrible slaughters it had brought to every region of the Reich smouldered in unforgiving and unforgiven hearts and minds. The psychic and moral damage enacted by Germany's war had not been repaired. A global Cold War would inflict renewed suffering on the lives of millions. Unquiet emotions and hatreds growled and roared in the minds and words of the men and women who had confronted the SS officers who came to Budapest in March 1944 to plunder and murder the Jews of Hungary. Brand would never forgive – and Kasztner could never quash the accusations that, to save lives, he had collaborated with the 'Nazi beast'.

To understand the persistent malevolence of this history and the power of these conflicted memories, we need to explore the puzzling and frequently misunderstood dynamics of Hitler's war against Jews – and how it came to engulf, with unprecedented savagery and at a very late stage in the war, one of the most fascinating Jewish communities in Europe.

3

DESPAIR DEFERRED

On the night of 15 January 1945, Adolf Hitler returned for the last time to Berlin. As the Führer's special train steamed into the shattered city, he had ordered that the window blinds be pulled down. He had no wish to observe what his war of destruction had wrought or to be seen by a people who had, according to police reports, lost faith in the Führer. Hitler was a sick and angry man who raged daily, his left arm trembling uncontrollably, at the generals who had, he believed, let him down. There could be no capitulation. He insisted to Armaments Minister Albert Speer that anyone even hinting that the war was lost would be 'treated as a traitor'. On the anniversary of the Nazi seizure of power on 30 January, Hitler insisted on broadcasting to the nation. He demanded from soldiers and civilians of the German *Volk* the most extreme sacrifices to combat the 'Jewish-international conspiracy' and the onslaught on Germany by 'Kremlin Jews' who had 'eradicated people in their tens of thousands' in the East. Most Germans who heard the speech, whether cowering in cellars or confronting the fire and fury of the Allied onslaught on the frayed borders of the Reich, responded with scepticism and sullen indifference. Inside the bunker, Hitler, his limbs shaking uncontrollably, ranted against defeatism. Schwerin von Krosigk, Hitler's Finance Minister, recalled that in order to comfort the Führer, Josef Goebbels read aloud passages from the British historian Thomas Carlyle's *History of Frederick the Great*, which describe how the great king faced disaster in the winter of 1761: how all his generals and ministers were convinced that he was finished, and the enemy already looked upon Prussia as vanquished. Then, Carlyle relates, on 12 February the Russian Czarina died … Prussia was saved. The Führer,

Goebbels claimed, 'had tears in his eyes' when he was reminded of the 'Miracle of Brandenburg'.[1]

Even the cynical Goebbels was convinced that 'for reasons of Historical Necessity and Justice a change of fortune must occur now just as it did in the Seven Years War'. He joyfully conveyed this message to General Theodor Busse and some of his staff officers. One of them enquired which Czarina was to die this time. Goebbels soon had an answer. 'My Führer,' he exalted. 'I congratulate you! Roosevelt is dead … It is the turning point.' These fantastical hopes were soon dashed. The passing of the president did not halt the destruction of the Reich.

A year earlier, in the winter and spring of 1944, the abyss of defeat and despair had yet to gape open. For Hitler and a few of his entourage, the benevolence of providence might still defeat the enemies of the Reich.

The Long Death of Hope

The temptation of hindsight is to imagine 1944, the last complete year of the Second World War, as the prelude to the certain defeat of Hitler's Reich. Many ordinary Germans experienced acute anxiety and depression about the fate of their homeland. But hope had not been extinguished and inside the cosseted and narcissistic world of the Nazi elite that still paid obeisance to Hitler, outcomes still appeared to be fluid. Optimism was hard to defend but for many who had pledged their loyalty to Hitler, the future was not yet settled. Since the encirclement and destruction of the German 6th Army at Stalingrad in the winter of 1942–43, Soviet armies had inflicted massive damage on Hitler's forces on the Eastern Front, breaking through German lines at multiple points and forcing a general withdrawal to a fragile 'Eastern Wall' along the Dnieper. Bad news poured into Hitler's military headquarters, the Wolf's Fort in East Prussia, from every overstretched front line. By May, North Africa had been lost; a quarter of a million German and Italian troops surrendered near Tunis. This calamity strained the already weakening bond between Hitler and the Italian dictator Mussolini. Allied troops were now poised to cross the Straits of Sicily to launch an attack on the strategic underbelly of Europe. In the Battle of the Atlantic the menace of the U-boat fleet was receding, thanks to the Bletchley code-breakers, and American supplies began to pour, almost uninterrupted, into British ports. In July, the Allies launched their long-feared assault on Sicily. Italian soldiers threw away their rifles and fled. At the end of the month, the Fascist Grand Council deposed Mussolini and had him arrested. Exultant anti-fascist demonstrators erupted onto the streets of Rome. As Hitler desperately made plans to send troops to Rome, RAF bombing fleets rained fire onto the cities and factories of the Ruhr. On 3 September, as British troops crossed the Straits of Messina to the Italian mainland, the new Italian Prime Minister, Marshal Pietro Badoglio, signed a secret armistice deal with the Allies. On the evening of 8 September, Hitler ordered Operation Axis and German troops, many brutalised by their brutal experience on the Eastern Front, crossed the Alps into Northern Italy. Two days later, the Germans seized Rome and the occupation was complete. Mussolini, much reduced, was rescued in a daring glider raid and brought to the Wolf's Fort. Hitler insisted that Mussolini, humiliated and wearied though he was, return to Italy. Here in Lombardy, on the shores of Lake Garda, he founded the 'Republic of Salò', a petty fiefdom of thuggish barbarism and rife corruption. The enfeebled Mussolini exercised little control over what has been described as a 'hodge-podge of municipalities, regional authorities and rogue gangs'. Overbearing German military and civil representatives, greedy for plunder, rode roughshod over local Italian officials.[2] The expedient military occupation of Germany's former ally fatally weakened the Eastern Front. Citadel, the last German offensive in the East, failed at Kursk. The Soviet Army now began to relentlessly push back German armies towards the mighty frontier of the Dnieper River. Further south, Romanian and German troops were cut off in the Crimea. By the end of the year, the German imperial fantasy of an empire in the east, a Garden of Eden for countless hordes of German settlers, was finished.

In the course of the following year, the facts on the ground of this titanic, unfolding catastrophe shifted and broke with ever more brutal speed. From the point of view of the combatant powers in Washington, London, Moscow and Berlin, the power of contingency reshaped, shattered and remade the order of things month by month. History was flowing in a single direction towards the downfall of the Reich, but its turbulent course was often unpredictable.

On 8 November 1943, the anniversary of the Beer Hall Putsch and a sacred date in the Nazi calendar, Hitler made a defiant speech to party diehards in Munich in the Löwenbräukeller in Munich. The bombast of his words that night reflected a perverse, even psychotic defiance, a solipsistic glorification of the German warrior spirit he embodied that might still turn back the flood of misfortune. Beset by the errors and miscalculations of his subordinates, he presented himself standing alone against the rising Bolshevik tide.

> The Americans and the English are right now planning the rebuilding of the world. I am right now planning the rebuilding of Germany! There will, however, be a difference: while the rebuilding of the world through the Americans and the English will not take place, the rebuilding of Germany through National Socialism will be carried out with precision and according to plan! … This is the first thing I have to say. The second thing is this: whether or not the gentlemen believe it, the hour of retribution will come! If we cannot reach America at the moment, one state is within our reach, thank God, and we will hold on to it.[3]

Throughout the speech, the last he would make in this mythologised place, Hitler returned obsessively to the mysterious workings of Providence and Fate – two mythic forces that would, he asserted over and again, deliver Germany from catastrophe. This semi-mystical conviction still had the power to sway his most loyal satraps.

In Hitler's mind, and in the thoughts of many Germans, two powerful delusions sustained this optimism in the face of crisis and catastrophe. There was the hope that the western Allies, Britain and the United States, would fall out with their natural foe, the Soviet Union. After all, Germany had launched its blitzkrieg in Poland and then Western Europe under cover of the Nazi–Soviet Pact that protected its eastern borders. Treachery was not unimaginable. To be sure, from the perspective of Washington and London, Soviet military triumphs in the East foreshadowed the enlargement of Soviet political power in the event of victory – but even this daunting prospect had so far failed to fundamentally damage the bonds forged between the 'Big Three'. Still, a damaging schism was not completely an irrational hope.

There is an irony here. In 1940, at a conference with his generals at the Berghof, his Alpine retreat, Hitler was mulling over Operation Sea Lion, the proposed invasion of Britain that was planned in the adrenaline-charged aftermath of the conquest of Western Europe. He explained to his generals that Britain had some grounds for optimism. Churchill was investing a great deal of energy trying to inveigle support from Roosevelt.

But Stalin had been shaken by the German blitzkrieg in the West – and Hitler suspected that Churchill hoped that Russia might abandon his pact with Germany and back Britain. The implications were startling. He told General Franz Halder that, 'With Russia smashed, England's last hope would be shattered …' In Hitler's mind, alliances were always expedient and potentially breakable. That the Allied warlords might turn against one another was a tantalising hope: 'the tension,' Hitler insisted 'between the Allies will become so great that the break will happen. In world history coalitions have always been ruined at some point.' Goebbels chimed in: 'the political conflicts will increase with the apparent approach of an Allied victory, and some day will open cracks in our enemies' house which can no longer be repaired.'

Even more seductive to both the Nazi leadership and ordinary Germans were reports and rumours of spectacular 'Wonder Weapons' whose destructive power would turn the tide of the war. This was not science fiction. The German atomic project, which provoked the Manhattan Project, was allowed to wither but sophisticated German missiles wreaked destruction in Rotterdam and London, and there was excited talk of new models of U-boats and tanks. As British and American bombers inflicted terrible damage on German cities, there was renewed interest in the Me 262, a jet fighter the development of which had been downgraded the year before. Now, Hitler believed, the new jets would give the much-diminished and widely despised Luftwaffe an edge against the Allied bombers. None of these new weapons could have conceivably altered the outcome of the war but remarkably, when the war was over, many Germans recalled the hope that these destructive wonders would snatch victory from defeat. These semi-mythological fantasies appear to have fed illusions of hope at every level of German society until very late in the war.

As the Soviet Army pressed relentlessly on the Eastern Front, and Allied armies pushed slowly, against fierce German resistance, north across the heel of Italy towards Rome, Hitler and his generals knew that Germany would soon confront another looming military threat. Despite the shrinking eastern borders of the Reich, he referred to the planned 'Anglo Saxon' attack on the Western front as the 'greater danger'. Huge efforts were invested in building the 'Atlantic Wall' to repel the attack and, perversely, Hitler began to regard the expected onslaught as an opportunity. He despised the British and confidently expected that superior German forces would deal the Allied invaders a death blow. In the early part of the year, Hitler was a great deal more preoccupied, in the aftermath of Mussolini's fall, with the faltering commitment of Finland and, even more important, of Germany's Eastern allies, Hungary and Romania. It was a long-festering crisis in relations between the Hungarian leader Admiral Miklós Horthy and the Reich that would set in motion the destruction of the last surviving Jewish community in Europe.

The origins of the crisis go back to the end of 1940 when Hitler's resolve to break the pact with Stalin and strike at the Soviet Union was hardening. As secret military plans for the invasion of Russia in spring of 1941, then code-named 'Fritz', gathered pace, it was essential to secure the south-east flank of the German Reich. In November, Hitler and Joachim von Ribbentrop, his Foreign Minister, had, after a long diplomatic offensive, won the agreement of the Balkan states Hungary, Romania and Slovakia to join the Axis powers. There was also strategic anxiety about British troops stationed in Greece and the Aegean. This threat would have to be eliminated – and plans were laid to occupy Greece and oust the British. When Yugoslav army and navy officers opposed to their country's drift into the German orbit staged a coup, Hitler postponed 'Fritz' and launched a lightning strike code-named 'Marita' against Yugoslavia. The Luftwaffe pounded Belgrade, killing 20,000 people. In a matter of weeks, the Germans had overrun the Balkans and smashed British forces in the Mediterranean. Like Czechoslovakia, the Kingdom of Yugoslavia was torn apart. Serbia was occupied and a pro-German regime seized power in Croatia. In Athens, the Swastika flag fluttered over the Parthenon.

On 22 June, the German army unleashed what would become the most destructive and brutal war in human history. It would be, Hitler vowed, a 'war of annihilation' that would crush the Bolshevik arch-enemy in Moscow and conquer a new German empire in the East. In his 'Table Talk' Hitler liked to argue that the conquest of India had made 'England' a proud nation and a world power; empire building was the cradle of national glory: 'What India was for England, the eastern territory will be for us.' His was a megalomaniacal vision founded on a crude pseudo-Darwinian philosophy of the survival of the fittest. Races advanced up the evolution-ary ladder through conquest and bloodshed. 'The dear God, once again … suddenly casts the masses of humanity on to the Earth and each one has to look after himself and how he gets through. One person takes something from the other. And at the end you can only say that the stronger wins.' He was to be proved right. Both Hitler and his generals, who collectively believed that the war with Russia would be like pushing in a rotten door, had grossly miscalculated the depth of Soviet human and technological reserves – and will to recover from the shock of attack. Despite spectacular early successes, the German plans began to falter as early as July. By the end of 1941, the premature onset of a brutal winter and the failure to seize Moscow sealed the fate of the German campaign. As it unfolded, the Wehrmacht's advance appeared unstoppable and the German occupation authorities wrought immense transformations in the ethnic topography of the East. Slavic and Jewish communities were liquidated, borders shifted, and countless millions of people herded into new 'Germanised' territories. As Hitler's armies plunged ever deeper eastwards towards the Ural Mountains and the Caucasus, the Reich became the arbiter of life and death on a monstrous scale and of territorial gain and loss. The authoritarian leaders and elites of the successor states that had been forged from the relics of former empires had a consuming and unsatisfied appetite for land. The new German imperialists had the means to feed or deny that appetite.

Satellites

The Kingdom of Hungary was a successor state to the vast and multi-ethnic Austro-Hungarian Empire. After 1919, the victorious Allied powers had dismembered the imperial corpse. In 1920, the Treaty of Trianon, which was imposed by the victorious Allied powers, punitively stripped away vast regions from what was seen as 'Hungary' within the defunct empire. It became an axiom to say that Trianon was 'the greatest catastrophe to have befallen Hungary since the battle of Mohacs in 1526', which had led to the destruction of the medieval Hungarian kingdom by the Ottomans. Under the terms of the treaty, the Kingdom of Hungary lost some 70 per cent of her territory – including all her seaports. This land was handed over to other states that had emerged from the wreckage of the empire: Romania, Czechoslovakia and Yugoslavia. Nearly 33 per cent of ethnic Hungarians now lived outside Hungary: close to a million in Czechoslovakia, 1.6 million in the Transylvania region that was now part of Romania and close to half a million in Serbia. The nation that took shape after 1919 was a landlocked state with a severely weakened economy. The shock of Trianon shaped and contaminated social and ethnic relations in Hungary for the next two decades. Hungary's new national leader, who called himself 'Regent' in anticipation of the return of the monarchy, was an Anglophile former admiral in the Austro-Hungarian Navy called Miklós Horthy. Through the figure of Horthy ran the turbid currents of Hungarian resentments and hopes. Horthy was courageous, obsessed by honour, often stubborn and suspicious of new ideas. He was a committed antisemite who both acknowledged and feared Hungary's enormous debt to its Jewish elites. In Budapest today, Horthy's bust looks out across Szabadság tér (Liberty Square) from a discreet glass case placed in the entrance to the Hazatérés church. On the plinth is inscribed a single word: Trianon. The myth of Horthy embodies the pain and trauma inflicted on Hungarians in the aftermath of the First World War – and an obsession with restoring what was lost. By the end of the 1930s, territorial restoration is precisely what Hitler could offer Horthy.

The temptation of Horthy began in the summer of 1938. Hitler invited the old admiral to Kiel to watch the launch of a new battle cruiser, the *Prinz Eugen*. After the celebrations, he invited Horthy to assist in the destruction of the hated state of Czechoslovakia. As well as exploiting the resentments of the German minority in the Sudetenland, and stirring up Slovakian fascists, Hitler encouraged Hungary to make claims against Czechoslovakia. This plan was thwarted when the French and British forced Hitler to accept a peaceful settlement of the Sudetenland question at the Munich conference in September 1938. The Hungarian government, led by Horthy's Prime Minister Béla Imrédy, now proposed invading Czechoslovakia. To secure German support, he offered to extract Hungary from the League of Nations and to join the Anti-Comintern Pact. Hitler and Italian dictator Benito Mussolini decided instead to mediate. At a conference at the Belvedere Palace in Vienna, the Italian and German foreign ministers Count Galeazzo Ciano and Joachim von Ribbentrop agreed to a revision of the Trianon Treaty. The 'First Vienna Award' gave Hungary part of Slovakia, including a strip of land north of the Danube with a Hungarian-speaking majority, as well as the towns of Kassa, Munkács and Ungvár. Roughly a million people were affected by the Award, in an area of 12,000 square kilometres.[4] Hungarians celebrated this snub to the baleful inheritance of Trianon and Horthy rode in triumph through his restored domains on a white horse. Hitler's award whetted his appetite for more. In early 1939, the Hungarian Foreign Minister István Csáky took Hungary out of the League of Nations and agreed to join the Anti-Comintern Pact. There was a morally expensive price to pay. Germany had already begun putting pressure on Horthy to 'solve Hungary's Jewish problem' and with territorial reward came bouts of anti-Jewish legislation – which will be explored in detail in a later chapter.

When the Germans occupied Prague on 14 March 1939, Hitler turned the Czech lands into a Protectorate. Slovakia became a pseudo independent state. Once again, Horthy seized an opportunity and Hungarian troops marched into the north-east region of Sub-Carpathia, which was in Ukraine. The people of the region identified as 'Ruthenes' not Ukrainians and welcomed Hungarian protection. The acquisition of more territory provoked another frenzy of jubilation in Budapest and another round of anti-Jewish legislation. Jewish property could now be legally stolen. Since the mid 1930s, Horthy had struggled to hold Hungary's most extremist parties and their most vocal leader, Ferenc Szálasi, in check. In 1938, the Hungarian police had arrested Szálasi and put him in prison. But even behind bars, he succeeded in fusing together Hungary's splintered and fractious extremist parties to form a single organisation, the Arrow Cross. Like the Romanian Iron Guard, the Arrow Cross was an avowedly national socialist party dedicated to 'cleansing' Hungary of Jews and Communists. 'I have been chosen by a higher divine authority,' Szálasi proclaimed, 'to redeem the Hungarian people.' In May 1939, Hungary held elections and, for the first time, the far right won 15 per cent of the vote, taking forty seats in the parliament. Szálasi and his new party could not be ignored. He was released from prison and set up an imposing new headquarters in a mansion on Andrássy Avenue, one of Budapest's grand boulevards. The building now houses the controversial museum known as the 'House of Terror'.[5]

When Hitler signed the non-aggression pact with the Soviet Union in 1939, the two powers secretly agreed to establish domains of influence in Central and Eastern Europe and the Baltic. In September, German armies invaded Poland – and Britain and France declared war on Germany. Hungary allowed the Wehrmacht to use railways east of Kassa to move goods to the front. Admiral Horthy strongly suspected that Hitler could not, in the end, win a war against the world's leading sea power – but in the early years of blitzkrieg and conquest, Germany appeared invincible. The Hungarians fervently hoped that some of the fruits of victory would fall into their laps – and so they did.

The Nazi–Soviet Pact was fragile from the start. Fearing Soviet intentions in Romania, the source of the Wehrmacht's vital oil supplies, Hitler adroitly offered to partition Transylvania in Hungary's favour. In August 1940, a second 'Vienna Award' handed some two-thirds of Transylvania to Hungary. Once again, Hungarians indulged in an orgy of jubilation and Horthy again mounted his white horse to ride in triumph through the streets of historic towns such as Kolozsvár and Marosvásárhely that had been lost by post-Trianon Hungary. 'I can hardly express how happy I am,' Horthy gushed to Hitler, 'I shall never forget this proof of friendship.'

Horthy was even more delighted when, a year later, Hitler hinted that Hungary would soon be offered more spoils. On the menu this time was Hungarian Voivodina in Yugoslavia. In return, Horthy would have to commit Hungarian troops to Operation Marita, the German invasion of Yugoslavia in the spring of 1941. To begin with, this seemed a small price to pay. In a gushing letter, Horthy pledged himself body and soul to the German Reich in 'unalterable loyalty'. His lust for Yugoslavian territory put him at odds with the British. But he and his new Prime Minister, Pál Teleki, defied warnings from London and the widely respected British minister in Budapest, Owen O'Malley, who made no bones about accusing Horthy of treachery. Teleki had a better understanding of what the British reaction implied and, tormented by the rush to war, shot himself. 'We have taken the side of scoundrels, the most rotten of nations …' he wrote in a note to Horthy. The Regent was untroubled, it would seem, and appointed the pro-German László Bárdossy de Bárdos to take Teleki's place. So it was that Hungarian troops played a minor role in Germany's destruction of Yugoslavia. By the time Hitler ordered Operation Barbarossa, the invasion of the Soviet Union in June 1941, Hungary had won back a good half of her lost territories and at least 5.3 million people, of whom less than half were Hungarian. Like Faust, Horthy and Hungary had sold their national soul to the devil.

A few weeks after German armies overran the Balkans, Horthy heard of Hitler's plans to attack the Soviet Union in the summer. It was an inadvertent discovery since the Hungarian leader was not privy to the most important decisions made by his friends in Berlin. The Regent took great pride in his reputation and experience as 'an old Crusader against Bolshevism' and now declared that, 'I count myself happy that my army can take part, shoulder to shoulder, with the victorious German army in the crusade for the elimination of the dangerous Communist horde'. Now he would be sucked even deeper into the Nazi maw. A mysterious bombing raid on a provincial Hungarian town was blamed on the Soviet Air

Force, although the aircraft were almost certainly Romanian – and taking advantage of this provocation, Horthy formally joined the German war on 26 June. General Ferenc Szombathelyi led an expeditionary force across the Soviet border into Galicia comprising two infantry brigades, a cavalry brigade and ten Alpine battalions. Thousands of ill-equipped Hungarian soldiers cycled to the front line. Szombathelyi's forces were assigned to the German 17th Army and the mobile corps reached the Donets River as the Soviet army retreated headlong towards Moscow.

Although tens of thousands of Hungarian troops would fight on until autumn 1944, obsolete weapons and equipment and continuous and heavy losses led to an early and severe collapse of morale. Szombathelyi himself had been sceptical about the war from the very beginning. So too was István Horthy, the Regent's eldest son, who was strongly pro-western and often accused of being a 'Jew lover' by Hungarian radicals. Szombathelyi drafted a memorandum summarising his views of the likelihood of a German victory. He concluded that the Russian war would be 'a long, drawn out, and bloody struggle, the result of which was completely uncertain'.

The report troubled Horthy. When he was summoned to Hitler's new eastern military headquarters, the Wolf's Fort at Rastenburg in the Masurian Woods, in early September, he was accompanied by Szombathelyi – and, with surprising determination, demanded that Hungary be permitted to withdraw the bulk of her forces. After a prolonged squabble, the first of many, Hitler agreed to the removal of the 'Fast Corps' – on condition that Horthy allowed four infantry brigades to remain in the now occupied Ukraine. In the first euphoric months of Barbarossa, Hitler was no doubt confident enough of victory to compromise: it was vital to keep Hungary firmly inside the Axis embrace. Horthy's resolve weakened again in December. At the beginning of the month, he fell seriously ill. It was rumoured he had cancer. He didn't – but while he struggled to regain his health, Britain declared war on Hungary and the Japanese bombed Pearl Harbor. Hitler made the fateful decision to honour his obligations to Japan and so declared war on the United States. Impetuously, Bárdossy announced that Hungary and the United States were at war without seeking approval from either the Regent or the cabinet. Hitler's other allies followed suit. The war was now a global conflict, but Horthy would never forgive Bárdossy. It would seem that Horthy was already uncomfortable wearing the German straitjacket he had blundered into strapping on his nation.

At the end of the month, as the German campaign ground to a halt just short of Moscow, Hitler wrote to Horthy admitting that due to bad weather and the 'fanaticism of Red Army soldiers' who fought with an 'Asiatic indifference to the loss of life' the German army had not dealt the expected 'annihilating blow' – and that a spring campaign would be necessary to win the war. When Ribbentrop flew to Budapest in early January to join the now recovered Regent's hunting party, he made less than subtle threats that Hungary's territorial ambitions would be thwarted if she did not contribute to the new offensive. The Romanian dictator Ion Antonescu, Ribbentrop emphasised, was promising to send his entire army to the Eastern Front. His appetite whetted again, Horthy capitulated and agreed to forming a 'Second Army' of some 200,000 soldiers that would be hurled against the Soviets.

Horthy was a pompous, vain and frequently deluded man. He was an avowed and unashamed antisemite with a virulent hated of Bolshevism. Like Hitler, he feared Soviet Communism as a Jewish conspiracy. But Horthy was also subject to bouts of pragmatism. To destroy the Hungarian Jews would be tantamount to crippling the Hungarian nation. To fight on with the Axis would hurl Hungary to the brink of extinction. After the acrimonious resignation of Bárdossy, Horthy persuaded Miklós Kállay, who had long feared the outcome of Hungary's commitment to the German war in the East, to accept the office. It was Kállay who on St Stephen's Day in August 1942 had to inform the Regent, as he led a procession through Buda, that István had been killed in a flying accident in the east. Horthy fainted. He never completely recovered from the loss of his eldest son.

Throughout 1942, Germany remained the dominant political and military power on the continent. German armies continued to advance into the east and across North Africa. Kállay was compelled to take a conciliatory line and Hungarian soldiers fell in their tens of thousands. Under pressure from radicals in parliament, his government passed another Jewish law in March that abrogated Jewish civil rights and authorised the confiscation of estates larger than 150 acres. Jews, who were forbidden to serve in the Hungarian Army, were also being conscripted into labour battalions and sent to the front. Many would perish in the terrible winter of 1942–43. In early 1943, the encirclement and destruction of the German 6th Army by Soviet forces at Stalingrad profoundly alarmed the Hungarian government. Worse was to come. Soon after the humiliation of the Wehrmacht at Stalingrad, Soviet forces broke through the German line on the Don – and fell on the Second Hungarian Army at Voronezh. Outnumbered and outgunned, men and animals starving on a 100-mile front line, many without boots in the dead of winter … the Second Army collapsed. Some 130,000 men were killed or captured – including 40,000 Jewish men conscripted into the labour battalions.

Kállay began to tentatively send out clandestine peace feelers to the Allies through emissaries in Bern, Stockholm and Istanbul – which, to begin with, met with unambiguous rejection. Only if Hungary severed her bonds with Nazi Germany would these shrill Hungarian entreaties get a hearing. Horthy knew that any such move risked all-out German occupation. Hitler knew all about these dalliances with enemy powers thanks to the sheer leakiness of the Hungarian intelligence services.

Since 1941, Hitler had called a succession of face-to-face meetings with the leaders of Nazi Germany's satellite states. His intent was, naturally, to make sure these temperamental authoritarians toed the Axis line. Hitler invariably pestered these nationalist bullies to solve their 'Jewish problems'. His preferred venue was the Schloss Kleßheim, located near Salzburg – and not far from the Berghof, Hitler's retreat in the Bavarian Alps. This baroque palace had originally been built for the Prince Bishops of Salzburg and in the 1920s became the temporary home of the Isadora Duncan School of Dance. After the Anschluss, the Germans had refurbished the castle as a kind of conference centre. That sounds quite innocuous but the purpose of Kleßheim was to intimidate and bully any recalcitrant heads of state. The palace was an elegantly designed theatre of power: a stage set for garrulous sessions of browbeating. In his 'Memoirs', the Italian Foreign Minister, Ciano, describes accompanying Mussolini to conferences at the Schloss: he recalled an oppressive atmosphere – and Hitler's repetitive and mind-numbing perorations. 'He talks, talks, talks, talks …' Ciano lamented. Even Hitler's most loyal generals sometimes fell asleep. At the meeting Ciano described, which took place as catastrophe overwhelmed German and Italian troops in North Africa, Hitler harangued a crumpled and exhausted Mussolini with uplifting tales of Prussian history. As a battering succession of crises began to engulf the Reich, the Schloss became an opulent arena in which to intimidate faltering allies. Here they all came, King Boris of Bulgaria, the Croatian dictator Ante Pavelić, the oleaginous French Prime Minister Pierre Laval, Marshall Ion Antonescu of Romania, President Tiso of Slovakia, and, of course, Vidkun Quisling. Hitler and his

Foreign Minister Ribbentrop, himself no stranger to bullying, exploited a cunning armoury of promises, flattery and threats. For the Reich, diplomacy was founded on the most corrosive self-interest.

When Horthy's turn came in April 1943, Hitler dispensed with any diplomatic niceties. In the course of an hour-long opening harangue, Hitler rammed home to the terrified old man the civilisational threat of Bolshevism. He repetitively compared the Soviet armies that were gathering strength in the East to Huns, Mongols and Turks. He reminded him that Hungary had once been overwhelmed by barbarians. Horthy had no choice but to perch on a gilded chair, his back ramrod straight, and listen to the rolling wave of rhetorical history lessons. Hitler denounced the performance of the Hungarian army and railed against the treachery of Prime Minister Kállay. Hitler and Ribbentrop repeatedly insisted that Horthy sack his prime minister. They flourished a folder of intercepted telegrams, evidence that Kállay was reaching out to the enemies of the Reich to strike a deal. Did Horthy not realise that anyone who tried to jump from a ship in a stormy sea would drown? Only 'fanatical determination' could save Hungary from the Bolshevik hordes.

Hitler's onslaught unfolded over a number of days. The sinister Hungarian military attaché in Berlin, Döme Sztójay, who had consistently urged Horthy to bond closer to the Axis, was often lurking nearby. At Hitler's invitation, he joined in the assault on his absent rival. Although Horthy stood up, as best he could, for Kállay, the Regent was a fundamentally weak man who, in the end, timorously agreed to 'investigate' Ribbentrop's evidence. Hitler pressed Horthy on the Jews. He was dangerously tolerant of these people and their demoralising influence. Horthy protested that Hungarian Jews were essential to the economy: they could not simply be 'clubbed to death'. Eventually, Horthy was permitted to return to Budapest. Hitler cut off contact with Kállay.

Hitler and his Foreign Minister had learnt to manipulate the 'Admiral on Horseback' with flattery. The Germans had no desire to oust Horthy, who still held sway over the majority of Hungarians, or commit troops to an expensive invasion. The Axis had, at least, to seem to be holding firm. When Horthy celebrated his 75th birthday in June, Hitler presented him with a new yacht that would be sailed along the Danube to Budapest. Horthy sent a gushing letter of thanks, the gift 'took his breath away', while privately sneering, 'What the hell can I do with a yacht? If he were a gentleman, he would send me a riding horse or a team of horses.'

Planning for Genocide

Shortly after that first bruising encounter at Kleßheim, Ribbentrop des-patched a German SS officer to Budapest to carry out an on the ground investigation of the activities and intentions of the Hungarian govern-ment. The name of the SS officer was Edmund von Veesenmayer – and he will play an increasingly significant role in this narrative. Impressively well educated, with a doctorate in economics, Dr Veesenmayer had taken a leading role establishing the new state of Croatia after the German conquest of the Balkans. Here he had sanctioned the persecution and murder of Jews by the fascist Ustaša militias and, in occupied Serbia, directly managed the deportation of more than 9,000 Jewish men accused of armed subversion. According to his biographer, Igor-Philip Matić, Veesenmayer was a pragmatic rather than emotional or dogmatic antisemite who had been trained to clinically evaluate the impact of occupation policy decisions. Matic argues that SS diplomats such as Veesenmayer believed that inciting and managing antisemitic persecu-tion in satellite nation states like Croatia and Romania was a means to bind their ruling elites to the Reich. This strategy of complicity would become increasingly significant as the German war faltered. To put it a different way, the mass murder of Jews and other minorities in Europe was represented to the different parties involved as a shared enterprise. While anti-Jewish actions are ruthlessly carried out to save Germany and the Europe it dominates from the menace of 'Jewish Bolshevism', it is nevertheless considered to be a crime against humanity by our enemies. Together, we are enacting this necessary purge. If you abandon your obligations to the Reich, the consequence will be defeat – and then retribution.

★★★

Following his exploratory visit to Budapest in April 1943, Veesenmayer reported to Ribbentrop on 10 December that Hungary was an 'arrogant' nation that was contributing 'a fraction of what it could' to the war effort.[6] He stressed that, 'The Jew is Enemy No. 1. These 1.1 million Jews are all sab-oteurs against the Reich, as are at least the same number of Hungarians … who are followers of the Jews.' Hungary had become an 'asylum of European Jewry' and the Regent's shilly-shallying was a consequence of a clique of

'Jews, and aristocrats related to Jews' who all exerted a 'nefarious' influence. Veesenmayer recommended that Hungarian officials with strong German ties should be encouraged to undermine Kállay while followers of known radicals such as Béla Imrédy and the Arrow Cross leader Ferenc Szálasi were encouraged to agitate for more radical policies. Veesenmayer urged that the 'Jewish question' must be tackled 'thoroughly'; this was 'a prerequisite for involving Hungary in the Reich's defensive and existential struggle'. The following spring, when his patience finally ran out, Hitler appointed Veesenmayer as the all-powerful plenipotentiary of occupied Hungary.

Until that fateful spring, Hitler refrained from further interference in Hungarian affairs even though Kállay remained in power and persisted in making what he believed were secret overtures to the Allies. Hitler seems to have understood that Horthy was genuinely reluctant to commit treason against an ally. It would, in his old-fashioned world of honour, be an ignoble act comparable to betraying a friend. At the same time, Horthy knew all too well that he could not trust members of his cabinet with close ties to Berlin not to betray to their friends in Berlin any discussion of taking Hungary out of the war. He did not seem to understand that the Allies had, since 1942, set in stone the principle of 'unconditional surrender', which would make any negotiations between the Allies and an Axis satellite a one-sided affair. At the same time, many on the British side had little sympathy for the plight of Hungary. This was largely the fault of Horthy himself as his public pronouncements were unequivocal in their commitment to the alliance with Germany. British sympathy was directed towards worthier causes such as the rival partisan movements in the Balkans.

Despite this, Kállay refused to give up. Through contacts in Switzerland, for example, he began discussions with Royall Tyler, an American expert on Hungary who had learned Magyar. The connection with Tyler would not become significant for another year but another envoy in the shape of a passionate young diplomat called Laszló Veress reached out to the British through connections in Istanbul.

These negotiations have an intriguing significance for our main story, the Zionist 'rescue missions' of the following year, for these puzzling events also involved secret contacts and negotiations in Istanbul. When Kállay reached out to the Allies, both the Americans and British were wary. The Soviets insisted on the principle of 'unconditional surrender'. By this stage in the war, as the military defeat of Nazi Germany became more certain, the Allies disagreed about the form of a post-war settlement of Eastern Europe.

Kállay's efforts had a negligible result. But following the Allied landings in Sicily and the downfall of Mussolini, he sent Veress back to Istanbul. This time the Hungarians decided to work within the framework of accepting unconditional surrender. Veress managed to get this message through to the British Ambassador in Ankara, Sir Hughe Knatchbull-Hugessen: the Hungarian army was ready to defend Hungarian borders against the Germans and would facilitate Allied occupation. It was an extraordinary offer and this time the Hungarians had the attention of the British Foreign Secretary, Anthony Eden, who passed on the gist of the proposals to the highest levels. Now Churchill, Roosevelt and Stalin's Foreign Minister Molotov Vyacheslav began haggling over how to respond.

A lot hinged on when Hungary should make an announcement – since no one wanted to provoke the Germans prematurely. On the night of 9 September, Veress was secretly taken to a yacht moored in the Sea of Marmora, where Knatchbull-Hugessen was waiting to meet him. The ambassador read out a number of preliminary conditions that Veress scribbled down. Hungary was expected to withdraw its troops from Russia and reduce military and economic cooperation with Germany. No announcement of the agreement would be made until Anglo-Saxon troops reached Hungarian borders. A week later, Veress arrived back in Budapest, where his discussion of the British conditions provoked rancorous debate. Unconditional surrender, of course, implied loss of sovereignty – which no one on the Hungarian side could stomach. Further negotiations followed in Lisbon – but the end game was a fudge. There was no real meeting of minds since the Hungarians desperately hoped to be 'struck off the list of enemies' and be given British protection while the British hoped to gain a military advantage in south-eastern Europe.

In the end, neither the British nor the Americans ever reached the Hungarian border and the agreement was never brought into play. There was one intriguing consequence of the negotiations. Veress returned to Hungary with two wireless transmitters. He returned to work in the Foreign Ministry and sent a stream of valuable information to the British. The other transmitter was secretly installed in Horthy's residence in the Castle and for the duration of the war Kállay stayed in touch with the British. At the beginning of the following year, there was another round of negotiations, this time with the OSS, the precursor to the CIA – which we will return to in a later chapter.

4

THE TWISTED ROAD TO GENOCIDE

Every tenth victim of the Nazi Holocaust was a Hungarian Jew. Two-thirds of Hungarian Jewry was destroyed between 1941 and 1945. Despite the ideological bigotry of Hitler and the Nazi elite, this escalation of barbarity was not inevitable; it did not evolve in a clockwork fashion. Before the spring of 1944, Hungarian Jews had suffered legalised persecution by the Hungarian state and, after Hungary joined the Axis invasion of the Soviet Union in the summer of 1941, significant levels of violence. Even before the war, the Hungarian state and society were pervasively antisemitic. And yet a significant proportion of Hungary's Jews remained alive when German troops marched into Budapest on 19 March 1944. After 1941, Hungarian Zionists including Joel and Hansi Brand had organised refuge for Jews fleeing occupied Poland and the puppet state of Slovakia. The murderous fury unleashed on Hungarian Jews in the aftermath of the German occupation was unprecedented. Every third victim of Auschwitz-Birkenau, the largest Nazi extermination camp, was Hungarian.

This has important implications for the study of the Holocaust. The German state murdered hundreds of thousands of European Jews in the last twelve months of the war. To the very end of the war, Hitler and the SS chief Heinrich Himmler oversaw the destruction of Jewish lives and exploited surviving Jews as hostages. In the course of 1945, huge numbers of Jews, as well as thousands of Sinti and Roma, perished inside the Auschwitz camp before its liberation by Soviet troops in early 1945. In the following months, at least a quarter of a million former camp inmates perished on death marches that were organised with immense cruelty from camps the Germans had been forced to flee in the east.[1] This slaughter was carried out with overwhelming speed but was not the expression of some kind of ideological frenzy. Mass killing was an integral part of a strategy of organised plunder of assets and properties as well as bodies exploited for slave labour. The hundreds of thousands of Hungarian Jews selected to be killed within hours of arriving at Auschwitz were deemed unfit to be exploited as workers in the German wartime economy: the sick, the elderly, many women and children. Seven decades after this unprecedented episode of state-sponsored mass killing and theft, Auschwitz has become the most potent contemporary symbol of the German genocide. And yet it was only in the late spring and summer of 1944 that the apparatus of mass killing and enslavement was so fully exploited in the archipelago of camps in occupied Poland.

It is impossible to understand the tragic events that took place in Hungary in 1944 – including the various rescue negotiations – if we fail to take into the account the fractured and opportunist unfolding of the Nazi genocides. The Holocaust was not a single, unitary event as the generalised use of the word could be taken to imply. European Jewry as well as other ethnic groups and marginalised individuals suffered a succession of blows of increasing lethality. Mass murder was never a priority for the agents and apparatus of the Third Reich. It was shaped by circumstance and opportunity. As the late historian David Cesarani argued in his final book, the Nazi Final Solution was carried out in a ramshackle, slipshod way and with inadequate resources. Recognising the contingent nature of genocide is not in any sense to belittle its consequences – on the contrary, by understanding the mechanics of the Holocaust we see more clearly the terrible results of cumulative persecution.

When Hitler confronted Horthy at the Schloss Kleßheim in April, he accused him of failing to solve Hungary's 'Jewish problem'. Ribbentrop referred to an intercepted message to the Allies in which the Hungarian Prime Minister, Miklós Kállay, appeared to promise to continue protecting the Hungarian Jews. Why, demanded Hitler.[2] The Jews had fomented the Bolshevik Revolution, both world wars and now were in charge of the bombing campaign that was killing thousands of women and children. Germany, Hitler insisted, was secure only because German Jews had been deported to the East. Hitler and Ribbentrop repeatedly brought up the 'Jewish Question'. 'What am I supposed to do with the Jews?' Horthy bleated, 'I can't have them shot.' Ribbentrop shouted, 'The Jews must either be annihilated or sent to concentration camps. There is no other possibility.' The Jews were 'parasites', 'like the tuberculosis bacilli …' And so it went on. Hitler lost few opportunities to spew the pseudo-biological clichés of racial hatred. 'Why would the beasts that want to bring us Bolshevism be spared.' Hitler had subjected the Romanian leader Ion Antonescu to the same kind of tirade a few weeks before Horthy's visit to Kleßheim. He simultaneously urged a more radical treatment of Romanian Jews and laced his harangues with innuendos that the Romanian government was, in any event, already complicit in the per-secution of the Jews. There can be no doubt that Hitler and his satraps such as Ribbentrop directly intervened to escalate the onslaught on Jews in satellite states that included Croatia, Romania, Slovakia and Hungary. Despite Hitler's explicit demands that leaders of these allied states find radical, invariably lethal, solutions to their 'Jewish problems', the precise nature of intent has proved puzzling and elusive.

★★★

Historians of the Holocaust have provided two key insights into the gen-ocides committed by agents of the Third Reich. The first is that while Hitler appears to have offered broad guidance and sanction, his expressed wishes were developed and acted on by competitive satraps who pre-sided over the many administrative entities of the Nazi state. Secondly, this atomised system of power provoked an uneven but inexorable radicalisation of strategy and action on the ground. The consequence of this chaotic system of rule was an escalation of lethality directed at human groups perceived as enemies of the Reich: as 'life not worthy of life'. That phrase reminds us that the origins of the genocide lay in the German euthanasia programme that had been sanctioned at the same time that German troops and special units swept across the Polish border. In this singular case, we have a Hitler 'order' typed on his own notepaper and dated 1 September 1939, 'commissioning' Reischsleiter Bouler and Dr Med. Brandt to grant 'mercy-deaths' to the 'incurably ill'. This was written authorisation to commit illegal acts of murder in the hospitals and clinics of a modern European state. No such document exists for the 'Final Solution to the Jewish Problem'.

Large volumes of ink have been spilled debating precisely when a decision was made to enact a Final Solution. There is no 'Hitler Order' and it is very unlikely one was ever issued. Arguments that an unrecorded decision was made by Hitler in, say, October 1941 or May 1942 are all tendentious. What we can perceive in the historical record is a succession of abrupt quantum-like escalations in what the historian Ian Kershaw has called the 'genocidal tempo'. As early as the Polish campaign in September 1939, the head of the Reich Security Main Office (Reichssicherheitshauptamt or RSHA) Reinhard Heydrich organised the dispatch of Einsatzgruppen, specialised police units that would accompany the army to attend to security matters, which in the case of Poland meant to begin with the liquidation of the Polish elites. The RSHA, which had been established by Himmler in 1939, was a huge organisation that would play a major role in the management of genocide. Heydrich's special units would simultaneously initiate the persecution of Polish Jews. Goebbels noted that, 'the Führer's judgement on the Poles is annihilatory'. This is not to imply that there was a straight line to mass murder from even the most vicious expressions of racial hatred like Hitler's notorious Reichstag speech, made on 30 January 1939: 'If international finance Jewry within Europe and abroad should succeed once more in plunging the peoples into a world war, then the consequence will be not the Bolshevisation of the world … but on the contrary, the destruction of the Jewish race in Europe.' To borrow and adapt terms used in quantum physics, Hitler's rhetoric generated a force field that was restrained by its initial conditions or circumstances but could, as time passed and these conditions changed, release energies in quantum bursts as pulses of mass killing. This surely is what we can observe taking place in the historical record.

It is not often remarked in histories of the German genocide that the invasion and occupation of the Balkans in the spring of 1941 inaugurated the mass slaughter of Jews and other ethnic groups by fascist militias such as the Ustaša in Croatia, the Hlinka Guard in Slovakia and the Iron Guard in Romania. The Balkan military campaign was a rehearsal, at the very least, for genocide. This is made very clear by Hitler's appointment of the Ustaša leader Ante Pavelić as the 'Poglavnik' or leader of an independent Croatia, the Nezavisna Država Hrvatska or NDH, carved out of the carcass of Yugoslavia. Although some German military commanders were wary of the extremist Ustaša, Hitler met with both Pavelić and his war minister, Marshal Slavko Kvaternik, at the Berchtesgaden and encouraged a national policy of 'intolerance'. The Croatian leadership took this as a green light for a campaign of ethnic cleansing of extreme cruelty carried out with knives, hooks, hammers, mallets and axes. Inside the Jasenovac camp complex in Slovonia, Ustaša men murdered or worked to death tens of thousands of Jews, Roma, Bosnian Muslims and Serbs. The camp became an alcohol-fuelled slaughterhouse. Some including Peter Brzica, a novice Franciscan monk, staged gruesome throat-slitting competitions using a curved knife known as a 'graviso'. It was only after the Ustaša squads had killed some 180,000 Serbs in the first four months after the creation of the puppet Croatian state that the Germans tried to restrain their bloodthirsty allies. In Romania, the Germans censured the equally frenzied killing of Jews by Iron Guard squads – but on the grounds that mass murder had to be orderly.[3]

As the German army prepared for Barbarossa, Hitler issued a number of 'Decrees' that stripped away legal constraints on the most brutal actions by German troops, such as collective reprisals and the peremptory shooting of guerrilla fighters or partisans. The notorious 'Commissar Order' of 6 June stated that '[Soviet] Political Commissars have initiated barbaric, Asiatic methods of warfare. Consequently, they will be dealt with immediately and with maximum severity. As a matter of principle, they will be shot at once'. These decrees carried a covert racialised message in the word 'Asiatic', which synthesised the myth that Bolshevism was in essence a mongrel product of inferior Slavs and all-powerful Jews, who were the progenitors of the criminal Soviet state. These Decrees need to be understood in the context of the 'General Plan East', which had been commissioned by Heinrich Himmler. This megalomaniacal scheme set out a plan for an ethnographic reordering of the East through the eviction of more than 30 million Slavs and other ethnic groups, above all Jews, from the vast regions stretching to the Ural Mountains earmarked for resettlement by the Germans. This plan was, as Ian Kershaw emphasises, 'plainly genocidal'. Deportation was invariably imagined as the prelude to extinction.

As Himmler busied himself with these schemes, his deputy Reinhard Heydrich was preparing to send the Einsatzgruppen brigades in the wake of the German army across the Soviet border to pacify conquered regions of the Soviet empire. The ferocious campaign of the Einsatzgruppen has been documented extensively. Soon Goebbels was reporting that 'vengeance was being wreaked on the Jews in the big towns of the Baltic'; they were being 'slain in their masses'. The Germans often tried to depict these 'wild killings' as revenge taken by local populations against the 'vile Jews'. This was murderous casuistry; none of these slaughters would have taken place without German incitement and connivance.

There is now a huge literature on the Holocaust and many aspects of the genocide enacted by the German state in the course of the Second World War remain contentious. It is broadly accepted that the unfolding of the Holocaust can only be understood in *evolutionary* terms. There was no simple enactment of a diabolical wish somehow expressed by Adolf Hitler. Instead, intent has to be examined through the ebb and flow of contingencies generated by a globalised war that began in Europe on 1 September 1939. For reasons that are still not clearly understood, Hitler and the elite of the Nazi Party that seized power in 1933 had come to envision Germany's position in the world through the lens of a Manichean struggle with a global enemy that posed an existential threat to the nation. How that enemy was to be engaged and finally destroyed would be shaped by war. In Nazi ideology, war and the shedding of blood was the highest expression of national destiny. War would forge a new Reich or empire that would feed in every sense the German people and war would provide the world stage on which the racial enemy would be confronted. War is necessarily a succession of contingent events where outcomes are shaped by interlocking patterns of circumstance and opportunity. The Holocaust was enacted in the crucible of war.

The destruction of the Hungarian Jews took place as Hitler's Reich reeled from the impact of crushing military setbacks and was in many ways a unique event within the overall unfolding of the Holocaust. The Hungarian tragedy underlines Donald Bloxham's insight in his important study *The Final Solution: A Genocide* (2009) that, 'The question is never about Hitler's extremism … it is about the alignment of the people and organisations that would give shape and substance to his violent fantasies, and about the course of events that opened new vistas of possibility.' Nazi ideologue Alfred Rosenberg recognised the unpredictable power of contingency when he said in November 1941 that 'the Jewish question is solved for Germany only when the last Jew has left German territory, and for Europe when not a single Jew lives on the European continent up to the Urals'. This chilling sentence implies that the enlargement of German power through conquest would at some point in the future threaten every Jew in Europe. At the end of November 1941, Hitler informed the Grand Mufti of Jerusalem, who had fled to Germany from Palestine, that,

'Germany has resolved, step by step, to ask one European nation after the other to solve its Jewish problem, and at the proper time, direct a similar appeal to non-European nations as well.'

The use of terms borrowed from evolutionary studies is not meant to imply a smooth ascent to the realisation of an intent. Biological evolution is shaped by chance and opportunity; so too is human history. In December 1941 a succession of shattering events would alter the course of Hitler's war. The attack on the American fleet in Pearl Harbor led President Roosevelt to declare war on Japan. At a speech to the Reichstag on 11 December, broadcast on the radio, Hitler announced his decision to fulfil his obligations to an Axis ally by declaring war on the United States to ecstatic cheers from the party faithful. In the same speech, he repeated his 'prophecy' that world Jewry would be punished for instigating a world war. By the time Hitler made this reckless decision, the Wehrmacht's advance into the Soviet Union had ground to a halt in the icy world of the front line. On the German side, many secretly concluded that Hitler's war had become unwinnable. In the midst of this crisis, there is compelling evidence that Hitler initiated an escalation of the war on Jews.

This evidence is, to be sure, circumstantial. Hitler issued many orders and decrees in the course of the war but not a single one concerned the fate of European Jewry. A paper trail definitively linking Hitler to the Holocaust has never been discovered. There is, however, strong evidence that the erratic evolution of the genocide was decisively shaped by Hitler's unrecorded interventions. This can be supported, though not proven, by scrutiny of the 'Wannsee Protocols', or conference minutes, a document discovered in 1947 and described by the American war crimes prosecutor General Telford Taylor as 'perhaps the most shameful document of modern history'. The Protocols is also, in the words of historian Mark Roseman, deeply mysterious, unfathomable and macabre. The Wannsee Conference was a gathering of fifteen high-ranking representatives of the SS, the party and various ministries convened by Reinhard Heydrich, the ambitious chief of the RSHA. Heydrich turned to the head of his 'Jewish Affairs' department Adolf Eichmann to organise the meeting, which was originally planned to take place in mid December. We will come back to Eichmann's role at the conference in a later chapter. Following the shattering developments of that month, the gathering was postponed and eventually took place on 20 January 1942 in the SS guest house at 56–58 Am Grossen Wannsee. As snow descended from a grey sky, one of the most cold-blooded discussions in human history took place inside the villa's opulently appointed rooms. As Peter Longerich has emphasised, the minutes are not a verbatim transcript of who said what. Closely supervised by Heydrich, Eichmann later edited his raw notes to compile a document that was distributed at the highest levels of the Nazi government. The purpose of the conference, as Eichmann admitted, was above all political. Heydrich needed to assert his authority as head of the RSHA over the management of the 'Final Solution of the Jewish Problem'.

What that phrase really meant to the Nazi elite has been much debated by scholars of the Holocaust. The German historian Christian Gerlach made a convincing case that in the period immediately following Hitler's speech to the Reichstag on 11 December, he had announced his decision to 'exterminate all Jews in Europe' at meetings of the party elite.[4] One of the most telling pieces of evidence, according to Gerlach, is a note made by Rosenberg on 16 December about a meeting with Hitler that explicitly refers to 'the decision'. Rosenberg notes: 'My position was that the extermination of the Jews should not be mentioned. The Führer agreed. He said they had brought the war down on us … so it should come as no surprise if they became its first victims.' Gerlach's case implies that the conference was postponed not because of the political and military crises that erupted at the end of 1941 but because Hitler's decision 'to exterminate the Jews' fundamentally changed the nature of the agenda that would need to be discussed. In December, Hitler addressed a meeting of party leaders. Goebbels' summary of Hitler's speech in his diary is unambiguous:

Regarding the Jewish question, the Führer is determined to clear the table. He warned the Jews that if they were to cause another world war, it would lead to their own destruction. Those were not empty words. Now the world war has come. The destruction of the Jews must be its necessary consequence … those responsible for this bloody conflict will have to pay for it with their lives.

Gerlach also cites a speech made on 16 December by the Governor of Occupied Poland, Hans Frank:

one way or another – and I can tell you this quite openly – an end must be put to the Jews … basically, my only expectation of the Jews is that they disappear. They must go … In any event, a great Jewish migration will start. But what should happen to the Jews? Gentlemen, I must ask you to arm yourselves against any considerations of sympathy. We must annihilate the Jews, wherever we encounter them and wherever it is at all possible, in order to maintain the overall structure of the Reich here …

This debate about a 'Hitler decision' and its timing may seem academic to readers who might reasonably assume that Hitler had from the very beginning of his political career intended to eliminate the Jews. His writings and speeches often use metaphors of biological eradication. Even proposals for Jewish emigration, such as the unrealised 'Madagascar Plan', had a lethal outcome in mind. The German planners of the scheme assumed that Jews deported to Madagascar would not survive. Physical elimination may well have been on Hitler's mind but there is a fundamental gap between uttering threatening rhetoric and commissioning the destruction of millions of lives. It was the globalisation of Hitler's war at the end of 1941 that finally extinguished restraint. Opportunist mass slaughter could evolve into genocide. As Goebbels' words implied, Hitler made a final break with rhetoric: 'Those were not empty words.' By the end of 1941, more than half a million Jews had already been murdered in the occupied regions of the East in a swathe of mass killing that stretched from Riga to Ukraine. Hitler's decision to 'clear the table' in mid December 1941 signalled a decisive intensification in a dynamic, evolving process that could, as the boundaries of the Reich expanded, encompass complete annihilation on a European scale. Whether or not we accept Gerlach's very convincing argument, there still remains a yawning gap between a decision, whenever it was made, and its implementation.

In the period after he fled Europe and before his capture in 1960, Eichmann made a number of statements that take on macabre significance. He recalled that Heydrich had called him to the RSHA headquarters on Prinz Albrecht Straße and informed him that Hitler had 'ordered the extermination of the Jews'. Heydrich then despatched Eichmann to Bełżec in occupied Poland to meet an SS officer called Odilo Globočnik. 'Globus', as Himmler affectionately called his close friend, was a ruthless killer. A convicted murderer, Globočnik had been appointed Gauleiter of Vienna following the Anschluss of 1938 but had been sacked for corruption. This mattered little to Himmler – or rather it provided him with a means to keep this odious man in check – and he appointed him SSPF for the Lublin district in occupied Poland. If Eichmann was telling the

truth, his mission is highly significant. In October 1941, Himmler had
ordered Globočnik to begin construction of a new camp whose sole purpose would be to murder Jews en masse. Himmler turned to Dr Christian
Wirth, a veteran of the German T-4 euthanasia programme, to develop
a technical solution. By November, Wirth had begun a series of lethal
human experiments using exhaust gases from a Russian motor engine.
At roughly the same time, mobile gassing vans were being used at another
extermination camp in Chełmno. The technology proved to be cumber-
some and not always effective as a means to kill on such a large scale. Since
Hitler's decision to 'exterminate the Jews' was a daunting technical challenge, Heydrich's interest in the new technology is highly significant. It is
conceivable that Heydrich postponed the conference not only because of
the different crises that erupted in December but because he needed more
time to prepare for a very much bigger task.

On that cold January morning at the villa on the shores of Wannsee,
Heydrich began by reminding the conference that the Reich Marshall,
Hermann Göring, had given him full powers to prepare the 'Final
Solution of the Jewish Question in Europe'. Heydrich had attached copies
of Göring's letter formalising this appointment to the original invitations
that had been sent out in December. It is important to note here that
Heydrich was the author of the letter and that he had gone to Göring to
secure a signature. The reason is that Heydrich needed a legal imprimatur
to carry out his plans and this could only be given by a government
official – not an SS or Party one. Göring was the government minister
responsible for the Four-Year Plan. Heydrich had called the meeting to
'obtain clarity on questions of principle' and to harmonise the work of the
different agencies and ministries represented at the meeting. He insisted
that responsibility for the management of the Final Solution lay with
Himmler and himself – and that their jurisdiction transcended 'geographic
boundaries'. At a stroke, Heydrich took managerial responsibility for
the fate of some 11 million European Jews. The representative of the
Foreign Office, Dr Martin Luther, made no objection to this astonishing
organisational coup. Heydrich then spelled out the astounding scope of
German plans for these millions of Jews. They fell into two categories – on
the one hand there were Jews in Germany, the Axis and client states and
occupied territories. On the other, Jews living in England, neutral or non-
belligerent states such as Turkey and Spain. He recognised that enforcing
German policy in the latter territories might encounter difficulties.

He observed that even states allied to the Reich such as Hungary and Romania were reluctant to tackle their 'Jewish problem' and could prove troublesome. Using a pseudo-biological metaphor, Heydrich promised that Jews would be 'combed through' (like lice) from 'West to East'. Heydrich then expounded on the fate of these millions of people. Those unfit for work would be immediately liquidated, but, 'Able-bodied Jews, separated according to sex, will be taken in large work columns to those areas for work on the roads, in the course of which action doubtless a large portion will be eliminated by natural causes.' Heydrich no doubt had in mind the use of thousands of Jewish workers on the construction of 'Transit Route 4' (Durchgangstraße 4), which was planned to extend from Lemberg (Lwow) in Ukraine deep into the East. The project was managed by the local SS and the high death toll among the Jewish labourers was well known to Heydrich. He went on to explain that Jews who survived such a merciless regime would be 'treated accordingly'. There was no ambiguity about what he meant. 'Special treatment' was a euphemism for murder. These hardy Jews, Heydrich stressed, would 'act as the seed of a new Jewish revival'. Naturally, the SS planners came up with a phrase to describe this process: *Vernichtung durch Arbeit*, annihilation through work.

Not a single objection was raised to Heydrich's plan by any of the officials who attended the conference. For Heydrich, their compliance was a political coup. He had expected opposition: there was none. In September one of the conference participants, Otto Hofmann, spoke at a meeting of members of the SS 'Race and Resettlement Office': future generations, he said 'will no longer recognise any Jewish problem. In twenty years, there may not be a single Jew left … I cannot believe that we have exterminated more than one million of them thus far.'[5] Other matters proved to be less tractable. There was a long and sometimes heated debate about the treatment of Jews with gentile partners and their children, or 'part-Jews'. This was left unresolved. Although Heydrich made it brutally clear that fit, male Jews would be forced to work 'building roads', this glib formula failed to satisfy State Secretary Erich Neumann (representing the Ministries of Economy, Labour, Finances, Food, Transport and Armaments and Ammunition at the conference) who argued that Jews already working in the armaments industry should be exempted from the Final Solution. This gruesome tug of war between demands for elimination on the one hand and exploitation on the other was a continuous source of friction between different Nazi agencies. Despite these loose ends, Heydrich was in a jubilant mood when the conference drew to an end. 'Happily,' he reported, 'the basic outlines of the practical implementation of the final solution' had been settled. When he returned to RSHA headquarters in Berlin, he approved a list of nominees for the War Service Cross, Second Class. The list included Paul Blobel, who had managed the slaughter of tens of thousands of Jews at Babi Yar in Ukraine, and Dr Albert Widmann, who was busy experimenting with the development of gassing vans.

As it turned out, Heydrich's plan to 'Europeanise' the Final Solution proposed at Wannsee was, for some time, frustrated. He himself would never see it fulfilled. Nevertheless, the Wannsee Conference had a ghastly consequence for Polish Jews in German-occupied Poland, known as the General Government. As noted, the governor of occupied Poland, Hans Frank, had made clear in a speech that 'an end must be put to the Jews'. Heydrich had invited Frank to the conference, but as it turned out he sent his deputy, Josef Bühler. After a break for cognac, a refreshed Bühler complained that Jews in the General Government were 'useless'. In other words, not fit for labour. Not only that, Jews undermined the economy with 'black market activities' and should 'disappear'. Frank too had ranted about Polish Jews being 'extraordinarily destructive eaters'. Bühler urged Heydrich to consider beginning deportations in the General Government. His only caveat was about methods. He did not care for the 'wild killings' that had reportedly taken place in the Baltic region, the Ostland. A new modus operandi had to be found. By the end of 1941, the Germans had begun experiments to replace mass shootings with murder by gas.

The Wannsee Protocols are riddled by ambiguities, but it is certain that Heydrich planned to secure a leading political role in the 'Final Solution to the Jewish Problem'. Heydrich was immensely ambitious – and evidently recognised that managing the Final Solution was a means to win valuable accolades in the Nazi state. Heydrich's machinations provide more evidence that Hitler had unambiguously sanctioned the 'Final Solution of the Jewish Problem' at the end of 1941. Heydrich would not have sought managerial control of the Final Solution if he was in any way uncertain about its importance to the Führer.

If the Wannsee Protocols reflected intent, the consequences would prove to be erratic. There was no immediate allocation of resources to the Final Solution and unresolved debates about the status of the Mischlings and feuding about the economic exploitation of Jews rumbled on for some time. In early 1942, Nazi Germany was waging war on multiple fronts – across the Russian steppes, beneath the Atlantic Ocean and in the deserts of North Africa. At the end of 1941, the crisis on the Eastern Front had provoked Hitler to sack his commander in chief as well as numerous generals and issue the notorious *Haltbefehl*, or Halt Order, which forbade any retreat. By then, Hitler's 'War of Annihilation' had killed some 830,000 men since the start of Operation Barbarossa in June. The Wehrmacht had suffered immense losses of equipment – and the German economy was now put under severe strain. Göring insisted that German industry must be reorganised to serve military needs and Hitler appointed Fritz Sauckel, a fanatical loyalist, as plenipotentiary for labour mobilisation. Under Sauckel's ruthless management, millions of foreign labourers were soon enslaved in German factories. This enormous influx had further repercussions. Workers needed to be fed – and this challenge fell on the desk of one of the lesser-known architects of genocide, Herbert Backe, the Reich Minister for Food and Agriculture who had devised the 'Hungerplan'. This chilling document envisaged the deliberate starvation of millions of Slavic civilians and the diversion of food supplies to the German *Volk*. Historian Timothy Snyder concluded in his book *Bloodlands* that as a consequence of the 'Backe plan', '4.2 million Soviet citizens … were starved by the German occupiers in 1941–1944.'[6] The nineteenth-century German philosopher Ludwig Feuerbach said, '*Der Mensch ist, was er ißt*': Man is what he eats. Food supply was closely linked to the evolution of the Final Solution – which is why Bühler, Frank's deputy, referred to Polish Jews as 'notoriously destructive eaters'. This apparently mundane preoccupation with food and the nutrition of the German *Volk* profoundly informed the evolution of *Judenpolitik*. So too did the fortunes of war – and the impact of blind chance.

In the spring of 1942, Himmler had much to be happy about. The SS was accumulating enormous new powers and had secured complete control of the Reich's Jewish policy. This reflected not just ideological fanaticism but Himmler's determination to make the SS both a military and an economic powerhouse, making it a semi-autonomous state within a state. He expanded the Waffen-SS to challenge the Wehrmacht and fused the many finance, business and construction departments of the SS into the SS-WVHA, the SS business and administrative head office. In March 1942, Himmler completed his reorganisation by merging the WVHA with the inspectorate of the concentration camps. This was entirely logical because the camps had become valuable reservoirs of expendable slave labour. The calculation behind Himmler's business plan was that Jews capable of work could be 'annihilated through labour'. In other words, they would be exploited to death. Jews fit for work would be spared so long as they could work; the rest eliminated. Himmler calculated that 60 per cent of Jews in the Lublin district of the General Government would be immediately despatched.

In the late spring, the sadistic logic of exploitation and selective mass murder took on new and even more lethal energies. As the 'Policeman of the Reich', Himmler was preoccupied by security matters. Like many of Hitler's satraps, he was convinced that mysterious Jewish cadres were inciting resistance to German rule in Europe. On 18 December 1941, Himmler made a list of matters he planned to raise at a meeting with Hitler. A rather enigmatic note read: '*Judenfrage | als Partisanen auszurotten*': 'Jewish question | to be exterminated as partisans'. Analysis of the note revealed that 'Jewish question' was written down at a different time than 'to be exterminated as partisans'. It is a reasonable conjecture that Himmler jotted down that phrase as a side note in the course of the meeting. In other words, the answer Hitler provided to the 'Jewish question' was 'exterminate them as partisans'.[7] Himmler's cryptic note may seem to be rather fragile evidence for a strategy of mass murder – but actual practice by SS murder squads shows that anti-partisan 'actions' in the field frequently targeted Jews. There were, of course, many Jewish partisans who took up arms against the Germans but the notion that partisan warfare was entirely engineered by Jews was a myth. Nevertheless, not only was the link expedient, Jews and threats to the security of the Reich were deeply connected in Himmler's mind and in the spring of 1942 two events reinforced his fears.

On 18 May, there was an arson attack on an exhibition in the Berlin Lustgarten of anti-Bolshevik and antisemitic propaganda that had been organised by Goebbels. The Gestapo quickly tracked down and arrested the perpetrators. They turned out to be members of a Communist cell led by a Jewish couple, Herbert and Marianne Baum. This little known and rarely celebrated resistance group had been founded by the Baums in the mid 1930s; most of the members were Jews. In 1940, Baum and other Jews had been arrested and enslaved at the Siemens-Schuckertwerke works. A year later, he and a number of other Jewish workers had escaped into the Berlin underground to avoid deportation. There was no doubt that the group had organised the attack; punishment was swift and merciless. Baum was tortured to death in Moabit prison; Marianne was executed in Plötzensee; and the Gestapo decapitated or hanged all the other members of the cell.[8] The arson attack by the Baum group was a gnat's bite, but it fuelled Himmler's anxieties about the security of the Reich: Jews had launched an attack in the capital. There was much worse to come.

On 27 May 1942, Heydrich, who had been appointed acting Reich Protector of Bohemia and Moravia, was shot in Prague by Czech and Slovak soldiers from the Czechoslovak army-in-exile that was based in London. The operation, code-named Anthropoid, was masterminded by the Special Operations Executive (SOE). The attack was botched. Heydrich clung to life for several days but died of his wounds on 4 June. For the Nazi elite, the assassination of this charismatic senior figure was a profound shock and a spur to take revenge. In the Protectorate, German military units liquidated the Czech village of Lidice: 199 men were shot dead and the women deported to the Ravensbrück concentration camp. This wave of terror came to be known among Czechs as the 'Heydrichiáda'. None of the assassins was a Jew, but Himmler was rattled. He lashed out at the racial enemies of the Reich. Thousands of Czech Jews were deported to Majdanek. At Heydrich's elaborately stage-managed funeral at the Invaliden Cemetery in Berlin, Himmler insisted to the heads of the SS offices who had gathered in Berlin to honour their slain leader that the Final Solution must be completed by the end of the year. He sent orders to Globočnik: 'The resettlement of the entire Jewish population of the General Government should be implemented and completed by December 31, 1942.' No Jews would remain alive after that date. Furthermore, 'all projects that employ Jewish labour must be completed by that date'.[9] The fate of more than a million Polish Jews was sealed in those words.

In mid July, Himmler met with Hitler at the Wolf's Fort, his eastern headquarters. Soon afterwards, Himmler reiterated his order to accomplish the murder of Polish Jews by the year's end: 'These measures are necessary … for the New Order in Europe, as well as the security and cleanliness of the German Reich and its spheres of interest'. These 'necessary measures' depended on a broadening circle of acquiescence. The SS intensified pressure on German state railways, through the Reichsverkehrsministerium or RVM. Since 1940, a special department known as E II: No. 21 Massenbeförderung (Mass Transport) had been responsible for providing special trains deporting Jews from Germany and the occupied territories, working closely with the SS Reich Main Security Office. In July, the transport minister, Julius Dorpmüller, promised that he would provide 'a train every day with 5,000 Jews from Warsaw to Treblinka and well as a train from Przemysl to Bełżec twice weekly'. On 17 and 18 July, Himmler travelled to Auschwitz. Here he witnessed a demonstration of a new gas chamber. He was, it was reported, in a happy and convivial mood.

In this period, Auschwitz was not yet the main site of mass murder in the Greater German Reich. The so-called Reinhardt camps, the first dedicated centres of extermination, are, as Mary Fulbrook writes in her remarkable book *Reckonings*: 'far less present in our later imagination'.[10] The first extermination camp had been constructed in December close to the village of Chełmno. It was staffed by veterans of the T4 euthanasia centres, led by Victor Brack, who used specially designed gas vans to murder Jews brought to the camp. The following year, Globočnik and Brack set up three more dedicated killing centres in the Lublin District at Bełżec, Sobibór and Treblinka. Building on lessons culled from their experience at Chełmno, Brack and his T4 colleagues developed stationary gassing equipment, using carbon monoxide as a poison. Unlike Chełmno, the three new camps were built close to railway lines. The gassing apparatus was carefully camouflaged – and the cruel deceptions were used to trick new arrivals and to disguise what was happening inside the camps. T4 expert Christian Wirth was in charge of the first Reinhardt camp at Bełżec. The camp was in operation for less than ten months. During that time, some half a million Jews, as well as a smaller number of Poles and Roma, were killed. Only a very few inmates survived the Reinhardt Camps – and first-hand accounts are rare. Rudolf Reder was deported from Lemberg in August 1942. He recalled arriving at Bełżec, after a long journey in an overcrowded train – and the momentary relief he and other passengers experienced when an SS officer called Fritz Irrman addressed the crowd of exhausted and terrified passengers: 'First you bathe, and afterwards you will be sent to work'. Irrman made the same speech many times every day. Soon afterwards, Reder went on 'the little ones were wrenched from their mothers, the old and the sick were tossed onto stretchers, men and small girls were prodded with rifle butts further and further along the path … straight to the gas chambers.' SS guards and their Ukrainian helpers used truncheons and bayonets to herd victims into the three gas chambers. When the chambers were each tightly packed with close to 1,000 people in each one, the

SS guards switched on the engines. 'I heard the desperate cries in Polish and Yiddish,' Reder remembered, 'the blood chilling laments of children and women, and then one communal terrifying cry which lasted fifteen minutes.' Throughout the slaughter, an orchestra played 'from morning till evening'. The SS used Reder and other Jews to drag out the corpses using leather straps – and to haul them to huge mass graves.

Deception and camouflage were essential to the operation of the Reinhardt camps. Day after day, Irrman welcomed new victims on the 'Road to Heaven'. Signs were attached to the gas chambers: 'Bathing and Inhalation Rooms'. Huge numbers of trees and shrubs were planted to disguise what was happening inside the camp behind a green veil. Camouflage was used at the camps. At Sobibór, the camp commandant, Franz Stangl, installed brightly painted boxes of flowers outside camp buildings that were visible from the train station. Tree branches were woven into a thick canopy to shroud the barbed wire fences. Reder remembered the arrival in October 1942 of a 'very important person' to inspect the camp. This was almost certainly Himmler. He inspected the camp accompanied by local dignitaries including the SS and Police Leader of the District of Galicia, Friedrich (Fritz) Katzmann, the author of an official report: 'The Solution of the Jewish Question in the District of Galicia'. Katzmann boasted:

> In the meantime, further evacuation was carried out vigorously, with the result that by June 23, 1943, all Jewish quarters could be dissolved. Apart from the Jews in camps under the control of the SS and Police Leader, the District of Galicia is thus free of Jews ...[11]

On 11 January 1943, the British secret service intercepted a radio telegram that had been sent from Lublin to Krakow. For unknown reasons, the British decoders failed to grasp the significance of the message. It was only very recently that historians realised that Globočnik's staff officer, Hermann Höfle, was reporting that no fewer than 1,274,166 individuals had been subjected to *Sonderbehandlung* (Special Treatment). He refers to the different camps by first letter:

> State secret! To the Reich Security Main Office, for the attention of SS Obersturmbannführer EICHMANN, BERLIN. To the commander of the Security Police, for the attention of SS Obersturmbannführer HEIM, KRAKAU. Re: 14-day report Operation REINHARDT. Reference:

radiogram from there. Recorded arrivals until 31 December 42, L[ublin] 12761, B 0, S[obibór] 515, T[reblinka] 10335 totalling 23611. Situation […] 31 December 42, L[ublin] 24,733, B[ełżec] 434508, S[obibór] 10,1370, T[reblinka] 71,355, totalling 1,274,166. SS and police leader of Lublin, HÖFLE, Sturmbannführer.[12]

To compile his brutally succinct report, Höfle used data supplied by German railways, the Reichsbahn. More than a million Jews and other victims of Nazi terror had, in short, been murdered in the Reinhardt camps.

By the end of 1943, the enactment of the Final Solution was fully under the control of Himmler and the SS. In the aftermath of the Italian collapse and with relations deteriorating with satellite countries such as Hungary and Romania, Himmler signalled another quantum escalation of the genocide. He did so explicitly. On 4 October 1943, he met with a number of SS group leaders in Posen.[13] Using terse, handwritten notes, Himmler spoke for some hours. Then he made this statement. He wanted to speak about a 'a very grave chapter … we shall never talk about it in public'. He meant the 'extermination of the Jewish people'. He went on to sympathise with SS men who had been forced 'to see 100 corpses lying side by side or 500 or a 1,000 of them …'

'To have coped with this and … to have remained decent, that has made us tough. This is an unwritten – never to be written – and yet glorious page in our history.' Two days later, in the same city, he spoke to the Nazi Party elite. He made the same points stressing again that Germany could not have coped with the severe stresses of war 'if we had still had this corrupting plague in our midst'. At the end of his speech, he discussed the killing of Jewish children. It was justified, he argued, because he could not have allowed to have 'their children … wreak vengeance on our children and grandchildren'.

It has been argued that Himmler's 'Posen speeches' were intended to bind the SS and the Nazi Party elite in a complicit fraternity. Shared knowledge meant shared guilt. This is not entirely convincing. The men who had come to Posen to listen to Himmler knew a great deal about the Final Solution; they shared complicity already. The speech can be understood as simple triumphalism. In any case, Himmler's rhetoric reflected an intensification of the Nazi war on Jews. Just a few days earlier, Himmler and Ribbentrop had ordered that Danish Jews must be deported. This plan to deport the Danish Jews was thwarted, for reasons we will return to in a later chapter – but as the Wehrmacht consolidated the German occupation of northern Italy, Himmler appointed the ruthless HSSPF Karl Wolff to supervise 'police operations'. His arrival immediately endangered the 43,000 Italian Jews who lived in the northern part of the country. In October, Himmler appointed Theodor Dannecker, one of the most brutal 'Jewish experts' in the RSHA, to oversee deportations to Auschwitz. In 1940, Dannecker had been sent to France as Eichmann's 'advisor' on Jewish affairs. An extreme antisemite, he obsessively amassed lists of French Jews, many of whom were arrested between May and August 1941. The following year, Dannecker promulgated a set of regulations to facilitate the deportation of both native-born French Jews and 'stateless' Jewish immigrants. Throughout his time in France, Dannecker had pressurised the Vichy authorities to accelerate deportations to the east. Now under Dannecker's fanatical leadership, the SS rounded up Italian Jews in Rome, Milan, Genoa, Florence, Turin and Trieste. As the Reinhardt camps were wound down, Himmler sent Globočnik to Trieste, his hometown. In Trieste, Globočnik and his Reinhardt team, reinforced by Ukrainians and Italian fascists, set up a Polizeihaftlager (Police internment camp) inside a disused rice husking factory known as La Risiera di San Sabba. At the rice factory, one of the least-known relics of the Holocaust, the SS managed the transit of deportees bound for Germany and Poland, stored confiscated property and interned, tortured and murdered hostages, partisans, political prisoners and Jews. The Germans converted the rice-drying apparatus into a crematorium with the capacity to incinerate large numbers of bodies. The plans were drawn up by another T4 veteran, Erwin Lambert, who had designed crematoria for the extermination camps in Poland. In the winter of 1942–43, the SS deported thousands of Jews to Auschwitz, Ravensbrück and Bergen-Belsen. Very few Italian Jews returned to their homes after the war.

As Himmler and the SS cast their net of persecution and mass murder ever wider in the aftermath of the German occupation of northern Italy, the destruction of Polish Jewry reached a ghastly climax in the Lublin District. Again, unforeseen events triggered another escalation of the slaughter. Inside the Reinhardt camps, the Germans employed Jewish inmates known as 'work-Jews' to assist with the task of burning the tens of thousands of bodies of victims on top of pyres. For week after week, these men inhabited hell – but as long as the killing continued, they were safe. Among the work-Jews, there was talk of rebellion. But the stringent security inside the camp made showing any sign of resistance extremely hazardous. In the autumn of 1943, the surviving Jews in Treblinka began to fear that the Germans were winding down the work of the camp. On 2 August, SS guards were taken by surprise when a group of prisoners staged a chaotic rebellion. More than 140 inmates escaped into nearby woods. A few months later, in mid October, the Jewish underground in Sobibór rose against their guards and stormed the perimeter fences. In the aftermath of the Warsaw ghetto uprising, the Treblinka and Sobibór rebellions alarmed Himmler and the SS leaders. If the SS was losing control of its own high-security camps, how could it guarantee the security of the Reich? Hans Frank, Himmler's rival, complained that 'the camps with Jews in the General Government constituted a great danger, and the escape of the Jews [from Sobibór] proved it'. Stung by criticism, Himmler ordered Friedrich Krüger, the HSSPF in the General Government, to eliminate all the Reinhardt camps. He code-named the operation *Unternehmen Erntefest* – Harvest Festival. Krüger and his subordinates feared that if they proceeded with the liquidations one camp at a time, it would give Jewish prisoners time to organise resistance: to make sure this didn't happen, they would strike at the camps in a single blow.

In the field, Harvest Festival was directed by SS Brigadeführer Christian Wirth, who was a veteran of the T4 programme. In 1971, Franz Stangl, who served as commandant of the Sobibór and Treblinka camps, described Wirth to the author Gitta Sereny:

Wirth was a gross and florid man. My heart sank when I met him … he addressed us daily at lunch. And here it was again this awful verbal crudity: when he spoke about the necessity of this euthanasia operation, he was not speaking in humane or scientific terms, the way Doctor Werner at T4 had described it to me … [*sic*] He laughed. He spoke of 'doing away with useless mouths', and that 'sentimental slobber' about such people made him 'puke'.[14]

The purpose of Harvest Festival was to complete the liquidation of Polish Jews in the General Government and to erase the camps where more than a million Jews, as well as thousands of Roma and Sinti, had been murdered. At the end of October, Jews in the Trawniki labour camp, where the SS trained Ukrainian auxiliaries, were ordered to start excavating anti-tank trenches. Some of them realised that they were digging their own graves. On 3 November, 12,000 Jews were marched to Trawniki. SS officers, their Ukrainian assistants and members of Reserve Police Battalion 41, most of them drunk, began shooting to the accompaniment of loud music. By early afternoon, the SS had completed their task and began the grisly task of cremation. For more than a week a sickening pall of burnt flesh and smoke hung over nearby Polish villages. In the meantime, Trawniki was destroyed and the site disinfected; crops were sown. Altogether some 43,000 Polish Jews were murdered that day. In the aftermath of the operation, the camp sites were abandoned. Clumsy efforts were made to erase evidence of mass murder but when the SS squads withdrew, hundreds of Polish villagers rushed to the ruins in search of valuables and dental gold. Their activities threatened to expose the terrible secret of what lay beneath − so a second campaign to purge the evidence was launched.

In the modern collective memory of the German genocide, Auschwitz has become the dominant symbol of industrialised mass killing. This macabre status is a consequence of the tragic events that took place in the spring and summer of 1944. Following the German invasion of the Soviet Union, the instruments of mass murder were the rifles and machine guns of the Einsatzgruppen murder squads and their collaborators. Excavated pits were the terrible places of death. Then it was the Reinhardt camps that became the arenas of mass killing in the accelerating horror that began unfolding in 1942. Although many tens of thousands of Jews, Sinti and Roma and other human groups judged to be unworthy of life were murdered in Auschwitz before the end of 1943, the camp reached a zenith of destruction after the German occupation of Hungary in March 1944. With terrible speed, Eichmann's SS commando, working closely with the Hungarian police, deported close to half a million Jews to Auschwitz. It was the destruction of the Hungarian Jews in the last complete year of the war that made this single place the nadir of the German genocide. This fact raises many questions.

By the time Eichmann and his SS Sonderkommando drove into Budapest in March 1944, the unprecedented barbarity of the Final Solution was known to the Anglo-Saxon and Soviet Allies. To be sure, many of the details remained obscure and the pattern and scale of the genocide was not fully grasped. But the brutal fact that human slaughter on an unparalleled scale was taking place in German-occupied Europe and the Soviet Union was indisputable. Yet knowledge of this monstrous and unique crime took on very little significance in the minds of the Allied war leaders and was not reflected in any strategic decision made to defeat Hitler's Reich. The Nazi genocide was not unknown to the Allied leaders but had no impact on the conduct of the war.

This was not simply a consequence of the imperatives of waging a global war. From November 1942, information about the mass murder of Jews and other ethnic minorities was available at the highest levels of the Home and Foreign Offices in Britain. The acquisition of this information preceded by nearly two years the widespread dissemination of the famous 'Vrba-Wetzler' report made in June 1944 by two Slovak Jews who had escaped from Auschwitz. The earlier evidence, mainly from Polish sources, was evaluated by British intelligence as 'reliable'. The reason is that, as historian Michael Fleming has shown, the British government, the Foreign Office, the Ministry of Information and the Political Warfare Executive (PWE) *choreographed* the release of news about the unfolding genocide in Europe. In 1941, government advice was set out in a document: 'Combating the apathetic outlook of "What have I got to lose if Germany wins?"' According to Fleming's forensic analysis, documents like this show that the British government wanted Jews and their suffering to be excluded from the unfolding narrative of the war. Fleming argues that British officials feared reinforcing antisemitism, which was known through Mass Observation and other surveys to be widespread – a fact testified to by George Orwell among others. In a prescient essay titled 'Antisemitism in Britain', Orwell wrote:

> it is generally admitted that antisemitism is on the increase, that it has been greatly exacerbated by the war, and that humane and enlightened people are not immune to it. It does not take violent forms (English people are almost invariably gentle and law-abiding), but it is ill-natured enough, and in favourable circumstances it could have political results.[15]

Government choreography of news had the result that any kind of 'Jewish Story', including reports of mass killings, often ended up on the inside pages – even in the *Jewish Chronicle*.

It was no different on the other side of the Atlantic. As late as 1944, the editors of the American army magazine *Yank* refused to print a detailed report about Auschwitz on the grounds that it was 'too semitic' and could provoke 'latent antisemitism in the Army'. It was claimed that Jews 'brought antisemitism with them' and this poisonous stereotyping influenced both the reluctance to publish vital intelligence about atrocities and to accept Jewish refugees. The censorship of information about the genocide by Allied governments quashes the trope that British and American Jews did not do enough to expose the full scale of what was happening. The Allied powers did not want their citizens to suspect that their soldiers were fighting a 'Jews' war'.

The German genocide was shaped and driven by a confluence of fanaticism and mercantile opportunism. Contingency in the shape of military conquest and disaster, the gain and loss of territory sharply influenced the unfolding pattern of the genocide. These evolutionary configurations provoked radicalisation among the highly ambitious agents of the Nazi elites, above all the SS, who opportunistically competed to enact the vaguely defined goals of the Nazi leadership. The extinction of millions of lives proceeded alongside the most egregious plunder of liminal human groups including Jews and Roma and the ruthless exploitation of their bodies for profit and labour. This mass robbery of European Jewry was, of course, founded in antisemitic obsessions with the imaginary wealth and power of Jews and the innate inferiority of Roma and Slavs. While racial ideologies made the Holocaust conceivable, quotidian realities determined its enactment – and escalation. At any moment, however, fanaticism could be tempered by erratic acts of pragmatism.

According to the racial ideology of the Reich, inspired by the hallucinatory pamphlet *The Protocols of the Elders of Zion*, the Allied powers were manipulated by a secretive cadre of Jewish politicians and financiers. This implied to both Himmler and Hitler that they could use Jews as hostages to gain leverage against the supposedly Jewish-dominated elites of the Allies. In early 1943, with mass killings escalating elsewhere in occupied Europe, Himmler ordered the construction of a special sub-camp at Bergen-Belsen, located between Hanover and Hamburg, to corral Jews whom they believed would be considered suitable for exchange. By December 1944, some 15,000 people, all of them Jews, had been transferred to this so-called Residence Camp (*Aufenthaltslager*) which swiftly degenerated into a maze of dilapidated barrack huts and tents. In June 1944, a few hundred prisoners were released and sent to Palestine in exchange for ethnic German settlers who had been interned by the British. Altogether, the Germans released just over 2,000 prisoners from the 'Residence Camp'. Almost the same number of Polish Jews were deported to Auschwitz when their Latin American citizenship certificates were pronounced unsuitable for exchange. All were murdered. We will return to the Residence Camp in a later chapter – for it was here that more than 1,000 Hungarian Jews would arrive on the 'Kasztner Train' in the summer of 1944.

In German-occupied Europe, the men and women of the many Jewish communities that were being liquidated one after the other appealed directly to the Allied powers for help but were ignored with the most callous rigidity. In the face of German terror and Allied indifference, some, like the courageous rebels of the Warsaw ghetto and the Sobibór and Treblinka death camps, turned to armed resistance. Others resorted to more subtle strategies. They had no illusion that they were dealing with individuals capable of compassion but fervently hoped that money or some other material reward could persuade a few venal officials to barter in human lives. It is not appropriate to condemn them, as Hannah Arendt did in her tendentious account of the Eichmann trial, for so passionately holding to this conviction. These negotiators could see the Germans' genocidal plans through a glass darkly. Their sense of history was shaped by the pogrom, not by genocide. They were powerless in the face of the agents of a state committed to violence, betrayal and deception. The radicalism of the Final Solution and the accelerating evolution of the means to enact it over the course of five years of a barbaric 'war of annihilation' was impossible to conceive. It defied the moral imagination even of its victims. How this clash of desperate hope and fanatical opportunism played out in the tragic events of 1944 is the subject of the chapters that follow.

5

THE WORLDS OF HUNGARIAN JEWRY

In 2014, it is alleged by journalists Hannes Grassegger and Eva S. Balogh
that the Hungarian Prime Minister and leader of the nationalist Fidesz
Party, Viktor Orbán, turned to American political advisers Arthur J.
Finkelstein and George Eli Birnbaum to find ways of bolstering his grip
on power. Finkelstein had won fame as advisor to right-wing Republicans
including Richard Nixon and Donald Trump. In 1995, he had advised
Benjamin Netanyahu, who had launched a political campaign in the
aftermath of the assassination of Yitzak Rabin. Finkelstein's speciality
was ruthless 'negative campaigning' – in effect, trashing the opposition
and finding bogeymen to alarm voters. When Finkelstein and Birnbaum
entered the Hungarian political battlefield, 'the search began for a fire-
breathing dragon that Orbán had to fight with the help of the people'.[1]
With remarkable prescience, Finkelstein devised a campaign idea strategy
that was 'so big and so Mephisphelean that it will outlive itself'. The
American strategists provided Fidesz with an enemy in the shape of the
Jewish financier George Soros. Birnbaum has not stinted in his praise of
Finkelstein's genius. If his partner was an artist, he has written, Hungary
was his masterpiece. The diabolical George Soros conjured up by the
Fidesz campaign was:

> a new antichrist. An old rich man, a speculator who caused [sic] the col-
> lapse of the British pound in 1992, the Asian crisis of 1997, the 2008
> financial crisis. He destroyed [sic] the Soviet Union and Yugoslavia.

He sponsors left-wing extremists … and lives from drug trafficking and financial crime …

The creation of this demonic figure fed on a pre-existing Soros mythology. The most egregious ingredient Finkelstein added to the mix was a scurrilous claim that 'even as a child [Soros] delivered Jews to the Nazis, although he is a Jew himself'. Soros is indeed a Holocaust survivor; Finkelstein's claim is a crass misrepresentation of Soros' experience during the war.[2] The mythic Soros was, as Birnbaum gloatingly put it: 'globalised, freely available, and an adaptable open source weapon'. It was said in Hungary that no one was more important to Orbán's politics than Finkelstein and that Finkelstein never had a better student. When I visited Budapest in March 2018, Orbán was leading Fidesz in a general election campaign. Everywhere, I noticed posters showing Soros as an interfering grand master of skulduggery. It was classic antisemitic propaganda that tapped roots deep in modern Hungarian history.

When Adolf Eichmann's 'Special SS Commando' drove into Budapest in the wake of the German army on 21 March 1944, he confronted a daunting organisational task. German strategy in Hungary with regard to 'solving the Jewish problem' evolved in rapid steps in the weeks that followed the occupation. But Eichmann and his superiors knew from the beginning that hundreds of thousands of Hungarian Jews would have to be deported swiftly from the provinces and Budapest. The Commando comprised a mere 100 SS men recruited from the different branches of the SS. This included drivers, secretaries and other administrative officials. Eichmann had just a handful of experienced 'deportation experts' at his disposal. This elite corps was, as Eichmann knew very well, hardly adequate to rapidly organise the deportations. What made Eichmann's mission feasible would be the zealous participation of some Hungarian government officials. The key was his close bond with László Endre, a minor provincial bureaucrat and a radical antisemite. His diary records the first meeting with Eichmann on 29 March: 'Afternoon … Eichmann and his associates at my place. Jewish affairs advisors, dinner'. The dinner, it seems, turned boisterous. The well-lubricated Hungarians and SS men began firing machine guns. Eichmann presented his own weapon to Endre as a gift.[3] In his 'memoir' published by *Life* magazine in 1961, Eichmann explains how he went about securing the dedicated cooperation of these eager Hungarians.

Soon after we arrived in Budapest I met a Dr László Endre, then a Budapest country official, who was eager to free Hungary of the Jewish 'plague', as he put it. One evening he arranged a little supper for me and my assistant, Captain Dieter Wisliceny. Two or three other Hungarian officials were present and an orderly in livery who stood at Dr Endre's side. On this evening the fate of the Jews in Hungary was sealed. As I got to know Dr Endre, I noticed his energy and his ardent desire to serve his Hungarian fatherland … Over the years I had learned through practice which hooks to use to catch which fish, and I was now able to make the operation easy for myself … Dr Endre, who became one of the best friends I have had in my life, put out the necessary regulations … And so it was no miracle that the first transport trains were soon rolling toward Auschwitz.[4]

Why did so many Hungarians become willing executioners of the German genocide? In modern Budapest, as in many other former Soviet Bloc nations, the past is not a foreign country but is continuously refracted through the social and political dynamics of the present. This is a nation whose Prime Minister, Victór Orban, has taken to invoking the spirit of divisive wartime leader Admiral Miklós Horthy, who led Hungary into the catastrophe of the Second World War as an ally of Hitler and who often proclaimed himself a proud antisemite. In the spring of 2018, I discovered that Horthy still haunts Budapest. From inside a bulletproof glass case enshrined in a church portico, he peers out across Szabadság tér (Liberty Square) – a public space that is on the front line of a struggle with and for the past. Here different versions of Hungarian history jostle argumentatively together.

Liberty Square was once the site of an enormous prison known as the 'Hungarian Bastille'. It was used to incarcerate and, in some cases, execute the leaders of the 1848–49 Hungarian Revolution. During the time of the Austro-Hungarian Monarchy, the prison was demolished, and the streets nearby named after the revolutionary martyrs. The empty space thus became 'Liberty Square'. After the signing of the Treaty of Trianon, Hungarians gathered here to mourn the loss of national territory. They planted trees in soil brought from the lost lands. Here today you will find the heavily defended American Embassy and, not far away, a bronze statue of Ronald Reagan. The Gipper appears to gaze defiantly towards a mighty stone monument dedicated to the Soviet Army soldiers who perished liberating Budapest from the Germans in 1945. The proximity of these monuments has an ironic significance. Both the Soviet Army and Reagan were, at different times and for different reasons, celebrated as 'liberators'. Here too is the Hungarian National Bank whose wartime directors had few scruples ingesting the plundered wealth of Hungarian Jews. On the opposite side of the square is the decaying hulk of Hungarian National Television. Fidesz has an iron grip on Hungarian media.

Since Orbán's party Fidesz won the parliamentary elections in 2010 and proclaimed a new era of unashamed nationalism, he has sought to imprint this new age in the fabric of the capital city. New buildings, refurbishments of old ones as well as new statues and monuments proclaim the ruling party's vision. On the south side of the square is the latest and most inflammatory addition to this crowded space, the 'Memorial to the Victims of the German Invasion'. In front of a colonnade of broken columns topped by a tympanum, a bronze eagle representing Nazi Germany hovers menacingly above 'Hungaria', represented as the Archangel Gabriel clutching an orb, the symbol of royalist power. A ring encircles one of the eagle's legs inscribed with the date '1944'. At the base of the monument is a text written in four languages (Hungarian, English, German and Hebrew): 'In memory of the victims'. The style of the memorial has been described by one art critic as 'Viennese neo-baroque mixed with social realistic kitsch'.

Few memorials have provoked such bitter debate. For Prime Minister Orbán it is 'morally precise and immaculate'. But for many Hungarians the memorial is imprecise and contaminated. His government, embarrassed by international criticism that it had failed to stem antisemitic tendencies, commissioned it as part of a plan to make 2014, the seventieth anniversary of the German occupation of Hungary, 'The Year of Holocaust Remembrance'. The plan turned out to be divisive and morally tone deaf. The intention of the planned memorial was to commemorate all Hungarians, including Hungarian Jews, who suffered or lost their lives as a consequence of the German 'invasion'. This is ingenuous for what the memorial implies is that the wartime Hungarian state and its agents can be absolved wholesale of any responsibility for the murderous onslaught on its own civilians. The wartime alliance between Hungary and Nazi Germany is elided. The banal iconography of the neoclassical memorial crudely expresses a version of history in which 'Hungaria' is caught in the talons of the Nazi Eagle and helpless to resist. A group of Hungarian historians protested: 'The monument is based on a falsification of history … By presenting the victims of the Holocaust and the collaborators as a single victim, it insults the memory of the victims.'[5]

★★★

From the moment the secretive plans for the memorial were leaked in 2013, they incited protest and argument. The local mayor denounced it as likely to 'damage the country's reputation, infuriate democratic states, and divide and offend Hungarians'. But two days after Orbán and his Fidesz Party won elections in April 2014, workmen moved into Liberty Square and cordoned off the area where the memorial would be erected. Hours later, hundreds of outraged Hungarians gathered to protest and tore down the cordon. Protests continued for weeks but construction of the memorial continued. In the meantime, a new initiative emerged on Facebook known as 'The Living Monument – My History'. This soon took physical form in front of the construction site. Holocaust victims, survivors and their family members placed memorial stones, candles and other objects on the barriers that enclosed the site: these included, according to a local journalist, 'a piece of railway track wrapped in ribbon with the colours of the Hungarian flag, family pictures, children's drawings, rolls of film … a copy of a 1944 letter of free pass that was issued by the Swiss embassy for Jews at the time …'

Then at midnight on 19 July, under cover of darkness and when many families had left Budapest for the holidays, hundreds of police closed off Liberty Square. Trucks arrived bearing the eagle and the angel wrapped in silver foil and workmen began soldering together the last components of the memorial. By sunrise, their work was finished. Budapest had a new memorial.

In front of the 'Hungaria', the 'Living Memorial', which is ever changing, has never been removed and ironically defines the meaning of the official state memorial it confronts. The living memorial is just that. Visitors contribute fresh flowers and family tokens, handwritten family stories and personal relics. There is note that states: 'My mother was killed in Auschwitz. Thank you Archangel Gabriel.' On the cold, spring day when I visited Liberty Square, I could see scores of shoes, suitcases and photographs that defiantly expressed a different and oppositional way of remembering. Integral to the design are two white chairs that face each other and are intended to invite discussion. It is the most moving memorial to an event of the Holocaust that I have experienced.

There is another ghost that haunts Liberty Square. Follow the sightline of the Angel Gabriel and you will see the façade of the Calvinist Church of the Homeland just a few hundred paces away from the memorial. Its pastor, Loránt Hegedüs Jr, is a divisive figure in the fractured Hungarian political landscape. He divides his time between the church and the seat he holds in parliament for the Hungarian Justice and Life Party, MIÉP. His wife is an MP for the far-right Jobbik Party. His father is a bishop. In September 2001, Hegedüs wrote an article for a party newsletter that many interpreted as calling for the expulsion of Hungary's Jews. Although he was officially reprimanded by the Synod, he retained powerful support, most notably from his influential father, Loránt Hegedüs Sr, who is a bishop. The Reform Church has deep roots in Hungarian history and has traditionally espoused anti-Communist nationalism laced with a distaste for Jews. On 11 April 2013, Jobbik MP Márton Gyöngyösi stood in front of a crowd of supporters inside the Church of the Homeland. He made a speech eulogising Admiral Horthy as a hero who had rebuilt Hungary after the ravages of the First World War and the Treaty of Trianon. Then Pastor Hegedüs emerged from the church and unveiled a bust of Horthy in front of a crowd of Jobbik supporters. Beneath the bust of Horthy is the single word 'Trianon'. Pastor Hegedüs was again reprimanded for a public gesture that many liberal Hungarians, disturbed by the vibrant resurgence of the demons of reaction in their midst, denounced as a stunt. Six years later, Horthy still gazes stubbornly across Liberty Square.

Hungary's 'Jewish Question'

At the dawn of the twentieth century, Budapest, the most youthful of the great metropolises of Europe, was ascending to its zenith as one of the twinned capitals, along with Vienna, of the Austro-Hungarian Dual Monarchy. According to the historian John Lukacs, who was born in Budapest, it was 'a city of dualities', both provincial and urbane, cosmopolitan and proudly Magyar. Buda-Pest is, tangibly, a dual city – divided by the River Danube. Just before the turn of the century, Henri de Blowitz, who was then the most celebrated journalist in Europe and a diplomatic correspondent for the London *Times*, described installing himself on a warm, bright day on a balcony of the Hôtel Hungaria overlooking the Danube. He admired the river's stately flow between the mighty piers of imposing new bridges and the vista of the 'ancient and lofty fortress of Buda' perched on its rocky outcrop on the west side. He wrote that 'Buda-Pest names an idea that is big with the future. It is synonymous with restored liberty … the future opening up before a growing people.' By 1900, Blowitz's hyphen was outdated. By then, Pest, Buda and Óbuda ('Ancient Buda') had become intertwined as the sixth largest city in Europe. In the final decade of the nineteenth century its population had grown by 40 per cent. Berlin was the only comparable European city that grew at such a spectacular rate. But deeply ingrained differences persisted. The people of Buda were Catholic, conservative and mainly German speaking. It was Pest that fomented the passions of Magyar nationalism that exploded in the Hungarian Revolution of 1848. In 1867, Emperor Franz Josef I was crowned twice in Buda *and* Pest but this division had become a lot less stark by 1873 when the Hungarian Jewish municipal spokesman Mór Wahrmann pushed through the law that joined Buda with Pest. In 1892, an imperial decree proclaimed Budapest to be a capital and royal seat equal in status to Vienna.

Castle Hill (Várhegy) is a mere 300ft in height but viewed from a tram rattling across one of the city's bridges it presents a striking outcrop of primeval rocky defiance confronting the quays and promenades of Pest on the other side of the Danube. Even today, Buda seems to glance backwards. On a terrace in front of the Castle stands the equestrian statue of Prince Eugene of Savoy, whose armies took Buda from the Turks in 1686. Here the mineral baths of the old Water District, fed by springs, testify to the inheritance of Ottoman culture. So too does Rózsadomb, Rose Hill – so named for a Turkish official who, half a millennium ago, planted a rose garden on its slopes. By 1900, Rose Hill was about to become one of the most fashionable parts of the city – brash new villas were rising from its slopes. It was in Rose Hill that, when he arrived here in March 1944, Adolf Eichmann seized an apartment at 13 Apostel Street, a grand villa built by the Jewish industrialist Leopold Aschner, who was deported to the Mauthausen camp. Eichmann established the SS headquarters not far away in a remote corner of the Buda Woods close to the former summer residence of Baron József Eötvös, the Villa Exclusion in the Majestic Hotel. It was in the garden of the Apostel Street villa that Eichmann was accused of killing an adolescent boy called Solomon for stealing cherries. He was, allegedly, heard to mutter the phrase '*übriges Mistvolk*', meaning 'superfluous rubbish people' as he cleaned up afterwards.[6]

While Buda seems to look back over its rocky shoulder, the eastern half of the city, Pest, was the dynamic engine of the modern. Only the Fourth District, the Inner City, has any claim to genuine antiquity. In 1900, Pest was bristling with the shock of the new. Here along the Danube Corso stood the finest hotels in the city, the Hungaria, the Carlton and the Bristol. In September 1848, in the square in front of the Danube Place, the Austrian Commissioner Count Lemberg had been dragged from his coach and murdered by a Pest mob. But it was in the same square that two decades later in 1867, Habsburg Emperor Franz Joseph took the coronation oath as King of Hungary, thus enshrining the Ausgleich, the Compromise that created the Austro-Hungarian Dual Monarchy that yoked together the states of Austria and Hungary under the same ruler, with shared institutions and a joint ruler. The Compromise created a vast, multi-ethnic conglomerate, a supra-national state, ruled by Franz Josef as emperor in Vienna and as apostolic king in Budapest.[7]

The young Crown Prince Rudolf recalled:

In the church there were many magnates and officers, then the music started and the Primate and many Catholic and Greek bishops and very many other priests. Then came Papa and Mama. Mama sat down on a kind of throne, and Papa went to the altar, where a lot of Latin was read out … Afterwards, the drums resounded and Andrássy and the Primate put the crown on Papa's head. Then the imperial orb and sceptre were placed in Papa's hands.

Rising from the flat landscape of the Danube's eastern flank, Pest was a city designed and planned to rival its more venerable imperial twin, Vienna. The most notable tip of the hat to Budapest's rival city is the Ring that connects the Margaret Bridge to the north and the Petőfi Bridge at its southern end. The Ring in turn gives rise to a succession of semicircular boulevards that ripple gently towards the Danube. The widest and longest of these was Andrássy Avenue, intended to rival the Champs Elyssee in Paris and Unter den Linden in Berlin, that ran through the city like an arrow pointed hopefully into the future. Beneath Andrássy Avenue, in a narrow tunnel dug out of the sandy soil, sped the boxy, yellow carriages of the electrified Franz Josef Underground Line that linked the City

Park with the Ring by way of the Budapest Opera House, the Octagon and its multitude of coffee houses and Heroes' Square with its statues of the ancient Magyar Chieftains and the Tomb of the Unknown Soldier. Between the Octagon and the City Park, Andrássy Avenue became the hub of an ostentatious villa district where in a bewildering melange of architectural styles resided members of the old Magyar aristocracy, diplomats such as the British Consul and some of the city's wealthiest Jewish families. Here it was that Manfréd Weiß, one of Hungary's most important and innovative industrialists who founded the huge Csepel Works on the outskirts of Budapest, built a villa for his family. In the 1950s, his granddaughter Marianne Szegedy-Maszak returned to 114 Andrássy Avenue and described the 'spectacular house' that had 'muscular, half-naked men supporting the sweep of the balcony'. When she visited, the villa had been turned into a guest house for the Russian Embassy next door. In 1944, SS Lieutenant Colonel Kurt Becher seized the villa from the Weiß family and set up offices to oversee the appropriation of the Manfréd Weiß Steel and Metal Works for Heinrich Himmler.

For reasons I will come to shortly, some Hungarian Jews were indeed very wealthy – for a time the wealthiest Jewish community in Europe. The majority of Budapest's Jews did not live on Rose Hill or Andrássy Avenue. In the Theresa and Elizabeth districts, Jews made up one third of a beleaguered community that fought a daily battle with hunger and poverty. According to one reporter, 'They were the simplest Jewish merchants … bushelmen, cleansers, poor women, peddlers.' Jews had lived in the region since Roman times and, like Jews everywhere, were vulnerable to unpredictable patterns of toleration, exclusion and persecution. They had been safer under Turkish rule; the return of Austria as a dominant power threatened to unleash a resurgence of antisemitism.

★★★

Despite this, Jewish immigration increased steadily as poverty ravaged Jewish communities in Galicia and other imperial domains. In the vast 'Pale of Settlement', demarcated in the Russian Empire, savage pogroms erupted in the wake of a peasants' uprising in Poland.[8] The persistence of pre-modern social relations, feudalism in short, excluded Jews from land ownership and so compelled many to take up occupations in trade and finance. The rapid modernisation of these sectors of the economy led to an expansion of new commercial and intellectual professions. These in turn rewarded investment in higher levels of education. Learning was traditionally valued in Jewish communities and so many Jews had the means to excel in the competitive new world of the professions. By 1900, Jews made up 5 per cent of the Hungarian population, but 57.9 per cent of trade and bank employees, 48.3 per cent of physicians and 34.1 per cent of lawyers. Many of Hungary's most vocal journalists were Jews. The most important literary journal, *A Hét*, was edited by the Jewish novelist and poet József Kiss. All the leading writers in Budapest wanted to be published in *A Hét*. Kiss celebrated emancipation in his early writings – but by the end of his life he was lamenting:

> He was free to pray in his homeland
> Disowned, destitute, and homeless
> Maybe the grave will bring him peace
> But maybe even that will reject him.[9]

In 1900, many Jews in the Austro-Hungarian Empire lived in a very different world from that their grandparents had made. At the end of the eighteenth century, the Orczy family constructed a rambling warren of interconnected buildings near what is today Károly Körút. Taking up an entire city block, Orczy House, as it came to be called, was the second largest building in old Pest after the Károly barracks and served a bewildering number of roles. The Counts of Orczy were sympathetic to Jewish immigration and the Orczy House was a kind of metropolitan *shtetl*, or Jewish town. Hundreds lived inside and rents brought in, it was said, one gold coin every hour for its owners, who for a time paid the highest taxes in Pest. Behind the walls of the Orczy House, visitors could find a synagogue, baths, schools, study houses, bookstores and storage cellars crammed with feathers, rags, wool, horn, oak apple, black pepper, Halina cloth, glue, starch and gum. There was a doctor in the house, a barber, an apothecary, a midwife and surgeons, corpse washers and dressers. In short, 'everything a traditional Jew may ever need throughout his life'. By the end of the nineteenth century, this rambling warren of rooms had become a reception centre for the thousands of Jews newly arrived from the eastern provinces of the Empire. At its chaotic, pulsing heart was the Orczy'sche Café opposite the market. According to one observer, the café was the centre of the world. It was also called a 'Noah's Ark in itself filled up with all kinds and forms of human existence'. The Café Orczy served as an exchange for Jewish cantors and teachers. Many came here desperate for a position. A description of the Orczy Café can be found in the autobiography of the Hungarian Jewish traveller and Turkologist Arminius Vámbéry:

> As an educational exchange, the Café Orczy […] enjoyed in those days a special popularity. [It] was crowded then with town and Country Jews of all sorts and descriptions … It was always a most painful scene, of which I have since often been reminded when visiting the slave markets in the bazaars of Central Asia. With a heavy heart and deeply ashamed I used to sit there for hours many afternoons together …[10]

Both before and after the First World War, there was a perilous pivoting in Hungarian politics and society between reaction, often violent, and acceptance, always ambivalent. There was a reason for this. The people of the Hungarian lands were astonishingly diverse. In many regions, Magyars were a minority of the population. They coexisted anxiously with Romanians, Croats, Slovaks and Germans who often far exceeded Magyar speakers. For Hungarian nationalists, the expanding Jewish community was ripe for demographic exploitation. For one of the provisions of emancipation was the opportunity for Jews to register as gentiles: in effect, this meant not just religious conversion but ethnic assimilation as Magyars. If Jews chose to identify as Hungarian, this promised to transmute the unbalanced demographics that so troubled nationalists. And many did. Only a small minority chose to become Christians, but by 1900 more than 70 per cent declared Hungarian as their mother tongue. Jews who embraced a Magyar identity in this way came to enjoy exceptional levels of social mobility. By the end of the century, for example, Jews made up nearly 20 per cent of the Austro-Hungarian army officer corps. Since there was no 'Jewish' or any other kind of ethnic political party, close to a quarter of Hungarian members of parliament were Jews: many of them reaching high office. The paradox of Hungarian history is that the success story of emancipation was entwined with the most vicious hatreds for the balance between toleration and rabid hostility was continuously shifting. The safety of Hungarian Jews was precarious, but it was rarely a straightforward task for many in the community to spot the perils that lay ahead – and even more difficult to predict when the balance would tilt the wrong way.

In 1859, when the Central Synagogue on Dohány Street was opened, Hungarian Jews formed one of the most religiously diverse communities in Europe. Many Hassidic Jews lived on the eastern margins of the Empire and preserved cultures very different from the Jews of the big cities. In the so-called Jewish triangle of Pest, which was an urban quarter not a ghetto, three synagogues or temples symbolise the three major wings of Hungarian Jewry. At the base of what is strictly speaking an inverted triangle, the Dohány Street synagogue is a magnificent building in the Moorish style. It remains the biggest synagogue in Europe and on high holidays its cavernous interior can seat 3,000 people. When it was completed, the synagogue expressed the desire of the Jews of Pest to become part of the Hungarian nation. On 20 December 1860, the festival of Jewish–Hungarian brotherhood was celebrated inside the temple, with the choir singing patriotic songs. A decade later, shortly after the Compromise had joined Austria and Hungary, the General Jewish Congress was held in the city's County Hall. Although emancipation remained legally moot, the Minister of Religion and Education, Baron József Eötvös, gave an opening address that promised 'the freedom, granted by the constitution of Hungary, will bind the Israelite citizens of our country to the homeland'. When the Baron sat down, the members of the assembly proclaimed, 'Long live the Homeland!'

While the city of Budapest fomented the dynamics of modernisation, the rest of Hungary remained semi-feudal. Here, Hungarian Jews were part of the complex mosaic of an Austro-Hungarian society marinated in ossified tradition. As Hungary stepped into the twentieth century, its history would be shaped by two very different kinds of aristocracy. One was the traditional nobility comprising landowning magnates whose wealth derived from their huge estates in the provinces. By the beginning of the twentieth century, the wealth of the old nobility was beginning to decline but was by and large intact. The wealthiest families, such as the Esterházys and Andrássys, had deep roots and divided their time between their great country houses and Budapest, where many served in the government. Count Frigyes Podmaniczky became vice president of the Council of Public Works. Some had houses in the most salubrious districts of Buda, but it became increasingly fashionable for princely families to invest in grand villas on Andrássy Avenue. By 1900, some of the nobility had begun intermarrying with the daughters of Hungary's other aristocracy, the new financial elite, many of whom were Jews. Sandwiched uncomfortably between the two aristocracies were the 'dzsentri' – the gentry, derived from the English word. They too derived their wealth from the land, but by 1900 the gentry was in decline. Profits from their property were falling and they were excluded from higher grades of the rigidly hierarchical Hungarian civil service. The nobility served as ministers, ambassadors, generals and judges; the gentry as lower-level administrators. They had security and pensions, to be sure, but little wealth – and this made many jealous and resentful. As a class, the gentry saw itself as the flag-bearer of Magyar nationalism and upholders of their Christian faith. They dominated the realm of the state and disdained private enterprise. As Hungary entered the modern age, the demand for financial managers such as auditors and accountants increased. Many educated Jews also took on newly professionalised jobs as lawyers and doctors. But even in rapidly evolving urban centres, the sons and daughters of the Hungarian gentry showed little interest in such mundane jobs. They took less interest in education and were thus excluded from many professions. In short, the gentry looked inward rather than outward and would come to fear and envy more cosmopolitan neighbours. Many of these neighbours were Jews. Before the catastrophe of the First World War, this envy was not yet full-blown antisemitism. But the virus of that malevolent prejudice had begun to seep into the national bloodstream.

The disdain for commerce among the self-appointed flagbearers of the Hungarian national cause meant that since the end of the eighteenth century, the captains of industry and finance were often ethnic outsiders – or more precisely, members of non-Magyar families. At the beginning of the nineteenth century, many Greeks fled the Ottoman lands to take advantage of new opportunities in Buda and Pest. Traces of this incursion can be found in common family names such as Haris, Lyka, Mannó and Agorasztó. Soon other Europeans followed in the wake of the Greeks, Norwegians, Swiss and, of course, Germans, who dominated many districts in Buda. Jews were latecomers. Most specialised in grain trading. Many were passionate about the Magyar cause and risked their wealth for the 1848 Revolution and War of Independence. That they were both Jewish and Hungarian was never in doubt. After the Compromise of 1867 and their emancipation by Franz Josef, a handful of Jewish families swiftly took the lead, modernising the Hungarian economy. The most enterprising moved away from grain trading to establish mills, factories and distilleries. They invested in banks and other instruments of finance. In less than four decades, the financial clout of Jewish families rivalled the old nobility and eclipsed the gentry.

Although the avowedly antisemitic Mayor of Vienna, Karl Lueger, disparaged Budapest as 'Judapest', before the First World War dynastic names such as Weiß, Chorin, Kornfeld and Hatvany-Deutsch had won respect among Hungarians whatever their faith or ethnicity. Contrary to the antisemitic shibboleth that Jews are always the rootless, cosmopolitan enemies of nationalism, Hungarian Jewry was the most assimilated Jewish community in Europe. A few families converted to Christianity, but the majority were devoutly committed to Hungary and to a Magyar culture. There is a reason for this. As Jews from Europe and then further east settled in Budapest, they encountered obstacles in the shape of the German guilds that dominated the lives of traders and artisans. In 1848, the year of revolution, guild apprentices led violent attacks against Jews in Buda. This was a powerful reason to identify with the Magyar cause – which led many Jews to take Magyarised names.

Modern antisemitism is an urban disease. While it is not a coherent ideology, the hatred of Jews tends to focus a repetitive cluster of prejudices and one of the most potent associates Jews with a deracinated modern sensibility that is expressed in the frictionless commerce of the modern city. In the eyes of antisemites, Jews are urbanised creatures devoid of more natural values. Such myths feed on distorted historical realities. During the nineteenth century, Jews, like many millions of others, migrated away from rural areas to embrace the opportunities of expanding cities. Unlike other provincial migrants, many Jews clung to traditional customs and rites: this meant that they remained visible as Jews. They came to be despised by some as the quintessence of a new rootless kind of urban life. Since nationalists tend to see their values embodied in rural life and customs, these urbanised Jews seemed to embody a threat.

Even at the end of the nineteenth century, Hungary was an exception. While in Austria, 90 per cent of Jews lived in Vienna, only 20 per cent of Hungarian Jews lived in Budapest. According to Lukacs, the majority were 'dispersed, many of them assimilated within the Magyar population in the small towns of the provinces'. Both Joel Brand and Rudolf Kasztner were born into provincial Jewish families. It would seem that in Budapest, the rising numbers of professionals who happened to be Jewish inspired trust among their patients and clients rather than resentment. It is telling that the founder of Zionism, Theodor Herzl, whose childhood home was not far from the Dardány Street Synagogue, came to fear violent antisemitism as an incurable condition only when he left Budapest to work as a reporter in Paris and Vienna.

Beneath the surface, the antisemitic virus was busily at work. It has never been purged.[11]

The Tide Turns

By the beginning of the twentieth century, the antisemitic virus had begun to take root in Budapest. Here it took on a chic modern garb, that of a populist democracy. It was modernised. It had little connection to tradition and was immensely dangerous. What went wrong?

For many Jews, the eruption of this new plague came like a bolt of lightning. There were sixteen Jewish members of parliament. Dozens of Jewish lecturers taught in the city's universities. A genre of novel celebrated friendships between Jewish and Magyar characters. Then, in 1901, a novelist called Miklós Bartha published *In the Land of the Khazars*. The book's title alluded to the myth that Ashkenazi Jews are descendants of a semi-nomadic Turkic tribe that converted to Judaism and thus had no connection to the ancient Jewish tribes of Palestine. The theory, which fascinated Arthur Koestler, who grew up in Budapest, has been thoroughly discredited and remains popular only among neo-Nazis and conspiracy theorists. For Bartha, the point was that Jews were an Oriental horde, a 'verminous pest'. In his story, the Jewish characters are all greedy shopkeepers and loan sharks who trick and exploit impoverished peasants. Although the novel is set in faraway Ruthenia, a region in the Carpathian Mountains, Bartha called Budapest 'Sodom'; he denounced the city as corrupt, corrosive and decadent. In other words, in Bartha's jaundiced eyes it was 'Jewdapest'.

Bartha's best-selling novel captures the moment when the tide turned against Hungarian Jews. Some of the more prestigious Budapest clubs banned Jews from membership. A younger generation of priests preached against the decadence of Budapest and the role of 'Jewish influences'. In universities, students turned against their Jewish fellows, accusing them of disloyalty. In the last decades of the nineteenth century, Hungarian Jews had taken a leading role in the modernisation of Hungary and the professionalisation of its elites. Now Christians accused Jews of arrogantly taking on the leadership of the nation. There were disturbing signs of some kind of awakening hostility. But in the prosperous world of Budapest in the years before the outbreak of the First World War, only a minority of Hungarians came to see Jews as a serious threat. Few Jews feared that the uniquely inclusive empire ruled by the reassuring figure of Franz Josef would close its doors to them. The catastrophe of the war and the humiliation that followed the defeat of the Central Powers would whet the knives of racial hatred.

The nation of Hungary was born in the ruins of empire. Hungarians were traumatised by the defeat of the Central Powers in 1918 and the abrupt disintegration of the Austro-Hungarian Empire. Hungary was shorn of its former imperial partner Austria and now became a kingdom. But it would be a kingdom that sacralised the searing pain of territorial loss – which, nearly a century later, is barely diminished in the rhetoric of the Fidesz government. Although many Jewish Hungarians embraced a nationalist Magyar identity in the years of the Dual Monarchy, the pathology of the Trianon obsession, which dominated Hungarian political culture in the aftermath of the First World War, untethered the fragile bonds of assimilation and made Hungarian Jews vulnerable to increasingly radical exclusion. It was the baleful spirit of Trianon that lay deep at the root of Hungary's Jewish tragedy.

During the course of the First World War, there were many opposition politicians who argued vehemently that Hungary had nothing to gain from the war being fought by the Central Powers. It was, they believed, the Austrian twin that was dragging Hungary to the brink of disaster. These Hungarians believed they had no quarrel with the Entente powers – but remained blind to the fact that, even before the end of hostilities, the French and British had made promises to rival states Romania, Czechoslovakia and Yugoslavia at the expense of Hungary. In fact, the question of Hungary deeply troubled the peacemakers gathered in Paris in 1919. This was not simply because the Hungarian armies, unlike the Romanians, had fought to the bitter end. The French and British expressed a liberal distaste for Hungary's aristocracy with its vast estates and a peasantry that had barely risen above serfdom. Even Hungary's history was dubious. The Magyars were barbarian invaders who had galloped out of Central Asia in the ninth century. Somehow Hungary was a poor fit in the new Europe that was being conjured up in Paris. The British Prime Minister Lloyd George opined that, 'I had a conversation with someone who has visited Hungary … the country has the worst system of landholding in Europe. The peasants there are as oppressed as they were in the Middle Ages.' He had not been misinformed. The new Hungarian Prime Minister, Mihály Károly, owned a 60,000-acre estate, a glass factory and a coal mine. He had enjoyed an indulgent youth and before turning to politics was a notorious playboy, with an insatiable passion for fast cars and casinos, who divided his time between a magnificent country estate and a villa in Budapest. What Lloyd George may not have understood is that behind the oligarchic trappings, Károly was, for his class, a progressive. Appointed Prime Minister in October 1918, he had no illusions about the storm Hungary would now have to endure as the European empires collapsed and so-called 'successor states' competed to extract maximum territorial advantage. As is often the case, peace provoked a cascade of petty wars and skirmishes. In that bitter winter, Károly had few cards to play. When he met the French General Louis Franchet d'Esperey in Belgrade, Károly was treated to a demeaning lecture: 'I know your history. You have oppressed those who are not Magyar,' the Frenchman declaimed. 'Now you have the Czechs, Slovaks, Romanians, Yugoslavs as your enemies. I hold these people in the palm of my hand. I have only to make a sign and you will be destroyed.' It is not surprising to discover that an American delegate at the Paris conference described Károly as 'permanently worried'.

So it was that in the gloomy days of November 1918, the Austro-Hungarian Empire fell apart – and, stripped of its imperial cloak, Hungary plunged into chaos. Violence engulfed Budapest and other cities. Crowds celebrating the end of the war drunkenly turned on Jews, looting shops and houses. During these months, more than 6,000 Jews were beaten or robbed by their neighbours. In Paris, Károly sought to make amends with the Allies, but was given short shrift. When he discovered that Romanian, Czech and Yugoslav forces had penetrated deep into Hungarian territory with the sanction of the Entente powers, Károly threw in the towel. His resignation threw open the door to a hitherto disregarded faction of Communists whose leader was in prison. This was Béla Kún. According to the once-celebrated American journalist Stephen Bonsal, who was President Woodrow Wilson's private translator at the Paris Peace Conference, Kún was an 'ugly man' with 'a flat nose and enormous ears, whose enormous head wobbled precariously on a thin body'. Born in Transylvania, his father was a non-practising Jew and a notorious drunk.

Kún would become for many Christian Hungarians the archetypal 'Jewish Bolshevik', but he himself said, 'My father was a Jew, but I did not remain a Jew, because I became a socialist, a communist.'

Before the war, Kún had built a reputation as a left-leaning journalist despite or perhaps because of his hot-headed vanity and narcissism. His sharp pen skewered wealthy Jews as well as gentile oligarchs. Class consciousness was more important than the shackles of heritage. During the war, he had fought on the Eastern Front and ended up in a Russian POW camp. At the end of 1917, Kún was caught up in the Bolshevik Revolution and ended up in Moscow, where he embraced the faith of Leninism. As the war ended, the Soviets sent him back to Budapest with false papers and a suitcase stuffed with gold to preach the doctrine of revolution. The timing was shrewd. As Budapest descended into chaos, Kún and a small cadre of fellow revolutionaries, many of them Jews, set about organising strikes and demonstrations. He may have lacked film star looks – but Kún possessed, it seems, a magnetic energy. Beaten up by the police and sent to prison, he consummately played the martyr. Then on 21 March, a little party of radical social democrats stepped into his prison cell and offered Béla Kún the keys to power. He seized them with both hands.

Kún and his comrades stepped into a chaotic power vacuum with the hope that the Bolshevik government in Moscow would rush to their aid. But the year-old Soviet government was engulfed in fighting civil wars on many fronts and Lenin curtly dismissed the Hungarian Communists' pleas for aid. To begin with, the Hungarian Soviet Republic won some popular support because it was aggressively opposed to the settlement that the Entente victors wanted to impose. Many former Austro-Hungarian officers joined the newly formed Hungarian Red Army for this reason. But the Kún regime soon squandered the fragile backing it enjoyed. In Paris, none of the peacemakers had any idea what could be done. They feared a kind of Bolshevik infection spreading from Moscow and Budapest like the influenza epidemic that was devastating communities all over the world at the end of the war. But the Allies lacked the will and the means to crush the Hungarian Soviet.

There is no doubt that the Kún regime deserves the harsh judgement of history. Kún and his cadre of young urban intellectuals issued a stream of decrees to cure, at a stroke, the ills of Hungarian society. It was a time, Lukacs writes, defined by 'imbecility, inefficiency and terror'. In the summer of 1919, as its people starved, chaos gripped Budapest.

As discontent mounted, Kún turned against those he regarded as arch enemies of the Soviet, the capitalists and the bourgeoisie:

> Power has fallen into our hands. Those who wish the old regime to return, must be hung without mercy. We must bite the throat of such individuals. The victory of the Hungarian Proletariat has not cost us major sacrifices so far. But now the situation demands that blood must flow. We must not be afraid of blood. Blood is steel: it strengthens our hearts, it strengthens the fist of the Proletariat. Blood will make us powerful. Blood will lead us to the true world of the Commune. We will exterminate the entire bourgeoisie if we have to!

The 'Red Terror' was exploited – and is still exploited – by Hungarian nationalists. In their propaganda, they portrayed the horrors of the Kún regime as the malevolent consequence of 'Jewish' power. The three main leaders of the Soviet were Jewish but that had nothing to do with the tyranny they briefly brought to Hungary: Jews were significantly overrepresented *among the victims* of the 'Red Terror' – even though many Christian Hungarians would recall the short life of the Soviet as a 'Jewish Uprising'.

As this grotesque farce unfolded, the French and the British could see that some kind of order had to be imposed. They insisted that all foreign troops must withdraw from Hungary and summoned a Hungarian delegation to Paris. On 4 June 1920, the delegation gathered inside the Grand Trianon Palace at Versailles and signed, with reluctance and shame – defining Hungarian borders to the present day. At a stroke of a pen, Hungary lost two thirds of its pre-war territory and the peoples that now lived behind new borders. The historian Deborah Cornelius succinctly sums up the consequences of the Paris treaties: 'the dissolution of the Austro-Hungarian Monarchy established a group of small, insecure and antagonistic states isolated from each other. The treaties disrupted the region of east central Europe'.

Just as the spectre of the Versailles settlement haunted Germany, Trianon symbolises for Hungarians, even today, the strategic malice of the victorious Allied powers. The treaty was despised as a 'stab in the back' that would fuel for decades to come a passionate obsession to undo its punitive provisions.

Salvation on a White Horse

In the meantime, salvation was at hand. Enter, on a white stallion, Admiral Miklós Horthy. The Admiral on Horseback would save Hungary … national pride would be restored. Hope would be rekindled. Or so it appeared to many Hungarians in the desperate summer months of 1919. Horthy came to represent, even embody, the dismemberment of Hungary in 1920 and the fervent expectation that the Kingdom could be restored. Revising Trianon became Horthy's obsession – but it was his *idée fixe* that acted as a national guarantee that the old Hungary would rise again.

Horthy had been born into the landowning nobility of the Dual Monarchy in Kenderes. He grew up on the great Hungarian Plan in a semi-feudal world where peasants worked the land in ways that had barely changed in centuries. His father lobbied to get his son a coveted place at the Naval Academy in Fiume on the Adriatic coast, where he learnt a brace of languages – he spoke a perfect cut-glass English – and the core value of *Ehrennotwehr*, which Hungarian historian Istvan Deak describes as 'the most onerous and dangerous of an officer's privileges' because it endorsed the necessity of defending one's honour at all costs. This archaic value system came to be bitterly attacked by liberals since the defence of honour frequently required the use of arms and the defiance of state law. When the ambitious Horthy was appointed aide-de-camp to the prickly Emperor Franz Josef, this antiquated value system was reinforced within the rarefied world of the Habsburg court in Vienna. According to Horthy's autobiography, these five years were the 'finest of my life'. After the outbreak of war in August 1914, Horthy's star rose even higher when he took command of the *Novara*, a cruiser in the Hapsburg navy. For much of the war, the fleet was trapped in the Adriatic by the Italian Nnvy – but Horthy won lasting if vacuous acclaim when he was wounded during the Battle of Otranto. By the end of the war the new emperor appointed him vice admiral. It was an empty appointment, for in October 1918, Horthy was forced to surrender his ship to the new Yugoslav navy. Horthy's gilded world sank almost overnight. Honour was compromised.

As Hungary descended into chaos, Horthy was psychically shattered. He fled to his family estate in Kenderes, where he tended to affairs in apparently rather rusty Hungarian. When he took the short train journey to Budapest, he was appalled by the alien new world he could see taking shape on the streets. He had long despised Mihály Károly, the new Prime

Minister, as an over indulged playboy and denounced his progressive democratic politics. He met with a group of army officers who opposed the new government and hoped the war hero would consider a political role. But Horthy resisted and took solace in his estate, where little was changing. Here even as the empire collapsed, the Roman Catholic Church and a handful of Hungarian aristocrats held firmly to their traditional lands. It would be the fall of the Károly government and the rise of Béla Kún that would take a blowtorch to Horthy's political diffidence.

Horthy now began to present himself as a Magyar warrior pledged to crush the Bolshevik enemy. When he travelled to Szeged, where the remnants of the Károly government had taken refuge, an anti-Bolshevik faction of army officers led by Captain Gyula Gömbös persuaded Horthy to join the new cabinet as Commander in Chief of a National Army that had yet to be mustered. As this alternative Hungarian government took shape, Horthy was appointed Minister of Defence. The so-called 'Szeged idea' began to absorb the ethos of fascist and other ultra-nationalist regimes. In Szeged, Horthy became the figurehead of a rabidly reactionary political world that preached the purification of Hungary, its liberation from 'international Jewry' – a 'White Terror'. He formed close bonds with racist ideologues like Gömbös and Pál Prónay, who deepened Horthy's instinctual antisemitism. Together they dreamt of ridding Hungary of the 'Bolshevik poison'.

For many months the cafés, barracks and squares of Szeged acted as a poisonous talking shop and echo chamber for the frustrated nationalists who gathered around Horthy. But when Romanian troops marched into Budapest and the hated Kún regime collapsed, Horthy rushed to Budapest, where a new right-wing government led by the Hapsburg Archduke Joseph had won power. On 15 August, he installed Horthy as the Supreme Commander of a new army he had mustered in Austria. In the meantime, special detachments of the National Army, led by some of Horthy's closest comrades, had marched out of Szeged under gleaming white flags and were wreaking a terrible revenge in the countryside. In every village the army set up 'People's Tribunals' to punish Communists and their supporters. Many Hungarians used the opportunity to denounce their Jewish neighbours. It was, in truth, a pogrom; the majority of those who were executed in this frenzy of revenge were Jews.

Then, on 16 November 1919, a 'wet and cheerless day' he recalled, Horthy rode on his white horse into Budapest, clad in his naval uniform, in an extraordinary display of nationalist fervour. Horthy spoke of his dismay that, 'Budapest had dragged the Holy Crown and national colours in the dirt and clothed herself in red rags'. After the lament came this disquieting warning. Hungarians must eliminate 'poisonous elements' from 'the soul of the nation' and rebuild the twin pillars of the national ideal and Christian morality. There followed an orgy of celebration led by Cecile Tormay, an outspoken antisemite who praised Horthy for the resurrection of Hungary after its 'horrible, bloody Calvary'.

For Horthy and his backers, the gateway to real power was the regency. This had been established by the Allied powers to prevent any restoration of a Habsburg. On 28 February 1920, the provisional government passed Law 1, which established that a Regent would be elected by secret ballot and act as 'temporary governor' – which meant that whoever took the position would wield the equivalent powers to a king. The Regent would have the power to appoint and dismiss the Prime Minister. On 1 March 1920, the parliament proceeded with the ballot. Horthy's comrades in the army established a cordon around the parliament and refused entry to delegates known to be hostile to their cause. Of the 141 votes cast, Horthy won 131, his single rival 7. It was, in effect, a 'soft coup'.

At his inauguration, Horthy appeared resplendent in his white admiral's uniform 'as if he was born to be king' in the words of one unhappy delegate. He took for himself immense powers as Supreme War Lord and insisted that he must be addressed as Serene Highness. For many Hungarians, the election of the new Regent heralded a time of renewed hope. The Regent embodied the propagandist cries of *Mindent vissza!* (Everything back!) and *Nem, nem, soha* (no, no, never!). In Hungarian schools, geography teachers displayed maps of the former Kingdom of Hungary and twice a day their charges recited this nationalist catechism:

I believe in one God
I believe in one Homeland
I believe in God's eternal truth
I believe in the resurrection of Hungary.

Hungarian Jews shared the same hopes, the same resentments about Hungary's humiliations. Why should they not? In these febrile months, the Kingdom of Hungary was broken and reshaped in the political storm let loose by the negotiations in Versailles. It would have been impossible to discern that the fragile pivot of Jewish security had already been knocked off kilter.

Since the Compromise, the majority of Hungarian Jews had committed to a kingdom that was being torn to shreds in a whirlwind of revolutionary change brought on by the uncontrollable forces unleashed by the peace negotiations in Paris. It is not surprising that for many Hungarian Jews the fury of the storm hid in plain sight the deepening perils of the way ahead. Many other Hungarians swiftly came to more certain conclusions. While most Jewish Hungarians reviled the Kún regime, the poisonous link between Bolshevism and Jews had been fixed deeply in many minds. Hungarians had given Jews emancipation. And yet it seemed they had turned on their benefactors by enacting a Red Terror.

6

THE POLITICS OF ENVY

By March 1944, when German troops rumbled menacingly across the Danube to secure Hungary for the Reich, the SS had managed the destruction of more than 4 million European Jews. In Budapest and in the cities, towns and villages of the Hungarian countryside many hundreds of thousands of Jews remained alive. The community was not unscathed; nor was it, even as Hitler's armies confronted defeat, in any way safe. As described, as Horthy deepened Hungary's alliance with Nazi Germany, he was rewarded with piecemeal revisions of the hated Trianon settlement. As Hungary lapped up the lost lands it coveted, borders were redrawn – bringing confusion and mortal danger to the many different ethnic communities whose lives were disrupted.

In April 1941, the Hungarian army took part in the German attack on Yugoslavia and occupied the southern province between the Danube and Tisza rivers. Following the destruction of Yugoslavia, Serbian partisans began causing havoc in the Bačka region of Vojvodina. The Hungarian Chief of the General Staff Ferenc Szombathelyi despatched troops under the command of Lieutenant General Ferenc Fehalmy-Czeydner to quash the partisans. During the Second World War, German military actions to combat partisan militias in both the former Yugoslavia and the occupied Soviet Union involved the indiscriminate killing of civilians. Many of the victims of these operations, most of them conducted by SS units, were Jews. It will be recalled that at a meeting with Hitler in mid December 1941, SS chief Heinrich Himmler jotted down this cryptic note: 'Jewish question to be exterminated as partisans.' Although this phrase is indeed enigmatic, there can be no doubt that mass killing by SS squads and militias of unarmed civilians, especially Jews, during anti-partisan operations was strategic, not inadvertent. Some historians regard this note as the single surviving reference to a 'Hitler Order'.[1] Be that as it may, the Hungarian military action in the southern province escalated after Serb partisans killed a number of soldiers. Even after the partisan threat had been eliminated, the Hungarian soldiers turned their attention to civilians and carried out mass executions. At the very same time, in January 1942, the German Foreign Minister, von Ribbentrop, had arrived in Budapest with the Supreme Commander of the German Army, Wilhelm Keitel, to discuss Hungary's wartime role. The Germans urged Horthy to contribute more to the war effort on the Eastern Front. To counter this bullying, Horthy and Szombathelyi brought up the threat posed by partisans on the Hungarian borderlands, which would be sharpened if they were compelled to send troops to the front line. When General Fehalmy-Czeydner reported that the Serb partisans had moved into the regional capital, Újvidék, Horthy demanded immediate and drastic action. With the assistance of local ethnic Germans, Colonel József Grassy prepared lists of local people, mainly Serbs, alleged to be associating with partisans. Then at dawn on 21 January, in freezing temperatures, Grassy closed the roads that led into the town and the raid began. The first victims were some fifty Serbs whose names appeared on the lists. They were swiftly court-martialled and executed. But the numbers failed to satisfy Fehalmy-Czeydner: he demanded better results to report back to Budapest. Now Grassy turned his troops and the local gendarmerie, the rural militias, on the Jewish community. By 23 January, a terrible bloodbath was unfolding enacted by soldiers and gendarmes who had been promised plunder and plied with copious volumes of alcohol. The killings took place in the streets and alleys of the town – and at execution sites on the banks of the frozen Danube. Soldiers and gendarmes forced Jews to stand on the riverbanks, then shot them in the back of the head. The bodies were hurled into the ice, which had been broken up by explosives. We have this eyewitness account from Julia Kolb, who was 21 in 1942:

> One of my neighbours came out and told me that the entire town was covered in blood. I did not know what had happened to my parents and set out for town. I was horribly afraid I would not find them alive. Along the way, there were bloody corpses lying on the road. I rang at my parents', and it was only then when I heard my father's footsteps that my horrible fear dissipated. Many people we knew were executed. They

sat on the cold pavement for 48 hours and then they were thrown into the Danube. Lots of our relatives died then. In some cases, a child disappeared and the parents survived, in others, the parents disappeared and a child was the only one left. The rabbi was also taken to the banks of the Danube, along the way. They kept beating him with a rifle butt …[2]

The Újvidék incident shows that both the officer corps in the Hungarian army and the rural gendarmerie had no compunction targeting and murdering Jews. Soon afterwards, news about the Újvidék incident reached Budapest and Jews who had relatives there pleaded for information about their fate. As a consequence, a few members of the Hungarian parliament (including representatives of the Serbian minority) protested to Horthy. Nothing was done. The slaughter in Újvidék also underlines that the Hungarian obsession with righting the wrongs of Trianon was closely connected to the fates of Hungary's ethnic minorities as borders were adjusted by Germany to favour Hungary. These revisions of the hated treaty burnished the status of Nazi Germany for many Hungarians – and thus strengthened the hand of extremists who were obsessed with the nation's 'Jewish question'.

Under Attack

As noted in the previous chapter, the national trauma that followed the collapse of the Dual Monarchy and the dismemberment of Hungary provoked violent onslaughts on Hungarian Jews. Jews suffered disproportionately during the White Terror that was incited by Horthy and radical factions in the Hungarian Army after the collapse of the Kùn regime. This wave of violence in the chaotic aftermath of the First World War fizzled out, but in the now diminished nation that emerged after the Paris negotiations Jews had become a lot more vulnerable to prejudice, persecution and attack. Now more than half of the pre-war Jewish population found themselves outside the new borders imposed by the treaty, and this would have far-reaching consequences.

The short-lived Kún regime and the 'Red Terror' it provoked was now enshrined by many Hungarians as a 'Jewish uprising'. For many, the mythical bond between the murderous Bolshevik and the conspiratorial Jew was set in stone. Several hundred thousand people joined a new and explicitly antisemitic party known as the Association of Awakening Hungarians, whose main demand was that Jews be resettled. By the early 1920s, between one quarter and one third of MPs belonged to the association. The fabric of the Hungarian nation was soon ingrained with hostility to Jews. On 26 September, the Hungarian government took a crucial step towards legalising antisemitism by passing Act XXV, known as the 'numerus clausus' law, which imposed a restriction on the number of Jews who could enter higher education. This single law abolished, at a stroke, legal equality for Hungarian Jews. Pressure to assimilate by converting to Christianity intensified and Jewish emigration increased.

Although Hungary was no longer the 'co-owner' of a vast multi-ethnic empire, there were aspects of the old imperial order that had remained intact. As we have seen, the modernisation of Hungary after the Compromise of 1867 had been led by German and Jewish minorities that had embraced the transforming energies of new industries, commerce, communications (from railways to newspapers) and, just as important, the emerging professions such as law, journalism and medicine. The majority of the Hungarian feudal nobility, with its huge rural estates, withheld itself from such demeaning occupations.

At the same time, the Hungarian political elite regarded the Jews as allies, not just in the cause of modernisation but as an ethnic counter-weight to its Slav minorities such as Slovaks, Czechs, Poles, Serbs, Croatians and Ruthenians. These bonds between the Hungarian elite and its Jewish communities were shattered by the international humiliation, as many experienced it, of Hungary in 1920. As in Weimar Germany, a national myth emerged that the Kingdom had been betrayed – not only by the so-called 'Peacemakers' in Paris but by disloyal, deracinated and opportunist Jews. These vindictive emotions proved stubborn. Eichmann's good friend and collaborator László Endre lamented in 1944:

> How could we have foreseen the grievous end and the consequences at a time when we had no idea of the diabolical scheme of things which started the war with the bullet of the Jewish Princip [sic], so that the Jews in this world war could then cause the poverty and ruin of millions of non-Jewish people while at the same time obtaining immeasurable financial gain for themselves … thereby promoting their second objective of driving the masses into such a state of discontent as to allow them to bring the war to an end by way of revolutions … How could we have

known then that this … had all been planned and decided long ago by the Jews in their Masonic lodges [*sic*].

It need hardly be pointed out that Gavrilo Princip, who assassinated Archduke Franz Ferdinand, was not a Jew but a Serb nationalist. Nor do many Jews meet in Masonic lodges.

There can be no doubt that Hungarian Jews were over-represented in the liberal professions, in the economy and trade and the financial sector by five to ten times compared to their proportion in the nation's population. Hungarian industry was dominated by Jewish family concerns, including the Vida, Perényi and Ullmann dynasties centred on the Credit Bank, and the Weiß, Chorin, Kornfeld and Mauthner dynasties that controlled the Commercial Bank. This handful of families, some of which had converted to Christianity, controlled a significant part of Hungary's industrial and commercial production. Since the traditional Hungarian elites had clung to their estates and disdained any capitulation to the modern, even after the end of the war, it is not surprising that these prominent Jewish families shaped Hungarian perceptions of national wealth. In the same way that the Communist regime was perceived as being 'Jewish' despite its brutal treatment of Jews, so too were industry and commerce defined as manifestations of 'Jewish wealth'. Capitalism as a globalised economic system was imagined to be a Jewish phenomenon.

★★★

This axiom led to the growth of a uniquely modern species of antisemitism in Hungary in the decades after the First World War. A significant number of Hungarians came to believe that the social stresses of the new nation could only be solved by confronting these supposedly all-powerful Jewish dynasties and redistributing their wealth. So it was that in the decades after the First World War, Hungarian Jews were ground between contradictory political factions that on the one hand feared and hated Jews as atavistic enemies of the Hungarian nation bent on its destruction, and on the other as the selfish and uncaring foes of social equality.

In the turmoil of a fracturing peace was born a new kind of hatred that was cradled, to begin with, in the universities. Students attacked Jews and demanded a 'Christian-Nationalist' Hungary and the banning of all Jews and Bolsheviks from higher education. At the Technical University in Budapest, Christian students formed armed squads to attack Jews. The authorities were powerless to halt the violence, which was taken up by extremists in the parliament. The consequence of this turmoil, whipped up by cadres of Christian students, was the 'Numerus Clausus' Act of 1920, which, in the words of one Hungarian intellectual, signalled the end of liberalism and an act of 'intellectual hara-kiri'. Strictly speaking, the Act was not explicitly directed at Jews. It was the executive implementation of the Act, drafted by the Prime Minister Pál Teleki, that made it antisemitic by limiting the number of Jews that could be admitted to the universities. Teleki would draft a succession of Jewish laws over the next two decades.

In the meantime, a rash of extremist organisations erupted in Hungarian political society. The most important was the Union of Awakening Hungarians, the ÉME, but there were many others such as the Hungarian National Defence Force Alliance (MOVE), led by Horthy's old comrade Gyula Gömbös, and the Double Cross Allegiance (KKV). These organisations shared the same political objectives, to overturn the Treaty of Trianon and 'protect the Hungarian race'. In 1921, the young László Endre joined the ÉME. At the time he was constable of the town of Gödöllű near Budapest and a convinced Jew-hater. Five years later, he had risen to become chief constable of the entire district. In this position, Endre launched a vitriolic campaign to prevent a Jewish company being awarded a contract for the installation of electric lighting.

As he rose to power in Hungary's rural hinterland, Endre became expert in the manipulation of legal loopholes to discriminate against Jews. He would, for example, lead inspections of Jewish-owned shops and businesses and often uncovered some sort of irregularity, like uncleaned windows, which would be punished by exorbitant fines and even in some cases closure and the arrest of the Jewish owner. Endre punished many Jewish businesses on the merest of pretexts, such as a letter of complaint from a neighbour.[3]

Many other ambitious regional bureaucrats used the same tactics. The majority of these antisemitic ideologues were followers of the statistician Alajos Kovács. In the 1920s, Kovács churned out pseudo-academic tracts that claimed to expose the baleful economic role of Jews. He presented 'hard facts' to proclaim a message: 'The nation is sick, because an alien body has pierced its organisation, and is sucking away more and more of its vitality. Either radical surgery is needed here or a lengthy and regular course of medication.' This was the new language of antisemites. The presence of Jews in the national body was a condition or disease that needed to be cured.

Endre became one of Kovács' most devoted followers and thoroughly absorbed these new-fangled biological metaphors. Theirs was the shiny new antisemitism of science and data analysis. In 1928, Endre travelled to New York. He was looking for new ways to promote the welfare of the people of Gödöllű and had meetings with leading figures in the Rockefeller Foundation to learn about innovations in healthcare and public hygiene. He applied successfully for a grant and when he returned to Hungary threw himself into developing a programme in the Gödöllű district to eradicate the incidence of TB and reform childcare. As a consequence, over the next decade, the district increased its birth rate to twice the national average. Endre's practical measures to improve the health of the race were widely admired.

But Endre had another and much more sinister reason to visit the United States. After he had completed negotiations with the Rockefeller Foundation, he boarded a private aircraft that flew him to the home of Henry Ford in Detroit. As Endre recalled: 'I had the opportunity to get to know Mr Ford in person … [He] is the greatest expert on the international Jewish threat.' The celebrated inventor of automobile mass production was the David Icke of his era. Ford was an extreme antisemite who used his immense wealth to promote his cause. He published a notorious and widely read tract called *The International Jew* and had the notorious forgery *The Protocols of the Elders of Zion* reissued. In 1918, he had purchased his hometown newspaper, the *Dearborn Independent*, and used this forum to unleash a barrage of articles disseminating his paranoid obsession that a global conspiracy of Jews was intent on global domination and the destruction of American values. One of Ford's closest friends admitted that he 'attributes all evil to Jews or to the Jewish capitalists … The Jews caused the war, the Jews caused the outbreak of thieving and robbery all over the country, the Jews caused the inefficiency of the navy'. Ford wielded tremendous economic and political clout through his factories and dealerships but his reputation was damaged when Jewish activist Aaron Sapiro filed a lawsuit for libel against the *Dearborn Independent*. The newspaper, Sapiro claimed, had made false accusations about his cooperative farming movement in California. According to the *New York Times*: 'Mr Sapiro was accused in the articles of being a cheat, a faker and a fraud, and there were animadversions against the Jewish people.' The court, however, refused to entertain any discussion of antisemitism. About a month after it began, the case ended when the judge declared a mistrial. Sapiro was bitterly disappointed but there was a surprising outcome to his legal crusade. Louis Marshall, a leading Jewish lawyer, engineered a compromise by persuading Ford to publicly apologise for his antisemitism.[4] For Ford, the admission was a blow: the *Dearborn Independent* closed in 1927 and his reputation in the United States was badly tarnished by the time Endre met the bitter old mogul in Detroit. His obsessive hatred was undimmed, and he encouraged his new Hungarian disciple to read and study the classics of hatred such as the *Protocols*. Ford also arranged that Endre travel to Munich, where he met a rising politician called Adolf Hitler.[5]

When Endre returned to Hungary, he paid his respects to one of Hungary's most celebrated scientists, who worked at the Zoological Department at the Hungarian National Museum. Born in 1862, Lajos Méhelÿ had spent many decades studying bees, crayfish and reptiles. Dismayed by the collapse of the Dual Monarchy and the chaos that came in its wake, Méhelÿ looked for a scientific explanation for the humiliation of his nation. He found it in the Jewish 'race'. Méhelÿ abandoned his crayfish and bees, throwing himself into a pseudo-scientific species of antisemitism. His publications echo the work of the German racial scientists such as Hans Günther which was flourishing at the same time and adding academic lustre to the bigoted rhetoric of emerging nationalist parties including the NSDAP. Like the German race scientists, Méhelÿ published obsessively about the dangers of racial mixing. 'The Jewish race must be regarded as an artificially bred, firmly established mongrel breed.' Rather than being a true race, like the Magyar peoples for example, Jews were bearers of 'negroid and Oriental blood'. If this impure strain entered the national bloodstream, Méhelÿ warned, the consequences would be 'tragic'.

As in Germany, the *language* of science – rather than its substance – energised nationalist movements and offered a way to demonise Jews and other inferior races with the trappings of modernity. Although he was still just a hard-working provincial bureaucrat, Endre played a leading role in the propagation of this new kind of racism. He was soon at the centre of a network of scientific racists who all revered Méhelÿ. Endre became involved with a new cultural society founded by a geography teacher called Zoltán Bosnyák. 'The Alliance Against Harmful Insects' would become a prolific ideas hub, publishing and translating a steady flow of popular pseudo-scientific works that found a fast-growing readership in Hungary. In 1935,

Bosnyák himself published The *Jewification of our Capital*, which would become an intellectual manifesto for Hungarian far-right nationalists. He demanded a boycott of Jewish-owned businesses, as well as cultural works created by Jews, to bring about the re-Magyarisation of Hungarian political life. Bosnyák yoked together statistical analysis with the science of race to forge a seductive amalgam of radical proposals. His ideas were taken up by the Hungarian government, which by the end of the 1930s became increasingly committed to antisemitic measures.

Until the mid 1930s, Horthy and his prime ministers had resisted the siren calls of the extremists. The brake on enacting further antisemitic measures was the chronic weakness of the Hungarian economy. Horthy, whatever his instincts, could not afford to do without the wealth and experience of industrial giants such as the Weiß and Chorin families. He regularly played bridge with Ferenc Chorin. Just as Austro-Hungary had been transformed by the energies of the same families in the revolutionary decades before the First World War, now, battered and diminished, the nation was in desperate need of the same investment in its future. The post-war recovery of Hungary owed everything to the dynasties that men like Endre and his coterie denounced as alien parasites. By the end of the 1930s, Hungarians felt more confident. Horthy and his prime ministers looked enviously at the political ascendancy of Nazi Germany, whose charismatic leader openly proclaimed his determination to exorcise the demonic spirits of Versailles. In 1938, Hitler swallowed up Austria – and Germany shared a border with Hungary. Between 1938 and 1941, Hungary regained nearly 40 per cent of its lost territories – thanks to Hitler. In early 1939, Hungary left the League of Nations and joined the Anti-Comintern Pact. The following year, Horthy agreed to join the Tripartite Pact with Germany, Italy and Japan.

The international turmoil that brought Hungary into a deepening relationship with Nazi Germany had dangerous consequences for Hungarian Jews. In May 1938, the government enacted the First 'Jewish Law' (Act XV), which was intended to reduce the proportion of Jews in business and various professions. As historian Lászlo Karsai has shown, in the next five years, between May 1939 and March 1944, the government passed no fewer than 22 antisemitic Acts, as well as 267 anti-Jewish decrees that banned, for example, marriages and extramarital sex between Jews and non-Jews. As Jews were pushed out of jobs, other Hungarians lapped up the rewards. During the debate on the Second Jewish Law in the

Hungarian parliament, the industrialist Ferenc Chorin, who had converted to Christianity, warned with astonishing prescience that 'according to our calculations, there is a group of approximately 90,000 people who need to be replaced. This means that approximately 200,000 people will be left without an income'. This Second Jewish Law explicitly referred to encouraging 'the emigration of Jews'. There was a way around the new laws – and, in 1944, it would have unforeseen consequences during the German occupation. This was to use the so-called 'Aladár' or 'Stróman' strategy to create shell or façade companies by formally transferring ownership to the names of Christian partners. Alternatively, Christian managers were given positions on the board of directors but without decision-making powers. This kind of deception was not without risks, since many Hungarians seized any chance to cheat Jewish partners.

At this stage, Hitler was exerting very little pressure on the Hungarian government. The war on Hungarian Jews was completely Hungarian, driven by Hungarian ideologues including László Endre and inscribed into law by Hungarian government officials with the approval of the Regent. The battery of a succession of anti-Jewish laws had a debilitating impact of Jewish communities at every level. By the end of 1942, the number of Jews who had lost their livelihoods had risen above 200,000.

A young man called Ernö Galpert recalled: 'Supporting oneself became very difficult. My father had his trade licence taken away. The owner of the workshop in which I worked also had his licence taken away from him, so the workshop closed down in 1940. My father and I had to look for jobs.'[6] As in many modern genocides, petty legalistic discrimination paved the way for extremist action.

Into the Maw of Death

As Hungarian troops marched into regions like Carpatho–Ruthenia that had been reacquired under the Vienna Awards, they encountered Jewish communities that had once been woven into the ethnic mosaic of the Austro-Hungarian Empire. Hundreds of thousands of Jews came under Hungarian rule. Many Jews welcomed the Hungarian soldiers – as Ernö Galpert explained: 'Older Jews recalled that within the Austro-Hungarian Empire, Jews used to have a relatively large degree of freedom and they hoped for the best … With time it became clear that this country was no longer the old Hungary but a fascist country.' Jews in Carpatho–Ruthenia and other territories gobbled up by Hungary would soon discover that they were no longer viewed as members of the Hungarian national community. At the same time, between 10,000 and 20,000 Jews fled to Hungary from Germany and German-occupied Austria, the Czech territories and Poland. Once they arrived behind Hungarian borders, many went into hiding using false papers, but others were interned by the National Central Authority for Controlling Foreigners, the KEOKH. For the antisemites in the Hungarian government, the sudden acquisition of so many Jews was an unwelcome downside of annexation. Some now called for more radical measures. The new commissioner of Carpatho–Ruthenia, Miklós Kozma, openly called for the deportation of Jews in his fiefdom. In the winter of 1940–41, soldiers and gendarmes launched a number of arbitrary 'cleansing' operations by expelling a few families across the Soviet and Romanian borders. Then in the summer of 1941, as Hitler launched Operation Barbarossa, the invasion of the Soviet Union, Kozma and other Hungarian officials seem to have realised that the tumult of war offered the chance to go much further. With the eager approval of the Prime Minister, Lászlo Bárdossy, as well as the Minister of the Interior, Ferenc Keresztes-Fischer, and the Regent himself, they set in motion the round-up of allegedly 'stateless' Hungarians in July. The operation was planned with brutality and mendacious cynicism. Officials forced the Jews to take only a small amount of cash and enough food for three days and were promised access to land that had been abandoned by Jews on the Soviet side of the border. This deception ensured that anyone deported would have very little chance of survival. Once they had left, neighbours would plunder and occupy abandoned property: deportation was a grotesque form of wealth redistribution. At first, the authorities targeted Jews who failed to produce papers proving Hungarian citizenship and were judged to be of 'uncertain citizenship' but soon began rounding up entire communities. Mrs Géza Sachs, who was then 32 years old: '1941, Jews who did not possess a certificate of their citizenship were considered foreigners, regardless whether they lived here, whether their father and grandfather were born here. Naturally, other countries gave them no admittance either, hence these Jews became stateless. We also belonged to this group.'[7]

István Weiß described how a chief constable called Imre Mogyoróssy handled the matter:

On the afternoon of August 8, 1941, I was returning from a business trip, and … Chief Constable Mogyoróssy had the [local] gendarme patrol unit arrest me … Because it was late at night by then, a group of 88 people was already on its way to the train station … I myself was born in Hungary as were my late father and even my grandmother … Most of them provided certificates to prove this, which the Chief Constable took away from them … The Chief Constable was depraved enough to take away these citizenship certificates, which were completely in order … And he had them expelled …

As the round-up accelerated in Carpatho–Ruthenia, Hungarian gendarmes launched deportation operations in Northern Transylvania and in the Lake Balaton region. The first destination of all the deportees was a collection camp set up on the border at Kőrösmező. As many thousands of Jews arrived every day, long convoys of trucks rumbled into the camp. In the next few weeks, nearly 18,000 Jews were driven across the border into the Galicia region of western Ukraine. This would become one of the most notorious killing sites in the German war of annihilation.

More than 10,000 of the deported Hungarian Jews ended up in a town called Kamenets-Podolsk, today in Ukraine. In 1900, a Jewish handbook referred to Kamenets as the 'mother city of the Jewish people, who are G-d fearing and esteem his name'. It was a bustling market town and regional trade centre. In the late summer of 1944, Kamenets, as it was called by its Jewish inhabitants, was in a German military zone, a highly significant factor in the events that followed the arrival of the deportees. A few found refuge with local Jewish families but the majority had to make do in the open. As the numbers of deportees rapidly escalated, conditions in these temporary camps deteriorated. There was little to eat; lethal infections spread unhindered. According to a Hungarian soldier who passed through Kamenets-Podolsk:

There are several Jews here, especially women, they are in rags, but they ask for bread wearing jewellery and with lips painted red. They would give any money for it. Some count their steps with the desperation shown on their faces, others are crawling on the road collapsed from exhaustion and hunger. Some others bandage the wounds on their feet with rags torn from their clothes … The Jewish quarter of the city is full of Jews, there are many from Budapest among them: they live in unspeakable and indescribable dirt, they come and go in scanty attire, the streets stink, unburied dead bodies are lying in some houses. The water of the Dniester is infected, here and there corpses are washed out to the bank.

In the paranoid view of the German military authorities, the chaos at Kamenets-Podolsk posed a serious threat to security. They protested to the Hungarian Minister Keresztes-Fischer – who very reluctantly agreed to stop the deportations. But he refused to allow any of the deported Jews to return to Hungarian territory. This obstinate refusal sealed their fate.

As the Hungarian Jews struggled to survive in this hellish environment, SS-Obergruppenführer Friedrich Jeckeln arrived in Kamenets-Podolsk.[8] As one of the Higher SS and Police Leaders (HSSPF), Jeckeln commanded a conglomerate force of Einsatzgruppen and Order Police (Orpo) battalions in the southern Soviet Union. The Einsatzgruppen and Orpo units were mobile militias that followed in the wake of the German armies to secure the rear areas as army divisions rapidly moved east into the Baltic region and Ukraine. In practice, the Einsatzgruppen and Orpo units acted as murder squads. In the months before the German invasion, the Einsatzgruppen leaders had attended training courses and received instructions about the categories of people who would need to be liquidated in order to pacify the rear of the invading army. These categories included Communist officials, Jews in 'party and state positions' as well as 'radical elements' including assassins and agitators.

This execution mandate, as historian Donald Bloxham argues in his important book *The Final Solution: A Genocide*, did not explicitly refer to the murder of all Soviet Jews but was couched in language that allowed the Einsatzgruppen leaders considerable latitude to respond to changing circumstances. The mandate referred with brutal specificity to executing Jews who were functionaries of the Soviet state but at the same time recommended inciting or at the very least not preventing local pogroms. The notion that Bolshevism was a 'Jewish' phenomenon was deeply rooted in Nazi ideology and it was well known among the SS leadership that nationalists in the regions of the east that had been occupied by the Soviets shared this hatred of 'Jewish Bolshevism' and were likely to seek revenge. In practice, the terms of the mandate permitted a broader assault on any adult male Jews in former Soviet territories regardless of their political role. Soon, the Einsatzgruppen leadership would dispense with constraints based on gender and age altogether.

The inevitable escalation is documented in the Einsatzgruppen Reports, which the unit commanders punctiliously sent back from the front line to be circulated among the SS leadership. It is evident that all the Einsatzgruppen units soon began to indiscriminately kill Jewish males of military age in increasing numbers. Only a few skilled and specialist workers were exempted. The killings were carried out using rudimentary but increasingly efficient and systematic means. A pit was dug, usually by local auxiliaries. A firing squad assembled. A group of victims was marched to the edge of the pit and shot. All the Einsatzgruppen commanders proved themselves to be dedicated killers. Jeckeln developed a method of mass execution he called 'sardine packing' that facilitated the killing of tens of thousands of victims in ever shortening periods of time by stacking the dead in layers after each shooting.

Himmler's desk diary shows that he travelled frequently across the Baltic region and Ukraine in this period and his meetings with SS leaders such as Jeckeln often preceded an escalation of mass killings. What took place in Kamenets-Podolsk at the end of August would prove to be a watershed moment in the evolution of the genocide. From this moment on, the German murder squads would slaughter all Jews regardless of race or gender.

When Jeckeln observed the disorder in the camp in Kamenets-Podolsk and learnt of the refusal of the Hungarian government to take back the deported Jews, he offered to take care of the problem. At the end of August, Jeckeln set about liquidating every Jew in the area, as well as the Hungarian deportees. He deployed Police Battalion 320, an Order Police unit, as well as Ukrainian militiamen and, possibly, a Hungarian sapper unit to carry out the first mass murder of the German genocide. In three days, Jeckeln's men shot 23,000 Jewish men, women and children. During this period, British intelligence were intercepting German radio reports and noted with some incredulity that:

> The execution of 'Jews' is such a recurrent feature of these reports that the figures have been omitted from the situation reports and brought under one heading. Whether all those executed as 'Jews' are indeed such is of course doubtful; but the figures are no less conclusive as evidence of a policy of savage intimidation if not of ultimate extermination.

Just weeks later, British intelligence analysts had no doubt that 'the police are killing all Jews that fall into their hands'. The report concluded that there was no longer any point continuing to make reports about these 'butcheries' 'unless so requested'. In other words, mass killing operations had become routine.[9]

Also present in Kamenets-Podolsk during these terrible days of slaughter were Jewish members of the Hungarian army, who were mainly serving as drivers. Gábor Mermelstein had once driven a taxi in Budapest; he now served as a driver for a munitions company based in Kassa:

> We saw hundreds of people undressing there … we were passing a row of maple trees – practically over the mess of naked corpses … suddenly we glanced at a square-shaped ditch, at all four sides of which people were standing. Hundreds of innocent people were machine-gunned down. I'll never forget what I saw and felt: the scared faces, the men, women and children marching into their own graves without resistance. I felt fear, outrage and pain simultaneously.

Many of the military drivers wept uncontrollably. A German calmly pointed out: 'Don't worry, there are enough Jews left in the world.'

There is a chilling account of the mass slaughters in a Soviet report held by the archives of Yad Vashem. It is a confession by one of the Ukrainian auxiliaries, the Schutzmannschaften:

> On the day of the shooting, in the morning, German soldiers and 'schutzmanner' went around the houses and drove the Jews out onto the street. Then they were lined up in a 4-row wide column and, under German guard, were taken to the shooting site in the direction of Belanovka. I personally did not participate in the round up of the civilians from their houses since I had the day off. After the civilians were taken outside the city by the Germans, police chief Razumovskiy met me and told me to join the other policemen at the shooting place outside the city. We got into cars that took us to a field in the Belanovka area, to which the civilians of Jewish nationality had already been taken. All the 'schutzmanner' who had arrived were placed in a cordon around the Jews to guard them and, under no circumstances, allow them to get away. We were armed with rifles. At that time the people we were guarding were forced to undress and were taken by Germans, in groups of 5–6, to a grave where two German accomplices shot them. In this way all of the people taken there were shot. Subsequently, the grave was

covered by [local] people mobilized for this task and we returned to the city. The Germans took for themselves the possessions of the people who were shot ...[10]

Another eyewitness recalled:

At this time in Kamenetz Podolski we also met 35,000 Hungarian Jews, who had been expelled of Hungary, and were shot and buried there. There are mass graves there. When we crossed this area by car, they were being collected and we were almost caught, too, but we managed to make the Germans believe that we were not Jews, so we were not touched. When we crossed that place on the way back home there was not even a single Jew alive. At the same time, as we travelled on, in each Ukrainian town (such as Proskorov or Vinnitsa) Germans caught the Jews and killed them. They are in mass graves now ...[11]

The Kamenets-Podolsk mass killings were carried out by German mass murder squads, commanded by Friedrich Jeckeln, the ruthless German *génocidaire*. And yet the origins of this momentous episode of mass slaughter lay in decisions made by Hungarian officials at the highest level of government that included state ministers and the Regent. These decisions reflected a political culture that had taken hold in the aftermath of the First World War and demanded an increasingly harsh and exclusionist treatment of the country's Jewish community. It was only the role played by prominent Jews as indispensable wealth creators in Hungary's development as a modern nation that offered tenuous protection.

The Hell of Labour Service

This chapter has tried to answer a question of incalculable significance for the catastrophe that overwhelmed Hungarian Jewry in 1944. Why did so many Hungarian state officials actively collude with the lethal demands of the German occupiers? We have seen that the punishment, as it was perceived, of Hungary by the victorious Allied powers in 1920 reacted with the experience of a brutal Communist regime interpreted as a 'Jewish uprising' to distil a pungent new variety of antisemitism that was, in turn, deepened by a statistical and pseudo-scientific sociology that constructed Hungarian Jews as barriers to social equality. This meant that well-informed and, in some ways, 'progressive' government officials such as László Endre accepted that Jews were at the root of Hungary's diminished status and domestic ills. By the end of the 1930s, these pervasive attitudes among state officials led them to give legal weight to their prejudices through the barrage of anti-Jewish acts and decrees. When Hitler's attack on the Soviet Union in June 1941 legitimated violent solutions to alleged racial enemies, Hungary and other successor states including Romania took the same path to mass murder.

The final part of the answer focuses on the introduction by the Hungarian army of labour service obligations. This would have a catastrophic impact on the lives of tens of thousands of Hungarian Jews – and, eventually, the entire Jewish community. Labour service turned out to be cruelly discriminatory towards the Jews, who were compelled to take part and, in the longer term, made the community more vulnerable by siphoning off its young men and sending them to the military front line. Many never returned.

This is how it worked. In 1939, the government introduced compulsory military service for all male citizens. Article 230 of the Act stated that anyone who was judged unfit for armed military service would have to perform labour service. A new Labour Service organisation was established. The new Act was not in itself discriminatory but the Second 'Jewish Law' made it so, because under its terms Jews could not serve as officers or NCOs or take on special responsibilities in administration or in the signal corps. Then, after spring 1941, Jews lost their right to bear arms. Other groups were also discriminated against – Romanians and southern Slavs, for example, as well as political radicals and Jehovah's Witnesses. But the Ministry of Defence brought in other measures that specifically targeted Jews – such as the establishment of special companies, the wearing of yellow armbands and the use of files marked with 'Z' standing for *zsidó*, Hungarian for Jew. The upshot was that Jews in the labour service were highly visible – and the consequences would be lethal.

★★★

On the front line, the readily identifiable Jewish Labour Service men were at the mercy of officers and guards. During the 1930s, the Hungarian officer corps was transformed in both ideological and operational ways by the infusion of a younger generation, many of whom were devoted followers of one of the most extremist members of Horthy's cadre – Gyula Gömbös. His brash young disciples sidelined the older generation of army officers, many of whom still honoured the polite tolerance of Habsburg times. They openly accused Jews serving in the army of treachery. And, when war came, they seized every chance to make the lives of Jewish officers intolerable. For many of these officers, torturing and executing Jewish Labour Servicemen was a matter of duty and honour. A survivor, interviewed after the war, provided this shattering narrative:

> Gendarme Lieutenant Csaba was whipping and kicking us with his boots while we were trussed. My brother-in-arms, who was trussed up for 15 days, was hanging from a tree, when that lieutenant climbed up and jumped on him. Then he took an iron stick and he was beating the poor man so badly that his face and body had swollen. After the torture he was hardly recognisable … We worked very much and suffered from the cold, because we did not have any winter clothes … Our sergeant, Domafalvi from Eger, treated us very badly. He was beating and abusing us. The most horrible thing was when we had to stand at attention outdoors in summer clothes for one or two hours in minus 36–38 degrees Celsius. At such a time he organised a boxing match whenever he felt like that. It meant he hit all of us in the face and we were not allowed to move …[12]

In the spring of 1942, as Hitler's armies renewed their onslaught on the Soviets, the Hungarian Second Army was despatched to the Eastern Front. Serving in its ranks were more than 50,000 mainly Jewish Labour Service men. More than half of these men, perhaps as many as 45,000, would not survive the war. Although not all Hungarian officers and guards acted with the same level of brutality, the Labour Service men were starved and murdered by their fellow Hungarians. Some officers sent Jews into minefields with long leashes tightened around their necks. When the Soviet army smashed the Hungarians in January, 1942 many soldiers scapegoated Jews. That winter, few survived the punishing retreat. They were often abandoned without supplies – and left to the mercy of German soldiers and Ukrainian partisans. A few months later, cholera swept through a Labour Service battalion deployed near the Ukrainian village of Doroshich. Hungarian soldiers set fire to their barracks and machine-gunned the sick who tried to escape:

The doors and the windows were closed, so that we would not be able to get out. When with great efforts we could open some of them, many people wanted to get out at once, so we were on top of each other: it was such a bedlam. People were treading on each other. Burning people were running out of the building just to face machine-guns waiting for them outside. I could get out only with burns, which later got healed.[13]

We have an account of the treatment of Jews in the Labour Service in the memoirs of General Vilmos Nagybaczoni Nagy, the Hungarian Minister of Defence between September 1942 and June 1943. Loyal to Horthy though he was, Nagy had fervently opposed Hungary's pact with Nazi Germany. In his memoirs, he admitted that: 'Anti-Jewish sentiment reigned in the Ministry of Defence'. As conditions on the front deteriorated, Nagy spoke out in the Hungarian parliament to protest about the treatment of the Labour Service men. At least within Hungary in areas under his direct control, his attempts at improving conditions were partly successful. He discovered that the ministry's antisemitic staff officers ignored his orders. There was little he could do when decrees were issued implementing a battery of discriminatory measures. Nagy was forced to resign when, in the summer of 1943, he tried to resist the German demand that Hungary provide servicemen to work in the copper mines in Bor in Serbia. In his memoirs, he recalled receiving reports, day after day, that the Labour Service guards 'went wild – and unfortunately the reserve company commanders followed suit – they introduced such cruel treatment that decent Hungarian soldiers were appalled. Because of the beatings, the extremely strenuous work, and the lack of adequate food many labour servicemen died.'

For daring to speak out, Nagy was sacked. His protests had little impact. According to a Hungarian officer, whose diary is held by the Hungarian National Archives, the most callous brutality was a daily norm. Many of the entries end with the words 'Filthy Jews':

We work here as ordered. The mood is stirred up because frozen Jews are dragged around. They are dragging them barefoot, on a child's sled. 17 were shot in the head ... We sentenced to death Emil Gyémánt, a Jewish Labour Service man, for pretending to be sick ... He deserved it ... Filthy Jews. What we saw on the Kotschatowka Road was awful. Vehicle upon vehicle, crowds of people pushing each other, horse cadavers, frozen Jews ...[14]

There are many eyewitness accounts by Jewish Labour Service men that substantiate the persecutory conditions on the front. 'E.J.', who was a tailor from Munkács, remembered:

> We met hardly a soul and we were at the mercy of the guards. Beatings and truss-ups were every day occurrences. The food was stolen and we got less and less every day. My comrades perished, one after the other ... [Lieutenant Barna Almásy] sent the intellectuals to the minefields. Thus, he managed to kill all intellectuals. He delivered speeches to us about the rising star of the Hungarian nation and the falling star of Jews. He planned to kill all Jews and he did everything in his capacity to achieve this goal.

'R.E.', another tailor, from Budapest:

> On January 18, 1943 I was called up for labour service in Nagybánya for the battalion no. X. We received a most hostile welcome. They called us communists and threatened to take us to Ukraine to pick landmines and to wrap up defence wiring. They called us 'dirty Jews' and told us we would not see the light of day much longer. In November 1943 they took us to Ukraine. We were travelling under fairly good circumstances ... In Ukraine, our guards were replaced and we got a new commander, 2nd Lieutenant Imre Friedrich, a person who you would call a real Jew-killer. He spoiled our well-intentioned guards, recruited from miners of Tatabánya, by turning them against us ... We were working 18 hours a day and got a very minimal food supply. We got a good share of beating and antisemitic slurs. We got infested with lice and spotted fever broke out ...[15]

The great Hungarian poet Miklós Radnóti was conscripted into a Labour Service battalion in 1941. Like so many tens of thousands of other Jews who served on the front line, Radnóti did not return home to Budapest – but he left behind heart-breaking evocations of the terrible experiences endured by Labour Service men. Radnoti's battalion ended up working as slaves in the Bor copper mines. In 1944, the Germans began to evacuate troops and auxiliary units from the Balkans. The Hungarians, numbering some 6,000 men, were marched north towards the Hungarian border – on foot. Among them was Radnóti. As the Labour Service battalions stumbled towards home, German and Hungarian guards beat the Jewish labourers and killed any who fell behind. When Radnóti himself collapsed by the side of the road on 9 November 1944, he was indifferently shot dead by a Hungarian soldier and his body kicked into a mass burial pit. Years later, the mass grave was exhumed, and, miraculously, a notebook discovered in the pocket of a decayed coat. The notebook contained Radnoti's final poems.

This one refers to the death of a friend who was a violinist:

I toppled beside him – his body already taut,
tight as a string just before it snaps,
shot in the back of the head.
'This is how you'll end too; just lie quietly here,'
I whispered to myself, patience blossoming from dread.
'This one's still moving,' the voice above me jeered;
I could only dimly hear
through the congealing blood slowly sealing my ear.

7

RANSOM AND THE SLOVAK TRICK

Modern scholarship of the Holocaust emphasises the uneven evolution of the Final Solution. Intent and the rhetoric of destruction vented in Hitler's speeches was continuously shaped, diverted or intensified by opportunity and chance. The apparatus of genocide embodied in the police agencies of Himmler's SS was, as David Cesarani emphasised in his masterly account of the Final Solution, frequently improvised and rickety. This is surely the case with many genocides. In real time, events are only dimly perceived and frequently misunderstood. For the victims of genocide, the landscape of slaughter is infrequently illuminated, perhaps never.

There is little doubt that by the end of 1941, the Allies and the Zionist agencies in the United States, Europe and Palestine suspected that the Nazi state planned the annihilation of European Jewry, and that what was happening was not merely a monstrous pogrom. What Churchill called 'a crime without a name' was shrouded by the fog of circumstance and strategic deceit. On the German side, as we have seen, there was uncertainty about the how and the when. There was debate about whether the final and complete solution of the 'Jewish problem' should be postponed to the end of the war and a German victory. Sheer opportunism and the initiative of lower-level SS commanders partially resolved the matter of timing as different Jewish communities fell prey to the Reich. The German occupiers, the civil authorities, the Wehrmacht and the SS regarded the presence of Jews within the borders of Hitler's expanding empire or close to the military front line as an intolerable security threat. This intolerance deepened as partisan militias, backed by the Allies, expanded operations in Belarus and the Balkans. Other factors led to a braking tendency. Among the planning agencies of the Reich, there was a never to be resolved dispute about whether Jews – and which Jews? – should be exploited as slave workers or liquidated. The formulation made explicit in the minutes of the Wannsee Conference, that Jewish slave workers would inevitably be 'worked to death', offered a provisional resolution. These bureaucratic quarrels and hesitations merely postponed or decelerated the plunder, exploitation and murder of hundreds of thousands of Jews across German-occupied Europe. The moral horror of genocide is not diminished if we see through the rhetoric of racial hatred to the banal managerial complexities of mass murder.

It has taken historians more than seven decades to grasp the realities of the Holocaust. Many puzzles remain unsolved and there are many uncomfortable points of debate. In this light, it is hardly surprising that in the course of the Second World War the Jewish and Zionist organisations in Britain and the United States confronted enormous dilemmas struggling to find appropriate and effective responses to the onslaught on Jews as it took place. The terrible plight of Jews was well known to the leaders of the Allied powers from the winter of 1941, when British intelligence intercepted and decoded German police signals explicitly referring to mass killings on the Eastern Front.[1] On 24 August 1941, when he was informed of these reports, Churchill denounced the 'most frightful cruelties … whole districts are being eliminated. Scores of thousands – literally scores of thousands – of executions are being perpetrated by the German police troops.' He did not refer to Jews. It has been argued that commenting on the identity of the victims might have exposed the fact that British intelligence had broken the German codes. Be that as it may, the catastrophe we now refer to as the Holocaust happened in cruel fits and starts within the shadowy interstices of a world war. As we have seen, the Germans refined many different ways of concealing the mass shootings in Eastern Europe and the function of extermination camps such as a Treblinka and Sobibór.

These deceptions, evoked by the phrase 'night and fog', hoodwinked with utmost cruelty the victims of the Final Solution, who went to their deaths often not knowing the fate that awaited them at the end of a railway journey.[2] Likewise, these deceptions confused the Zionists in Palestine and other Jewish agencies elsewhere. Deception enabled the Final Solution.

Trickery obscured the nature of German strategies and rendered impotent effective reaction. Out of this maelstrom of deceit came the obsession with ransom. German-occupied Europe resembled a medieval citadel that had been seized by enemy forces. From within its steel walls issued horrifying rumours alongside tantalising offers to barter, to exchange unwanted prisoners for money or commodities. Like any kind of exchange, ransom depends on good faith. But in the struggle to save Jewish lives, the only party to the process with power had no interest in either respecting or following the rules.

'Willy'

To understand how this trickery worked, it is instructive to look at the case of SS officer Dieter Wisliceny, a representative of Adolf Eichmann's Department IVB4 of the RSHA. Wisliceny was an avuncular *genocidaire*, a kind of Nazi Falstaff. His activities reveal how many of the SS officers involved with the destruction of different Jewish communities both exploited and deceived their confused and frightened victims. When Wisliceny arrived in Budapest, he took a leading role establishing a 'Jewish Council'. The purpose of establishing the Council, as will be explained in detail later, was to impose order and discipline on Jewish communities and to disguise their fate. SS men such as Eichmann and his subordinates were past masters of such cynical trickery. One of the leading members of the Jewish Council in Budapest was Fülöp Freudiger.[3] When his brother, Sámuel, was arrested shortly after the beginning of the occupation, Freudiger sought, to begin with, the help of the President of the Council, Samu Stern; he never replied. Sámuel was being held at the National Rabbinical Institute – a building that Wisliceny had procured as an internment camp. So Freudiger appealed directly to the SS officer – who recognised him as one of the Jewish Council leaders in Budapest. For Wisliceny such a plea from a member of the German-appointed Council was an opportunity. He assured Freudiger that he would have his brother released. And so, it came to pass. Sámuel was freed a few days later.

Soon after this first meeting, Wiliceny summoned Freudiger and another member of the Jewish Council to a meeting at the Institute. He showed them a remarkable document. It was a letter, written in Hebrew, from Rabbi Michal Dov Ber Weissmandel of the Rescue Committee

(Va'adat Hatzala) in Bratislava. In it Weissmandel warned Freudiger that it was now the turn of the Hungarian Jews to suffer the same fate as other Jews in occupied Europe. He urged Freudiger to look into a scheme he called the 'Europa Plan' and to 'trust Wisliceny'. This exchange was a pivotal moment in the relationship between the Hungarian Jews and the German occupiers. Wisliceny used Weissmandel's letter as a cruel bait that Freudiger and other members of the Jewish Council swallowed whole. To understand why, we need to turn the clock back to the period after the Wanssee Conference in the spring of 1942 – and examine the fate of the Jews of Slovakia.

The nation of Czechoslovakia was spawned by the great reordering of Europe that followed the Paris Peace Conference of 1919. The new republic, which, as Margaret Macmillan notes, resembled a tadpole with its head in the west and its tail tapering off in the east, yoked together the prosperous Czech lands of Bohemia and Moravia with the mountainous and less-developed region of Slovakia. It was a marriage of unequal partners. While the Czechs had effective advocates in Edvard Beneš and Tomáš Masaryk and could glory in the golden age of the Kingdom of Bohemia and a time when Prague was the capital of the Holy Roman Empire, Slovakia had been a backwater for centuries. The immense upheaval of the Reformation had little impact in its deep valleys and mountain pastures. Slovaks were accustomed to Hungarian rule; Czechs by Austrians. The majority of the sober and industrious Czechs were Protestant; the Slovaks resolutely Catholic. During the 1920s the peoples who inhabited these relics of the Austro-Hungarian Empire struggled, despite sharing closely related languages, to find a shared national identity. It was a state created from different nations, wrote one commentator, 'all filled with hatred one against the other, arrested in their whole economic and social development and in the progress of their civilisations by hate and national strife, nourished by tyranny and poisoning their whole public life'.[4] This was a decidedly bleak analysis but there was no doubt that the new state confronted mighty challenges. Within its borders, minorities comprising Germans, Hungarians, Ruthenians, Poles and Roma made up one-third of the population; Czechs and Slovaks together made up two-thirds but shared little in common. The Czechs assumed a semi-colonial conception of their status as bringers of civilisation to a benighted backwater. This was deeply resented. Many Slovaks began to envy their wealthier Czech cousins and resent the small Jewish community in Bratislava. In 1919, an obscure Catholic priest called Father Andrej Hlinka vented Slovak resentment: 'We have lived alongside the Magyars for a thousand years. All the Slovak rivers flow towards the Hungarian Plain, and all out roads lead to Budapest, their great city, while from Prague we are separated by the barrier of the Carpathians.' Slovaks, he proclaimed, were true Catholics, 'innocent and without stain'. The Czechs were infidels. Just over two decades later, fanatical members of the 'Hlinka Guard' herded Slovakian Jews onto trains bound for Auschwitz.

As in the rest of post-war Europe, the collapse of empire and the emergence of new nation states fomented a rising tide of antisemitism. In Slovakia, these resentments fuelled the rise of a new party founded by Hlinka, the Slovak People's Party, which was nationalist, antisemitic and anti-Czech. The sharp edge of the party was a militia known as the 'Hlinka Guard' that, like other such organisations, mimicked far-right militias in Italy and Germany. The party rapidly became the most important political movement in Slovakia. In 1918, at an extraordinary convention bringing together Czechs, Slovaks, Poles, Ukrainians and even Zionists was held in Pittsburgh, on the eastern seaboard of the United States where many Slovaks had settled. The Czech nationalist Tomás Masaryk signed an agreement that promised considerable autonomy to the Slovaks in the new state: their own language, courts and parliament. The Pittsburgh agreement was conveniently forgotten. In May 1938, a group of American Slovaks arrived in Bratislava with the original agreement. Hlinka staged a huge rally to demand that the government in Prague honour the promises made in 1918. When Hlinka died in 1938, another conservative Catholic priest, Jozef Tiso, became party leader. By then, Hitler was ratcheting up pressure on Czechoslovakia by exploiting the grievances of the German minority in the Sudetenland. Abandoned by the western powers at Munich, the republic became increasingly fragile. Tiso demanded autonomy and the beleaguered Benes gave in. Hitler, realising that Czechoslovakia was in a terminal state, bullied Tiso to demand complete independence. When German troops marched into Prague in March 1939, the brand new state of Slovakia was born from the prostrate corpse of the Czechoslovakian republic. Hitler punished the Czechs by dismembering and occupying the rest of the cadaver as the Reich Protectorates of Bohemia and Moravia. Hitler invariably took a frugal line on the costs of conquest and occupation. For the Germans, an obedient puppet state was the cheaper option and they believed that Tiso and the Slovak People's Party could deliver.

As president, Tiso immediately abolished all other parties, but his new Slovak state was deeply split between antagonistic factions. Tiso himself led a traditional conservative wing of the government with strong links to the Vatican. Opposition was led by the Prime Minister, Vojyêch Tuka, a former law professor, and the Minister of the Interior, Alexander ('Sano') Mach, who was the head of the Hlinka Guard. Both Tuka and Mach were deeply influenced by Nazi ideology. Both factions were antisemitic but while Tiso and his followers sought ways to expropriate Jewish property, their opponents demanded a more radical solution. These distinctions meant little to the Jewish communities of Slovakia as the Tiso government began bringing ever more radical legislation to deprive them of their rights and property. On 28 July 1940, just under a year before the German invasion of the Soviet Union, Hitler met with Tiso, Tuka and Mach at the Schloss Kleßheim in Austria. He insisted, as he always did at these conferences of the unequal, that the Slovaks step up action on the Jewish question. On the Slovak side, Hitler's insistence on a more radical Jewish policy turned into a licence for plunder. On 9 September 1941, a 'Jewish Codex' authorised the acquisition of Jewish-owned property and its distribution to members of the People's Party – and the Hlinka Guard. A Jewish Council was established and a special department, the Central Office for the Economy, was established to enact this blatant act of robbery. Plunder, of course, implied expulsion and in the same month between 10,000 and 15,000 Jews had been driven out of Bratislava to the east.

A month after Hitler's meeting with the Slovak leaders, the SS sent Dieter Wisliceny to Bratislava as an advisor on Jewish Affairs attached to the German Embassy. His task was apparently to push for more radical solutions to the 'Jewish problem' and he found sympathetic listeners in the Tiso government. Despite this meeting of minds, action against Jews was confused and sporadic. While the more radical Slovaks frequently pushed for the expulsion of Jews, the German side resisted. Even Eichmann spoke against adopting a piecemeal solution. But this chaotic state of affairs began to change after the Wannsee Conference at the beginning of 1942. It was noted at the meeting that 'political problems', that is resistance, were not anticipated in Slovakia and so deportations could begin immediately. At the beginning of the year, Germany had demanded 20,000 Slovak workers for the armaments industry. Tuka then offered 20,000 able-bodied Jews. In mid March, a Slovak representative attended a meeting in Berlin with Eichmann and Wisliceny and an agreement seems to have been reached to begin the deportation of Slovakian Jews at the end of the month with Himmler's approval. Eichmann planned to use the young Jewish workers to continue work on the Birkenau camp at Auschwitz, replacing Soviet prisoners who had died in the course of construction. The Slovaks would pay 500 Reichsmark per deported Jew to cover German expenses.

Although the Slovak government had insisted on the expulsion of Jews, Himmler was concerned that the deportations might still provoke the Slovaks. The reasons for his concern are not easy to explain. The Slovaks applied a lot of pressure to persuade the Germans to rid the nation of its Jews, but Himmler may have been aware that Tuka had negotiated without informing Tiso. When Tiso found out about the talks he tried to force Tuka to resign – a move resisted, of course, by the Germans. Whatever the reasons for Himmler's anxiety, Eichmann insisted that Wisliceny make sure that the deportations happen quickly and efficiently to head off any second thoughts on the Slovak side. As it turned out, Tiso offered no resistance at all and turned a deaf ear to some half-hearted protests from the Vatican. In this, he was supported by a group of Slovak bishops who cynically defied Papal authority by issuing a pastoral letter that denounced Jews as murderers of Christ.

The first transport of Jewish deportees left for Auschwitz on 26 March 1942. Crammed inside cattle cars were 999 young women. Under Wisliceny's guidance, the Hlinka Guard and another paramilitary organisation comprising members of the Slovak German minority, the 'Freiwillige Schutzstaffel' (FS), seized Jews in their homes and herded them onto trains to Žilina, a railway junction on the Polish border. From here, they were despatched to ghettos in the General Government or straight to Auschwitz and Majdanek. Some were murdered in the Bełżec death camp.

By the end of June 1942, Wisliceny and his Slovak collaborators had deported close to 52,000 Slovakian Jews. Most had ended up in Auschwitz; the majority had been murdered. Then the deportations slowed. Tuka was outraged and insisted that the pace was accelerated. Tiso hesitated. The German minister to Bratislava, Hans Ludin, reported: 'Evacuation of Jews from Slovakia has reached deadlock … Prime Minister Tuka wishes to continue the deportations, however, and requests strong support by diplomatic pressure on the part of the Reich.' At the end of the month, Ernst von Weizsäcker replied: 'You can render the diplomatic assistance requested by Prime Minister Tuka by stating that stopping the deportation of the Jews and excluding 25,000 Jews would cause surprise in Germany, particularly since the previous cooperation of Slovakia in the Jewish question has been much appreciated here.'Weizsäcker had first written instead of 'cause surprise': 'would leave a very bad impression'.[5]

Why did the deportations from Slovakia grind to a halt at the end of June? The answer is a tangled story that would be exploited by the SS in Hungary two years later. Although some puzzles have not been completely answered, the basic facts established by historians Yehuda Bauer and Schlomo Aronson are as follows. On 26 September, the Slovak government had compelled the divided and diverse Jewish community to establish a Jewish Council – the Ústredna Židov, known as the ÚŽ, or Jewish Centre. Two weeks before the deportations were scheduled to begin, Wisliceny planned to force members of the Centre to assist with the round-ups and had begun developing a relationship with a Jewish engineer called Karel Hochberg. As Bauer puts it, 'Hochberg was in the mould of Jewish traitors during the Nazi period' such as Abraham Gancwajch, the police chief in Warsaw and Szpiro, the head of the Jewish police in Cracow. Hochberg willingly became Wisliceny's assistant. In the meantime, the group of Zionist Jews led by the Rabbi Weissmandel and his secular cousin, the redoubtable Gisi Fleischmann, responded to the growing threat to Slovakian Jews by establishing the Pracovná skupina, or Working Group. Weissmandel referred to the organisation in Hebrew as the Hava'ad Hamistater, the Hidden Committee. Weissmandel and Fleischmann desperately began to search for ways of rescuing at least some of the Jews. Weissmandel had heard rumours that Wisliceny had released a single Jew after the payment of a ransom. In mid June, he proposed to the Working Group that they send Hochberg to Wisliceny with a more lucrative offer – to persuade him to stop the deportations. When a committee member warned that Hochberg would betray them to the Slovaks or Nazis, Weissmandel insisted that he was certain that the traitor would seize the chance for redemption. This was remarkably naïve.

And Weissmandel went further. He was convinced that Wisliceny would not be sufficiently impressed by an offer from a Slovakian organisation so he *invented* a representative of World Jewry, called 'Ferdinand Roth', who was, he told Wisliceny, based in Switzerland. It was a shrewd, if hazardous calculation. As we will see again in Hungary, Jewish rescue organisations often tried to exploit Nazi fantasies of vast Jewish wealth hidden in Swiss bank accounts. Using an old English typewriter and paper with Swiss watermarks, Weissmandel composed a letter, addressed to himself, from the fictitious 'Ferdinand Roth'. Whether or not he was seeking redemption, Hochberg now approached Wisliceny with the new ransom offer. We have no idea what kind of discussion took place but Hochberg returned to Weissmandel a few days later with a price for Wisliceny's cooperation: $50,000 in dollar bills, to be paid in two instalments of $25,000. Hochberg also suggested bribing the Slovak officials who were managing the deportations and Weissmandel agreed.

The Zionist rescue organisations like the Working Group simply did not have access to the riches the Germans imagined they did. Weissmandel faced formidable difficulties finding the funds Hochberg had promised Wisliceny – and succeeded in drumming up only the first instalment from Slovakian businessman Solomon Stern. Hochberg handed the money to Wisliceny. At the same time, other members of the Working Group made contact with Anton Vašek, the head of the 14th Department in the Slovak Ministry of the Interior that was responsible for organising the deportations on the Slovak side. Soon after the money was handed to Hochberg, the deportations halted.

It is completely to be understood that, from the point of view of Weissmandel and Fleischmann, the halting of the deportations was the miraculous consequence of their ransom payments. Now came the problem of the second instalment. Weissmandel and Fleischmann turned to a non-fictional Swiss individual in the shape of Saly Mayer – who was head of the philanthropic American Jewish Distribution Committee (JDC, or simply the Joint) which was based in Geneva, as well as other Swiss Jews. None had the funds to spare – certainly not the hard cash in dollars that Wisliceny had insisted on receiving. Weissmandel was bitterly angry with Mayer but there was little he could do and by the time discussions had ended, the second ransom payment was late. As a consequence, or so it seemed, the deportations resumed with a transport to Auschwitz on Yom Kippur, the Day of Atonement: 21 September. Shortly afterwards, Weissmandel acquired funds from a Hungarian businessman. When Hochberg at last handed over the delayed second instalment to Wisliceny, the Slovak government halted the deportations. They would not be resumed until the autumn of 1944.

For Weissmandel and the Working Group committee, the pattern of events was proof that the Germans could be bribed, and lives saved. But a closer examination of the timing of the stop-start deportations reveals that he was mistaken. As Bauer points out, after Yom Kippur *two additional transports* were despatched from Bratislava to Auschwitz on 23 September and 20 October. Arguably the planning of the first might have been too far advanced, but *the October transport* casts grave doubt on the claim that the bribes were the main factor in the halt.

It should be noted here that no one on the Slovakian side, including Weissmandel and the Jewish Council, had any certainty about what had happened to the tens of thousands of Slovakian Jews who had been deported. The Germans had muddied the water with requests for 'Slovak workers'. It would seem that only the Hlinka guard members who stayed on the trains after they crossed the Polish border at Žilina knew that many of the Jews deported from Slovakia would be killed. These Hlinka men had no interest in warning Slovak Jews what happened in the camps in occupied Poland.

Despite this fog of uncertainty, the members of the Working Group in Bratislava began to fear the very worst about the fate of Slovak Jews. This deepening apprehension about German plans for European Jewry led to the next and most crucial development in the Group's enigmatic bonds with Wisliceny. Weissmandel and Fleischmann were completely convinced that the bribes had persuaded Wisliceny to order a halt to the deportations. Other members of the Group were sceptical, but Weissmandel pressed ahead. He now came up with a plan to ransom all the Jews of Europe. He called this the 'Europa Plan' and presented it to Wisliceny in November, once again through the treacherous Hochberg. Weissmandel insinuated that huge sums could be made available – at least $2 to 3 million just to begin with. He was certain that the avaricious Wisliceny would take the bait – but it was at this moment that Weissmandel's plans nearly came unstuck. The Slovak police arrested his go-between. They accused Hochberg of extorting money and valuables from Jews who were listed for deportation – in return for promises of release. The circumstances of the arrest are murky. It is possible that he was betrayed by another member of the Group called Andrej Steiner, who had spoken out against using Hochberg, but it makes a lot more sense that the Slovaks had found out what was going on and resented the flow of Jewish funds into German pockets. In any case, the arrest was a headache for Wisliceny, whose shady dealing was threatened with exposure, and for Weissmandel, who had come to rely on Hochberg. He made futile efforts to get Hochberg released but Gisi Fleischmann, who was equally committed to the 'Europa Plan', persuaded

Weissmandel that Hochberg's unexpected removal from the negotiations was a stroke of good fortune. The Working Group committee asked Steiner to take over as go between to push forward the 'Europa Plan'. According to Steiner's own account, the negotiations began immediately. Wisliceny informed Weissmandel that he would need high level approval for what he called the 'Grossplan' to proceed. He claimed to have travelled to Berlin and met with Himmler. It is more likely that he informed Eichmann, who then went to his superiors in the RSHA, who then talked to Himmler. There is no record of any of these discussions but, in any event, Himmler signalled his approval. As he would again in Hungary, Himmler made clear that any promises made to Jewish organisations need not be made in good faith. As we know, Hitler had already approved Himmler's proposals to fleece small numbers of wealthy Jews of hard currency or other valuables in exchange for their lives. This kind of high-level skulduggery to plunder Jewish 'treasure' would have little impact on the overall plan to proceed with the Final Solution.

It is not necessary to follow all the twists and turns of the duplicitous 'Europa Plan'. What is important for our purposes is to find out why the deportations were halted. Had Weissmandel's plan to bribe Wisliceny worked? Many members of the Working Group believed this was indeed the case. According to a Jewish representative in Switzerland: 'the possibility of stopping the scourge of the deportations … the [Working Group] tell us that [Wisliceny] will now become the chief official for south-eastern Europe, and that until now *he has kept all his promises to the fullest extent*' [my italics]. Weissmandel would convey the same message to the Va'ada, the Rescue Committee in Budapest, in March 1944. *Ransom worked; Wisliceny should be trusted.* This 'story' of what happened in Slovakia had a decisive impact on shaping the strategy adopted by the Va'ada. Some SS officials accepted bribes; Jews could be ransomed. Furthermore, the details of the negotiations in Slovakia were well known to Himmler and the 'Jewish experts' in the RSHA. Eichmann and his masters had learnt a crucial lesson in deception.

The hard evidence shows that the bribes paid to Wisliceny by the Working Group had little or no impact on the decision to halt the deportations from Slovakia. The most telling evidence is in the timing. Deportations were stopped between the end of July and 18 September. But although Weissmandel hatched up the plan to bribe Wisliceny in early July, Hochberg did not approach him *until August* when he handed over the first instalment. In the course of the *next six weeks*, two transports, crammed with Slovakian Jews, departed Bratislava for Auschwitz. It would seem that Wisliceny received the second payment shortly after that. As noted earlier, transports were not discontinued in the period after Yom Kippur until October. If bribes paid to Wisliceny did not halt the deportations of Slovakian Jews, what really happened?

A clue can be found in a diplomatic telegram sent by Hans Ludin, the German minister in Bratislava, to the Foreign Office in Berlin on 26 June. He wrote that the 'evacuation' of Jews had reached 'deadlock', 'because of clerical influence and the corruption of individual officials'. It will be recalled that while the Slovakian government was dominated by conservative Catholics with a strong tradition of antisemitism, there were deep divisions between the president, Jozef Tiso, and his Prime Minister, Vojtech Tuka, who was a radical pro-Nazi. By the end of June, Tiso was becoming increasingly wary of cooperating with German demands. This may have reflected moral scruples or more likely the fear of retribution if the Allies prevailed. More than 52,000 Jews had already been deported and it was becoming evident that few of them had survived. The Vatican Secretary of State, Luigi Maglione, had voiced concern and a handful of religious authorities in Slovakia demanded that Jews be 'treated as human beings'. By September, when three further transports departed for Auschwitz, just 20,000 mainly baptised Jews remained alive in Slovakia. While Tuka pressed to complete the task of solving Slovakia's 'Jewish problem', ever louder protests from clergy and from Slovak intellectuals persuaded Tiso to call a halt.

The issue flared up the following spring, when Tuka once again pushed for the complete removal of all Slovakian Jews. He complained to Ludin that 'the naïve Slovak clergy was prone to believe such atrocity fairy tales and [Tuka] would be grateful if they were countered from the German side by a description of conditions in the Jewish camp'. He proposed that a Slovak delegation comprising Catholic priests and journalists be allowed to visit Auschwitz and other camps to allay such fears. It is unclear whether Tuka really believed that the slaughter of Slovakian Jews was a 'fairy tale'. Nothing came of Tuka's suggestions and in April, Hitler summoned Tiso to the Schloss Kleßheim once again to harangue him about 'finishing the job'. Ominously, he ranted at length about Horthy's stubborn 'protection' of the Hungarian Jews. Under enormous pressure, Tiso, on this occasion, refused to promise that he would take any further action. The Slovakian Jews who remained alive would be safe – for now.

The Germans did not give up. In June, Eichmann suggested that Tiso should be shown 'favourable reports', illustrated by photographs, of conditions in Jewish camps to counteract 'fantastic rumours circulating in Slovakia'. None of these deceitful strategies persuaded the Slovakian government to resume deportations. As Friedländer points out, the Germans may have refrained from more drastic action because of a 'bottleneck' that had developed at Auschwitz as the camp authorities struggled to cope with the final transports from Germany and occupied Poland. At the same time, Wisliceny was busy in Salonika organising deportations of Greek Jews, which would cause yet more management problems on the ramps at Auschwitz.

For now, the Slovakian Jews were safe. In Berlin, they had not been forgotten.

Wisliceny, with the blessing of the SS chiefs in Berlin, had carried out a spectacular sting. He posed as the master of ransom – with the power to save tens of thousands of lives at the right price. The 'Europa Plan' was simply a cynical means to raise the level of rewards by setting a price on the heads of all European Jews. A price that could never be paid. The oleaginous 'Willy' proved himself to be a master of such scams. When Wisliceny arrived in Budapest with the Eichmann Commando in March 1944, his reputation as a venal power broker went before him. Leading figures in the Jewish Council such as Freudiger would often seek his succour with this favour or that, which Wisliceny would, it appeared, happily gift. He knew he could afford to save a handful of relatives or friends of the influential Jews he had to impress so that the deportation trains kept on rolling without interruption.

There is an anecdote that perfectly encapsulates this perilous bond. At every one of their meetings, Freudiger presented 'Willy' with boxes of sweets, chocolates and select items of the family jewels or cash. For Freudiger, this sweetening of the SS palate paid off. Wisliceny helped him and his family escape to Romania in August 1944.

8

THE TRAP

It would be the last German invasion of the war and began with a trick.

By the spring of 1944, Hitler and his military commanders had run out of patience with the barely concealed vacillations of the Horthy regime in Budapest. On 3 March, Hitler summoned Goebbels to his Alpine Fort in Berchtesgaden. By then, he feared Allied attacks from the air and the Berghof was draped with camouflage netting and the vast rooms inside were dimly illuminated. The atmosphere was gloomy but Hitler, Goebbels discovered, was in a robust frame of mind despite the crisis on the Eastern Front and another simmering confrontation with the Finnish government, another unwilling ally. According to Goebbels' diary account of the conversation, Hitler was bullishly confident that the front line in the East would be held and discussed plans for a summer offensive; he was confident that the long-expected Allied attack in the West would be repelled. He even spoke of ordering Göring to launch aerial counterattacks against the British bomber fleets that were nightly raining death and destruction on German cities. 'You feel some scepticism rising up within you,' Goebbels confessed in his diary.[1]

It was the 'treachery' of Hungary that cast the deepest shadow over Hitler's plans. Horthy had 'smelled a rat', Hitler suspected, meaning that he had realised that Hungary had chosen the losing side. Miklós Kallay, Horthy's Prime Minister, had never disguised his hostility to Germany. The deteriorating military situation sharpened Hitler's fears about the intentions of his ally. By early 1944, the Soviet Army was advancing across Ukraine ever closer to the Carpathians and the Hungarian border. Earlier in the year, Horthy had written to Hitler requesting, not for the first time, the withdrawal of battered and demoralised Hungarian forces from the front. If the Soviets made contact with the Hungarians, Horthy's commanders might seize the chance to defect.

The portents were troubling. According to Goebbels, Hitler now planned to crush the government of the hated Kallay and arrest Horthy. Hitler gloated over Hungary's barely tapped resources of weapons, oil and foodstuffs, which would be confiscated for the Reich. He denounced the Hungarian aristocracy, which he blamed for sabotaging Hungary's war efforts. He blamed the Hungarian and Romanian armies for the debacle at Stalingrad. And the Hungarians had failed the most important test of all: they had failed to solve the nation's 'Jewish problem'. In the most venomous language, Hitler blamed any setback on the 'Jewish enemy'. In the case of Hungary, he told Goebbels: 'We shall make sure that they don't slip through our fingers.' There was a perverse rationality behind the obsessive hatred. As Goebbels noted: 'He wants to put the 700,000 Jews in Hungary *to activity useful for our war services*' [my italics]. Hitler was motivated not only by ideological obsession but by an urgent need to exploit in one way or another Hungarian resources, including its peoples. He may not have been aware that large numbers of Hungarian Jewish men of military age had already been conscripted into the Labour Service. The case for tackling the Hungarian problem was overwhelming: there was no doubt in Hitler's mind that action had to be taken, soon.

On 11 March, Hitler issued orders to launch a military operation to occupy Hungary code-named Margarethe I that had been planned in September the previous year. Because of the massive pressure on German military forces in Italy as well as the Eastern Front and the simultaneous preparations for the expected Allied invasion in the west, the Oberkommando der Wehrmacht (OKW) had planned to deploy Romanian, Slovak and Croat units. Hitler was also planning to put Horthy under arrest and to disarm the Hungarian army and police. At the last moment, the SD head of intelligence for Central and Southeast Europe, Wilhelm Höttl, with the connivance of Walter Schellenberg, convinced Hitler that such extreme measures could be catastrophic. The deployment of troops from these hated neighbours would provoke unpredictable political blowback and to arrest the Regent would be to pour fuel on the fire. Höttl recommended instead a political solution backed by military force. Horthy would remain at his post; the Hungarian army and police would be kept on side. This plan for a 'soft' occupation, which

Höttl convinced Hitler was the wisest solution, was not in any sense an act of benevolence. Keeping Horthy as a symbolic head of state would dampen resistance and, as it transpired, the Hungarian Interior Ministry, and the police and gendarmerie units it controlled, would become the very willing executioners of Himmler's SS. In any case, the Romanian dictator, Ion Antonescu, had refused to take part in any military venture against Hungary unless former Romanian territories, gifted to Hungary, were returned. Only German troops would be sent across the Hungarian border. Hitler also agreed that the Hungarian army should not be disarmed – so long as Horthy could be persuaded to comply. A plan was now hatched to ensnare Horthy.

In Hungary, it was carnival season. Streets were crowded in Budapest and shops were busy, even the ones specialising in luxury items. The most affluent Hungarians still enjoyed a daily round of dinners, cocktail parties and entertainment. Many, including Jews, seemed to be convinced that the war would soon be over. The Hungarian national holiday of independence, celebrating the fiftieth anniversary of the death of the Hungarian patriot Kossuth, was to be held as usual on 20 March, and Prime Minister Kallay would address parliament on an important matter. There were many Hungarians who hoped that Kallay would proclaim a Hungarian surrender and announce the imminent arrival of British or American airborne divisions. On 15 March, Horthy and his wife, Magda, attended a performance of the opera *Petofi*, which had been put on by university students. During the intermission, the German Minister, Dietrich von Jagow, arrived with an urgent letter from Hitler requesting a meeting at the Schloss Kleßheim. The Minister insisted that neither Kallay nor the Minister of the Interior, Ferenc Keresztes-Fischer, both of whom he distrusted, accompany the Regent.

On Saturday, 18 March, Horthy, his chief of staff, Ferenc Szombathelyi, and a clutch of anxious ministers arrived at the Schloss on the Regent's special train. In his memoirs, Horthy describes the 'usual procedure'.[2] He was greeted at the station by Hitler, his Foreign Minister Ribbentrop and Field Marshall Wilhelm Keitel. Döme Sztojay, the sycophantic Hungarian Ambassador in Berlin, was also in attendance. Hitler, Horthy noted, 'stooped more and looked much older'. The Hungarian party was driven in a gleaming Mercedes to the Schloss along roads lined with hard-faced SS men in black uniforms. The atmosphere was intimidating, as Hitler intended.

Hitler got down to business straightaway. He took Horthy into the room he used as a study and refused to allow the other Hungarians to join the discussions. Horthy retaliated by demanding that Paul Schmidt, Hitler's interpreter, leave the room. Horthy's German, like his English, was excellent. Schmidt and a handful of colleagues waited nervously outside the study. Raised voices could be heard muffled by the thick baroque doors. Then suddenly, the door was wrenched open and Horthy, flushed and angry, strode into the corridor, followed in an instant later by an irate Hitler, who pursued Horthy to his rooms. The door remained firmly closed. Hitler rushed away to find Ribbentrop. Later, Horthy would say that he regretted not having his revolver: 'I would have shot the scoundrel!'

Behind closed doors, Hitler had, without any preamble, launched a frontal assault. He accused Horthy of negotiating with the Allies and warned of taking 'precautionary measures'. Horthy responded with vacuous flimflam about Magyars never being traitors but Hitler then switched to Hungary's stubborn protection of nearly a million Hungarian Jews. They threatened the security of Germany's forces, he shouted. After this sustained browbeating, Hitler insisted that Horthy sign an agreement to accept German occupation. The tension in the room was escalating; Horthy refused to sign; Hitler insisted that there was no alternative: Hungary would be occupied whether Horthy agreed or not. Hitler piled on the humiliation. Any resistance, he lied, would be crushed by Romanian, Slovak and Croatian forces. This was too much for Horthy: 'If everything is decided, there's no point staying any longer!' It was at this moment that he threw open the study doors and rushed away – to the astonishment of Schmidt and his colleagues waiting outside.

Horthy announced that he and his party would return to his train. The negotiations were over. At that moment, an air raid siren wailed, and thick smoke billowed across the Schloss gardens. He demanded a telephone but was informed that a storm had damaged communications and the telephone line was down. Horthy and his party were trapped.

The theatrics provided a gangster-style deception that Hitler had planned in advance. Hitler's plan was to delay Horthy's departure from Austria as German troops mustered on the border. The simmering Hungarian party now sat down to lunch with their hosts. The atmosphere was 'not cordial' as Hitler picked 'nervously' at a vegetarian lunch. When the discussions resumed after the meal, Hitler insisted that German troops would withdraw as soon as a suitable new government had been installed to replace

Kallay. According to Horthy, Hitler persisted with unsettling game playing. He summoned Keitel and enquired whether the occupation order could, even now, be rescinded. 'Impossible,' replied Keitel, 'our troops are already crossing the border.' It was all a sham. Horthy's last card was to offer to resign. He understood that Hitler needed him to stay on only to quell any signs of a national uprising. But Horthy played this last card half-heartedly: he feared that, if he stood down, the Germans would turn to the extremist Arrow Cross to impose order. This was probably a miscalculation. Hitler resisted making political use of ultra-radical nationalist factions, as he had shown when he spurned the Romanian Iron Guard. Horthy and his party stood up from the dinner table. 'Am I a prisoner?' he demanded. Hitler needed more time. He reassured the Hungarians that their train would be ready to leave 'in a few hours'. Ribbentrop then presented Horthy with the text of a communiqué that stated he had agreed to the stationing of German troops in Hungary by 'mutual consent'. Horthy angrily refused to sign. Ribbentrop had the document published in the German newspapers without comment or revision. It seemed to all intents and purposes that Admiral Horthy had fallen on his sword.

Hitler had got what he wanted but his game of deception had not yet run its course. He accompanied the Hungarian party to the station and sent them off 'with a friendly smile'. As Horthy's train steamed towards Budapest, it was held up for long periods in Salzburg and then in Linz. Sometime after midnight, the German Minister von Jagow entered Horthy's compartment and announced that he had been recalled. His successor had just boarded the train and wished to meet with the Regent. The successor was none other than Edmund Veesenmayer who, it will be recalled, had already spent some time in Hungary studying the 'Jewish problem'. Veesenmayer was not merely a successor to von Jagow. Hitler had provided him with extensive powers as plenipotentiary and Ambassador of the Reich, Bevollmächtiger des Großdeutschen Reiches und Gesandter in Ungarn. He was also a Brigadeführer in the SS. Veesenmayer was accompanied by Ernst Kaltenbrunner, the head of the RSHA.

His presence on Horthy's train, as it clattered through the night towards Budapest, was just as ominous.

Kaltenbrunner had replaced Heydrich as head of the RSHA. He was Eichmann's superior and a rabid antisemite. He had risen to power in the Austrian SS alongside fanatics such as Globočnik and won the favour of Himmler as a self-proclaimed 'intelligence expert' who reported efficiently on the activities of the Austrian Nazis. But Kaltenbrunner made the bad mistake of falling out with Heydrich, who despised him as a crude 'subaltern type'. Proud of his own Aryan physique, Heydrich poked fun at Kaltenbrunner's odd appearance and the size of his rear. He was, to be sure, a huge, intimidating man. Topping out at 6ft 4in, with the broad shoulders and thickly muscled arms of a circus strong man, his equine visage was engraved with an ugly and intimidating maze of fencing scars. He had won these insignia of Teutonic pride as a fanatical member of a reactionary student fraternity at Graz University where, like so many Austrian Nazis, he had studied law. Ever since his days of fraternity carousing in Graz, Kaltenbrunner had been a dedicated chain smoker and semi-alcoholic, who often drove at reckless speeds through night-time Vienna. He had a reputation as an insatiable seducer. Wilhelm Höttl, who was a member of Veesenmayer's staff, was astounded by what he regarded as Kaltenbrunner's unfathomable appeal to women and astonished by the 'variety' of his conquests. Höttl remembered Kaltenbrunner's 'remarkably broad shoulders and claw-like hands – whenever he shook hands with me, I worried'. The SD intelligence chief Walter Schellenberg described 'a real lumberjack ... square heavy chin ... a thick neck forming a straight line with the back of his head ... the eyes of a viper seeking to petrify his prey'. And those hands again: 'I always had the feeling I was looking at the hands of an old gorilla ... he made me feel quite sick.' Schellenberg added: 'He had very bad teeth and some of them were missing so that he spoke quite indistinctly. Himmler also found this extremely unpleasant and eventually ordered him to go to a dentist.' The shock experienced by the unfortunate *Zahnarzt* when Kaltenbrunner opened his mouth can only be imagined.

Despite such low standards of dental hygiene, it was to Kaltenbrunner that Himmler turned in the turbulent aftermath of Heydrich's assassination in Prague. In the view of Himmler's quack masseur, Felix Kersten, he admired Kaltenbrunner as a 'fighter, an ideological fighter who would shrink from no task'. Like many of the Austrian officers in the SS, Kaltenbrunner was a spiteful and single-minded antisemite who was very deeply involved in the Final Solution. Interrogated after the war, Kaltenbrunner ranted to his captors: 'All partisan activity, every resistance movement, every form of espionage had the Jew as its organiser; he was the decisive element in every hostile action.' As soon as he was appointed head of the RSHA, Kaltenbrunner made no bones about his commitment and managerial talents to push forward the task of 'evacuating' Jews to the East. Throughout occupied Europe, he consistently backed Eichmann's deportation teams to round up and ship Jews to the concentration camps. If Eichmann ran into difficulties, he turned to Kaltenbrunner to remove any roadblocks.[3]

Kaltenbrunner would have been a menacing presence on Admiral Horthy's train as it steamed slowly through the night towards Budapest. Like Veesenmayer, he had a passion for forensic pseudo-legalistic detail that he would exploit to ensnare Horthy and reshape the Hungarian government to serve the murderous ends of Hitler's Reich. There was cunning logic behind the presence of these two men on the train. The hulking Kaltenbrunner acted as the enforcer; Veesenmayer took on the role of the suave, politely spoken diplomat. Both believed that the treachery of the Hungarians was inspired by Hungary's Jewish citizens. After his visit to Budapest at the end of 1943, Veesenmayer reported that members of the government and the Hungarian middle class expected, in the event of an Allied victory, 'clemency and benevolent treatment' from the British and Americans because they believed, with little justification, that they had shown a 'hospitable attitude towards Jewry' and even worse, in Veesenmayer's view, regarded this as a *guarantee* of Hungarian 'concerns'. In other words, he perceived that Hungarian national sovereignty was entwined with the protection, fragile though it was, of Hungarian Jews. Veesenmayer argued that this 'guarantee' must be 'torn up' to force Hungary to remain loyal to the Axis. He concluded that solving the Jewish question in Hungary would be a 'rewarding and compelling task' and the 'precondition for the engagement of Hungary in the Reich's battle for defence and existence'. He interpreted the Hungarian government's reluctance to pursue a solution to its Jewish question as a gauge of diminishing loyalty to the Reich: so the removal of the Jews was a 'definitive solution' that would divest Hungary of its guarantee of clemency.[4]

Horthy seems to have been blind to the diabolical intent of Hitler and his enforcers. He was much more preoccupied with his own status and repute than with the fate of Jews. His priority was to defend his own power base. Hitler's interpreter, Paul Schmidt, was also on the train and Horthy plied him with dinner and a stream of colourful stories. For Schmidt, this was a very different Horthy from the enraged and red-faced man who had angrily rushed out of Hitler's study. He no longer seemed to care a great deal about what lay ahead for his country and its people.

In his memoirs, Horthy portrayed himself as a victim of Nazi Germany, but there is ample evidence that his opportunist resistance to Hitler's demands could be easily overcome. At his trial in Nuremberg, Veesenmayer testified that: 'Horthy himself told me that he was interested only in protecting those prosperous, the economically valuable Jews in Budapest, those who were well off. However, as to the remaining Jewry – and he used a very ugly term here – he had no interest in them'. According to László Baky, who took a leading role in the deportations, Horthy confessed: 'Baky, you are one of my old Szeged officers. The Germans have cheated me. Now they want to deport the Jews. I don't mind. I hate the Galician Jews [i.e. Eastern Jews] and the Communists. Out with them, out of the country!'[5] While it might be said that Veesenmayer and Baky had a vested interested in vilifying the Regent, there is a consistency that runs through all his many pronouncements about Jews. His wealthy bridge partners had value; they were friends; the rest were dispensable.

Horthy's train pulled into the Vienna Hauptbahnof shortly after midnight. Here it was again held up. At 4 a.m., the train steamed out of Vienna towards Budapest. At that moment, German troops began marching across the border.

Sunday, 19 March was a beautiful spring day. The invasion was led by the parachutists of the elite Brandenburg Division, who were dropped close to Budapest to seize key positions. Once the paratroopers had done their job, eleven divisions under the overall command of Field Marshall Maximilian von Weichs crossed Hungarian borders from the north-west through Eastern Slovakia, and from Syrmia and the Banat region of Romania. The occupation forces had been cobbled together from ethnic German units and a Croatian Mountain SS Division that included many Bosnian Muslims. For many bewildered Hungarians, especially in Budapest, the first day of the occupation was deceptive. In the capital, Operation Margarethe resembled a smart military parade. Elite German troops marched smartly into the city, bands playing. Many Hungarians watched impassively. A student called Sándor Kiss took a tram to the Castle on the ridge above the Danube and was shocked to see two German soldiers 'their weapons at the ready'. He remembered: 'I got cold shivers up my spine. I knew there was big trouble and it suddenly hit me: the Germans.'

In their account of the occupation of Hungary in 1944, German historians Götz Aly and Christian Gerlach tease out what they term the 'rationality' of German strategy.[6] The principal objective was to prevent

Horthy defecting to the Allies and withdrawing Hungarian troops from the front. Just as important, the Germans planned to exploit the country's natural resources such as food, fuel and raw materials for the increasingly desperate war effort. Since the great Jewish dynasties still controlled a significant proportion of industry and manufacturing, Jews would inevitably become targets of plunder on a huge scale. Finally, Aly and Gerlach argue, Germany was buckling under a crippling manpower shortage and coveted Hungarian Jews as a vast pool of slave labour. The task was to round up and deport Hungarian Jews considered to be fit for work. Those who were deemed unfit would be eliminated.

The problem with this argument is that the Hungarian Army Labour Service, described in the previous chapter, had profoundly distorted the demographics of the Hungarian Jewish population. The Hungarian government had already enslaved tens of thousands of young Hungarian men and many Jewish communities had much higher proportions of women, children and the elderly. In the same rational terms, the Labour Service had severely depleted the economic value of the Jewish community as a manpower resource. Whether this was known to Hitler is uncertain. In any event, the rationality of the German treatment of the Jewish community becomes less convincing when the terrible human damage wrought by the Labour Service is taken into account. It is very clear from the aggressive language used by Hitler and his apparatchiks like Veesenmayer that the most fundamental intention was mass slaughter.

9

WHO WAS ADOLF EICHMANN?

The capture of Adolf Eichmann by Israeli agents in May 1960, the trial that followed in Jerusalem, and his conviction and execution two years later are pivotal events in the European narrative of the Holocaust. The trial, as Mary Fulbrook points out in her important new book *Reckonings*, was 'of momentous importance … the Eichmann trial redefined Nazi criminality in terms of the mass murder of Jews.' The trial was a global event: it took place in a converted theatre and was recorded by an American camera team. It was attended by hundreds of journalists from all over the world sitting in the courtroom or following proceedings on screens in the press room. The prosecutors, led by the attorney general Gideon Hausner, made 'path-breaking' use of emotive survivor testimony 'to make the Jewish catastrophe vivid'.[1] The Eichmann trial generated a rich trove of eyewitness accounts, which I have made extensive use of in this book. But it also left behind a historiographic patina of myth. Many remember the trial through the lens of Hannah Arendt's phrase 'the banality of evil' – words that have hampered understanding of the agents of the Nazi genocide ever since. What is less well known is the role taken by the West German government. Eichmann's arrest took the West German government by surprise. The Chancellor, Konrad Adenauer, feared that Eichmann would incriminate cabinet ministers and officials in Bonn. The Defence Minister, Franz Josef Strauss, threatened the Israeli government with cancellation of arms deals if they did not protect Bonn. The West German intelligence service, the BND, was instructed to find out how much Eichmann knew about public figures in the Federal Republic – and sent Rolf Vogel, one of its agents, to attend the trial. Vogel sat with the reporters in the courtroom and was officially accredited to the *Deutsche Zeitung* newspaper. This was camouflage. Vogel was being paid 2,000 Deutschmarks a month by the Federal Government, plus per diems and first-class plane tickets, to attend the trial. As a reserve officer in the West German army, the Bundeswehr, Vogel had formed a close relationship with the Chancellery Chief of Staff, Hans Globke, who had served the Reich as a senior official in the Interior Ministry. He had taken part in the drafting of the Nuremberg Laws in 1935 – and was now extremely anxious about what the Eichmann trial proceedings could reveal.

Journalist Klaus Wiegrefe discovered that:

> [Vogel] fed the Israeli prosecutors exonerative material on Globke and did everything he could to ensure that the prosecution remained limited to Eichmann. He wanted to ensure that the Israelis did not empha-size, before the world public, the roles played by many other Germans. Together with a journalist for the tabloid newspaper Bild, Vogel even stole documents from an East German attorney in Jerusalem who was trying to capitalize on the Eichmann trial's propaganda value for East Germany. Vogel feared that the documents could incriminate West German politicians or officials.[2]

In other words, it was essential for Adenauer's government that the fallout from the proceedings in Jerusalem did not spread too far and contaminate the international status of the West German government. The theatre of the trial, with the isolated figure of the accused inside a bulletproof glass booth, played a crucial propagandist role in making sure that only Adolf Eichmann was on trial. The Eichmann trial, in short, was pivotal both for what it revealed about the Holocaust but also for the way in which the proceedings were represented.

The trial was about the *facts* of the Holocaust – but at the same time, a crucible of mythology.

Adolf Eichmann has often been depicted as the most important German protagonist in the murderous assault on Hungarian Jewry in 1944. At the time, this was how the members of the Va'ada rescue committee such as Joel Brand and Rudolf Kasztner understood his role. He was the arbiter of life and death. And it was a role that Eichmann cultivated assiduously.

From what we know about the encounters that took place between Eichmann and the Va'ada, it is evident that he took pains to perform the part of the all-powerful 'master of deportation'. 'You know who I am?' he ranted at Brand. Some historians have echoed Eichmann's disingenuous role playing. Rudolf Braham for example, wrote that when Germany occupied Hungary and Hitler demanded a solution to the 'Jewish problem', Eichmann 'saw his life's dream come true. He finally had a chance to test his well-oiled apparatus on a massive and grandiose scale in a lightning operation … the "master" proved to be at his best in Hungary'.[3] Eichmann, to be sure, played a vital role in the onslaught on Hungarian Jews in 1944 and proved himself as a fanatical organiser of mass murder. There can be no doubt that Eichmann was a staunchly devoted functionary working within a many layered and competitive bureaucracy of occupation that brought together both German and Hungarian power-brokers. There is nothing banal about his role. His self-aggrandisement was a theatrical act of strategic deception designed to dupe the Va'ada rescuers and, at the same time, a peacock display of arrogant narcissism.

This is not to say that Eichmann was a mere cog in a murderous machine who 'just followed orders'. This was the self-image that he assiduously cultivated at his trial in Jerusalem. The German philosopher Hannah Arendt reported on some of the trial proceedings and her account has bedevilled many attempts to understand Eichmann and his role in the Holocaust ever since. Arendt was struck by the shabby appearance of the former SS colonel, who obsessively shuffled papers inside the bulletproof glass booth constructed for his protection in the courtroom. She hatched up the celebrated phrase 'the banality of evil' to pin down the disquieting asymmetry between the mediocre man and the horror of his deeds: 'Except for an extraordinary diligence in looking out for his own personal advancement, he had no motives at all. It was sheer thoughtlessness … that predisposed him to become one of the greatest criminals of that period.' And yet this slavish mediocrity was evil. Arendt was no ordinary journalist. She was a major thinker who had completed a revolutionary political study, *The Origins of Totalitarianism*, two years before Eichmann was brought to trial. She argued that totalitarian societies were pyramidal. At the top is a leader figure and a secretive cadre of elite apparatchiks. The commanding heights of the totalitarian state rest on a succession of layers built from the state apparatuses and mass organisations. The many layers of the pyramid are fully integrated and support and protect the leader. We now know that in the case of Nazi Germany, Arendt was wrong. Hitler's state was a jerry-built and ramshackle edifice thrown together from competitive power brokers and state organisations that often acted autonomously, albeit in the service of a charismatic power. Arendt's analysis of totalitarianism led her to see Eichmann as a functionary of the Nazi pyramid. In another memorable paragraph, she wrote that he 'never realised what he was doing'. For Gideon Hausner, the prosecutor at Eichmann's trial, who rejected Arendt's analysis, the defendant was the 'personification of satanic principles'.

Can any human action, however destructive, be explained by the theological if not mystical idea of evil? One of the most disturbing lessons of any genocide is that, to borrow the title of a classic study of a Nazi police battalion, 'ordinary men' can willingly commit crimes of the utmost cruelty. The motivations of perpetrators of genocide or *génocidaires* are too complex for any theological explanation. 'Evil' can never be an explanatory term. In any case, Arendt's notorious words appear to imply that evil persons should be in some way be *extraordinary* rather than banal. This suggests perhaps the allure of cultural icons such as John Milton's 'Satan', who in *Paradise Lost* is among the most charismatic characters in all literature. It is reassuring to believe that people who do terrible things are afflicted by some kind of demonic character flaw. The evidence of history is a lot more disturbing. Doing terrible things to other people requires no special qualities. It is both more enlightening and challenging to view a *génocidaire* such as Eichmann as an ambitious middle manager with unusually sharp elbows who clawed his way to power by slavishly adopting the corporate values of his superiors. He was neither cog nor evil mastermind – and in Hungary, Eichmann had to negotiate a labyrinthine network of competing Nazi power brokers.

As the plenipotentiary of the Greater German Reich, it was Edmund Veesenmayer who had overall responsibility for both political and economic decision-making and reported directly to the Foreign Minister, Joachim von Ribbentrop. Hitler empowered Veesenmayer to fulfil his 'police duties' to solve once and for all 'the Jewish problem'. His civilian staff included a number of 'experts' on Jewish matters such as Adolf Hezinger, Theodor Horst Grell, Franz von Adamovic-Waagstaetten and SS Captain Ballensiefen. Although Veesenmayer had 'full powers', as his official title implies, Himmler had hoped to seize such plenipotentiary powers for a representative of his ever-expanding SS empire. This had been resisted: Hitler refrained from giving the SS chief all the powers he craved so that the SS could act behind the screen of a pseudo-civilian occupation administration. Hitler preferred to cultivate rivals he could manipulate to courtiers such as Himmler, who might conspire to build their own power bases. It was a strategy of despotic rule that invariably provoked fierce turf wars among the Nazi occupation powers.

This was the case in Hungary. Thwarted by Veesenmayer, Himmler immediately began to build his own semi-autonomous security apparatus, which itself had confusing duplications of authority. During the first few days of the occupation, Himmler ordered the baleful chief of the RSHA, Ernst Kaltenbrunner, to oversee the SS and police units that entered Hungary with the German army. Kaltenbrunner's most important role, however, was political. As soon as German troops entered Hungary, he would shape a compliant new government to reflect Himmler's particular intentions. Once this had been achieved, Kaltenbrunner returned to Berlin. Following his departure, Himmler appointed SS Obergruppenführer Otto Winkelmann to the all-important role of Higher SS and Police Leader (HSSPF) in Hungary.[4] He would soon become a bitter rival to Veesenmayer, whom he frequently denounced for being 'too soft'. Winkelmann was the only child of a town clerk. He attended the Faculty of Law at Kiel University for a term, but his studies were interrupted in 1914 when he enlisted in the Reichswehr. In 1918, Winkelmann joined the State Security Police – and successfully pursued a career as a professional policeman. He joined the SS in the early 1930s, and by the end of the decade was a committed and trusted major in the Order Police. Although on paper, Winkelmann's career and personality are colourless, his steady rise within the SS ranks would not have been possible if he had not joined in the murderous activities of the Order Police units in the occupied territories of the Soviet Union.

Winkelmann's second in command was the same SS Sturmbannführer Wilhelm Höttl whose shrewd memorandum had changed Hitler's mind about the strategy of occupation and was now responsible for counter-espionage operations. When Kaltenbrunner returned to other duties in Berlin, the RSHA he headed was represented by SS Standartenführer Hans Geschke, who was appointed BdS, *Befehlshaber der Sipo-SD*, meaning commander of the security police and security service in an occupied territory. Although, strictly speaking, Eichmann and his men were attached to Geschke's headquarters, it was the HSSPF, Otto Winkelmann, who had the final word on the actions to be carried out by the commando.

Himmler's continuously expanding SS empire was a ramshackle amalgam of competitive offices, each with its own chieftain and acronym. He mimicked Hitler's strategy of appointing competitive empire builders to senior roles, who jockeyed for power and attention. After the occupation of Hungary, Himmler made another crucial appointment that reflected his colossal ambitions. By this stage in the war, the SS was both an instrument of terror and a fast-expanding, militarised corporation that exploited the vast slave labour reserves of the concentration camps. In the empire of the SS, plunder and exploitation went hand in hand with mass murder. To this end, he despatched SS Standartenführer Kurt Becher to Budapest with instructions to seize Hungarian industrial and commercial assets. Becher was, in effect, a corporate raider. His activities in Hungary would have remarkable consequences for the Zionist rescue organisation, the Va'ada – as we will soon discover. The ambitious Eichmann soon clashed with Becher, the suave SS cavalry man who had the same SS rank but, as a special envoy, had a direct line to Himmler.

Who was Adolf Eichmann? One answer might be that there were many Eichmanns. A hard-working file clerk in an obscure SS office. A 'Jewish expert'. The 'Master of Deportations'. The bean counter of genocide. In exile, he signed photographs for admirers: 'Adolf Eichmann – SS-Obersturmbannführer (retired)'. The cowed prisoner in the courtroom in Jerusalem. From the moment Eichmann pledged his loyalty and honour to the SS he took ownership of the 'Jewish question'. His career reflected the evolving status of Jewish persecution in the priorities of Hitler's Reich. As a recent biographer, Bettina Stangneth, emphasises: 'Every time the persecution of the Jews entered a new phase, he was in the vanguard.' Like most lives, his biography reveals an interplay of ambition and opportunity. His rise to prominence was tied to the evolutionary rhythm of the Nazi war on Jews. His first job for the SS was as a kind of filing clerk. When he fled Germany at the end of the Second World War, he had become notorious as the SS 'deportation expert'. This career arc was shaped by both ideological commitment and cunning.[5]

Otto Adolf Eichmann was born in Solingen in western Germany, but he grew up in the Austrian city of Linz, where his father Karl moved his family to take up a lucrative job offer. Karl and his children kept their German citizenship. Although Linz was a predominantly Catholic city, Karl was a committed Protestant who devoted a lot of his time to the local religious community. The Eichmann family was relatively prosperous and had a house on the elegant shopping street of Bischofstraße. Although his mother died when he was 8, Adolf and his siblings had sheltered and privileged childhoods. He was provided with lessons in riding, fencing, dancing and the violin. Despite this, he hated reading and failed to shine at school. One of his schoolmates was a tall young man called Ernst Kaltenbrunner. Karl was disappointed. After leaving school, Adolf took a trainee position but soon gave that up too. Nevertheless, there seems to have been no serious rift between father and son. Adolf soon found a job as a petrol salesman for the Vacuum Oil Company of Vienna. The job provided a decent income and a company motorbike, and was not without glamour: the rise of the automobile in Germany meant that peddling petrol and engine parts had become a 'sunrise industry'. Even with a motorbike, Adolf continued to live with his family and his decision seems to have reflected significant affinities with his father. Karl was staunchly conservative and like many Germans begrudged the way the Allied powers had diminished and humbled the Second Reich. His son inherited his father's resentments. In the early 1930s, Adolf joined a nationalist militia called the 'Austrian Legion' and then the Austrian NSDAP. This was hardly youthful rebellion – his father followed his son into the party. Many of Adolf's other relatives were active party members. In 1933, Eichmann decided to return to Germany where he joined the SS and took part in basic training at Camp Lechfeld. He showed ambition as well as a tendency to 'overstep his competences', as Stangneth puts it. On one occasion he was reprimanded for abusing another guest at a coffee house who was listening to 'Jewish music'. It turned out that the unfortunate individual was an SS officer, who did not take kindly to Eichmann's admonishment.

The young Eichmann was precociously arrogant and a convinced national socialist. As he deepened his commitment to extremist politics, he either gave up his well-paid job or was sacked. It was at this moment that his old school friend Kaltenbrunner stepped back into Adolf's life. Armed with a law doctorate, Kaltenbrunner had opened a legal practice in Linz. He was one of the many German or Austrian lawyers who threw themselves into the Nazi cause. If, as Hitler promised, Germany would be refashioned root and branch, it followed that the legal professions had a vital role to play. New states need new laws; lawyers must become servants of the state. The Nazi state transformed lawyers and other professionals such as doctors into political warriors. Kaltenbrunner persuaded his old school friend to join the SS and got him a position in the SD, the security arm of Himmler's fast-growing elite that was headed by Reinhard Heydrich.

The SS had its origins in a 'Guard Squad' of ruffians who protected Hitler at rallies and meetings. When Himmler was appointed Reichsführer-SS, he turned a rabble into an elite organisation of Aryan warriors – a kind of Nazi Camelot. He recruited bright young men, fresh out of university, who were somewhat wet behind the ears. Eichmann was older than most of his new colleagues; his scholastic accomplishments were mediocre. It was by chance rather than conviction that he ended up in the SD's department of Jewish Affairs. It has been suggested that he got the job because he knew that Hebrew is read from right to left. It was rumoured, falsely, that he had been born in Palestine. His new job description referred to the 'constant perusal of the Jewish press' and 'surveillance of Jewish assemblies'. The work he did was desk bound, petty and barely professional but by the mid 1930s, Eichmann was the SD's go-to expert on all Jewish matters. His boss at the time was an SS-Unterstturmführer called Dieter Wisliceny, who was the spoilt son of an estate owner and a failed theology student. As it had been for Eichmann, the SS was for young Dieter a refuge from career mediocrity. In a note Wisliceny set out the role of the SD department Referat II-112. He argued that 'the solution to the Jewish question' was a large-scale 'Zionist Exodus' of German Jews by any means possible. In 1937, Eichmann and Wisliceny's successor, Herbert Hagen, embarked on a mission to the Middle East to establish contacts with 'Arab politicians such as the Mufti of Jerusalem'. The study trip turned into farce. In Cairo, the SD men were refused visas to enter Palestine and no meetings, let alone negotiations, ever took place. The fiasco had little impact on Eichmann's career; he slowly climbed the SD ladder.

It was the German invasion of Austria in March 1938 that would propel the SD and petty bureaucrats such as Eichmann into new roles as managers of the Nazi war on Jews. Even before the German army's entry into Vienna on 12 March, radical nationalists had launched an orgy of terror directed at anyone believed to be Jewish. The Austrian Jewish writer Carl Zuckmayer called this 'the revolt of envy; malevolence; bitterness; blind, bitter vengefulness'. The annexation, or *Anschluss*, of Austria was followed by immediate regime change. Austria was now part of the Greater German Reich and almost overnight Jewish citizens became objects of violent humiliation and plunder. Jewish men and women were forced into so-called *Putzkolonnen*, cleaning columns, and forced to scrub sidewalks with soap and water. Viennese Jews were robbed and beaten, their homes expropriated. As this orgy of violence and plunder spiralled out of control, an SD Sonderkommando (Special Unit) comprising Eichmann and Hagen arrived in Vienna on 16 March. Eichmann's first task was to seize documents from various Jewish organisations and private citizens based on lists prepared in Berlin. When Hagen was ordered back to Berlin, Eichmann was left on his own. He began to work out the details of a strategy to seize control of the Jewish community in Vienna through its own cultural and economic organisations. He reported to Hagen that: 'I'm in total control here. [Jewish organisations] don't dare take a step without checking with me first … At least I lit a fire under these gentlemen, believe you me'. At the same time, a steady barrage of financial expropriations rapidly caused severe impoverishment of many Austrian Jews. The intent was to compel Jews to emigrate – Eichmann set an annual target of 20,000, which he soon exceeded. He was now the 'master of deportation'.

Eichmann was described in one SD report as 'energetic and impulsive': in Austria after the Anschluss, he had found a perfect vehicle for his temperament and ambitions. He was promoted to SS-Hauptsturmführer and allocated a small staff. Then in August, the German occupation authorities established the *Zentralstelle für jüdische Auswanderung*, the Central Bureau for Jewish Emigration. The nominal head of the *Zentralstelle* was Dr Walter Stahlecker, another lawyer who in 1941 would lead one of the Einsatzgruppen murder squads that followed in the wake of the Wehrmacht. As it turned out, Eichmann would be the Bureau's de facto chief. He set up an office in a palace on Prinz Eugen Straße that had been owned, until 1938, by the Rothschild family. Eichmann had by now acquired valuable skills hacking through bureaucratic red tape. In just over six months, he and his colleagues engineered the emigration of 110,000 Austrian Jews.

After the invasion of Poland in September 1939, Eichmann and Stahlecker used the same kind of managerial skills to organise deportations of Jews from the Protectorate of Bohemia and Moravia, the relic of the former Czechoslovakia, and occupied Poland, now known as the General Government, to the Lublin district. The evolution from enforced emigration to deportation to a 'reservation' was a crucial turning point in the evolution of Nazi race policy. The new plan was devised by Hitler's 'Eastern expert', Alfred Rosenberg – and involved the participation of Himmler, the Governor of the General Government Hans Frank, who was Hitler's personal lawyer, and the Gestapo boss Heinrich Müller. Eichmann was charged with organising and managing the deportations to the new camp; Odilo Globočnik, who had been Gauleiter of Vienna, was put in charge of the reservation. A site was chosen in a remote corner of the General Government, in a low-lying area between Nisko and Lublin on the Galician border. This was deliberate. As another German administrator Artur Seyss-Inquart put it: the site was 'swampy in its nature' and would cause 'considerable decimation' of the Jews deported there.[6] He was proved correct. Many thousands of Jews died of cholera and typhus in the reservation – and when the plight of deported Jews was exposed in some European newspapers, including the *London Times*, the disastrous scheme was abandoned. The decision was entirely pragmatic. The failure of the Nisko Plan would inspire a more drastic and secretive scheme. Territorial solutions to the 'Jewish problem', like the Madagascar Plan and the Nisko reservation, would be abandoned. From the disaster of Nisko would come the notion of a Final Solution.

In 1939, Himmler and Heydrich had rationalised – or tried to rationalise – a plethora of SS and police bodies as the Reich Security Main Office, RSHA. This monstrous bureaucratic empire was the fiefdom of Reinhard Heydrich and would become the main instrument in the persecution of the racial enemies of the Reich. Heydrich appointed Eichmann as head of RSHA Referat or section IV D 4, which was responsible for so-called *Räumungsangelegenheiten,* meaning 'Clearing Activities'. This was a crass euphemism that, in reality, meant forcibly expelling unwanted ethnic groups from territories considered fit only for Germans. In March 1941, Eichmann was appointed director of Referat IV B 4, with a broader remit of 'Jewish Affairs'. This apparently pettifogging obsession with tweaking bureaucratic labels meant that, at different times, Eichmann's Referat was known as the IV R, then the IV D 4 and finally the IV A 4b … Many simply referred to the Referat as the 'Eichmann Department'.[7]

This may seem bewildering but there was a logic to this shuffling of labels. Throughout the war, Eichmann was doing the same kind of job working out of the same office at Kurfürstenstraße 116 in Berlin, but – and this is the crucial point – on a continuously escalating scale. The so-called 'Eichmann-Männer' (Eichmann's men), such as his deputy Rolf Günther, Alois Brunner, Theodor Dannecker and Dieter Wisliceny – who was now working under his former subordinate – managed the deportation of Jews from Slovakia, the Netherlands, France and Belgium. Then in the last years of the war, Eichmann's men applied their well-honed skills to deport Jews from German-occupied northern Italy and Salonika in Greece.

When Eichmann arrived in Budapest in March 1944, he and his men had considerable proficiency as masters of mass deportation.

According to Bettina Stangneth, Eichmann was respected and even *liked* by colleagues. He was, in contemporary jargon, a skilled people manager. He treated all his staff, who usually stuck with him for the long term, with scrupulous fairness and put a lot of thought into devising ways to boost camaraderie. He organised musical evenings at which he often played second violin, comfortable that one of his subordinates was the better player. This bonhomie is macabre but offers an insight into the enactment of mass murder. Himmler, at the pinnacle of the SS hierarchy, frequently acknowledged the psychological challenges of, as he put it, 'to have this people [Jews] disappear from the earth'. It was a supremely hard but necessary task that was essential to save the German *Volk* from its racial foes. Carrying out the task of mass murder, Himmler recognised, required a special kind of psychic toughness. Shirking could not be tolerated. For middle managers in the SS such as Eichmann, career success depended on instilling camaraderie and demanding loyalty. Staff turnover in the Eichmann Department of the RSHA was low. Even Wisliceny, who had once been Eichmann's boss, remained loyal to the bitter end. And since Eichmann's men tended to stay put, the Referat accumulated an unrivalled set of skills. These would be used on an unprecedented scale in Hungary.

Vital to Eichmann's success in the eyes of both his staff and superiors was his reputation as an authority on 'Jewish Affairs'. While he often indulged a malevolent fascination with artefacts such as old Torah scrolls, his much-touted expertise was sham. What he did know very well was that data was the key to influence. How many Jews were resident in France? Spain? England? He had the files. If he didn't know the right answer, then he was happy to make up the numbers. Eichmann won a reputation for ruthlessly untangling the convoluted chains of bureaucratic command that proliferated in the Nazi state – and making sure things happened. This skill was amply demonstrated at the Wannsee Conference.

As described in a previous chapter, at the end of 1941, Reinhard Heydrich began planning a conference of state-level ministers to assert the central role of the RSHA in the planning and enactment of the Final Solution. The purpose of the conference was a power grab – or to use a German word, a *Machtvollkommenheitserweiterung*, the expansion of absolute power. As Judenreferent, Eichmann was the logical choice to organise the meeting and compile the documents Heydrich would need to make his case. The conference eventually took place on 20 January 1942 at a villa on Wannsee, a lake south-east of Berlin. Here representatives of the different state ministries gathered to discuss the cold task of the Final Solution. The day before proceedings were scheduled to begin, Eichmann had been conducting an inspection of the Theresienstadt concentration camp. It was a bitterly cold winter – and he had been driven back to Berlin through a snowstorm. Eichmann had no doubt in his mind about the importance of the meeting he had organised for Heydrich.

At his trial two decades later, Eichmann claimed that he had attended the conference as a 'minor expert'. 'I sat in a corner with the stenographer,' he claimed 'and no one bothered us. No one. We were much too insignificant'. This was a lie. He took a leading role organising and managing the conference and, crucially, drafting Heydrich's keynote speech and supplying the reams of facts and figures that supported his case. To be sure, Eichmann may not have spoken. But the all-important minutes that he compiled later would provide a blueprint, albeit confused, for an expansion of deportation and mass murder plans that would take place under the auspices of the RSHA. When the conference came to an end and the delegates trotted out into the snow to their waiting Mercedes, whose exhaust fumes rose into the freezing air, Eichmann and Müller invited Eichmann to stay behind. Heydrich was a very happy man. He had taken personal charge of the Final Solution. In a stomach-turning statement at his trial in Jerusalem, Eichmann recalled, 'Heydrich, Müller and my humble self sat cosily around a fireplace. For the first time, I saw Heydrich smoking a cigar or cigarette, something I never saw. He drank cognac, which I hadn't seen for ages. Normally he didn't drink alcohol.'[8]

Eichmann, to sum up, staged the Wannsee Conference. It was a pivotal moment in his career. In the years that followed, he and his staff of 'Jewish Experts' managed and enacted the persecution of Jews and other minorities across the Greater German Reich. In March 1944, Gestapo Chief Heinrich Müller ordered Eichmann to organise a Sonderkommando and proceed to Budapest.

10

MANAGING THE WHIRLWIND

At the beginning of 1944, heavy bombing badly damaged the Prinz Albrecht Straße headquarters of the SS in Berlin. Gestapo chief Heinrich Müller called Eichmann and instructed him to oversee the construction of a make do office located outside Berlin. Eichmann seized 235 Jewish labourers from the Theresienstadt camp and set them to work. Temperatures were close to zero, Eichmann was a relentless taskmaster – but these men were fortunate. Many 'work assignments' meant deportation to Auschwitz and near certain death. In early March, the Gestapo chief Heinrich Müller visited Eichmann at the new offices. Spring was stuttering from the broken hulks of tenement blocks and piles of rubble. For many Berliners, the consequences of Hitler's war were expressed by the pulverised urban landscapes of the capital city of the Reich. But Müller had thrilling news. Himmler had chosen Eichmann, who was called the 'Tsar of the Jews' by his admiring subordinates, for a new task. It would be the most important, the most daunting of his career. He was to organise a Sonderkommando (Special Unit) – and make his way to Budapest. Hitler would shortly order German troops to occupy Hungary and solve this treacherous nation's 'Jewish problem' once and for all. Eichmann's commando, Müller promised, would have many important tasks to carry out for the Reich. Dieter Wisleceny claimed that Eichmann liked to boast that there 'certain to be a monument erected to me in Budapest'.[1]

A decade later, for the enlightenment of his sympathisers in Argentina, Eichmann explained the kinds of problems he had needed to solve:

Have you seen 25,000 people in a pile? Have you seen 10,000 people in a pile? That's five transport trains ... Loading a train is a tricky business anyway, whether it's with cattle or flour sacks ... and so much more difficult to load it with people ...[2]

The Sonderkommando mustered at the Mauthausen concentration camp not far from Linz in Austria. This massive archipelago of camps and sub-camps served as a reservoir of slave labour for Himmler's economic empire. Mauthausen and a neighbouring camp at Flossenbürg had been constructed to exploit local granite quarries. The camp architecture was, uniquely in the SS camp world, extravagantly expressive of economic function. Mauthausen was enclosed by giant granite walls and dominated by forbidding stone watchtowers. A granite stairway led up to the quarries. The majority of prisoners were, in Himmler's words, 'criminally recidivist and asocial', professional criminals, socialists, communists and homosexuals. Many wore green triangles. At Mauthausen, the Germans 'worked to death' many tens of thousands of these prisoners, who were forced to carry out brutally harsh labour, dragging huge granite blocks, in searing heat in the summer and bitter cold in the winter conditions. It was to Mauthausen, this hell on earth, that Kaltenbrunner, the head of the RSHA, sent SD, Sipo and SS units to prepare for the occupation as German army divisions massed on the Hungarian border. Eichmann's relatively small commando brought together his most experienced staff, such as Dieter Wisliceny, Hermann Krumey and Otto Hunsche.[3] These hardened *génocidaires* relished their new assignment. Deportations from Western Europe had, by the spring of 1944, slowed to a trickle. The frenzied killing that had erupted a few months after the Wannsee Conference had subsided. Since the end of 1943, Eichmann's staff had feared transfer to other offices in the RSHA. Now they would become very busy indeed. On 19 March, as German columns marched across the border, Krumey led an advance party of the SS commando towards Budapest. The following day Eichmann followed with 140 vehicles and staff. Before the commando crossed the Austrian border, he stopped to celebrate his birthday. It was, he recalled at his trial, a memorable occasion.

When Eichmann arrived in Budapest on 21 March, he and his staff took over the Majestic Hotel in the Schwabenberg (Svábhegy in Hungarian) district on the Buda side of the Danube. Other SS officers and administrators took rooms in the Hotel Astoria in the centre of Pest and set up offices in the Iron Workers Building on Magdolna Street, but Schwabenberg was the feared stronghold of SS power. The district was not far from Castle Hill and the Citadel, where Horthy and his court resided and which looked out over the Danube to the parliament. From the steeply inclined streets of Schwabenberg rose the swanky villas of the Hungarian elites. Any Jewish owners could be summarily evicted and their properties put to use by the SS. Fortress though it was, Schwabenberg was a bucolic urban landscape that delighted the new German occupiers. SS officer Otto Hunsche recalled that 'around there it was green, and one could sing a little'. Schwabenberg had other advantages. The district was accessible by only one or two roads so was easy to secure. A week after his arrival, Eichmann took over a villa, seized from the Jewish Aschner family, on Apostol Street in Rozsadomb (Rose Hill) for his living quarters. He may have been aware that he was living close to the beautiful sixteenth-century tomb on Mecset Street of Gül Baba, the Ottoman dervish and poet who had been so fond of roses. Eichmann would live at Apostel Street, as well as other purloined villas, in high style, attended by servants and drivers, for the next ten months.

We can get a sense of the occupiers' acquisition frenzy from the 'SS Request Lists', written in Hungarian:

Herr Müller!

Villa buildings for Obersturmbannführer Krumey and Eichmann

The reports which came in so far suggest the following addresses:
Viranyos street 32. Owner is Antal Berczeller, V. Honved 22. Vth floor. Large, empty villa, six rooms upstairs, two connected rooms downstairs. The upstairs area is suitable for Sturmbannführers, the downstairs for deputy officers since there are two bathrooms available. One of the two kitchens in the basement is a bomb-shelter at present. Garage and servants' room are separate.
Kutvolgyi ut 44. Owner is Mrs Dr Miksa Fenyo. Eight rooms with bathroom. The villa is unoccupied but furnished. There is a garage.

[Eichmann chose a different villa.]

Kohlbach engineer, Svábhegy [Swabian Hill]

District II.Aposton 13 [i.e.Apostol 13, Eichmann's villa] He is asking for tools to build a bomb shelter there (pincers, hammers, shovels).

Two door name plates are to be made in very nice quality with the following names:

Obersturmbannfuhrer Krumey
Anmeldung

Obersturmbannfuhrer Eichmann

The plates must be made in a way that they can be unhooked from the door from time to time.

21 April 1944, 14.00

Requesting: Kohlbach

5 pots of green plants
5 pots of blossoming plants
to be transported to Melinda street 14, to colonel Freiwirth

Done.

24 April 1944. 14.30

Requesting: Schmidt Hauptmann, Obergruppenführer from Gellert Hill, the HQ of the Sicherheitspolizei (Berc street 15.)

(…)
5. Ten pieces of identical quality cattle skin boucle carpet in various sizes.
6. He requests a trained, German speaking Jewish gardener and landscape gardener to mend the garden. He should take seed and plant samples, and the Obergruppenführer will discuss things with him.

31 May 1944

Requesting: SS Untersturmführer Vierthaler, SS Feldlazarett 500.

10 goldfish

(available from breeder Ignac Gabor, Kiraly street 14, attached is a receipt.)[4]

It was important to be comfortable.

In the course of the next fifty-six days from 20 March to 9 July, Eichmann and his Hungarian allies would manage the destruction of the last intact Jewish community in occupied Europe. Eichmann, according to Wisliceny, set out to 'beat the record' set by Globočnik's deputy, SS Major Hermann Höfle, who had deported more than a quarter of a million Polish Jews from the Warsaw ghetto to the Reinhardt extermination camps in just fifty-three days.

That spring, as the SS men put down roots in Budapest, a number of troubling events preoccupied Eichmann and his bosses in the SS. As professionals of mass murder, they faced a formidable challenge in Hungary. They had learnt from bitter and indeed humiliating experience that deporting large numbers of people was fraught with risk. The successful management of genocide depended on making sure the victims did not fight back and ensuring that the 'native instruments of state power', to borrow a phrase from historian Tim Cole, backed the 'action' with hearts and minds. While it was fuelled by German ultranationalist fanaticism, the enactment of genocide depended on non-German collaborators – above all state actors in the semi-autonomous governments of allies and occupied nations. As we will discover, many Hungarians went further and deeper than the word 'collaboration' encompasses. Many had their own exclusionary agendas – which the German occupation facilitated. After the war, Eichmann gloated that: 'Hungary really offered the Jews to us like sour beer, and Hungary was the only country where we could not work fast enough.' The only country – it's a telling phrase. Historian David Cesarani insisted in his final book, *Final Solution*, that the Holocaust was ramshackle, improvised and often sidelined by more pressing matters. Genocide was, in short, contingent on a broader pattern of events and forces – and the SS managers of mass murder struggled with many different kinds of obstacle and setback. As described earlier, Himmler terminated 'Action Reinhardt' in occupied Poland after Jews and other ethnic prisoners rebelled against their guards. In 1943, a succession of unforeseen events knocked off course the management of the Final Solution.

In the middle of June 1942, a number of SS commanders met with district governors in occupied Poland to review the progress of the Final Solution. In the minutes, we discover that: 'Jews have already been evacuated in rather large numbers,' and hope is expressed that 'the city of Warsaw will be freed of the burden of Jews unable to work in a reasonable period of time'. 'Evacuation' meant deported to one of the Reinhardt extermination camps. The report concludes that: 'the Jewish operation had been prepared down to the last detail'. A month later, Höfle travelled from Lublin to Warsaw. On 21 July, he ordered SS cars to block the entrance to the Judenrat (Jewish Council). The plan was to liquidate the ghetto and any Jews who remained inside. Höfle had no inkling of what was about to unfold.

It was a warm, sunny day. As SS men set up a gramophone in the street and played the 'Blue Danube Waltz' over and over again, Höfle ordered the chairman of the Council, Adam Czerniaków, to summon all Jewish department heads and Council members. The Polish-born Marcel Reich-Ranicki, who worked as a translator in the ghetto and would survive to become a celebrated literary critic in post-war Germany, took minutes. Without any preamble, Höfle announced that deportations would begin that day. Reich-Ranicki recalled a strained silence, punctuated by 'the rattle of my typewriter, the clicking of the cameras of some SS officers, and gentle melody of the 'Blue Danube' wafting in from the street'. That evening, Czerniaków returned to his office and closed the door. He wrote a short farewell note and took poison. He died in seconds. He was the first victim of the deportation. On the following day, starving Jews gathered, as instructed, in the *Umschlagplatz* or gathering place. They had been lured there by promises of bread and marmalade. More than 5,000 Polish Jews were crammed into a freight train that steamed north-east from Warsaw towards Treblinka. Children were not spared; all the orphanages were emptied. By 21 September, more than 10,000 Jews had been killed in the ghetto. The Germans deported more than a quarter of a million to Treblinka, where drunken Ukrainian guards pushed and shoved them into the 'Himmelstraße', the road to heaven, which led to the gas chambers.

The task had not yet been completed; the ghetto had not yet been completely emptied of its starving denizens. The Germans had no idea that a few hundred militant Jews, who had refused to kowtow to the German controlled Judenrat, had evaded the SS round-ups. On 28 July, a small group of leftist Jews established the Jewish Fighting Organisation, ZOB.

They purchased a few pistols and hand grenades from Polish communists and laid plans to assassinate the hated leader of the Jewish Order Police, Jósef Szerynski. A Jewish policeman recalled:

> During the second half of August, the attempt on Szerynski's life was carried out. A man dressed in a policeman's cap rang the bell of his private apartment. He told the woman who opened the door that he had a letter for Szerynski. When Szerynski walked out toward him, his head slightly turned to the side, the man shot at him and wounded him in the face. In a rare fluke, the bullet penetrated his left cheek, a bit high, and exited through his right cheek without touching the tongue, teeth, or palate ...[5]

Szerynski committed suicide soon after the attack.

In the aftermath of the botched operation, the Gestapo arrested a number of ZOB members soon afterwards. They were tortured and killed. Despite these setbacks, ZOB survived. Right-wing Zionists established another armed group known as the Jewish Military Union, the ZZW. The Union issued this remarkable 'appeal to resist':

> Six months of constant fear of death have passed without our knowing what the next day will bring. We received reports left and right about Jews being killed in the General Government, Germany and other occupied countries. As we listened to these terrible tidings, we waited for our own turn to come – any day, any moment. Today we must realise that the Hitlerian murders have let us live only to exploit our manpower, until the last drop of blood and sweat, until our last breath. We are slaves and when slaves no longer bring in profits they are killed. Each of us must realise this, and always keep it in mind. Jewish masses, the hour is drawing near. You must be prepared to resist, not give yourself up to slaughter like sheep. Not a single Jew should go to the railroad cars ...

By the spring of 1943, just over 40,000 Jews remained alive in the Warsaw ghetto in the aftermath of the July 'Aktion', but in April Himmler demanded that the SS strike a final blow against the survivors. He scheduled the onslaught to take place on 19 April, the eve of Passover. This time, the SS would get a nasty surprise.

As German tanks and militias advanced into the ghetto, they encountered empty streets and an eerie stillness. The silence lasted for only a short time. ZOB fighters began launching fierce attacks on the German columns. So too did members of the ZZB. The first wave of German attackers fell back. Polish flags and the colours of the ZZB flew from rooftops. When the astonishing news of the revolt reached his headquarters, Himmler was thoroughly alarmed. He sent for one of his most fanatical SS generals, Jürgen Stroop, to crush the ghetto fighters. When he was interviewed by Kazimierz Moczarski after the war, Stroop revealed how the defiantly fluttering flags terrified the SS:

> The matter of the flags was of great political and moral importance. It reminded hundreds of thousands of the Polish cause, it excited them and unified the population of the General Government, but especially Jews and Poles. Flags and national colours are a means of combat exactly like a rapid-fire weapon, like thousands of such weapons … The Reichsführer [Himmler] bellowed into the phone: 'Stroop, you must at all costs bring down those two flags!'[6]

For several days, the Jews resisted the German onslaught. But by 28 April, most had been forced into underground bunkers. They fought hard, turning Warsaw's underground into a nest of fortresses. Stroop's battle-hardened soldiers, which included many Jew-hating Ukrainians, were forced to use flamethrowers, hand grenades and tear gas bombs to root out the fighters from their forts under the city. Some of the ZOB fighters escaped through the sewers to the 'Aryan side' of the city. When they returned later, they found no one alive. Stroop recalled:

> I witnessed an extraordinary scene that day. A group of prisoners had been herded into the square. In spite of their exhaustion, many of them held their heads high. I stood nearby, surrounded by my escort. Suddenly I heard shots. A young Jew – in his mid-twenties I'd say – was firing a pistol at one of our police officers – one … two … three … fast as lightning. One of the bullets hit the officer's hand. My men sprayed the Jew with fire. I managed to whip out my own pistol and hit him as he fell. As he lay dying, I stood over him, watching his life ebb away.

German posters informed Poles that anyone discovered hiding Jews would be executed. 'For the most part,' reported an SS general 'the Polish population approved the measures'. The Germans issued proclamations that linked the destruction of the Jewish ghetto to 'the mass graves found in Catyn [*sic*]' – referring to the discovery of the remains of the Polish officers and members of the intelligentsia murdered in Katyn Forest by the Soviet NKVD in 1940. This terrible crime, which was a macabre gift to Nazi propagandists, had nothing to do with Polish Jewry but the Germans could rely on smearing any Jewish community with the scurrilous myth of 'Jewish Bolshevism'. On 1 May, Goebbels, who had seized on the Katyn killings, responded to the alarming news of 'exceptionally sharp fighting in Warsaw': 'the fighting there is very hard; it goes so far that the Jewish command issues daily military reports'. Goebbels emphasised, '*what one may expect from the Jews when they manage to set their hands on weapons*' [italics inserted]. News of the uprising, as the historian Saul Friedländer shows, reverberated through the Nazi hierarchy. There was widespread anxiety that Jews had fought back hard.

It took Stroop and his multi-ethnic forces weeks of very tough urban combat to crush the uprising. On 16 May, he made the notorious announcement that: 'The Jewish quarter in Warsaw no longer exists.' To celebrate victory over 'the racial enemy', Stroop ordered his men to place explosives charges in the beautiful Great Synagogue on Tłomackie St. At exactly 8.15 in the evening, he gave orders to set off the charges. Stroop never repented. He was a fanatic to the end:

> What a marvellous sight it was. A fantastic piece of theatre. My staff and I stood at a distance. I held the electrical device which would detonate all the charges simultaneously. I glanced over at my brave officers and men, tired and dirty, silhouetted against the glow of the burning buildings. After prolonging the suspense for a moment, I shouted: 'Heil Hitler' and pressed the button. With a thunderous, deafening bang and a rainbow burst of colours, the fiery explosion soared toward the clouds, an unforgettable tribute to our triumph over the Jews … The will of Adolf Hitler and Heinrich Himmler had been done.

Stroop was hanged in Mokotów Prison in 1952.

The will of Hitler and Himmler may have been done in Warsaw, and in the next months the 'evacuation' and killing was relentless from ghetto to

ghetto in occupied Poland, but the ghetto uprising and the fierce determination of the doomed Jewish fighters shook the Nazi elite. Armed Jews
had disrupted the management of forced evacuation. In the thick dark
smoke that now hung in the air above Warsaw, Himmler and his subordinates discerned portents of catastrophe. Armed revolt could not be allowed
to erupt again. The model of using the Jewish Councils and Jewish Order
Police to control ghetto inmates was evidently flawed.

This meant that the lesson of Warsaw was to look deeper into the
Jewish communities to hunt out any organisation that might throw the
Final Solution off course. In Hungary, Eichmann feared that the Rescue
Committee, the Va'ada, might be the kind of unpredictable association of
Jews that could threatened to upset his plans. We will discover shortly how
that anxiety profoundly influenced the way Eichmann dealt with members
of the committee such as Joel Brand and Rezsö Kasztner. And the Warsaw
ghetto uprising was not to be the final warning to the SS managers of the
Final Solution. In October 1943, an entire Jewish community had been
rescued from destruction – how and why that happened offered other
important lessons to Himmler and his SS satraps.

On 9 April 1940, the Germans invaded Denmark. For the Danes, the
occupation that followed was for some time a painless experience. The
Germans eschewed draconian tactics for a number of reasons. Few Danes
resisted the invasion, which was swift and relatively bloodless compared
with the attack on Norway, which was fiercely resisted. Restraint and
acceptance would be rewarded. The Danes would be permitted to keep
their armed forces and most of the apparatuses of power, above all the
monarchy. King Christian X reassuringly stayed put in his palace. It was no
small matter that Denmark exported huge volumes of meat and dairy produce to Germany. The Danes fed the *Volk*! A velvet glove occupation was a
lot less costly since there no need to install an expensive garrison. What this
meant for the Germans in practice was that occupation strategy required
the subtlest pragmatism and a light touch. It was not only about economics. German racial theory accepted Danes as Aryan kinfolk. Some Danes
welcomed Hitler's attack on the Soviet Union and the Bolshevik menace
in the East. In November 1941, Denmark joined the Anti-Comintern
Pact and allowed Himmler to recruit 6,000 Danes, selected from 12,000
volunteers, to serve in one of the foreign legions of the Waffen-SS.

In one fundamental respect, this cosy accommodation had an inbuilt
limit. At the Wannsee Conference, a representative of the German Foreign

Office warned that the Danish government would resist any attempt to deport Danish Jews. This official knew that the Prime Minister, Erik Scavenius, had told Göring, in no uncertain terms, that there was not a 'Jewish problem' in Denmark. The King openly backed his Prime Minister: Danish Jews would be protected. In his diary, the King wrote:

> When you look at the inhumane treatment of Jews, not only in Germany but occupied countries as well, you start worrying that such a demand might also be put on us, but we must clearly refuse such this due to their protection under the Danish constitution. I stated that I could not meet such a demand towards Danish citizens. If such a demand is made, we would best meet it by all wearing the Star of David.

German minister Cécil von Renthe-Fink was a committed Nazi but he resisted Himmler's repeated efforts to seize control of the occupation. Under the Quisling regime in Norway, the SS secured a much tighter grip on power with terrible consequences for Norwegian Jews. For some years, Denmark's Jewish minority endured only minor indignities. There was, to be sure, a Danish Nazi party, the DNSAP, led by Frits Clausen, that published a newspaper called *Kamptegnet*, which pedalled bilious anti-semitism. Throughout the occupation, Himmler used Clausen and others to maintain a steady drumbeat of racial propaganda. The impact was minimal outside the Nazi community, and in any case the DNSAP was just one of many fractious and competitive far-right parties whose membership fell steeply throughout the war. When, in March 1943, the Germans permitted a free general election, the DNSAP won a derisive 2 per cent of the vote. As noted, a small number of Danish Nazis volunteered to join the Waffen-SS, but even these diehard militants had no opportunity to vent their racist spleen on other Danish citizens. So completely assimilated were Danish Jews that, as Renthe-Fink calculated, the majority of Danes would judge any kind of attack on Danish Jews as assaults on fellow citizens. As Leni Yahil reveals in his account of the Danish occupation, Renthe-Fink frequently alluded to a 'Jewish problem' in Denmark, perhaps to mollify the DNASAP, but he consistently resisted attempts to purge Jews from commercial and government posts. It is telling that during the period of occupation, no order was ever issued that Jews must wear a special mark. For Renthe-Fink, occupation meant cooperation – in Germany's interests.[7]

The velvet glove suited both sides. For many Danes, standards of living rose as their produce flowed into Germany. German soldiers relished a comfortable posting far from the horrors of the Eastern Front. This delicate balance was shattered in the autumn of 1942. The *casus belli* was the 'Telegram Crisis': in September 1942, the King replied to an effusive birthday message from Hitler with provocatively subdued enthusiasm: '*Spreche Meinen besten Dank aus.* Chr. Rex' ('Giving my best thanks, King Christian'). Hitler was furious. He expelled the Danish ambassador and recalled the German ambassador from Copenhagen. The King offered to send the Crown Prince to Berlin to apologise; Hitler spurned his offer. Now he turned his ire on Denmark.

It is likely that Hitler was waiting for a cue, however trivial, to tighten the German grip on the overindulged Danes. Be that as it may, Hitler reacted with tantrum-like speed. The Germans forced a change of government and recalled Renthe-Fink to Berlin. He was replaced by an SS Gruppenführer, whose reputation implied that he would impose a harsh new regime in Denmark. Dr Werner Best was a lawyer and devout Nazi who, as a senior official in the RSHA, had provided legalistic rationales for Himmler's pursuit of a Final Solution. Best's vaunting ambition goaded Heydrich – and he was banished to Paris, where he joined the military administration. His commitment to the persecution and deportation of French Jews earned him a reputation as the 'Butcher of Paris'.

For Denmark's Jewish community, Best's appointment as plenipotentiary was troubling. To begin with he made few changes to his predecessor's policy but in September 1943, as Hitler's armies stumbled from crisis to setback to catastrophe, the Danish resistance seized on the developing crisis in the Reich to launch a campaign of sabotage. Thousands of workers went on strike. The new German commander of the German garrison, General Hermann von Hanneken, declared martial law and began to disarm the Danish armed forces. The government resigned in protest. Hitler, as was his custom, pointed the finger of blame at Denmark's tiny Jewish community.

Himmler finally had his chance and despatched SS-Standartenführer Rudolf Mildner from Auschwitz to quash the Danish resistance. But Ribbentrop urged caution. He knew that an assault on the Danish Jews would offer his rival, the SS chief, an opening. As his own influence in Hitler's court waxed and waned, he had come to fear and resent the growing power of the SS. Ribbentrop was also cautious about upsetting the intricate status quo in Denmark. His qualms were echoed by the German military authorities. General von Hennecken cabled his reservations about taking more aggressive action: 'No cooperation can be expected afterwards from the civil administration or from the Danish police. The supply of food will be adversely affected'. Best was taken by surprise when Himmler's man, Mildner, also recommended postponing any anti-Jewish action. Frustrated, on 8 September, Best despatched his notorious telegram No. 1032 to Ribbentrop, 'begging' that 'measures should now be taken toward a solution of the problems of the Jews and Freemasons'. Hitler brushed aside Ribbentrop's doubts and agreed to Best's demands. Although the Final Solution was shaped by chance and opportunity, there was a logic to Hitler's decision. By then, 'Action Reinhardt' had been terminated. More than 1.5 million Jews had been killed in the extermination camps at Treblinka, Sobibór and Bełżec. Himmler and other SS leaders were pressing to broaden the Final Solution to the rest of the German empire, even where implementation carried a freight of diplomatic risk. So it was that at the end of September, an SS officer from Eichmann's office called Rolf Günther arrived in Copenhagen to begin preparations for the deportation of Denmark's Jews. He chartered a ship for this purpose and drafted in 1,800 Order Police.

Dr Best's telegram was not what it seemed. Or rather, it was more than it seemed, a parry in a game of smoke and mirrors. Rather than a call to action, it was a play of Machiavellian hedging. Because Best had fallen foul of power struggles within the RSHA, he was desperate to impress Himmler. Hitler considered him too soft: according to Goebbels' diary, he complained that Best 'knows only the velvet glove'. During his time in Paris, Best had tried to beef up his reputation with an eager commitment to interning and deporting French Jews. As plenipotentiary in Denmark, his telegram was a fit of assertiveness that laid claim to a leading role assaulting the Danish Jews. At the same time, Best understood that he could not hold power in Denmark on a long-term basis, as he hoped to do, if he threw away the velvet glove. He feared that any aggressive persecution of Danish Jews would be certain to arouse the opposition of many Danes. In the long term, this would make governance impractical. The inappropriate exercise of power, the iron fist, would in the end eviscerate German power.

So, as far as we can interpret his motives, Best 'begged' Ribbentrop to authorise anti-Jewish action while covertly looking for ways to thwart the SS.

Hitler's mind was, nevertheless, made up. Deportations, he ordered, would commence on 2 October. The date set was the eve of Rosh Hoshanah, the Jewish New Year, and the timing of the plan would lead to unforeseen consequences.

On 22 September, General Jodl, the Chief of Operations Staff of the German Army, informed General von Hanneken: 'The deportation of the Jews will be carried out by the Reichsführer SS, who has transferred two police battalions to Denmark for this purpose'. Overnight, Danish Jews went from being fellow citizens to hunted prey. This was anathema to the majority of Danes. As Eichmann's man Rolf Günther pressed ahead with preparations for the deportations, Best made his move. On 11 September, he summoned the maritime attaché of the German Embassy to his office. Georg Ferdinand Duckwitz was a lapsed National Socialist who had lived for many years in Denmark and had close links to a number of Danish politicians. The conventional historical narrative, which has seen considerable revision, continues with Duckwitz's revelation of the German plans to Hans Hedtoft, the leader of the Social Democrats – who in turn passed the alarming news to Carl Henriques, the chairman of the Jewish Board of Representatives in Copenhagen.

This narrative is correct as far as it goes but obscures the convoluted interaction between different German factions who feared that the deportation plan threatened to undermine their exercise of power in occupied Denmark. This unprecedented opposition to Hitler's orders and the power of the SS had no ethical dimension at all but was a calculated strategy to preserve German power in the longer run. Best did not doubt the legitimacy of the Final Solution and was fully aware of what it implied, but the consequence of his opportunist political manoeuvring was to create a space of opportunity for Danes and their Jewish fellow citizens. There was one other vital factor. During the Second World War, Sweden, like Switzerland, Turkey and Portugal, was in theory a neutral power. But just as Swiss bankers permitted Germans to hoard purloined riches in their vaults, Swedish industrialists and even the National Bank made enormous profits from the German war. Swedish journalist Arne Ruth, who wrote a book exposing the myth of Swedish 'neutrality', showed that:

Sweden was not neutral, Sweden was weak. Its sales of iron ore made an important contribution to the German effort. It allowed German troops and weaponry through its territory to Norway. In 1943, its government told the central bank to ignore suspicions that German gold Sweden received was looted ...[8]

A number of historians argue that Sweden was a 'de facto ally' of Nazi Germany. But by 1943, some members of the Swedish government were beginning to question the value of these lucrative bonds with Germany – and, above all, the persecution of Jews all over Europe. Many Jews had already found refuge in Sweden and, as historian Paul Levine has shown, many influential Swedes took action against German racial persecution through their foreign legations. When Duckwitz was informed about the German plans, he also passed the information to the Swedish ambassador, who informed Henriques, the Jewish community leader, that 'Sweden was open'. Sweden made no secret of its offer of refuge. News of the offer was broadcast on Swedish radio and a pastoral letter from Sweden's archbishops demanding freedom for 'our Jewish brothers and sisters' was despatched to parishes across the country. The Swedish government also informed American diplomats, who promised that the United States would offer funds to Jewish refugees.

The day 29 September was the eve of Rosh Hoshanah, when most of Denmark's Jews attended synagogue, so word spread quickly among them that the community was in grave peril. Remarkably, almost every Jewish family gathered together their belongings and made for the Danish coast. They had no doubt about the truth of the rabbis' messages and the imminent threat to their lives. Thousands of Danish Jews gathered their families together and departed to an unknown fate without hesitation. On the eve of the planned deportation, Danes from all walks of life came to help ferry 7,000 Jews across the narrow stretch of water, the Øresund, that marked the border between Denmark and Sweden. Leo Goldberger recalled:

> We came to this little fishing village and we were instructed to go down to the beach which was right next to the harbour and to wait for a signal and we were hauled up aboard by the fishermen and then put into the hold, where the fish used to be, so you can imagine the smell. The smell was absolutely the worst part of the immediate experience, plus the fact that it was very crowded down there. There must have been 18 to 20 people as the fishermen started to move out into the sea, we, luckily, were not discovered and we went off into the night.[9]

Danish coastguards allowed the flotillas of little boats to pass. So too did the German navy. Events would have had a very different outcome if the escape route had been overland: the German army was unlikely to have shown the same restraint. On the other side of the Sound, Swedish naval patrols shepherded the flotilla of refugees to safely.

As this remarkable escape was unfolding, during the night of 1 October, the SS and Order Police battalions began to round up Jews who had not, for many reasons, been able to flee. The German security forces consisted of 1,300 to 1,400 police officers, together with Danish volunteers and the 'Schalburg Corps', a Danish SS unit. Several hundred Jews fell into their hands. The majority were deported to Theresienstadt and all but a few survived the war.

The following day, Best proclaimed that Denmark had been successfully 'de-Jewed'. His devious plan had worked out in his favour: he remained in power until the end of the war.

In the offices of the SS, the lessons of the Danish rescue that came just months after the Warsaw ghetto uprising were stark. Jews were capable of organising resistance and its consequences could be catastrophic. Stroop and his SS superiors gloried in the destruction of the ghetto but the campaign to put down the uprising had been long drawn out and expensive. In the Danish case, Best's secretive betrayal was known only to a handful of other Germans, who, in any case, sympathised with his deceit. From the perspective of Himmler and his courtiers, the failure of the Danish deportation plan must be laid at the door of the unbowed Danish resistance that had organised the rescue. At a deeper level, Himmler understood that the Final Solution depended on the cooperation of the national community – both active and passive. Throughout occupied Europe, the SS had secured the involvement of tens of thousands of willing executioners who threw themselves into the tasks of mass murder. The Final Solution could not be enacted without trustworthy collaborators – such as the Milice in France and the many fascist militias in Eastern Europe. This partnership, in turn, depended on the passivity of bystanders who cared little for their Jewish neighbours and benefitted from their removal.

For the managers of genocide such as Eichmann, these then were the clear lessons. Neutralise any known Jewish cells that might foment resistance and compel the compliance of the general population. The irony of the Danish rescue is that such an event was never to be repeated. Rescue of Jews in German-occupied Europe was not a myth – but depended on a unique concatenation of circumstances. The German occupiers of Denmark understood that the small community of Danish Jews was rooted in the Danish national body and that their fellow citizens would not tolerate their persecution. Despite his record as 'The Butcher of Paris' and commitment to Nazi racial policy, Dr Best attached much greater importance to his position as the plenipotentiary of occupied Denmark than to the fanatical fulfilment of racial ideology. Whether we accept or not that his telegram to Ribbentrop 'begging' for permission to solve Denmark's 'Jewish problem' was a strategic feint, his actions suggest that he hoped to sabotage the deportation plan. Best's anxieties about the unpredictable consequences of an all-out assault on Denmark's Jews were shared by a number of other German powerbrokers and even Mildner, Himmler's SS representative. Furthermore, rescue would have been impossible to achieve without a refuge – and the rapidly changing circumstances of the war meant that members of the Swedish government willingly agreed to offer a place of greater safety. Finally, there are the simple facts of geography. It is not to belittle the Danish rescuers to point out that the determined men and women who navigated their Jewish neighbours to safety had to contend with the narrow waters of the Sound.

In the aftermath of the flight of Denmark's Jews, it seems that Hitler and the SS chiefs failed to see through Dr Best's stratagems. He remained unchallenged until the end of the war. They blamed the abject failure of the deportation plan on the Danish resistance and the way a tight-knit Jewish community had so quickly responded to warnings of danger. In just about every way the situation in Hungary was profoundly different from the Danish case – and incalculably more hazardous for the nation's Jews. In the aftermath of the Warsaw ghetto uprising and the Danish rescue, Eichmann and the SS men he commanded would exploit every one of those differences with tragic consequences.

A Question of Management

When Hungarian Prime Minister Miklós Kallay met Admiral Horthy at the railway station in Budapest, he noted that the Regent was 'deathly pale' and 'worn out'. The bonhomie that Hitler's translator Paul Schmidt had enjoyed had evaporated. As Horthy and Kallay were driven across the Danube to the Castle, Horthy made it clear that the Germans would insist on appointing a pro-German government. Resistance was not an option. The Hungarian army had been shattered on the Eastern Front and at the Kleßheim meeting, Hitler had threatened to deploy Romanian, Croatian and Slovak troops if the Hungarians refused to accept the reality of occupation. Horthy clung to the tattered shreds of sovereignty that Hitler dangled. As long as the Regent appointed a government that Hitler could trust, German troops would be withdrawn. Kallay understood what Horthy was implying and how little room they had for manoeuvre, and immediately offered his resignation. That afternoon, Kallay and other advisors tried to persuade Horthy to resign and have nothing to do with any German-approved government. He refused. According to Kallay's memoir, Horthy insisted that he would not 'abandon the Hungarian people'. Who would defend a 'million Magyar lads from being dragged away to the Russian shambles … Who will defend the Jews or other refugees'. His decision was supported by the Jewish elites, who were on good terms with the Regent. On the day after the Germans marched into Budapest, Ferenc Chorin and Móric Kornfeld rushed to the Castle and pleaded with Horthy not to abdicate. They told him that if he did, they feared 'certain extermination'.

The Germans, of course, needed Horthy to stay put. His presence in the Castle would ensure that the bogus promise of sovereignty dampened resistance. The members of the government who counselled Horthy to spurn the German offer knew better. Count István Bethlen argued that any new government would become a puppet regime. Horthy's abdication would expose that the Germans had put an end to legitimate government.

Veesenmayer, who was soon being referred to in Budapest as *Reichsverwesenmayer*, acted quickly against Hungarian politicians known to be pro-Western or worse, sympathetic to Jews. Within days, the Germans rounded up scores of dissenters and threw them into prison camps in Germany. Bethlen fled in disguise; Kallay found sanctuary, at the last minute, inside the Turkish Embassy.

On the other side, Veesenmayer was fuming and frustrated. He was contending with warring factions in the Nazi elite who each favoured a different political outcome to the occupation. Himmler and the RSHA chief Kaltenbrunner pushed for a fully pro-Nazi government under the leadership of László Baky of the Hungarian National Socialist Party. Veesenmayer, backed by Ribbentrop, favoured a less extreme solution. No one yet wanted to hand power to the Arrow Cross leader Ferenc Szálasi, who was busy importuning anyone who would listen that he was ready to lead the nation in the struggle against Bolshevism.

Ribbentrop prevailed and Veesenmayer proposed that Horthy appoint the former Prime Minister, Béla Imrédy, to take office. He calculated that a known and widely respected politician would bolster the façade of Hungarian sovereignty.

The problem, he soon discovered, was that Imrédy was anathema to the Regent: 'What, you want Imrédy, the Jew?' sneered Horthy. He could not forget that Imrédy, when he served as Prime Minister at the end of the 1930s, was in favour of pushing Hungary to become what he called a 'gentlemanly Fascist dictatorship'. He admired Hitler and tried to curry favour with the Germans by promising to bring in even tougher anti-Jewish laws. As it transpired, Imrédy's efforts to 'streamline' the Hungarian government, as he put it, would end with his downfall. Horthy was, for all the usual pragmatic reasons, uncomfortable with Imrédy's proposals for new anti-Jewish laws: he could not, he said, accept 'butchering a cow while continuing to milk her'. He feared too that Imrédy's authoritarian streak might threaten his own power. In a bizarre turn of events, Horthy confronted his Prime Minister with evidence implying that one of his great-grandmothers had been Jewish. It reveals much about the ever more hostile attitude to Jews in Hungary that Imrédy immediately accepted that he must resign.

This murky chain of events now led Horthy to dig in his heels. Imrédy was not acceptable. Veesenmayer bitterly complained to Berlin that Horthy was 'not up to his tasks any more'. After two days of wrangling, the Regent and Veesenmayer finally settled on a compromise. On 23 March, it was announced that Hungary's representative in Berlin, Döme Sztójay, would be appointed to head the new government. For Horthy, blocking Imrédy was a Pyrrhic victory. Hitler and Ribbentrop knew and trusted Sztójay – who immediately appointed a pro-German Cabinet crammed with ultra-nationalist extremists. As Sztójay got on with the job of satisfying Veesenmayer and his masters, Horthy sulkily withdrew into the gloomy salons of the Buda Castle.

Like Werner Best in Denmark, Veesenmayer had to balance exercising power with making concessions that disguised or smoothed over the abrupt loss of sovereignty. The presence of the German military divisions would not be permanent. By the end of April, the bulk would be returning to front-line service. Power could not be enforced at the end of a gun. In the Hungarian situation, Veesenmayer had no reason to fear the reaction of the majority of Hungarian citizens to his pursuit of a radical solution to the 'Jewish problem'. Although Veesenmayer despised Szálasi as a 'buffoon who alternately swaggers and grovels', he recognised that the Arrow Cross was a formidable and widely popular force. For now, the Germans held Szálasi and the Arrow Cross fanatics at arm's length. Veesenmayer believed that Hungary's police and gendarmerie were up to the task in hand. And he was right.

At his trial in Jerusalem, Eichmann claimed that when he was ordered to Budapest, he arrived with no clear plan for deporting the Jews of Hungary. He may have been telling at least a partial version of the truth. Eichmann knew that he would have to depend on the cooperation of Hungarian antisemites in the Ministry of the Interior. We have encountered these men in earlier chapters. Soon after he took over the government, Sztójay appointed Andor Jaross as Minister of the Interior. Jaross in turn appointed László Baky, a virulent antisemite, as State Secretary for Political Affairs. Neither Jaross nor Baky, who was a retired major in the gendarmerie, had any administrative experience – so they brought in Lászlo Endre, who had long experience in local government. These appointments sealed the fate of the Hungarian Jews. It will be recalled that Endre was a devout racist and hater of Jews who had travelled to the United States to pay homage to the antisemitic industrialist Henry Ford. Eichmann's superior, the HSSPF Otto Winkelmann, stated that Eichmann had no need to educate Endre for 'he fulfilled his task out of his own convictions'. At his trial in Jerusalem, Eichmann laid all responsibility for the murder of Hungary's Jews onto Endre's shoulders: 'Laci did everything,' he claimed. 'He wanted to eat Jews with paprika.' It need hardly be said that Eichmann enabled his good friend's monstrous hatreds. The poisonous zeal demonstrated by men such as Baky and Endre had seeped downwards into many levels of the Hungarian police forces and gendarmerie. In the spring of 1944, the Germans had no need to unleash the fanatics of the Arrow Cross.

'On several occasions,' Eichmann recalled, 'I would say to myself "*Wau!*" Till now you thought that in Germany there is a certain precision reigning, and here you are seeing the same painstaking accuracy. I admired the Hungarian public administration'.[10]

The stage was set for the last and most murderous spasm of the Final Solution.

11

THE DOGWOOD
CONNECTION

There is a mystery at the heart of the Blood for Trucks story. Why did the Germans send Joel Brand and his companion 'Bandi' Grosz to Istanbul? This simple question is rarely asked. Turkey was a neutral country – so too were Portugal, Spain and Switzerland. The Rescue Committee of the Jewish Agency (in Hebrew, Va'ad ha-Hatsala be-Kushta) had offices in Istanbul from late 1942 through 1944 – but Zionists were also active in Geneva. Istanbul was a kind of playground for German, British and American intelligence agents. But Portugal was even more pivotal. Lisbon was the only European city in which both the Allies and the Axis powers operated openly; the city was a crowded refuge for more than a million refugees hoping to escape to the United States as well as a multitude of spies, secret police officers, stateless Jews, prisoners of war on the run and black marketeers. So why was Brand despatched to Istanbul? The answer to this question casts surprising new light on the entire affair.

To begin to decipher the events of 1944, it is essential to recognise how and in what way the façade of German power in Hungary was by strategy and intent deceptive. Those courageous yet powerless individuals who opposed the actions and decisions of the occupiers confronted a confusing array of Nazi agencies and duplicitous individuals that masked the identity and intentions of the decision-makers.

This is hardly surprising. It is broadly accepted by most historians that the Nazi regime was inherently polycratic, with many different courtiers competing for Hitler's attention. The chaotic Nazi state reflected Hitler's warped social Darwinism. In a world of perpetual competition, the most powerful and ruthless won out and rose to the top to 'work towards the Führer'. By the spring of 1944, the conflicts that defined the Nazi state and its agents were reaching a point of extreme stress. The state apparatus was fracturing, and its elite power brokers were groping for ways to survive. The Hungarian Zionists who confronted the German occupation authorities in Budapest had only the vaguest sense of the power struggles that were gathering momentum behind the façade of Nazi power. Nor did they understand the distribution of powers among the many different individual agents of the Nazi state in occupied Hungary. This was especially significant in the case of Eichmann who, for political and personal reasons, staged semi-theatrical displays of power to impress and manipulate the fragile organisations that he used to achieve his aims. Many different cross-currents of power in the Nazi state impacted on the Zionists' desperate efforts to save lives from destruction.

It is for this reason that the Blood for Trucks negotiations and the intent and motivation of the parties involved appear to be so baffling. There is no single key that unlocks the puzzle. The ransom negotiations served different aims and purposes for different protagonists at different times. If this is recognised, then many of the puzzles begin to appear less intractable. What were these aims and purposes and how did they interact?

Let us begin not with Brand but with the Hungarian Jewish convert Gyorgy Andor, alias 'Bandi' Grosz. At one of the final meetings with Eichmann and other SS officials, Brand was astonished to be told that Grosz would be accompanying him to Istanbul. The SS officers made it very clear that Brand had no choice in the matter. When he was interrogated by British intelligence agents in Cairo, Grosz insisted that the Germans had entrusted him with a separate and, he claimed, more important mission: Blood for Trucks was merely camouflage. He was acting on behalf of a German faction that was looking for ways of initiating peace negotiations with representatives of the Allied powers. This secret mission had been authorised by none other than Heinrich Himmler. Many historians have accepted that there was some truth in what Grosz told his interrogators.[1] Was he telling the truth?

There are very good reasons to conclude that Grosz was spinning a farrago of half-truths. Let us begin with the fact that Grosz had another identity. He was 'Trillium' – the code name of one of the most active members of an intelligence network based in Istanbul in Turkey. The head of the network was Alfred Schwarz, who had settled in Istanbul at the end of the 1920s. He was a polished, cosmopolitan Czech Jew who had studied philosophy and psychology in Prague and Vienna. An OSS agent who compiled a report on the Dogwood affair at the end of 1944, which we will come to in more detail shortly, described Schwarz as 'ponderous in his manner. He is vain in a German way [sic] and is impressed by people of position or political power. His vanity is probably his weakest point especially when hooked up to his mild reverence for what we call a big shot. He is brainy and thorough, which is best illustrated by the following …' Unfortunately, the next paragraph is redacted so we have no idea precisely what it was that demonstrated Schwarz's brainy thoroughness.[2]

Soon after finishing his studies, Schwarz won a competition set by an advertising company and was offered a job by the same company in Turkey. Here he put down roots, set up his own business and made a lot of money. Schwarz was a consummate maker of useful friendships. He was on good terms with the Vatican envoy or Nuncio Angelo Roncalli. Roncalli, who would later become Pope Pius XII, helped to rescue Jewish refugees during the war. Schwarz was a passionate anti-Nazi, but fiercely hostile to Communism. Schwarz gave all his agents flower code names. Although American agents referred to him as 'Blacky', he was 'Dogwood' – and the network is referred to in the records of other intelligence agencies as the Dogwood network.

Until February 1945, Turkey remained neutral. Its strategic importance to both the Allies and the Axis powers was immense. It offered Germany an eastern foothold in its war against the Soviet Union and a base from which to infiltrate the Middle East. The British and Americans too needed bases in Turkey as a staging post to liberate the German-occupied Balkans. For more than a century, the Russians had depended on Istanbul and the Straits to control the Black Sea and secure access to the Mediterranean. In October 1943, when Turkey celebrated National Day, the President İsmet İnönü invited representatives of the belligerent powers to a reception. When the delegates arrived at the presidential palace, they discovered they had been allocated separate rooms. When the Italian ambassador was led into the Axis room, the German ambassador, Franz von Papen, refused to tolerate the presence of a 'traitor' and stormed out of the reception. The Greek and Yugoslav envoys also cold-shouldered the hapless Italian, who ended up disconsolately pacing the corridors. Istanbul was not just a diplomatic hornets' nest, it was a refuge for victims of persecution in occupied Europe, a haven for fugitive German dissidents plotting the downfall of Hitler – and a busy hub for Zionists searching for ways to smuggle Jews out of danger. It was to Turkey that Romanian, Hungarian and Bulgarian emissaries came to explore secret surrender deals to Allies. Intelligence, genuine, forged or faked, was a precious commodity. Istanbul fizzed and bubbled with intrigue.

It would be rather too conventional to romanticise Istanbul in the 1940s. It was an ancient city where in wartime the most lucrative merchandise on sale was intelligence. Agents and spies with information to trade lurked in Taksim Square at dusk or strolled along Istiklal Boulevard in search of buyers. Others lurked in the city's busy nightclubs and dance halls, or met in the shadowy corners of the famous Abdullah's restaurant. In the lounge of the Park Hotel, the house pianist would often pointedly play a popular hit 'Boo Baby, I'm a Spy'. The song lyrics celebrated a mythical spy who was '10 per cent cloak and 90 per cent dagger'. It was rumoured that the Turkish counterintelligence agency, the Emniyet, used Istanbul's ubiquitous lemonade sellers as street lookouts. Even a fly-infested pastry shop might be a façade for an espionage operation. The backstreets and bars of Istanbul reeked with the sour odours of hope and betrayal.

This was world that Alfred Schwarz inhabited. Like Rudolf Kasztner, he had tremendous self-regard. This made him overconfident about the trustworthiness of the men he recruited as agents. Schwarz relied on his gut and it would often let him down. He made some disastrous misjudgements. His spider's web of connections spanned the German, Austrian and Czech émigré worlds in Istanbul and Ankara. He had excellent Turkish and was on good terms with a number of agents in the Emniyet. His fascination with information nourished his businesses but he could not forget the menace of Hitler and when war came in 1939, Schwarz began casting around for ways to contribute to the struggle against Nazi Germany. He began deepening his ties with the German and Austrian exiles to find out more about the groups who opposed Hitler. A good number of the German exiles had cosy jobs in Turkish universities, where they vented their loathing for the uncouth gangster regime in Berlin.

Developing contacts in this world of shadows and masks was fraught with risk. Schwarz industriously cultivated his friends in the émigré community in Istanbul, but he would find out to his cost that few could be completely trusted. Some inside the German community had connections to the German military intelligence service, the Abwehr. These shady, treacherous connections would come play a crucial role in the story of Blood for Trucks.

The Lure of Dogwood

Involvement with the agents of the Abwehr could be an opportunity or a trap. Sometimes it was both and many British and American agents discovered that it was rarely possible to be certain of the difference. It was a perplexing organisation. The other Nazi intelligence agencies, above all Reinhard Heydrich's SD, suspected both the competence and loyalty of the Abwehr head, Admiral Wilhelm Canaris, and many of his agents. It was suspected, rightly, that in 1940 Abwehr agents had leaked German plans for the attack on Western Europe. In the spring of 1943, the Gestapo tracked down and arrested a number of dissident Germans who had found refuge inside the Abwehr. According to Walter Schellenberg, who headed the rival Office VI in the SD, Canaris 'overinflated his organisation, indiscriminately enrolling serious workers and dubious riffraff'. He characterised Canaris as a pessimistic weakling.[3] For Allied agents and anti-Nazis such as Schwarz, the lesson should have been to exercise extreme caution. Schwarz was not careful enough.

In neutral Turkey, Istanbul became a front line in the intelligence war between the Germans and the Allies. In the city's watering holes, British, American and German agents worked and played in a shadowy dance of secrets and lies. Schwarz proved himself very useful to British intelligence and cultivated a close bond with the head of the MI6 station in Istanbul, Colonel Harold Gibson. In April 1943, the American Office of Strategic Services, the OSS, the precursor to the CIA, appointed Lanning Macfarland as chief of mission in Istanbul. 'Wild Bill' Donovan had founded the OSS just a year earlier in mid 1942 and in these early years, the American agency was a junior partner to the more mature British foreign intelligence apparatus. When Macfarland took up his posting in Istanbul, Gibson introduced him to Schwarz, who was happy to offer his assistance and the services of his secretary, a young Polish exile called Walter Arndt. Soon after making contact with Macfarland, Schwarz sold his company and became an OSS operative code-named 'Dogwood'. For the OSS, Macfarland worked out of an office in the American Consulate in Istanbul but it would have been absurd for agents or informers to be observed visiting him there. So Schwarz/'Dogwood' agreed to set up a 'ghost' subsidiary of the US Western Electric Company at his office, where he and OSS agents could covertly meet members of a rapidly growing network. Schwarz used his many business contacts across the Balkan region to begin recruiting agents and sub-agents. Each one had to be swiftly trained, with OSS assistance, in a bewildering number of spy craft disciplines that included elaborate security procedures, coding and concealing messages, and making use of radios. All this while conducting business as usual.

What Schwarz offered to the grateful American OSS agents was a teeming garden of other flowers such as Austrian businessman Franz Josef Ridiger ('Stock'), Alexander Rustow ('Magnolia'), a university professor and Hans Wilbrandt ('Hyacinth'). 'Dogwood' reported to OSS agent Archibald Coleman, who was code-named 'Cereus'. Coleman was a former Treasury Agent who had been based in Mexico. Sent back by the OSS, he had been quickly unmasked by the Mexican police and despatched to Spain. Here Coleman got on the wrong side of the American ambassador and had been transferred to Turkey, where he assumed the cover of a correspondent for the *Saturday Evening Post*. Coleman, then, had an undistinguished record and the arrogant Schwarz was not impressed. His opinion of Macfarland was not much better – the neophyte OSS agents lacked, he complained, the polish of 'Middle Europeans' like himself, born and educated in cities like Prague and Budapest. He was impressed by the glamour of the OSS – and no doubt imagined he could refine the skills and manners of his new American friends.

Dogwood's ready-made network began feeding the OSS a gush of information that seemed to justify Coleman's investment. It soon became the most important American spy ring in Europe. Macfarland reported:

> Most important of all is action! We are now on the spot with all of them, British, Greeks and Turks. They have done everything we have asked of them (much to my surprise) and now we must produce. Our whole future here depends now on whether we can deliver the goods.

Relations between Dogwood and the OSS in Cairo soured early in the relationship. According to a top secret OSS report about the 'Dogwood Project, Istanbul Mission' submitted in December 1944 and released by the CIA in January 2001, a few OSS agents expressed doubts about

Dogwood from the beginning.[4] The author of the report, whose name is redacted, met 'Mr Dogwood' in the second week of July 1943. Schwarz informed the OSS agents that he been working for British intelligence on an informal basis for a year and had become increasingly unhappy that he had not been given any official role or status. He informed the OSS agent that he would now prefer to offer his services to the Americans rather than the ungrateful British. The author of the report concluded that Schwarz was 'exceedingly able, clever, shewed, calculating and cunning' and completely loyal to the Allied cause. Another OSS agent took a contrary view: Schwarz was a 'German spy playing the boldest of games in an attempt to penetrate our own secret service or services'. The writer goes on 'it was easy for me to fall into line with his conviction; and we decided then and there that perhaps Dogwood was too dangerous.' But when the agents consulted Macfarland, he pointed out that Schwarz had been cleared by the British. So after some further discussion, it was agreed to take Schwarz on and 'give him a try'.

There is no convincing evidence that Schwarz was 'playing the boldest of games'. There is no reason either to question his passionate commitment to the anti-Nazi cause. When the American historian Barry Rubin tracked down the 83-year-old Schwarz to his home in Lucerne in 2001, he met an articulate and hospitable man who convincingly defended the record of his network. His entire family had perished in the Holocaust. His bitterness was reserved for the British and Americans, who had refused to respond to German peace offers. When Rubin presented Schwarz with evidence that some of his most prized Flowers had been enemy agents, Schwarz refused to accept that he had been betrayed.[5]

For an intelligence organisation, Dogwood had crippling flaws. Both the British and American agencies wanted one commodity more than any other and that was a flow of information from inside the fortress of German-occupied Europe. But Schwarz had grander plans that clashed with one of the fundamental axioms of the Allied war. Shortly after the Allied landings in French North Africa at the beginning of 1943, President Roosevelt and Winston Churchill met in Casablanca between 14 and 24 January to coordinate Allied strategy. Because the Soviet Army was launching a major offensive against the German army at Stalingrad, Stalin was unable to attend. On the final day of the Casablanca Conference, Roosevelt announced that he and Churchill had resolved that the only way to ensure a post-war peace was to insist on a policy of unconditional surrender. The reasoning was that in the aftermath of the First World War, many Germans had come to believe that rather than being defeated fair and square, they had been 'stabbed in the back'. This national myth fed the Nazi onslaught on Jews, Communists and other 'enemies of the people'. By insisting on unconditional surrender, the Allied leaders hoped that the eventual defeat of the Axis powers would finally extinguish these malevolent ideas. The main war aim was, in Roosevelt's words, 'the destruction of the philosophies in those countries which are based on conquest and the subjugation of other people'. Acutely conscious that the absent Soviet leader was furious that the western Allies had so far failed to open a second front in Europe and feared that some kind of secret deal might be struck with the Germans while millions of Russian soldiers were dying on the Eastern Front, Roosevelt and Churchill made it clear that neither the United States nor Great Britain would seek a separate peace. The implication of the declaration of 'unconditional surrender' was that any kind of negotiations with any representative or faction of the Axis powers could not be contemplated.

For Alfred Schwarz, the message of Casablanca was unwelcome. For him, the purpose of the network was not merely to acquire and convey information, it was to actively undermine the Nazi state by seeking out the German opposition and backing plans to topple or assassinate Hitler. This implied that it was necessary to open furtive negotiations with dissidents inside the Nazi state and, furthermore, to imply that in the event of the collapse of the Hitler regime the terms of surrender could be negotiated. The fissiparous German resistance was united by an abhorrence of Bolshevism and dread that Europe would be overwhelmed by Slavic hordes. Many of its leaders hoped to make some kind of deal with the western Allies to stave off the nightmare of Bolshevik conquest. This was delusional: neither Roosevelt nor the fiercely anti-Bolshevik Churchill had any illusions about whether they could win the war without the involvement of Stalin's increasingly formidable armies. Stalin may have feared that the western Allies might turn against the Soviet Union and make a pact with Germany, but the reality was that such a course was impossible to contemplate in London and Washington. On that side of the Grand Alliance, no effort would be spared to reassure and placate the paranoid Soviet dictator.

Schwarz took a different view – one that would put him on a collision course with the OSS.[6]

In July 1943, Count Helmut James Graf von Moltke and another German aristocrat, Wilhelm Wenger, travelled to Istanbul on an official mission to request the return of a fleet of merchant ships impounded by the Turkish authorities in the Sea of Marmara. Von Moltke was born into Germany's most esteemed military dynasty, but his mother Dorothy was a South African and both his parents were practising Christian Scientists. Although Helmuth was confirmed in the Lutheran Church, he seems to have inherited, as well as a huge estate in Kreisau in Silesia, a stubbornly ethical world view that, to some degree, ran counter to his family's martial pedigree. He studied law and political sciences and with the outbreak of war became a legal advisor to Admiral Canaris, the Abwehr commandant. In the course of his work, which required him to travel and report from different regions of German-occupied Europe, he observed the consistent and violent abuses carried out by the German army and the SS.

Von Moltke openly protested to Canaris and other high-ranking officers in the Abwehr. He wrote to an English friend:

> Today, not a numerous, but an active part of the German people are beginning to realise, not that they have been led astray, not that bad times await them, not that the war may end in defeat, but that what is happening is sin and that they are personally responsible for each terrible deed that has been committed – naturally, not in the earthly sense, but as Christians …

His knowledge of the horrors wreaked by the German occupation inspired him to found with like-minded colleagues a resistance cell known as the Kreisauer Circle, so-called because its members met occasionally at the Moltke family estate in Kreisau in Silesia. We should remember that the German resistance was not a liberal movement: it was dominated by deeply conservative members of the old Prussian elites who were terrified that Hitler was dragging Germany into a catastrophe that could only end in submission to the godless Bolsheviks.

Moltke had no intention of wasting time haggling with Turkish officials about the German merchant ships. His colleague would sort out the matter. His real purpose was to meet with German anti-Nazis in the city who could in turn introduce him to British and American agents. He had excellent connections and no doubt assumed that he would get through to the right people. Through his mother he had been introduced to Field

Marshall Jan Smuts; he was acquainted with the United States Ambassador in Cairo, Alexander C. Kirk; he was a friend of the American journalist Dorothy Thompson. Moltke had a good idea whom he could trust in the German community. When he arrived in Turkey, he immediately contacted Paul Leverkühn, the head of the Abwehr station based in Ankara, who despite a fussy, scholarly manner had proved himself a tough operator in the treacherous waters of the Bosporus. His operational success blunted but could not completely bury questions about his loyalty. These were not just a matter of rumour and innuendo. He had studied law in Edinburgh and the United States, where he made the acquaintance of another ambitious law student called William Donovan. When he returned to Germany to set up a law practice in Berlin, his office was at 7, Pariser Platz, the same building where von Moltke worked.

It would seem that Leverkühn was willing to take the plan further. He introduced Moltke to Alexander Rustow who, it will be recalled, was 'Magnolia'. He already knew Hans Wilbrandt, 'Hyacinth': he had advised von Moltke about the management of his family estates. Soon he began to have secret meetings with the network ringmaster, 'Dogwood' himself, and revealed his masterplan. He proposed persuading the western Allies to launch an immediate and crushing attack on the Nazi stronghold. In the meantime, he and his fellow conspirators would depose Hitler and his satraps from within the Reich. In the aftermath of this palace revolt, Germany would be occupied swiftly by the Anglo–Americans, stalling the Soviet advance from the East. The dramatic 'One Blow' plan was ambitious and grossly delusional, but it began to gather momentum across the Dogwood network and among the more naïve OSS officers. On 9 September, Macfarland sent a report to Washington about the 'Founding of a Free German Movement in the Service of the Western Allies': 'an organization of Germans who have united to work for the liberation of Germany and her reconstruction along democratic lines, in close co-operation with the Allies in the common struggle against Hitlerism.' The movement, Macfarland claimed, had 'valuable contacts with like-minded men inside Germany, with circles in the Wehrmacht and all sectors of German economic life'.

Schwarz was even more enthused. He informed General R.G. Tindal, the American military attaché in Ankara, that 'the magnitude of the promise held out by the proposed collaboration can hardly be overstated. No limited intelligence effort can offer even a remotely comparable chance of ending the war in the West at one stroke.' The historian Schlomo Aronson points out that although Schwarz wanted to believe that the downfall of Hitler would end the persecution of Jews, he was careful not to make any mention of his hopes to save Jews. This strongly implies that he suspected or knew that it would be unwise to seem to taint the plan with 'Jewish concerns'.

On the American side, in Washington, Donovan was thrilled by reports of the plot and travelled to Istanbul in person to meet his old friend. Claiming that he was acting on behalf of the German resistance, Leverkühn presented the wide-eyed Donovan with a memorandum, bearing the letterhead of the German Embassy, which stated that German military commanders in the west would not resist an Allied invasion of France. The content of the memorandum should have strained credulity to breaking point but in any event the conspiracy was doomed. Both the British and the Americans had long distrusted the German resistance – and after the Casablanca Conference, the mantra of unconditional surrender had been set in stone. When von Moltke returned to Istanbul in December hoping to set up a meeting in Cairo with his old friend Kirk, the Ambassador replied: 'I would always be glad to see you but I do not see any good purpose would be served by our meeting now as it is my personal conviction that nothing short of unconditional surrender of the German armed forces will terminate the war in Europe.' Kirk explained his decision to General Tindal: 'the war must end by the military defeat of the German armed forces and *not by any dickering on our part with factions within Germany*' [my italics].

Donovan sought other opinions. A German expert at the New School of Social Research in New York concluded that von Moltke's group was 'worthy of consideration' and offered the only 'practical and politically permissible way to keep Russia out of Central Europe'. That precisely was the problem. Roosevelt feared that 'dickering about' with Germans would come to the attention of his Soviet allies and he was loath to anger Stalin. In Washington, the OSS Planning Group decided not to transmit Donovan's report to the Joint Chiefs of Staff for action 'at this time'. If the Moltke Plan was holed below the water line, in March 1944 Allen Dulles, the OSS Chief in Bern, sent it to the bottom. He informed Donovan that a few months earlier in January, the Gestapo had arrested Helmuth von Moltke and charged him with treason.

As Rubin discovered, Alfred Schwarz was unforgiving, decades later, about the failure of the Americans to take the plan seriously and, as he fervently believed, end the war. The terrible irony is that von Moltke was almost certainly betrayed by the Dogwood network.

This brings us back to the question raised at the beginning of this chapter. Who was Dogwood agent Bandi Grosz? Why did the Germans insist that he accompany Joel Brand to Istanbul? Is Grosz the key to the puzzle?

It is a truism that the world of spies and intelligence networks rests on a rotten foundation of deception and counter-deception. The currency of intelligence is mined from the veins of truth that run through a bedrock of lies. The most successful spymasters owe their mythical success to the esoteric craft of sifting the glittering shards of signal from the detritus of mere noise. They must listen but not believe. The glitter of secret information must be resisted until it has withstood the corrosive power of doubt. This means that any head of an intelligence network must be a master of distrust. The Dogwood network and its bonds with the OSS foundered on an excess of trust. Schwarz was too eager to believe in the integrity of his agents. Even when he knew that they served two or more masters, he assumed that their primary loyalty was to him. When Macfarland reflected later on the Dogwood misadventure, he admitted that:

> the complete integrity of agents thus selected can never be assured. It was obviously necessary to recruit agents having the possibilities of travel between Central Europe and Turkey which of necessity required that the individuals were persona grata [*sic*] with the German authorities. Furthermore, in order for them to be particularly useful, they had to have access to German officials on a sufficiently high level to obtain useful intelligence.

Growing in Schwarz's garden of flowers were some poisonous weeds which he was unwilling to uproot. Many of the weeds had entwined links to Hungary. This was the fatal flaw of the Dogwood network and it would have catastrophic consequences for the Jewish rescuers in Budapest.

Let us follow now the chain of connections that would break up the Dogwood network and, in the spring of 1944, fatally compromise the Brand Mission. It begins in Brazil with an Austrian Catholic called Franz Josef Messner. As general director of the huge Semperit rubber and chemical works, Messner was among Austria's most powerful industrialists and had a reputation as a benevolent employer. Dismayed by the rise of Nazi-allied forces in Austria, he had taken refuge in Brazil, which supplied his factories with rubber and other raw materials, and took Brazilian citizenship. When war broke out in 1939, he decided to return to Austria, now part of the Greater German Reich, to make sure the reforms he had introduced at the Semperit factories were not overturned. But he was immediately ordered to return to Brazil by the Reich Ministry of the Economy to secure rubber for the German war machine. Several months later, in June 1940, Messner boarded an Italian steamer, the *Conte Grande*, bound for Europe. Halfway across the Atlantic, a French destroyer intercepted the *Conte Grande*, impounded it in Casablanca and arrested Messner. After his return to the Reich, Messner was increasingly disenchanted with the Nazi regime and became involved with the Austrian resistance. Many of the most active were Communists or leftists – but others, like Messner himself, were staunch Catholics. A few members of the group began passing information to the British, mainly to do with the location of armaments and ball bearing factories in Austria. Messner made sure that none of the information passed to British intelligence agents revealed the location of the Semperit factories. This was not simple opportunism. Messner was protecting a number of Jewish workers in some of the factories, and as an OSS report reveals:

> he built up his own intelligence and sabotage chain by appointing as warehouse managers men whom he trusted implicitly. These various warehouse men could report to [Messner] directly through codes which they had devised concerning any military movements or combat intelligence that came their way. It was an extensive and dangerous organisation – dangerous for the personnel.

Even as he protected his factories, Messner was looking for ways to expand the Austrian resistance network. His chance came when he met the director of the Semperit office in Istanbul, Gustav Rüdiger, who was already deeply involved with Dogwood. In early 1944, Messner travelled to Istanbul, where he was introduced to Schwarz and he eagerly welcomed him into the network as 'Cassia'. On 4 February, he signed a formal agreement with the OSS to assist the Allies in the defeat of Nazi Germany. On his way home, Messner stopped off in Zürich to meet Dulles. He made a very favourable impression: 'I wish to offer my congratulations to [Macfarland] in developing this line … We are convinced that [Messner] is worthy of all our support'. It was a huge risk for

Messner to make this commitment on behalf of his colleagues in Austria – and it would prove to be his downfall.

As part of his agreement with the OSS, Messner agreed to receive a radio to keep in touch with the OSS when he returned to Austria. He arranged to pick up the radio in Budapest from another Dogwood agent code-named 'Iris'. When Messner and his secretary arrived in Hungary on 25 March, he was immediately arrested. Tortured, he gave up the names of his colleagues and the Cassia Ring disintegrated. A broken Messner was hanged on 23 April 1944 in Dachau.

When the hapless 'Cassia' arranged to meet 'Iris' in Budapest he could have no idea who or what he was dealing with. 'Iris' was a tall, blond-haired and imposing Czech called Fritz Laufer. Like Grosz, he used a ready supply of false identities. He was at different times Ludwig Meyer, Ludwig Hermann and Karl Heinz. He had been born František Laufer in Prague; his parents were converted Jews. It is said that he worked as a waiter. In 1938, after the German invasion of Czechoslovakia, Laufer was threatened with deportation and had saved his skin by becoming an informer for the Abwehr in exchange for 'Aryan papers'. He seems to have betrayed a number of Czech operatives and was sent to Budapest as a fully fledged agent. According to an intelligence report filed by the OSS counter-intelligence unit X-2, 'Friedrich [sic] Laufer is popularly regarded as a Gestapo [sic] agent … as he appears to be persona grata with the Germans in spite of being a Jew and has suddenly shown signs of great wealth.' His superiors in the Abwehr and later the SD included SS Captain Gerhard Clages, who would take a significant part in the Brand Mission.[7]

In another OSS report, Schwarz tells a very different tale. Under pressure from the OSS, he must have wanted to present his friend Laufer in a better light to justify why he trusted him. He says that Laufer was born in Prague in 1900, attended a gymnasium and studied agricultural science. He was employed by his father in his food import business and as an administrator of the family estate. Laufer moved on to take a position in a Prague company that specialised in textiles. In 1938, the company sent Laufer to Belgrade to manage its export business. In the spring of 1941, the German Luftwaffe bombed the city and Laufer fled to Budapest. Schwarz then explains that Laufer pursued various unspecified business affairs in Bulgaria and Turkey and developed 'ties with the Allies'. He visited Istanbul first in 1941 and at least three times in 1943 'under the instructions of one who is now a close collaborator of ours'. This individual is not identified. Schwarz's version of

Laufer's story is undoubtedly an elaborate cover concocted by Laufer and his German contacts in the Abwehr. It convinced Schwarz, who came to trust and admire 'Iris' as the jewel in the crown of the Dogwood network.

We may never know the full story of Fritz Laufer. We glimpse him only in the slippery manufacture of identities by warring intelligence agencies. It is clear only that he was motivated by fear and greed. At any moment Laufer could be betrayed and dispensed with by his bosses in German intelligence. He could make himself useful slipping back and forth between aliases and allegiances – and between Budapest and Istanbul. He was a broker of information. If he had any sliver of loyalty to his origins as a Czech Jew or to his friend and admirer Alfred Schwarz, it was always overshadowed by his dependency on his German masters.

The Mysterious World of Bandi Grosz

It is Laufer who finally brings us back to Bandi Grosz. Grosz too was a master of fabricated identities. He was Andre Giorgi, Andreas, Bondi or Antal. For the OSS and Schwarz, he was 'Trillium'. He had something else in common with Laufer: he was a Jewish convert to Catholicism. Since the period of the Habsburg monarchy, many Hungarian Jews had converted to one of the Christian faiths, including members of some of the wealthy dynasties. In many cases, the decision to convert was made for purely pragmatic reasons in order to overcome the severe restrictions imposed on Jews in the aftermath of the First World War. For others, conversion sprang from the desire of people treated as outsiders to proclaim a deeper attachment to a nation. The decision may or may not be rewarded by acceptance. Conversion, as it turned out, rarely protected converted Jews from the poison of antisemitism. Grosz, Laufer and a handful of others made a living from trading information – in contemporary jargon we might say monetising data. They plied their trade in near continuous motion between the hostile camps of Hitler's 'War of Annihilation'. For its agents, the intelligence trade was high risk. Survival depended on adopting many different roles. Betrayal was a constant risk. So too was the inadvertent slip of a mask. Grosz and the other agents who flitted between the agencies of the belligerent powers had to be accomplished shapeshifters. As converts, they had a unique sense of the fluidity of the identities we present to others and the power of the actor's craft.

We know very little about the life of Grosz before the war. The British agents who interrogated him in Cairo in 1944 left us with a word portrait that, although undoubtedly tainted with ethnic disdain, brings Grosz memorably to life. He was well dressed, 'small, rather thin'; his frizzy, combed back hair was 'grey mixed with black'; he wore spectacles; his voice was hoarse and medium pitched; his nose was long and hooked; he had a mark like a deep cut on the right side of his upper lip; all in all, Grosz was 'ugly, but not repulsive'. The agent concluded that:

> One of G's personal weaknesses lies in his inability to tell the truth. Possessed of a remarkably agile and inventive mind, he is never at a loss to explain away the many inconsistencies in his story. His attitude on the surface is the sincerest imaginable. But he defeats his own ends, for he is just that much too glib and too eloquent to be taken seriously ...[8]

The British record reveals that Grosz was born in 1905 in the Hungarian city of Beregszasz in Transcarpathia, now in Ukraine close to the Hungarian border and known as Berehovo. He went to a Jewish School in Budapest, where he met Samuel (Samu) Springmann – who, decades later, would persuade Grosz to work as a courier for the Jewish Agency.

Evidently a mediocre student, Grosz transferred to a vocational school to study banking. Two years later, we find him working for a transport company called Feketr. It is unclear what kind of 'transport' but the job was certainly rewarding. By the time he turned 21, Grosz owned a café in Budapest that was a rendezvous for thieves and fences with money or goods to sell and sanitise. In 1930, Grosz set up his own transport business. This was without any doubt a smuggling business because, as he told the British, the company was fined for customs offences and forced to shut down. But Grosz was learning. In the next decade, he rose to become a kingpin in the Budapest underworld, an international smuggler dealing in diamonds, gold and Persian carpets. Grosz married a Hungarian Catholic woman in 1937 – which is when he converted. There is no evidence that Grosz had any kind of religious convictions.

His story now takes a different turn. In 1941, Grosz was arrested, probably not for the first time, and sent down for eighteen months. The police granted him a 'grace period' of three months to wind up his affairs, which was extended to six because Grosz claimed to have heart trouble. During this period, Grosz bribed an Abwehr officer referred to as 'Dr Grovitcs' to give him work and a way to avoid his prison time 'serving the German war effort in the fields of commerce', as he put it to his British interrogator. His task was to 'use his connections and influence with international transport firms to buy up goods for Germany in Switzerland and arrange for their transport to the Reich'. In the British report, the names of the Abwehr agents are queried in the text and were perhaps misheard, so it is difficult to identify the actual agents. The sequence of events is nevertheless convincing. 'Dr Grovitcs' informed Grosz that his superior 'Dr Gustav Busse' (Bueckel? wonders the interrogator) will travel to Budapest to check whether Grosz is 'suitable for the job'. All went well and Busse/Bueckel let Grosz know he has been taken on. To celebrate, Grosz escorted his Abwehr friend on a bibulous tour of the 'alcoholic sights' of Budapest. He paid his new friend's enormous bills.

★★★

The introduction to the Abwehr may have come through another professional crook and dissimulator, Rudolph 'Rudi' Scholz. Born in Vienna, Scholz was a strikingly handsome, elegantly attired and coiffured fellow with a scholarly manner who specialised in safe cracking. Robbery fed his sartorial passions, but he eventually ran out of luck. 'The good times were over,' he told a friend. With the police hard on his heels, he fled Vienna and washed up in Paris. Here he took refuge among 'professional acquaintances' in the criminal underworld but appears to have led a quieter life and perfected his French. When Germany occupied France in 1940, Scholz, as a Reich subject, was drafted into the German army and ended up assigned to the Abwehr station in Stuttgart that monitored resistance groups in occupied France. Because he spoke perfect French and had made no secret of his underworld connections, Scholz was sent back to Paris to investigate illicit currency exchanges that the Germans suspected were being organised by members of a resistance cell. He must have impressed his superiors. Two years later, Scholz was posted to Budapest to take over the Abwehr's Budapest station. Posing as an Austrian 'merchant', Scholz set about seducing a young Jewish woman who worked as a typist for Samu Springman. She was charmed by Scholz's old-fashioned attentions and enthralled by his tales of globe-trotting exploits. The young woman told Springman all about her new beau and suggested that he might be useful as a courier. Springman needed little persuading – and Scholz readily agreed to help

– and gratis. He now had access to a key Jewish network that linked the Yishuv and the Rescue Committee in Budapest.

In the meantime, Grosz had served his German employers well – and he used his powerful new friends to rebuild his business career using a complicated arrangement of shell companies that the Abwehr used to get around the embargo against Germany. For Grosz and his Abwehr masters, the arrangement proved to be highly profitable. The British file on Grosz gives us some idea of how this worked. In Budapest, Grosz had got to know Ilona Talas, the mistress of an Abwehr officer called Josef Baumruck. Through Baumruck, Grosz was introduced to an Austrian Jew called Richard Kauder, code-named 'Klatt', who controlled a network of wireless stations for the Abwehr in Sofia, Bulgaria, and had run into financial difficulties.[9] Baumruck proposed that Grosz lend money to 'Klatt' in return for potentially very lucrative 'smuggling rights' between Sofia and Budapest. Both made it very clear that they knew everything about Grosz's problems with the Hungarian police and his relationship with the Abwehr in Stuttgart. Grosz agreed to go along with the plan and began spending a lot of time in Sofia. He was, he told his interrogators, impressed by the activities of the Klatt Dienstelle: he was 'doing masterly work for Germany'.

In August 1942, the plan began to unravel. The Hungarian police had not forgotten Grosz and the sentence for customs offences he had not yet served. When he returned to Budapest after a short business trip to Sofia, he was arrested. In some desperation, he turned to an 'influential' lawyer, who managed to get him released after fourteen days. His sentence was again postponed for three months. Grosz was angry that his Abwehr friends had not lifted a finger to help him 'because he was a Jew'. Klatt urged him to go to Stuttgart and sever his relations with the Abwehr station and work full-time for him. Grosz followed his advice. On his return from the showdown in Stuttgart, Grosz was summoned to the Hadik Barracks to meet Colonel Sillay, the chief of the Hungarian Counter Espionage Service. He received a brutal dressing down. He was called a 'bad Hungarian on account of his smuggling activities and connections with Germans'. Sillay threatened Grosz with deportation to Ukraine. There was one way he could redeem himself. He would continue working with the Klatt Dienstelle in Sofia but report everything he knew back to the Hungarians. It was not an offer he could refuse. Sillay introduced him to Lieutenant Colonel Anton von Merkly, known as 'Uncle

Toni', and Lt Ferenc 'Feri' Bagyoni. They would be his contacts. Hungary was, of course, a German ally and Merkly was a liaison officer with the Abwehr – but there was deepening distrust between Berlin and Budapest. Discovering who knew what and who was talking to whom and why was an obsessive preoccupation for both sides. As the Germans already knew, the Hungarians kept open back office channels to the Allies.

No sooner had Grosz signed up with the Hungarians to spy on the Germans than his story took yet another turn. Sometime in October, his old school friend Samuel Springman walked into the Café Pariset, where Grosz spent a lot of his time. Springman had a proposal to make. He had heard that Grosz was a rich man with many connections. 'He was doing very well for himself.' Springman told Grosz something about his Zionist activities and the work of the Rescue Committee and lamented that there was so little that could be done for Jewish refugees. He then came to the point. The Rescue Committee in Budapest needed ways and means to communicate with a Zionist group in Istanbul established by the Jewish Agency in Palestine, which had, he revealed, 'mail and money' ready to send. He asked Grosz to travel to Istanbul with a letter for one of the Zionists based there, Venja Pomeranz (whose Hebrew name was Ze'ev Hadari), who would hand over a sum of money to take back to the Rescue Committee in Budapest. Grosz agreed – in return for 10 per cent of any money entrusted to him. He introduced Springman to a new friend whom he had 'met at the races' called Erich Wehner, alias Eric/Erik Popescu, who had agreed to travel to Istanbul with the letter. The British SIME report refers to Wehner as a 'Romanian Jew'.

Two weeks later, Popescu returned from Istanbul with a sum of money for Springman. As the British report states, Grosz and Popescu had agreed to split the 10 per cent commission, but, much to his annoyance, Popescu handed over just 2.5 per cent. It is not clear from his account whether Grosz realised this immediately or found out later that he had been cheated. In any event, Popescu informed Grosz that having met Pomeranz and the other Zionists, he had concluded that they would 'not make much money out of them', meaning the Zionists in Istanbul. Despite this shabby beginning, by March the following year Grosz was deeply involved in the thick tangle of intelligence networks that had been woven between Budapest, Sofia and Istanbul. He had become 'Trillium'.

The different players in Grosz's circle of couriers had strikingly similar profiles. In early 1943, Grosz was looking for someone to take Zionist mail and money to Poland and Slovakia. Through his contacts in the Abwehr, he was introduced to 'Joszi' Winninger, who readily agreed to take on the job. Winninger was rumoured to be half-Jewish and worked as a courier and agent for the Abwehr station in Vienna. Friling says that Winninger 'worked for the Jewish Agency in Istanbul, and for the British and Americans in Turkey'. The deal Grosz worked out with his new courier was all about money. Winninger first sought the approval of the Abwehr station chief, Dr Schmidt – who agreed to the arrangement for a 40 per cent cut of the Zionist money. The rest was divided between Grosz, Popescu and Winninger himself. According to Aronson, Winninger also cheated the Zionists on exchanges from gold or dollars into Reichsmark – he became quite wealthy on the proceeds. As was his custom, Grosz played a duplicitous game. According to the OSS report quoted earlier: 'Winninger was also used by DOGWOOD who TRILLIUM reports to have warned against subject, saying that he told everything to his Nazi masters. DOGWOOD is said to have replied that subject [Winninger] was doing excellent work and that he had "complete faith in him".' The trust Schwarz repeatedly placed in Abwehr agents such as Laufer and Winninger is truly remarkable.

Both British and American agencies in the Middle East took a keen interest in what they called 'Jewish refugee traffic' that was flowing between a number of different organisations. In April 1943, a report by an American military attaché in Cairo sounded 'a note of warning' about the possibility that various Jewish refugee organisations might be exploited for espionage purposes: *'their operations must be closely scrutinised, (1) because of the unsavoury character of certain individuals connected with them; and (2) because of the undoubted opportunity afforded the enemy for making use of them in introducing agents into America'* [emphasis in original]. There have been suggestions that Hitler permitted Canaris to use refugee Jews in the United States for intelligence work but no evidence at all that this was ever carried out.

What may have confused the Allies, with good reason, is a plot hatched by Dr Hans von Dohnanyi and Dietrich Bonhoeffer, dissidents in the Abwehr, to recruit Jews threatened by deportation as agents. According to a recent book, *No Ordinary Men* by Elizabeth Sifton and Fritz Stern, a dozen or so elderly Jews whose names appeared on the deportation lists were designated as Abwehr agents and sent, with the Gestapo's consent, to Switzerland. By September 1942, fourteen Jews had found safe haven. The fear of inadvertently providing sanctuary to an enemy has always fuelled hostility to refugee policy, as it does to this day. Dohnanyi and his co-conspirators acted in good faith but seen from the perspective of the Allied agencies, plans such as Operation 7 risked tainting all refugees and their backers as potential spies and saboteurs. It was inevitable that the activities of 'unsavoury' characters such as Grosz and the other agents trafficking intelligence between Europe and Turkey would generate alarm and distrust.

By the beginning of 1943, Grosz had woven an elaborate web of connections with Abwehr agents and Hungarian intelligence. His work for Samu Springman introduced him to the Zionist network in Istanbul, and the Hungarian intelligence chief Merkly urged Grosz to 'to establish a connection through the Zionists with Allied representatives with a view to future discussions on cooperation between them and members of the Hungarian General Staff'. His main Zionist contact in Istanbul was Theodor 'Teddy' Kollek. The British report tells us that Kollek 'gave him [Grosz] the Zionist mail, including a letter from SCHWARZ, a Czech immigrant who had a high position with the Americans for a certain Fritz LAUFER'. On his return to Budapest, Grosz gave Springman the letter and other messages from the Zionists in Istanbul to hand over to Laufer. This is a remarkable revelation. Merkly was thoroughly alarmed when, after returning to Budapest, Grosz told him about the letter from Kollek that he had handed over to Springman. Merkly insisted that Grosz retrieve the letter, and warned him that Laufer was 'a first class German agent'. This is prima facie evidence that the Zionists in Istanbul and Springman's Rescue Committee were deeply compromised. When Grosz returned to Istanbul in July, Kollek introduced him to Schwarz, presumably for the first time. Grosz confronted Schwarz about Laufer and the fiasco with the letter. Schwarz's reaction was entirely predictable. According to the British report: 'Schwarz said Laufer could not be a double crosser as he was his best agent and had given him most valuable information.' The almost comic irony in this exchange is that Grosz too was an Abwehr agent. Indeed, he leaked in every direction. We have to assume that by now Grosz had become 'Trillium' in Schwarz's network. What is remarkable about the story of the Dogwood network is that the Americans kept faith in the clumsy machinations of its flowers for so long. The rococo plots and schemes spun by Schwarz's team of sloppy liars and thieves would play a calamitous part in the destruction of Hungarian Jewry.

Slippery Lieutenant Colonel Hatz

At the same time that Grosz was deepening his links with 'Dogwood' and other flowers, he continued to make frequent and lucrative visits to Sofia to meet Klatt. It was here that Merkly introduced him to Otto Hatz de Hatzsegy, who had recently been appointed as the Hungarian military attaché. Merkly wanted Grosz to introduce Hatz to his contacts in the OSS in Istanbul. Now the stakes were raised much higher. As OSS agent Major Roger Pfaff reported to Donovan a year later:

> the ['Dogwood chain'] was to penetrate Germany and the Balkan Axis powers (Austria, Hungary, Romania and Bulgaria). In addition to obtaining military intelligence, it was hoped that this chain would be able to collaborate with resistance groups, and eventually affect the overthrow of Axis governments and their satellites …

Hatz was a handsome, smooth-tongued young man who spoke German, Russian, Bulgarian and basic French and English. He had, however, run up crippling debts lavishing money and gifts on a succession of young women. He was admired for his fencing skills and daring sense of humour; it was said that his comic impression of Hitler was a star turn at diplomatic parties. Hatz claimed to have no politics. In truth, he was greedy. To feed his expensive habits, he was just as amenable as Grosz was to the profits that could be squeezed from the intelligence trade. The same Major Pfaff also reveals that as early as December 1943, Macfarland was warned that: 'Hatz was in collusion with the Abwehr'. The same report also reveals that none other than 'Iris'/Laufer had initiated the first contact with the Hungarian General Staff.[10]

So it was that on a balmy September evening in 1943, Lieutenant Colonel Hatz was strolling across the Pera Bridge in Istanbul. He had been sent to Turkey by his superior, Colonel Gyula Kadar, to seek contacts with the Allies. The mission had been approved by the Hungarian Chief of Staff, General Ferenc Szombathelyi. As a cover, he attended the famous Turkish trade fair in Izmir. A few yards ahead of him, he noticed a large black car halted by the side of the road. As he peered into the back seat, the rear door was opened and a smartly dressed little man with a scar above his upper lip gestured him to join him. As the black car sped off in the direction of one of Istanbul's smartest neighbourhoods, Grosz chattered amiably to the suave young Hungarian officer. In an OSS safe house, Grosz introduced Hatz to Coleman and Schwarz. There was another Hungarian present at the meeting. This was Lothar Kövess – who was 'Jacaranda' in the Dogwood network. Schwarz entrusted him with running the network's Hungarian operations. He also had, as it turned out, many close German contacts and frequently expressed pro-Nazi views – and yet, it seems, he effortlessly misled both Macfarland and Schwarz, who stubbornly sealed their eyes and ears to the dubious loyalties of their human assets.

Hatz readily agreed to gather intelligence for the OSS. He now became 'Jasmine' in Schwarz's network. Coleman hinted at a much bigger plan, to draw Hungary away from the Axis. For now, Hatz returned to Hungary with a suitcase that contained radio equipment, which he showed proudly to Colonel Kadar. He boasted that the transmitter could be used to get in touch with President Roosevelt. As it turned out, a nervous Szombathelyi forbade the use of the transmitter but approved further discussions with the OSS. Kadar hid the radio equipment inside a piano owned by his mistress, the actress Katalina Varga-Karady. It is not at all surprising that when the Germans occupied Budapest in the following year, they knew exactly where the radio was hidden. Everyone connected with it was arrested.

What the Hungarians and the OSS did not know is that on his way back to Budapest, Hatz had stopped off in Sofia. Here he had dinner at the house of Otto Wagner, the Abwehr chief who was code-named 'Dr Delius'. Hatz told his friend all about the meetings in Istanbul and claimed that he had resisted the lure offered by the OSS. Wagner informed the German minister in Sofia, Adolf Beckerle, who in turn reported to the Foreign Office in Berlin. The plot thickens once again. Beckerle's report fell into the hands of Fritz Kolbe, who was the 'Referent' for Karl Ritter, the ambassador for special assignments. The Foreign Minister Ribbentrop depended on Ritter to sift through the huge volume of cables and reports that flooded in from German diplomats all over the world. A punctilious German Catholic, who was fond of wearing Lederhosen, Kolbe led a perilous double life: he was a spy.

Every day, Kolbe read and secretly photographed top-secret diplomatic and military cables that crossed Ritter's desk. After hours, he frequently stayed late in his office as Allied bombers pounded the city. For a long time, it was impossible for Kolbe to send the information he had gathered out of Germany. His breakthrough came in 1943. After many unsuccessful attempts, the hard-working paper shredder was appointed to serve as one of the Ministry's hand-picked couriers, which enabled him to travel outside the Reich with diplomatic protection. In Switzerland, he met an exiled Jewish businessman who put him in touch with Allen Dulles. Until the end of the war, Kolbe met Dulles in Bern every three months and passed on a trove of secret documents that provided details about German foreign policy, as well information about industrial plants and weapons development. Kolbe was perhaps the most important spy of the Second World War.

★★★

Kolbe had immediately recognised the significance of Beckerle's report about his meeting with the Hungarian officer. It revealed that: 'Hatz is a reliable pro German. However, he is short of funds and has numerous affairs with women. There is also an unconfirmed report to the effect that he is in touch with Jews who are paid by Hungarian intelligence and that he shares in the profits which he makes from smuggling currency.' This was dynamite but Dulles failed to recognise the significance of Beckerle's revelation and did not send on the report to Washington until the beginning of January 1944. In the meantime, in the last months of 1943, Hatz was shuffling back and forth between Istanbul and Budapest – always breaking his journey in Sofia to have dinner with Wagner/Delius. He would pass on the latest proposals from the OSS and again insist he had righteously refused to play ball.

There are many other revealing details in the British SIME reports. In December, Grosz informed his interrogators, he returned to Istanbul, where he met with Hatz. This time, Hatz gave Grosz the brush off. He told him in no uncertain terms that he alone would continue his discussions with Schwarz and Lothar Kövess. There were a number of possible motivations for Hatz's break with Grosz. It may have been simple dislike. All they had in common was an addiction to lying. It is also clear from Grosz's account that his own discussions with the British intelligence agent Captain Johnson might have annoyed Schwarz and Macfarland, who evidently wanted to keep the Hungarians inside the OSS fold. It is not at all beyond the realms of possibility that Hatz had discovered that Grosz was informing Merkly and the Zionists about the meetings with Wagner in Sofia.

Turning up the Heat

By now it was early 1944 … From Berlin, Hitler and Ribbentrop stepped up a barrage of bellicose warnings to the perfidious Hungarians. The threat of occupation loomed. At meetings in Istanbul, Macfarland pressed Hatz to persuade the Hungarian army leaders to find ways of pulling Hungary out of the grip of the Germans. There was talk of Hungarian soldiers seizing airports so that American parachutists could land … This is presumably why so much discussion between the OSS and the Dogwood agents focused on supplying radios. Hatz and Kadar took these ideas directly to the Hungarian Prime Minister, Miklós Kallay. But Kallay, who understood better the belligerent mood on the German side, firmly opposed any actions that would provoke countermeasures. He nevertheless advised Hatz to continue discussions with the Americans in Istanbul not, it would seem, to seek military assistance but to explain Hungary's perilous situation.

At the same time, Hitler had also run out of patience with the intelligence failures of Canaris and the Abwehr. The coldly efficient SD chief Walter Schellenberg was preparing to strike. Unaware of these ominous developments, on 9 January, Kadar and Hatz both travelled to Munich to meet with Canaris. It is unclear what they hoped to gain – but in any event, Canaris, who knew, of course, that Hatz was playing both sides, refused to get involved. He knew that the SS vultures were gathering. What happened next defies rational understanding. When Hatz returned to Istanbul a few days later, Macfarland confronted him about his meetings with the Germans. Hatz had a ready reply. He claimed that he had become aware that the Germans knew about his meetings in Istanbul and that he had been forced to appear to come clean with his Abwehr contacts. This was nonsense, of course. He had met with Wagner in Sofia to reveal his dealings with the OSS long before anyone in the Abwehr was aware of his activities. Hatz then returned to Sofia, where he again met with Wagner – who reported their discussions to Beckerle, who reported to Berlin. Hatz revealed that the OSS knew all about his reports to Wagner – a revelation that might have put Fritz Kolbe in grave danger. But no one on the German side seemed to understand the implications.

Hatz's journey to Munich did not go unnoticed. When Grosz returned to Istanbul the following month with Springman he met Captain Johnson and Schwarz and informed them all about Hatz's secretive meeting with

Canaris. Schwarz refused to believe him and turned the conversation to wireless sets. Macfarland and Schwartz had further meetings, Hatz until the eve of the German invasion of Hungary in March. In the course of these final discussions, the OSS provided new radio sets to take back to Hungary. One of these was provided to Fritz Laufer – who, it will be recalled, used the radio to trap Messner and the Cassia Circle.

Soon after German troops occupied Hungary, Hatz, Kövess and Bagyoni were recalled to Budapest. On 3 May, they were arrested after the radio set was discovered: it was still hidden in the piano owned by Kadar's mistress. Hatz confronted Wagner about his arrest – and was set free at the end of May. He returned soon afterwards to Istanbul, where he again met Macfarland. Hatz had all kinds of plausible stories about his arrest and sudden release, but by then Dogwood was on its last legs.

Hatz returned, tail between his fine officer's legs, to occupied Hungary. He ended up serving with the Seventh Hungarian Corps – but in November he deserted to the Soviets. Following the liberation of Budapest, he was appointed military commander in the city, but was then arrested by the Soviets. He spent the next ten years locked up in Soviet prisons and returned to Hungary in 1955. He became a fencing trainer to the East German and Hungarian fencing teams. Had Otto Hatz de Hatzsegy, formerly 'Jasmine', discovered at last the virtues of loyalty?

The Germans were well aware of a secret Hungarian mission to sound out the Allies. When he summoned Horthy to the Schloss Kleßheim, Hitler angrily and at length denounced the Hungarians for their treachery. He and Ribbentrop insisted that they knew everything about the secret contact with the Allies. Since the German Minister in Sofia, Adolf Beckerle, had sent his report about Hatz to the Foreign Office, it is very unlikely that Hitler was not informed about his contacts with the OSS – and so we can say with reasonable certainty that the rickety Dogwood network played a forgotten role in provoking the occupation of Hungary.

Ensnared

We must now return to Grosz's story. By the end of 1943, the Dogwood web had drawn in other members of the Rescue Committee. Fearing exposure, Springmann and his family fled to Istanbul. At the beginning of January, Joel Brand and Rezsno Kasztner took over his work and Grosz made the introductions to the most important couriers and agents in his circle – Rudi Scholz, Eric/Erik Popescu alias Erich Wehner, 'Joszi' Winninger and Fritz Laufer. So it was that through Springmann and Grosz, the Rescue Committee became entangled in a sticky and treacherous web that linked the Dogwood network and the OSS to the Abwehr. In the SIME report, Grosz is reported to have observed:

> BRAND had become closely acquainted with Dr Schmidt [head of the Abwehr station in Vienna], WINNINGER [Abwehr agent and 'Dogwood' courier] … and G. [Grosz] noted on his return that he [Brand] was continually in their company drinking and playing baccarat, Dr. KASTNER [*sic*], too, had become very thick with GARZULY [Hungarian military intelligence].

The OSS report on Dogwood adds more detail:

> WINNINGER and SCHMIDT are reported to have extorted vast sums of money out of the Zionist representatives in Budapest BRAND and KASZTNER. Finally they were stopped by IRIS [Laufer] of the SD, *who wanted to make use of BRAND and KASZTNER and also wanted to prove the SD's authority over the Abwehr personnel* … [my emphasis]

When the historian Schlomo Aronson interviewed Springmann, he claimed that it was *Laufer* who had, sometime in 1943, first brought up the idea of ransoming Jews in occupied Europe for military goods, such as trucks. This claim can be substantiated by a few sentences in Schwarz/Dogwood's OSS interrogation where he refers to Laufer/Iris proposing a 'Jewish refugee deal' involving exchange for either 'material or money'.

How did Laufer's scheme become Eichmann's? In these statements and reports, we have vital clues to the true story of the Brand Mission. We will explore their significance in the next chapters.

In the febrile world of wartime intelligence, Grosz and his fellow couriers and agents had a rare value. They were men without loyalties. They cared not a jot for ideologies or humanitarian values. Some of these shady characters had Jewish roots but there is no evidence that any one of them had the slightest interest in saving the lives of other Jews. Neither were they patriots in any real sense. Loyalty was never at issue; they had none. Grosz could be bought and used. Betrayal was merely a better deal.

When I met Daniel Brand, he referred to the Dogwood network and its bewildering cast of shape shifters as 'noise'. I can't agree. I have shown in this chapter that most of the players in the Blood for Trucks negotiations were entwined in many different ways with one or more of the Dogwood network and its affiliates. All the actors in the drama were driven by conflicting ambitions and needs that often overlapped in the same person. There is no doubt that many hoped to rescue individuals threatened by one of the most violent terroristic states in human history. But in the world of intelligence motivations are rarely pure and greed and opportunism had the same potency as idealism.

At the centre of the maze is the German Abwehr. Commanded by an intimate friend of Heinrich Himmler who had lost all conviction but was paralysed by indecision, the ramshackle organisation had become a refuge for dissidents and opportunists on the make. By the beginning of 1944, Hitler had run out of patience. Canaris had failed too often. The new head of the RSHA, Ernst Kaltenbrunner, was eager to strike and rid the Reich of a decayed and blunted force. His intelligence chief, Walter Schellenberg, was an empire builder and the Abwehr was prime intelligence real estate. The crisis came to a head at the beginning of the year. A succession of intelligence failures and the defection to the Allies of Paul Leverkühn's assistant in Turkey, Erich Maria Vermehren, enraged Hitler. The final blow came when Abwehr agents planted a bomb on a British ship carrying Spanish oranges. Germany depended on Spain for supplies of tungsten and the Foreign Office feared that this reckless act of sabotage would drive Franco into the hands of the West. Hitler decided that it was time to create a unified German intelligence service and dispense with Canaris and his incompetent Abwehr once and for all. Its agencies would be abolished or absorbed by the RSHA intelligence service, the SD. The process of eviscerating the Abwehr and transplanting its healthier organs to the sprawling new service was a formidable task and took many weeks. For RSHA head Kaltenbrunner, the hostile acquisition of the Abwehr and its agents was a spectacular coup. The architect of the plan was the SD chief, Walter Schellenberg, who had long hoped to see the fall of his rival, Canaris.

The consequences of the fall of the Abwehr and the aggressive expansion of the SS would be catastrophic. The cast of characters whose enigmatic activities and allegiances we have been tracing in this chapter now fell into the hands of the SD chieftains, who answered to Himmler and Kaltenbrunner. Schellenberg vowed that the new organisation would honour a 'clean National Socialist, Germanic world view'. Using more pretentious rhetoric, Himmler promised Hitler that the SS/SD would offer a service founded on, 'Blood and race and state form and imperial will; these are the preconditions for an intelligence service.' He informed former Abwehr agents, 'if one wants to know what the SD is, one needs to know first, what the SS wants'.[11]

By joining forces with the Dogwood network, the Budapest Rescue Committee had become even more deeply ensnared in a trap. We must now find out how it closed.

12

OCCUPATION AND DECEPTION

Many accounts of the Blood for Trucks mission take Brand's depiction of his first meeting with Adolf Eichmann at face value. In his post-war accounts of the encounter, he described how he was picked up at a café in Budapest by a German staff car and driven to the SS headquarters at the Majestic Hotel in Schwabenberg. He recalls Eichmann barking:

> You know who I am? I ran the actions in Germany, Austria, Poland, Slovakia and so on. I was assigned to run the actions in Hungary. I want to do business with you: goods for blood, blood for goods. I'm willing to sell you a million Jews …[1]

Putting to one side for now the contradictions between Brand's many different versions of this infamous encounter, what has been overlooked is the *theatricality* of Eichmann's speech. He puts on a show — as he had done for the Jewish Council — using melodramatic gesture and inflated language to convey menace and power. This was, to be sure, a display of *ego*. But there is more to Eichmann's act than the strutting SS peacock. He imposes his will by convincing Brand and other members of the Rescue Committee of the extent of his power over life and death. By doing this he is reinforcing the enticement to negotiate. 'I can take but I can also give.' At the same time, Eichmann is also signalling to the other SS officers that it is *he* who is in charge of Jewish matters in Hungary. The display is theatrical because Eichmann had always to refer upwards to his many

German superiors: Winkelmann, Müller, Himmler and Kaltenbrunner. Eichmann was dependent too on the cooperation of many Hungarian accomplices, from state ministers to gendarmerie officers, to manage the deportation of many hundreds of thousands of Hungarian Jews. At the first meeting, he needed to convince Brand and the Rescue Committee that he, Adolf Eichmann, was the most important decision-maker. His performance was a way to control interactions with Brand and through him the activities of the Va'ada – and, even more importantly, to dominate his rivals in the SS. As I hope to show as conclusively as possible, Eichmann had no interest whatsoever in Brand succeeding in his mission. To be precise, he would make sure that he failed. What is revealed by Eichmann's notorious words, 'You know who I am?', is a malicious stratagem to dominate and to deceive.

In May 2018, I arrived in Tel Aviv to meet and interview Daniel Brand. He had recently published a book about his parents, Joel and Hansi – and is a fervent advocate of their commitment to rescue in the midst of slaughter. As I would soon discover, Daniel is an angry man. He is convinced that the Zionist establishment let down his father in 1944 and that his memory continues to be traduced by the historians at Yad Vashem, the Holocaust Memorial in Jerusalem. Long ago I had visited Israel for the first time as a student. Then I had been captivated by its landscapes and the vision of a socialist utopia in the Kibbutz movement. Israel has been transformed fundamentally since then and so have my own naïve views of its conflicted society. The posthumous reputations of Brand, Kasztner and many of the men and women who confronted the Nazi terror seven decades ago have also been argued over and reshaped in the furnace of history. Were they heroes, dupes or even, as one recent book by Paul Bogdanor claims, criminal collaborators? This reshaping of the meaning of people and events as the new state of Israel struggled to come to terms with the national memory of the Holocaust for its own citizens and their allies and enemies was not merely bitter. Kasztner was murdered outside his new home in Tel Aviv. His punishment for allegedly collaborating with the German perpetrators of genocide haunts Israel. On 12 April 2018, the Knesset chose to honour Kasztner during the official Holocaust Remembrance Day ceremony. His daughter, Suzi, and granddaughter, the leftist lawmaker and 'feminist firebrand' Merav Michaeli, lit and dedicated a candle to his memory. It was a highly charged moment. As Michaeli and her mother stepped forward, Likud minister Ofir Akunis stalked out of the hall in protest. A youth activist of the same party had written of his 'disgust and disappointment' that Kasztner's memory should be honoured, citing Kasztner's actions 'to save Nazi murderers'. Michaeli tirelessly defends her grandfather. He chose, she frequently insists, not to be a victim. The memory of Kasztner in modern Israel remains a troubled and restless one.

There can be no doubt – no moral doubt – that Kasztner and the other members of the Rescue Committee had to make ethical and practical choices in circumstances none of us can conceive of. None was a passive agent of blind historical forces. But, as we have seen, they lived and struggled in a world that was built on foundations of unequal power, violence and deceit. Confronting the enemy meant engaging with the agents of a state who so despised the objects of its terrorist policies that any kind of truth was dishonoured and eviscerated in the maw of power. Rather than talking of Kasztner's *crime*, we should insist instead on the tragic mistake of his blindness to the institutional bad faith of his enemies.

The mendacious nature of the Nazi regime was not only directed at those it chose to destroy as enemies of the *Volk*. It drove the power struggles that unfolded within its own state institutions. This reflected, as noted, Hitler's crassly malformed pseudo-Darwinian convictions about the eternal struggle of races and individuals, but was also a calculated and opportunist strategy of weakening opposition to his own power. The turmoil of this polycratic state eviscerated truth-telling and sanctified falsehood. So not only were the agents of the Nazi regime conditioned to lie to their enemies, they lied to each other. To talk of 'Kasztner's crime' is to mistake the kind of interaction that was possible with the agents of the Nazi state. His tragedy was to misunderstand the malevolent power he confronted.

The members of the Rescue Committee had no illusions about the likely consequences of the German occupation. After March 1944, Hungarian Jews were in mortal peril. This must be qualified. It has taken specialist historians many decades to grasp the nature of the genocide enacted by the Nazi regime – and some puzzles remain intractable. Although Hitler frequently alluded to a clear intent to eliminate European Jews as well as other minorities, how that intent was realised was to a significant degree improvised and contingent on the unfolding of a globalised war. Genocide was localised and opportunist – and no more so than in Hungary. Hitler often harassed and bullied allies like the Romanian dictator Antonescu and the Hungarian Regent Admiral Horthy to act more decisively against

Jews in their national territories – and in Hungary the Labour Service and a succession of new laws discriminated with lethal consequences against Jews. Despite this deeply ingrained and institutionalised racial hatred, nearly a million Hungarian Jews remained alive when German troops marched into Hungary in March 1944. There is evidence that many Hungarian Jews found it difficult to accept that their lives were in danger. This complacency is, at the very least, comprehensible. The military defeat of Nazi Germany appeared to be not only inevitable but imminent. It was hard to imagine that this beleaguered state could possess the wish or capacity to embark on the destruction of Europe's last Jewish community. In any case, the Jewish community in Hungary was not a single entity capable of acting against the occupier and their collaborators. The majority of Hungarian Jews who perished in Auschwitz were deported from the provincial towns, cities and villages. Many Jews who lived in Budapest survived the German onslaught as well as the murderous gangs of Arrow Cross fanatics that rampaged through the city in the autumn of 1944.

The Zionist members of the Va'ada, the Rescue Committee in Budapest, took a very different, much more pessimistic view than many other Hungarian Jews. They had extensive contacts with representatives of a number of Jewish organisations in Istanbul and Switzerland. Joel and Hansi Brand had assisted many hundreds of Polish refugees who had fled across the Hungarian border. These men and women brought with them horrifying reports of the mass killings in German-occupied Poland and Ukraine. Such reports consistently demonstrated that ghettoisation was a prelude to deportation to mass killing centres. Brand and other members of the Committee had developed contacts with German and Hungarian intelligence agents, some of whom confirmed the reports of the refugees.

In short, the Germans were killing European Jews on a systematic and unprecedented scale. Nor did the German occupation catch the Rescue Committee by surprise. Brand was warned about Hitler's plans by the Abwehr agent Josef Winninger five days before German troops crossed the border. The leaders of the Rescue Committee, as Braham points out, 'were among the best-informed persons in Budapest'. At the postwar trial of Edmund Veesenmayer in Nuremberg, Kasztner testified: 'we had a unique opportunity to follow the fate of European Jewry. We had seen how they had been disappearing one after the other from the map of Europe'.

The Rescuers

Paul Bogdanor sums up what the Rescue Committee members had learned about the German Final Solution, from a number of different sources, as follows:

> The death toll ran into several millions
> Children and the elderly were being wiped out
> The SS was in charge of the slaughter
> Mass killing was industrialised in death camps, such as Auschwitz
> The technology of mass murder consisted of gassing and the burning of corpses.[2]

But a chasm would come to divide this privileged knowledge from the decisions that the Rescue Committee decided to take in the spring of 1944.

At the time of the German occupation of Hungary, the Va'ada leadership comprised Ottó Komoly as president, Kasztner as executive officer, Dov Weiss as secretary, Joel Brand, Sámuel Springmann and a handful of others who represented the major Zionist parties in Hungary. For some time, the Budapest Committee had been a fractious organisation, which had provoked a succession of reproaches from the Zionists in Istanbul and Jerusalem. This argumentative tendency was to a significant degree a consequence of the way Joel Brand and Kasztner came to dominate the Va'ada. They were close friends and yet rivals with starkly different personalities and life experiences. Brand had been born in Naszòd in Transylvania – but had grown up in Germany. A bright boy but a less than committed student, he had joined the Communist Party in Thuringia and quickly risen in the ranks. He may have become a Comintern agent – and in this capacity travelled widely to the Soviet Union, the United States and as far as the Pacific. Brand returned to his native Transylvania, now part of Romania, in the mid 1930s. The Romanian government soon expelled Brand, most probably because of his political activities, and he fled to Budapest. Here he married Hansi Hartmann and the couple set up in business together manufacturing gloves. After the German occupation of Poland, the couple became deeply involved with refugee affairs. In 1941, the Brands rescued Hansi's sister and brother-in-law after they had been deported to Ukraine. They had been assisted by a Hungarian intelligence officer called József Krem who, in return for substantial rewards, worked with the Brands over the next few years organising human smuggling operations. The Brands financed all this with profits from their business. When I talked to Daniel Brand, he often spoke of his father's open, gregarious personality and natural talent for making useful friends and keeping them. It is not difficult to imagine him drinking and playing baccarat with German agents if he believed that such dubious 'false friends' helped him to save lives.

Kasztner had a rather different character.[3] Like Brand, he had been born in Transylvania. He had grown up in Kolozsvár, now Cluj-Napocar in Romania, one of the great centres of Jewish culture in the region. While Brand had fled school as a young man, Kasztner was a natural scholar who shone at school and university and forged a professional career as a lawyer and a journalist for the *Új Kelet* (*New East*), the Hungarian Jewish daily paper. Kasztner was very ambitious. His standing in the Jewish world of Kolozsvár rose even higher when he married Elizabeth, the daughter of Dr József Fischer, who was the president of the Jewish community and representative of the Jewish Party in Romania's Chamber of Deputies. Soon after his marriage to Elizabeth, Kasztner was appointed chairman of the party's parliamentary group. He had arrived. Kasztner had a very sharp mind but according to Brand was a 'snobbish intellectual who lack[ed] the common touch'. He was, it was widely agreed even by his closest friends, dictatorial and overbearing; he was jealous of the successes of others. He also had a 'Bohemian' reputation. It is difficult to say precisely what this word meant but Kasztner was evidently a seducer of other men's wives.

Kasztner's rise to power and influence in his hometown came to an abrupt and humiliating end in 1940. Hungary annexed North Transylvania following the Vienna Awards and Kasztner's parliamentary role was extinguished. New antisemitic laws passed by the Hungarian parliament forced the closure of his newspaper. He was, overnight, a nobody. Soon afterwards, Kasztner moved his family to Budapest. Here he made a precarious living as a Zionist fundraiser. Worse was to come. In 1942, Kasztner was drafted into the Labour Service and ordered to the Eastern Front. As we have seen, service in a Jewish labour unit was often tantamount to a death sentence. But in December the unit was discharged; Kasztner never served on the front. There were rumours of bribery and embezzlement that, as Brand recalled, 'hung in the air long afterwards'. Although he was exonerated by a commission that happened to be chaired by his father-in-law, Dr Fischer, Kasztner was fired from his fundraising job. In 2010, Israeli researcher Eli Reichenthal published evidence that Kasztner had indeed used Zionist funds to bribe the Hungarian military authorities. It was a murky affair to be sure, but Kasztner did not save merely his own life but every one of his comrades in the labour unit. What should we choose to remember – the fact that he misused the Zionist funds or that he saved so many lives? Kasztner provoked conflicting judgements to the end of his life. He was, according to Moshe Krausz, a 'megalomaniac' with delusions of grandeur. Sámu Springmann remembered 'a very capable and experienced Zionist of the cold intellectual variety'.

With the exception of Ottó Komoly, the majority of the committee were in some respect outsiders in Hungarian Jewish society. They spoke German more naturally and readily than Hungarian. Most were convinced Zionists who had little in common with the majority Jewish communities in Hungary. Even though the Rescue Committee members were better informed than many other Hungarians about the monstrous scale of the German mass murders of Jews in Poland and the occupied Soviet Union, and suspected that Hitler threatened the safety of every Jew in Europe, it was a formidable challenge to warn an entire community and be believed. The younger generation of Zionists, known as *Halutzim*, paid little heed to these obstacles. They repeatedly and courageously tried to warn Jews in both Budapest and the countryside about the murderous intent that drove the new anti-Jewish measures. Few listened. We should recall that the Jewish community had already been shattered by the Labour Service measures, which had removed so many young men from towns and villages across Hungary.

Brand, Kasztner and the others had come to believe – and believe fervently – that the fate of Jews could be negotiated. They had been persuaded that the mercy of a handful of powerful Germans could be bought; lives could be traded and bartered. Furthermore, the close entanglement of the Rescue Committee leaders with Abwehr agents of uncertain loyalty appeared to show that some anti-Nazi individuals or factions might have the desire and means to obstruct Hitler's murderous plans. In the critical months leading up to the German occupation, the Rescue Committee leaders struggled to grasp the significance of the destruction of the Abwehr and the absorption of many of its agents by the SD. These confounding experiences and misperceptions deeply impacted on the thinking of the Rescue Committee leaders in occupied Hungary. The tortuous and corrosive relationship between Jewish activists and avaricious German agents of the Nazi state was driven by opportunism and evolved through happenstance – but its consequence was the irrevocable disruption of rational norms, making every decision a bad one.

The Plan to Deceive

In an interview published by *Life* magazine in 1960, Adolf Eichmann described his task in Hungary in this matter-of-fact way: 'my basic orders were to ship all Jews out of the country in as short a time as possible. Now, after years of working behind a desk, I had come out into the raw reality of the field.'[4] The acute stress brought on by these 'basic orders' would drive Eichmann, as his recent biographers revealed, to strong drink and uninhibited promiscuity to soothe his demons. He was under enormous pressure from his masters in Berlin. 'Shipping out' hundreds of thousands of people in record time was daunting enough. Himmler and the other SS chieftains such as Kaltenbrunner were preoccupied by the humiliation of the Warsaw Ghetto Uprising and the flight of the Danish Jews. These catastrophes could not be allowed to happen again. The deteriorating military situation in the spring of 1944 aggravated Himmler's anxieties. As Eichmann testified at his trial, Himmler feared that 'as the front came closer', the Soviets would make contact with 'the Jewish masses'. There might be uprisings that would weaken German defences. The German army commanders shared the same fears. Since the attack on the Soviet Union in 1941, the Wehrmacht had frequently encouraged the liquidation of Jewish populations in strategic locations to ensure security. By 1944, as the borders of the Reich shrank inexorably under Soviet assault, Himmler's fears of a Jewish revolt had deepened. Mass murder would need to be managed with the most duplicitous means. For Eichmann, in the 'raw reality of the field', fulfilling his orders depended on subterfuge and deceit.

The campaign of deceit began with the Jewish Council. From as early as 1939, the head of the RSHA, Reinhard Heydrich, stressed the importance of establishing Jewish Councils or Judenrat that would be 'fully responsible for the exact execution of all instructions'. In practice, this meant that the heads of the Judenrat were obligated to keep the peace and to manage selections of their fellow Jews for deportation. They became 'involuntary accessories to German crimes', in Braham's words. The leaders of these Jewish Councils have, even today, left a bitter and divisive historical legacy. In her book about the Eichmann trial, Hannah Arendt wrote: 'To a Jew this role of the Jewish leaders in the destruction of their own people is undoubtedly the darkest chapter of the whole dark story.' She implied that had Jews ignored the instructions of the Councils, many more lives might have been saved. She was not a lone voice. Historian Raul Hilberg described the Councils as 'self-destructive machines'. Historian Yehuda Bauer has led an impassioned defence. Writing of the posthumously excoriated head of the Judenrat in Warsaw, Adam Czerniaków, he writes:

> [his] ordinariness was his most notable characteristic. Yet his diary shows him to be anything but ordinary. His basic decency is striking in a time of unbridled ruthlessness. Not only did he devote every single day to his community, but he particularly cared for the humblest and the weakest among his four hundred thousand wards: the children, the beggars, the insane.[5]

Few modern historians judge the Judenrat leaders as harshly as Arendt.

The leader of the Jewish Council in occupied Hungary was 70-year-old Samu Stern – a successful businessman and a former counsellor of the Hungarian Royal Court. He was chairman of the Jewish Community in Pest and head of the National Bureau of the Jews of Hungary. He was close to the Regent, Admiral Horthy, or imagined himself to be, and had many friends among the Hungarian aristocracy. Even though the Jews of Hungary had been battered by a succession of anti-Jewish laws, Stern remained convinced that he was still a member of the club. He was deluded. After the war, Stern struggled to explain why he accepted the invidious role as head of the Judenrat: 'it would have been a cowardly, unmanly and unjustifiably selfish flight on my part to let down my brethren in the faith during the very instant they were in dire need of being led'. Stern was highly respected. He was also conservative, respectful of authority and obsessive about doing things the right way. He hoped, to begin with, that Horthy could be persuaded to step in and help the Jews: 'that man whom I knew for two decades'. As Stern would soon discover, Jews were in fact perilously isolated in Hungary.

Eichmann's Sonderkommando struck fast. On the morning of Sunday, 19 March, the first day of occupation, Herman Krumey and Dieter Wisliceny appeared at the Jewish community's headquarters at 12 Síp Street and demanded to meet with Stern, who happened to be elsewhere. In his absence, the SS men ordered the community officers to call a meeting for 10 a.m. the next day. When he heard of the SS order, Stern punctiliously consulted the Hungarian Minister of Religious Affairs and Education and was informed in no uncertain terms that, 'The demands of the Germans must be obeyed.' It could not have been clear to Stern and his colleagues that there was already an understanding in place between the German and Hungarian leaders regarding the 'Jewish Question'. They could expect no sympathy from the Minister.[6]

The following morning, the Jewish community leaders returned in a state of great apprehension to Síp Street. Some, fearing the worst, had brought their wives and had valises packed with essential items. A lawyer called János Gábor, who spoke the best German, waited in the entrance for the German party to arrive; he would become the liaison between the SS and the Jewish Council. When Krumey arrived in Stern's office on the third floor of the community headquarters, accompanied by the corpulent Wisliceny, he noticed the packed valises. He smelled fear; for him, it was the odour of power. Smiling obsequiously, he reassured everybody gathered in the cramped little room that there would be no arrests. There would merely be 'certain restrictions' because it was wartime. No one would be deported. No need to pack … A German stenographer arrived shortly afterwards and Krumey began issuing instructions. By noon of the following day, the community must, he insisted, appoint members of a new Jewish Council that would exercise jurisdiction over Jewish affairs subject to the approval of SS-Obersturmbannführer Alfred Trenker, head of the Security Police in Budapest. Krumey was insistently reassuring. No Jew would be harmed; everyone should continue his work. Then Krumey came to the point. The new Council, he demanded, must act to calm the Jewish masses to stem panic. To do this they would publish the right kind of stories in their newspapers and insist that rabbis convey the same soothing message in synagogues. Krumey's performance must have been impressive. One of the community leaders called his wife immediately after the meeting and told her breathlessly, 'everything is all right, the Germans even want to help us'. Eichmann's men were expert deceivers.

With reassurance came tangible favours: the gifts of the powerful. The SS, Krumey explained, would issue 'Immunity Certificates' (Immunitäts-Ausweis) that would exempt members of the Jewish Council from many anti-Jewish measures. These certificates allowed the holder to move freely – a crucial privilege that provoked resentment among Jews who were subject to increasingly vexing measures. It was widely said that the members of the Jewish Council 'separated themselves from the community as a whole'. The SS conferred the same privileges on Brand and Kasztner. In August, the German authorities exempted members of the Council from the obligation to wear the Yellow Star – which intensified criticism from within the Jewish community. At least one member of the Council defied the privilege and chose to openly wear this mark of racial exclusion.

It is always perilous to judge behaviour under terrorist regimes with the unquantifiable benefits of hindsight. When I met Tomi Komoly, Otto's nephew, who has lived in the United Kingdom since 1956, at his home near Manchester he told me: 'they [the Jewish Council] decided poorly because it was impossible to decide well'. In other words, Stern and the other members of the Jewish Council made the wrong decisions in circumstances that made bad decisions unavoidable. Stern insisted later that it would have been 'cowardly' to defy the SS demands. He would be abandoning his community. In one sense, he used the same argument that the Regent had to justify holding the frayed and empty reins of power after the occupation. Horthy claimed that it was morally right to remain 'at the helm'. As Braham concludes, 'the historical fact remains that the members of the Jewish Council … unwittingly and unwillingly cooperated with the Nazis and their Hungarian henchmen'. Stern believed that since Germany faced inevitable defeat, he was buying time by cooperating. What he meant by this was that since the military defeat of Germany was inevitable, it was a matter of fending off the SS until the Allies won.

By the time the fallacy of his argument became evident, as the Germans and their Hungarian collaborators swung into action against the Jews, it was too late. The Germans relied on the Judenrat to reassure Jewish communities throughout Hungary, to issue internment summonses, to requisition Jewish apartments, to distribute the Yellow Star badges, and, finally, to herd Jews into special 'Yellow Star Houses'. As one of the judges at the Eichmann trial declared: 'no matter how the Judenrat acted, they served the interests of the Nazis. Even those who served the interests of the Jewish communities assisted the Nazis.'

The case of Fülöp Freudiger who, it will be recalled, assiduously cultivated SS officer Wisliceny and plied him with chocolates, shows how the SS strategy proved so seductive. By bribing Wisliceny, Freudiger had managed to get his brother released from the detention centre in Rökk-Szilárd Street. Now he told other members of the Jewish Council that: 'I do not believe that we shall suffer the same fate that befell the Polish Jews.

We shall have to give up our wealth, we must be prepared for many sorrows and deprivations, *but I am not worried for our lives*' [my italics].[7]

Eichmann in Auschwitz

Soon after his arrival in Budapest, Adolf Eichmann welcomed an old friend to his offices at the Majestic Hotel. Later, in the evening, he would invite his visitor to his purloined villa in Schwabenberg to relax and to drink. SS-Obersturmbannführer Rudolf Höß was a convicted murderer and a veteran of the SS camp system. After a period serving as a sentry at the Dachau camp, he had risen fast through the KL system. 'I wanted to become notorious for being hard,' he wrote in his memoir, 'so that I would not be considered soft.' In May 1940, Himmler had appointed him commandant of a new camp built on the former Polish border at Oświęcim, south-east of Kattowitz. The chosen site lay at the marshy confluence of two rivers, the Sola and the Vistula, and was infested with insects and prone to flooding. But it lay close to a railway hub and the low, flat landscape where the camps would be constructed permitted the concealment of whatever happened behind the barbed wire perimeters. Auschwitz would become the biggest and, in the summer of 1944, most lethal of the German camps; the word is synonymous with tyranny, terror and the mass murder of more than a million people. Now a symbol of the Holocaust, Auschwitz was in fact three very different camps inside an archipelago of horror: it was a concentration camp, a killing centre and a conglomeration of scores of satellite camps that fed slave workers to the voracious German armaments industry. It was a machine to kill exploit and plunder – and the men and women who ran it became deeply corrupt. Rudolf Höß was one of the most important architects of the Auschwitz system, and he would be hanged inside the camp perimeter on 16 April 1947, just a few hundred yards from the comfortable villa he built for his family. Nikolaus Wachsmann writes: 'For over a million prisoners, Auschwitz was death. For Höß it was life.'[8]

In 1941, Höß began experimenting with a new method of killing Soviet POWs using prussic acid, known by its trade name, Zyklon B. Although Auschwitz is now the most powerful symbol of the Holocaust, the camp was not built to annihilate the Jews. Nor was it ever a single-purpose camp like Treblinka or Sobibór. Even as late as the spring of 1942, Auschwitz was a peripheral camp in the KL world, not yet the 'Capital of the Holocaust'. From May that year, increasing numbers of Jews were deported to the camp. The unfit would be murdered immediately; the survivors worked to death. As the numbers arriving at Auschwitz escalated, Höß began constructing new killing facilities in a birch forest near Birkenau. Himmler was impressed. He now regarded Auschwitz-Birkenau as a key site for the secretive mass murder of Jews brought from all over Europe. Auschwitz would become a world of gas and fire. Himmler and other SS top brass often visited the camp to observe and admire the ceaseless work of the crematoria. Primo Levi wrote that the camp became an inverted factory: in went trains laden with human beings, out came 'the ashes of their bodies, their hair, the gold of their teeth'. Höß was elated: the camp he had raised from the Polish swamp had been given an important new task, 'the solution of the Jewish problem'.

As Auschwitz evolved into a factory of death, Höß often entertained his esteemed colleague and friend Adolf Eichmann at his family home that overlooked his empire of mass murder. Both men were rising managerial stars of the SS hierarchy. Both were pragmatists preoccupied with systems. Eichmann referred to Höß as a 'dear comrade and friend'. He admired the camp commandant's modesty and 'exemplary family life'. During these visits, Eichmann and his friend would work hard inspecting camp facilities or driving to new sites in the flat, marshy landscape that encircled Oświęcim. In the evenings they relaxed in the opulent, wood-lined villa where Höß lived with his family next to the camp. Here a Polish prisoner had created a 'paradise of flowers' for Frau Höß, who enjoyed the services of numerous other camp inmates. At weekends, his four children played happily or swam in the Sola river 'with daddy'. In this perfect bourgeois world, Höß plied his friend with cigarettes and copious volumes of alcohol. The following morning, they tucked into a hearty breakfast before returning to work. Their discussion would focus on the camp's 'capacity': in Eichmann's words, 'how much human material I was planning to send'.

In his post-war testimony, which was published as *Commandant at Auschwitz*, Höß wrote warmly about Eichmann:

Eichmann was a vivacious, active man in his thirties, and always full of energy. He was constantly hatching new plans and perpetually on the lookout for innovations and improvements. He could never rest. He was obsessed with the Jewish question and the order which had been given for its final solution …

He noted that Eichmann was required to make frequent reports to his masters, Himmler and Kaltenbrunner, but 'kept almost everything in his memory. His memoranda consisted a few pieces of paper which he always carried with him, inscribed with signs which were unintelligible to everyone else.'[9]

Höß was a diligent, obedient and efficient manager. He was notoriously hard headed, but he was unwilling or unable to remedy the epidemic of corruption that infested the members of the SS staff at the camp. In 1943, Himmler, who liked to imagine the SS as an incorruptible elite, ordered a special commission headed by Dr Konrad Morgen to investigate abuse in the camps. More than 700 SS men were discharged from active service or put on trial in SS courts. Morgen uncovered massive corruption at Auschwitz. He purged senior staff, many close to Höß, but did not bring the camp commandant himself to account. Instead, he was moved sideways to head a department of the SS Business and Administration Office, the SS-WVHA, the Economic and Administrative Office (SS-Wirtschafts und Verwaltungshauptamt) – which Himmler had established as a kind of 'SS corporation'. SS enterprises depended on the exploitation of slave labour, so it was a logical move for the ambitious Höß. At Auschwitz, he was replaced by another KL veteran, Obersturmbannführer Arthur Liebehenschel who, unknown to his SS masters, was hiding a secret that would turn out to be his undoing.

In the early spring of 1944, as German troops marched into Budapest, Auschwitz was running at reduced capacity. The number of transports to the camp was falling and, in March, the new commandant received orders from Berlin to put off any planned work to expand the camp. When Eichmann visited Auschwitz sometime in late March or early April he was dismayed. As he toured the Birkenau site, he observed neglected crematoria and the incomplete state of a new structure known as the 'Judenrampe'. So Eichmann turned to his old friend. Soon after Eichmann's inspection, Höß was back in charge – and rushing to prepare the camp for the arrival of a huge volume of 'human material'. He immediately made radical changes. Official complaints from the RSHA head Kaltenbrunner as well as Eichmann led to the removal of Liebehenschel. The commandant had, in any case, been exposed in a relationship with a woman who, it was discovered, had once 'consorted' with a Jew. She was a 'race defiler'. On 1 May, Höß cancelled all vacations and leave for SS staff at Auschwitz – and recruited some of the most brutal SS officers in the camp system, such as Josef Kramer and Richard Baer. He accelerated the construction of a new railway branch line to carry trains right into the camp and completed building the 'Judenrampe'. Höß expanded the hated Sonderkommando units – the special squads of Jewish prisoners who were compelled to assist the SS with the gassing process and disposal of corpses. The 'Kanadakommando', which processed valuables stolen from murdered prisoners, was also enlarged. The SS men hoped to reap a rich harvest of plunder from the Hungarian Jews.

In his autobiography, Höß reveals that he 'made three visits to Budapest in order to obtain an estimate of the number of able-bodied Jews that might be expected'. He also mentions that a 'fanatical Zionist leader' tried to persuade Eichmann to exclude any Jews with large families from the transports. He alleges that 'this man had up to date knowledge concerning Auschwitz and the number of transports and the process of selection and extermination'. Was this Zionist leader Kasztner?

Dieter Wisliceny was another participant in the discussions between Eichmann and Höß. In a sworn affidavit made after the war, he revealed:

On numerous occasions, Eichmann told me that Jews had no value as except as laborers and that only 20–25 percent were able to work. I was present in Budapest in June or July 1944 at a meeting between Eichmann and Hoess, Commandant of Auschwitz concentration camp, at which they talked specifically about the percentage of Hungarian Jews that would be strong enough for labor. On the basis of transports previously received at Auschwitz and the supply of Jews inspected by him in collection centers, Hoess stated that only 20 or at the most 25 percent of these Hungarian Jews could be used for labor. Hoess said that this percentage also pertained to all Jews transported to Auschwitz from all over German occupied Europe, with the exception of Greek Jews who were of such poor quality that Eichmann and Hoess said that all Jews unfit for labor were liquidated. Among the able-bodied were women and some children over the age of 12 or 13 years. Both Eichmann and Hoess said that all Jews unfit for labor were liquidated [spellings retained from original document].[10]

When he returned to Auschwitz, Höß, with his long experience of the mechanics of mass murder, immediately realised that the crematoria that comprised dressing halls, gas chambers and furnaces were no longer fit for purpose. He calculated, after his fact-finding visits to Budapest, that many of the Hungarians would be of little use to German industry. At least 75 per cent would have to be murdered and disposed of. This meant that the crematoria needed an urgent overhaul. A Sonderkommando worker called Filip Müller, who survived the camp, recalled:

> Cracks in the brickwork of the ovens were filled with a special fireclay paste. New grates were fitted in the generators, while the six chimneys underwent a thorough inspection and repair, as did the electric fans.

Müller and the other Sonderkommandos repainted 'the walls of the four changing rooms and eight gas chambers …'[11]

Elevators were installed in two of the crematoria to connect the gas chamber with the incineration room; another was equipped with new ventilation fans to accelerate the killing. Höß introduced other efficiencies. Müller describes how 'day and night many hundreds of prisoners were busy laying railways tracks right up to crematoria 2 and 3' and the construction of a 'loading and unloading ramp complete with a three track railway system … to provide a direct link between the death factories, Auschwitz and the outside world.' Müller understood that: 'Quite obviously all these efforts were intended to put the places of extermination into peak condition to guarantee smooth, and continuous, operation.'

Müller observed the return of Höß to Auschwitz at the beginning of May, accompanied by another SS officer, Hauptscharführer Otto Moll. The arrival of the chubby-faced Moll, known to the prisoners as 'Cyclops' because he had a glass eye, filled Müller 'with fear and foreboding'.[12] In the meantime, Eichmann's deputy in Berlin, Rolf Günther, began ordering supplies of Zyklon B from the manufacturer, Degesch. By the end of May, 990kg of the 'Desinfektor' had been supplied to the camp.

In their offices in Berlin, the heads of the SS-WVHA looked forward to reaping huge returns from the new 'Große Aktion'. Whether they worked or were killed, the Hungarian Jews would be stripped of everything they possessed that had not been pocketed by the Hungarians. Yet, like the SS chief Himmler, they abhorred theft by others. At the camp, SS men were required to sign a statement of responsibility regarding their participation in the operation against Hungarian Jews. The statement demanded 'unconditional confidentiality' in the 'swift and smooth' execution of the tasks. 'I am aware,' the document read, 'that should I acquire Jewish property of any sort through unauthorised means, I will be condemned to die.'[13]

By the time the SS men signed this document pledging to carry out mass murder efficiently and honestly, the death camp was ready.

Eichmann Meets the Jewish Council

On 31 March, Eichmann summoned the leaders of the Jewish Council to his headquarters in the Majestic Hotel in Schwabenberg. He delivered one of his most outstanding and deceitful performances. His task was to lie, intimidate and cajole. By the time he stepped in front of the Council, the Hungarians had issued decrees, for example making wearing the Yellow Star compulsory. The police had arrested many Jews in Budapest and incarcerated them in the camp at Kistarcsa. According to the minutes of the meeting, Eichmann began with the practicalities of the Yellow Star. The Jewish Council were responsible for manufacturing at least 3 million of these from 70,000 metres of fabric. The Council should charge 3 pengős per star. Rich Jews could pay for stars for the poor.

Then Eichmann made this statement:

He declared in principle that his major concern was that industrial and war production be expanded … If Jews showed a proper attitude, no harm would befall them … He declared in general that he was no friend of force, and he hoped that things would go well without it … According to his experience so far, violence and executions had occurred only where the Jews took up opposition … But if the Jews understood that he expected only order and discipline from them … not only would they not come to any harm but they would be protected from it …

With great cunning, Eichmann recommended that every Jewish household subscribe to the newspaper *A Magyar Zsidók Lapja*, which must promote the same message that Jews would be protected if they 'behaved'.

At the end of the meeting János Gabor, the Council's liaison with the Germans, rose to his feet. He told Eichmann that his late father had served

Hungary in the Great War. His grandfather had fought the Austrians in 1848. Now he feared that by wearing the Yellow Star he would be attacked and mocked by riffraff in the streets. In the 'moving scene' that followed, Eichmann declared that he would never tolerate the harming of Jews for wearing the Star. If any incident was reported to him, he would 'deal with the attackers'.[14]

The Council leaders seem to have been impressed by Eichmann's crocodile tears. Some it seems were convinced that the community was in safe hands.

In the meantime, Eichmann and Höß brooded over the schedules of deportation. How many trains could Auschwitz accommodate every day? Who would live and who would die?

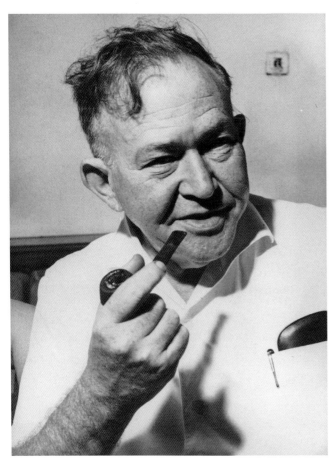

Joel or 'Jeno' Brand, one of the founding members of the Hungarian Va'ada, (Va'adat ha-Ezra ve-ha-Hatzala e-Budapest), or Rescue Committee. Brand flew to Istanbul to negotiate the notorious 'Blood for Trucks' ransom offer that had been instigated by Adolf Eichmann.

Joel Brand's son Daniel, indefatigable defender of his father's work as a rescuer during the Holocaust, at his home in Tel Aviv. (Author's collection)

SS officer Kurt Becher seized this villa on Andrássy Avenue in Budapest as a headquarters to organise the plunder of Hungarian Jewish assets ordered by SS Chief Heinrich Himmler (Author's collection)

The Dohány Street Synagogue in District VII in Budapest is the temple of Hungary's Neolog Jews, this magnificent building was consecrated in September 1859. (Author's collection)

The Dohány Street Synagogue is the largest in Europe with seating for 1,497 men downstairs and 1,472 women on the two upper balconies. (Author's collection)

The Orthodox Kazinczy Street Synagogue in District VII. It is part of a building complex that includes a school and community hall. This beautiful Art Nouveau building was desecrated by the Arrow Cross militias, who used it as a stables in 1944. (Author's collection)

A former admiral, Miklós Horthy was appointed Regent of Hungary in the aftermath of the First World War. He vowed to restore Hungary's pre-war borders stripped away by the Treaty of Trianon. In the chaos that engulfed Hungary at the end of the First World War, Admiral Horthy posed as a national saviour – often riding on a white horse. (Courtesy Robert Speller & Sons)

Admiral Horthy still gazes across Szabadság tér (Liberty Square) in the centre of Budapest.

The propagandist new memorial
erected by the Orbán government
in Szabadság tér (Liberty Square).
It shows 'Hungaria' as an angel
victimised by the Nazi occupiers.
(Author's collection)

Rabbi Michael Dov Weissmandel
was one of the leaders of the Jewish
'Working Group' in Slovakia. He
negotiated with SS officer Dieter
Wisliceny and was convinced that
bribes paid to SS officers led the
Slovakian government to stop
deportations of Jews in 1943.
He was mistaken. (Yad Vashem)

הרב וויסמנדל בשבת 1944 .ג-199/2692

Adolf Eichmann moved into this villa at 13 Apostol Street, appropriated from its Jewish owner, Ascher Lipot, in March 1944. (Sándor Csukás)

Portrait of SS-Obersturmbannführer Adolf Eichmann, specialist in 'Jewish affairs'. (Getty Images)

László Endre and László Baky under arrest after the war; Eichmann had worked closely with them in the Hungarian Interior Ministry. Both were later executed. (Yad Vashem)

Adolf Eichmann relaxing with his son, Horst, in Prague, 1942. (Getty Images)

SS-Hauptsturmführer Franz Novak, the 'Station Master of Death', was a key figure in the Eichmann Sonderkommando. He was responsible for managing and timetabling the railway transports. (Yad Vashem)

Hitler despatched SS-Obersturmbannführer Otto Skorzeny to engineer the removal of Horthy in October 1944. Skorzeny had previously rescued Benito Mussolini from captivity in a daring glider raid. (Bundesarchiv)

The fanatical Austrian
SS-Obergruppenführer Ernst
Kaltenbrunner, who was head of
the RSHA. He took a leading
role initiating the destruction of
Hungarian Jewry. (Getty Images)

Adolf Hitler summoned Miklós
Horthy to the Schloß Klessheim
near Salzburg in Austria in
1944 to forcefully persuade him
to keep Hungary in the Axis.
(Getty Images)

Hitler bids farewell to Horthy. As the Regent travelled back to Budapest, German troops entered Hungary on 19 March 1944. (Getty Images)

A Hungarian Jewish family, wearing compulsory Yellow Stars in the summer of 1944. (Fortepan)

Many thousands of Hungarian Jewish men were conscripted in Labour Service battalions and suffered brutal treatment on the front line. Many thousands did not survive the war.(Fortepan, László Hächter)

Orthodox Jews arriving on the Judenrampe at Auschwitz II–Birkenau. (Fortepan, Lili Jacob)

This photograph clearly shows the process of 'selection'. Behind the SS officers in the foreground, the deportees have been separated into two columns. On one side, men fit for work; on the other women, the elderly and children. The latter will be taken straight to the gas chambers. (Fortepan, Lili Jacob)

26 May 1944: brothers Sril (Israel), who is looking straight at the camera, and Zelig Jákob – both were murdered soon after this picture was taken. (Fortepan, Lili Jacob)

In October 1944, two days after the Szálasi government seized power, Adolf Eichmann returned to Budapest. He now had the opportunity to begin deporting Jews from Budapest. (Bundesarchiv)

Hitler appointed Edmund Veesenmayer as plenipotentiary in Budapest following the German occupation. Veesenmayer was a fanatical antisemite who had spent time in Budapest in 1943 and recommended a radical solution to Hungary's 'Jewish problem': but his colleagues in the SS concluded he was 'too soft'. (Bundesarchiv)

SS-Reichsführer Heinrich Himmler visiting Waffen-SS troops in the autumn of 1944. Himmler remained loyal to Hitler throughout 1944 – and was obsessed with the destruction of European Jewry until the very end of the war. (Bundesarchiv)

Rezső Kasztner with Otto
Komoly, the head of the
Va'ada (Rescue Committee),
in 1944. (Yad Vashem)

Komoly was a First World War
veteran. However, honourable
military service did little to
prevent persecution of Jews in
post-First World War Hungary.
(Tomi Komoly)

Members of the Va'ada Rescue Committee: from left to right: Otto Komoly, Hansi Brand, Rezső Kasztner, unknown man and Peretz Révész.

Kasztner's apartment block in Tel Aviv. He was shot and fatally wounded outside the entrance by a squad of right-wing extremists as he arrived home on the morning of 4 March 1957. (Author's collection)

13

DECEIVING THE RESCUERS

Eichmann and the other members of his Sonderkommando were well informed about the Hungarian Jewish world. This knowledge gave them power. Power to deceive, to manipulate – and to murder. Eichmann could be confident that the leaders of the Jewish Council could be cheated into doing his bidding. But the Germans were aware that the Hungarian Jewish community was not a homogeneous entity and that the Council alone could not be relied on to bridge the different factions. Eichmann was most concerned about the Zionist activists of the Relief and Rescue Committee, the Va'ada. It has been argued that the handful of Zionist Jews who established the Rescue Committee simply did not have the power and means to challenge the SS under German occupation. This is to look at the issue through the wrong end of the telescope. After the Warsaw ghetto uprising and the rebellions in the Reinhardt camps, Himmler and the other SS chieftains had very good reason to fear secretive Jewish cells.

By the spring of 1944, the SS and their Hungarian collaborators knew a great deal about the activities of the Va'ada – and the identity of the most important members of the group. The Va'ada had few secrets thanks to years of interaction with the agents of the Dogwood network and German military intelligence, the Abwehr. Now that SS intelligence, the SD, had reassigned many of the key Abwehr agents in Vienna, Budapest and Istanbul and weeded out any suspected traitors, Himmler and Kaltenbrunner took ownership of a huge volume of intelligence about the activities and characters of the Va'ada committee, what they knew about camps such as

Auschwitz and what they knew of the Final Solution. As described in an earlier chapter, Joel and Hansi Brand had built an extensive network of supporters that extracted thousands of Jews from occupied Poland and smuggled them into Hungary. The Brands' factory and home served as hubs in this highly successful network. Refugees brought with them important information about the fate of Jews in occupied Europe – and the rescue network was also an intelligence highway. Naturally, the SS feared that this knowledge could pose a serious threat to their plans in Hungary.

The SS may also have been aware that at the end of 1943, Brand had tried to persuade the Va'ada leadership to set up an armed unit to be called the Hungarian Haganah, inspired by the Jewish paramilitary organisation in the British Mandate of Palestine. Daringly, he proposed to 'steal weapons left carelessly aside by soldiers in such places as restaurants and barbers' shops' and to carry out raids on 'small police stations and military posts'. He reached out to other armed Jewish movements in Slovakia and the Balkans. Brand, with little support, devoted a lot of time, energy and money to the Haganah project. He and a group of refugees identified strategic targets and even started constructing bunkers and stockpiling food. Secret training exercises were organised. The Jewish Agency in Istanbul approved and donated a substantial sum to assist the Hungarian Haganah. So armed resistance was contemplated by the Va'ada and Brand worked hard to build such a movement. His most intractable problem was weapons. His plan was to arm some 2,000 insurgents but after months of effort, he had managed to build an arsenal of '150 pistols of various ages', '*c.*40 grenades', '3 small carbines and just one serviceable machine gun'. It was this disappointment that made Brand and the other Rescuers vulnerable to the seduction of an alternative strategy to armed resistance – that of negotiation and bribery.[1]

Although Eichmann would have known from Wisliceny about the duplicitous success of the Slovak trick and the 'Europa Plan', he could not be completely confident that the Va'ada could be neutralised in precisely the same way. He was aware that the Warsaw Ghetto Uprising had been fomented by a few hundred young Jewish fighters who ambushed German troops using a tiny cache of guns, grenades and Molotov cocktails. In the aftermath of the Uprising, he had toured the ruins of the ghetto with Jürgen Stroop, the SS commander who had, with difficulty, crushed the action. In his interview with Willem Sassen, Eichmann described seeing 'resistance nests where the fighting had been intense, I had never seen in war such devastation'. Stroop provided Eichmann with a set of photographs that commemorated the destruction of the ghetto and its synagogue. Eichmann told Sassen that he used these images as a travelling salesman would have done 'who sells an article all the more easily by showing a special advertising attraction'. Stroop's photograph collection demonstrated the savage might of the SS but it also conveyed a warning. Later, in the Sassen interview, Eichmann boasted that his boss, Müller, had sent 'the master' (that is, Eichmann) to Budapest 'to be quite sure that the Jews would not rebel'.[2]

It was these concerns that led Eichmann and the members of the Sonderkommando to focus their guile on the leaders of the Va'ada Committee. From Eichmann's point of view, this was an organisation that had acquired a great deal of knowledge about the German treatment of Jews in occupied Europe and might have the motivation and means to provoke resistance. In short, the Rescue Committee could not be disregarded. With this in mind, we can now turn to the events that unfolded after 21 March 1944 that would lead to Brand's calamitous journey to Istanbul. We have a number of archival sources to piece together what happened and why it happened. The most important are Brand's own account to his British interrogators, which can be read in the UK National Archives and *The Kasztner Report: the Report of the Budapest Jewish Rescue Committee, 1942–1945*, which is available in English. These records are not impartial. Both Brand and Kasztner felt compelled, for different reasons, to defend the decisions they made and the actions they took. When he wrote his report, Kasztner was already under attack as a 'collaborator' and Brand was burdened with a punishing sense of having failed in his mission to 'save a million lives'. But cross-referenced with other sources, these documents allow us to follow, encounter by encounter, meeting by meeting how the German trap closed.

On 10 March 1944, as Eichmann was briefing the members of the Sonderkommando at the Mauthausen camp, another meeting was taking place at an elegant restaurant in Budapest. Five days earlier, the former Abwehr agent, Josef Winninger, who was involved with the Dogwood network, had introduced Brand to his commanding officer, Dr Johann Schmidt. Brand described Schmidt as 'an unpleasant, sexual, sadistic, disgusting character'. He must have overcome his revulsion for a second meeting was arranged with the two Germans. So it was that on 10 March, Brand met with Winninger and Schmidt at a 'certain small café'. When the two Austrians appeared at midday, each driving their own cars, they took Brand to the elegant Lukacs Bad restaurant. Schmidt said he had 'various things to tell him officially'. He requested that Brand take detailed notes and send a memorandum, to be approved by Schmidt, to the Jewish Agency in Istanbul. Then the two Germans regaled Brand with an astonishing farrago of lies. They said that a 'difference of opinion between the SS and the Army' (meaning the Abwehr) had been finally resolved 'in favour of the Army'. This meant that there 'should be no further mass executions of Jews'. The Army regarded Jews as 'very important labour power, just as other peoples' – and they would be well treated in 'big camps in Poland'. He demanded that Brand arrange to send additional funds to improve the conditions in the camps. Schmidt went on to say that in Italy, Jews would be 'normally treated' provided a sum of money was provided. Here Brand interjected that Jewish affairs in Italy were handled by 'Switzerland', presumably meaning the 'Joint'. Schmidt then promised to free Gisi Fleischmann, one of the leading members of the Working Group in Slovakia and well known to Brand, who had been held in a prison in Bratislava for some time. Finally, he proposed a simplified way of paying the sums of money: each one of his 'various things' came with a request for money.

It is astonishing that Brand accepted much of what Schmidt claimed at face value. He was, however, sceptical whether this 'disgusting character' could be trusted. He questioned neither the nature of the man nor the veracity of his claims, that the Army (meaning the Abwehr) had defeated the SS and that there would be 'no further executions of Jews'. This was, of course, grotesque nonsense. Nevertheless, Brand's report to the Va'ada committee about the meeting led to a flurry of meetings with Kasztner and others to work out what to say to the Jewish Agency and how to arrange the payments. At another meeting with Winninger, Brand, Kasztner and Otto Komoly discussed Schmidt's offer. According to Brand's account, 'If Schmidt's offer were genuine, it was a wonderful opportunity, but he felt he could not trust Schmidt'. It was decided to fudge the issue by sending *two* reports to the Jewish Agency – one to be sent secretly by courier to Istanbul that described the German offer without requesting funds, the other a false report that would be submitted to Schmidt but not sent. This convoluted response shows that, sceptical though they were, Brand and the Va'ada had been gulled by the tissue of lies spun by Schmidt and Winninger.

At a final meeting of the Va'ada that took place a day before the German occupation, there was another crucial development. According to Brand:

[we] knew from the SCHMIDT Group that the Germans were coming. They knew that a year previously Gisi Fleischmann had undertaken negotiations on behalf of the Jews in SLOVAKIA with Wili von WISLIZENI [*sic*], Hauptsturmführer of the S.D. [*sic*], a relative and confidential friend of Himmler. Since all WISLIZENI'S promises had been kept [*sic*], they asked WININGER [*sic*] to get them in touch with him. WININGER was against this but said he would consult SCHMIDT.

The last sentence is telling. Evidently Schmidt's Abwehr group was hoping that the SS, in the rotund shape of Dieter Wisliceny, could be prevented from appropriating their scheme and its likely rewards. We don't know what Schmidt advised – presumably he urged Winninger to keep Wisliceny away from the negotiations – but it was inevitable that Eichmann and his men would do everything in their power to get a grip on the negotiations with the members of the Rescue Committee.

On 19 March, the Brand household was in turmoil. At that moment, Admiral Horthy was on a train slowly steaming towards Budapest in the unwanted company of the new plenipotentiary Edmund Veesenmayer and the RSHA chief Kaltenbrunner. German troops had begun to cross the Austrian border into Hungary. That spring, the Brands had accommodated hundreds of Slovakian refugees in their home, and as Daniel Brand informed me when I interviewed him in Tel Aviv, 'it needed fumigating'. So Hansi took her two sons across the Danube to Buda and paid for a room at the Majestic Hotel. Joel himself had taken refuge in a second house rented by the Brands. At 9 a.m. on the morning of the invasion, Winninger, who knew of this second address, arrived at the front door and told Brand he must come with him immediately. He was not being arrested but placed in 'protective custody'. He left a note for Hansi and was driven to Schmidt's office. 'The SS or Army know your address, they will arrest you,' Brand was told. He wished only to protect him. Schmidt was, for his own devious reasons, telling the truth. Some 3,000 Jews and other suspect Hungarians were rounded up and arrested in the first days of the occupation. Brand's name may well have been on lists of suspects that had been prepared by the planners of Operation

Margarethe. Schmidt's real motivations became evident soon enough. He insisted that Brand hand over any money he had brought, promising to return it later. Brand asked permission to telephone Kasztner – and urged him to keep calm. He asked his friend to stay at Brand's home 'since Mrs Brand would be alone with her two children'. Schmidt and Winninger then drove Brand to an apartment rented by Rudi Scholz – who, it will be recalled, was another Abwehr agent involved with the Dogwood network.

There is another important point that becomes clear in the detailed account Brand gave to his interrogators. When he suggested that Kasztner too should be offered protective custody, Schmidt informed him that his friend was 'not so important'. So it would seem that on the German side, Brand and not Kasztner had been marked out as the key contact in the Va'ada committee. This may simply have been because Brand spoke the best German and took the lead at the meetings with Winninger and Schmidt. Whatever the reason, Brand would become the most important liaison with the Germans until his departure to Istanbul. During his incarceration at Scholz's apartment, Brand finally realised that it was the Abwehr group that had been quashed by the SS not the other way around. This was a shattering revelation – and he decided to try and make contact with Wisliceny.

On Wednesday, a few days after German troops entered Budapest, Brand persuaded Winninger to release him from custody. Once home, Brand called a meeting of the Rescue Committee to thrash out what to do in the changed circumstances he had discovered during his days in 'protective custody'. The other committee members agreed with his proposal to contact Wisliceny by offering Winninger a 'large sum of money'. The convoluted relations between the various Germans must have been bewildering. It is important to note that, according to Brand's report, the committee also agreed to 'redouble their illegal work' to get Jews out of Hungary, to produce more false identity papers *and to obtain arms*.

Brand continued to deal with the 'unpleasant, sexual, sadistic, disgusting' Winninger. This made sense because the former Abwehr agents who now acted for the SD offered the only direct access to the SS and Wisliceny. It would be wrong to judge Brand for not completely seeing through the new order of affairs. In fact, the reorganisation of the Abwehr under Kaltenbrunner's RSHA would not be fully completed for some time. Relations between former Abwehr agents like Schmidt and their new SS colleagues remained strained but fluid. The rescuers were caught in an unequal power struggle between different German agencies. For Schmidt, Brand and the other Va'ada committee members were assets that he hoped to retain.

The Onslaught

The German blitzkrieg against the Hungarian Jews began immediately after the occupation. The arrival of the German troops had appeared rather low key. The new measures that fell on the Jews were anything but …

German heavy hitters Veesenmayer and Kaltenbrunner, who escorted Horthy when he returned, humiliated, to Budapest, wasted little time. In a matter of days, they could assure Hitler that the new Hungarian government they had imposed, led by Prime Minister Döme Sztójay, would unleash a savage anti-Jewish campaign with immediate effect. Among the Hungarians, there was no debate or hesitation. For the new state secretary at the Ministry of the Interior, László Endre, the radical new policies were not mere duplicates of German examples but the culmination of the Hungarian struggle against the 'Jewish enemy' that had been incubated over a quarter of a century. Just a few days after Sztójay took office, the government issued a decree ordering Jews over the age of 6 to wear 'a canary yellow, six-pointed star'.[3] In the following weeks, a barrage of further decrees pushed Hungarian Jews to the margins of society and then beyond. They were banned from restaurants and beaches; food rations were reduced; radios and bicycles had to be handed in to restrict the flow of information. Travel for Jews was severely restricted – and the unending flow of decrees stripped Jews of moveable property and real estate. Between March and August 1944, the Sztójay government issued more than 100 anti-Jewish decrees. Stigmatisation with the Yellow Star was a step to social isolation.

Next came ghettoisation. On 7 April, representatives of the German and Hungarian governments assembled to work on the managerial details. Present at the meeting were the state secretaries Endre and László Baky, their new friend Adolf Eichmann and representatives of the Hungarian army. They issued Confidential Decree No. 6163/1944, which explicitly stated that:

The Hungarian Royal government will within a short period of time cleanse the country of Jews. I order the cleansing by regions, as a result of which the Jews, regardless of sex and age, will have to be transported to designated collection camps ... The collection of the Jews will be conducted by the police with regional authority and the Hungarian royal gendarmerie ... The German police will be present on the scene as an advisory agency ...

On 16 April, Hungarian authorities began rounding up and 'collecting' the Jewish population of the north-eastern part of the country. 'Collection camps' were established in mills, barns, brick factories and pig sties.[4]

As the Sztójay government began issuing the first anti-Jewish decrees following the German occupation, Brand, Kasztner and the other members of the Va'ada committee became preoccupied with getting a meeting with Wisliceny. They pinned enormous hopes on the man who had, as they believed, halted the deportations in Slovakia. As described, the first contact with Wisliceny was made not by Brand but by Jewish Council leader Fülöp Freudiger, who had boldly approached Wisliceny at the Astoria Hotel, where the SS had set up a temporary headquarters, to secure the release of his brother, Sámuel. Like many other members of the Jewish community in Budapest, Freudiger had been gulled by the story of the bribe paid to Wisliceny by Rabbi Weissmandel. He had no doubt, like so many other Jews, that Wisliceny was amenable to bartering – and so it proved. Sámuel was released.

Wisliceny had arrived in Budapest with the Sonderkommando on 19 March. He was an important member of Eichmann's group. It was he, along with Krumey, who had met with Jewish leaders soon after the occupation began and ordered them to set up the Judenrat. Wisliceny played the role of an avuncular bon vivant very well – and was aware of his reputation as a genial soft touch. He would now exploit that false front to run rings around the Hungarian Jews. His actions in that first week of the occupation show how Wisliceny performed his fatal role. On 23 March, he rushed to Bratislava, where he obtained the codex of antisemitic legislation that the SS had used to legalise the deportation of tens of thousands of Slovak Jews to their deaths and would now be recycled in Hungary. The SS would have wanted the codex to make sure that all the requisite laws were passed and that the legislation met the requirements of the Nazis and not just the Hungarians. Wisliceny had another task in Bratislava. As the

SS Sonderkommando set to work in Budapest, Wisliceny paid a visit to Rabbi Weissmandel.

According to Weissmandel's autobiography: '[Wisliceny] said that he found that Friediger [*sic*] was the only person receptive enough for this [dealing], but he still found the bargaining very slow and suspicious … If we did not expedite matters, not only would the 320,000 [Jews] from east of the Tisa River [in Hungary] be lost, but we would lose everything'. Wisliceny persuaded Weissmandel to write a letter to leading members of the Jewish community in Hungary stating his view that 'von Wisliceny was the saviour of the Slovakian Jews and was well disposed towards them. We [Hungarian Jews] should trust him completely and fulfil his wishes.'[5] The letter, which was almost certainly dictated by Wisliceny, was the opening move in the SS plot to ensnare the Jewish rescuers.

Back in Budapest, Wisliceny called Freudiger to a meeting. In his memoir, Freudiger described what happened next:

[Wisliceny] closed the door and told me to sit down … He told me: 'I have a letter for you, read it!' It was a letter from Rabbi Weissmandel of blessed memory. It was written in Hebrew and was a short letter. He wrote to me that 'finally fate has caught up with Hungarian Jewry' … this was a letter expressing confidence in Wisliceny that we could negotiate with him … Wisliceny asked me… 'Did you understand?' 'Yes.' 'Return the letter to me,' he said … He tore it into small pieces and threw it into the stove … 'What do you have to say to this letter?' I answered: 'I am at your disposal.' He told me: 'From now on we need all the money arriving from abroad.'[6]

There is a remarkable twist in the story of the letter. Remember that Weissmandel was a man of high integrity and acute intelligence. By the time Wisliceny came calling that spring, the rabbi had few illusions left about the good faith of the apparently genial German SS man: Wisliceny should not be trusted. Weissmandel decided, as he describes in his autobiography, to write a second, secret letter *in Hebrew* warning about the grave perils of negotiating with the Germans. In his autobiography he described the contents of this secret letter:

I described the new developments and warned them that the Germans' plan may have been formulated to lull us into a false sense of security.

We had to make great efforts to tell the Jews in these districts [he was referring to Subcarpathia] that they were slated for murder, and to warn them not to enter the ghetto, even under threat, and that they should rather be killed than transgress [he meant disobey German orders] … I wrote that they should make great efforts to escape from there while there was still time …

Weissmandel also set a test. He explained that: 'the killing began with the gathering of everyone into a ghetto'. In other words, ghettoisation was not an end in itself but a preparatory stage in mass deportation. If the Germans discussed negotiations but at the same time began herding Jews into ghettos, it was definitive proof of their bad faith.

In his account of the episode, Freudiger admits that he had some difficulty deciphering Weissmandel's secret letter but, nevertheless, passed on its troubling message to members of the Jewish Council and the Va'ada committee. But Weissmandel's warning had little or no impact. The gathering momentum of negotiations in preference to any other strategy swept away all doubts. Why?

It is possible that Freudiger made a poor job of conveying Weissmandel's secret message. Neither Brand nor Kasztner spoke Hebrew. Another reason is that the pivotal shift to a strategy of negotiation reflected the increasing dominance of Kasztner over other members of the Rescue Committee. In the confusing aftermath of Brand's meeting with Winninger and Schmidt, different options had been put on the table, including organising armed resistance. Under pressure from Kasztner, the committee had already begun to shift towards the negotiations option. Now the tantalising possibility of meeting a senior officer in the Eichmann Sonderkommando, namely Wisliceny, together with the reassuring message from Rabbi Weissmandel slammed shut the door on every strategy except negotiation. Kasztner had prevailed. This was the moment when, by falling for the German bait, Kasztner led his colleagues towards calamity and humiliation. His intent was not criminal as Bogdanor argues. Instead he was tempted, in my view, by the chance to dominate the Rescue Committee and to seize the baton from the Brands. He had come to believe that he alone possessed the intellectual and personal qualities to successfully barter with agents of the Nazi state – unscrupulous men who claimed to possess power over life and death.

Now Kasztner sent a message to Schmidt that the Va'ada wanted to meet with Wisliceny. This offer from an illegal organisation was discussed by Eichmann and the Sonderkommando leaders and a swift decision was made to agree to a meeting. This was, of course, *their game*. Wisliceny's visit to Rabbi Weissmandel and the letter of recommendation baited the line. The Zionists, members of an illegal organisation, had swum to the surface and bitten.

In the following weeks, a macabre charade was performed that would prove to be very lucrative for the former Abwehr agents and their SS masters. Brand's report reveals that the Va'ada offered Schmidt and Winninger US$20,000 to facilitate the meeting and 'maintain the status quo'. What he seems to have meant by this phrase was that there should be agreement to halt the hitherto low-level harassment and persecution of Hungarian Jews. At that moment, the German and Hungarian authorities were spewing out a barrage of anti-Jewish measures. As well as the fees demanded by Schmidt and Winninger, Wisliceny himself demanded US$200,000 for his time. His motivation was greed, but he knew from his experience in Slovakia that demands for large sums in American dollars would be almost impossible to fulfil and have the effect of tying up the Jewish organisations in desperate appeals to Jewish organisations outside Hungary.

On the same day that Hungarian Jews were required to wear the Yellow Star for the first time, the long-anticipated meeting with 'Willi' took place. Brand and Kasztner arrived at Winninger's apartment – where Schmidt introduced them to the corpulent Wisliceny, who, Brand recalled, was 'too fat to sit in a chair'. The meeting seems to have been attended by a shady cast of other characters such as Dr Sedlaczek, the former dentist and Dogwood courier. Also present was a Gestapo/SD officer called Erich Klausnitzer.[7] Once half of the money demanded by the Germans had been handed over, Kasztner asked Wisliceny directly what the Va'ada could do to persuade the SS not to carry out its plans to set up ghettos and deport Jews. Wisliceny replied that although Jews would have to wear the Yellow Star, no deportations would take place 'unless the Hungarians appealed directly to Berlin over the head of the Sonderkommando'. He was implying that it was the new Hungarian government not the SS that was demanding that Jews should be deported. There was a murky semi-truth behind Wisliceny's claim: the new Prime Minister, Döme Sztójay, and his Interior Minister,

Andor Jaross, were fanatical antisemites who were already plotting to rid Hungary of its Jews. Wisliceny's devious equivocation seemed to offer an opening. Brand demanded an end to executions, no further deportations, no further concentration of Jews in special areas and that 'permission to emigrate should be granted'. Wisliceny's replies to Brand's demands beggar belief. The SS officer agreed to every one of the requests – only querying the last about emigration. When Brand tentatively suggested that there might be just a few hundred emigrants, Wisliceny scoffed that he was only interested in 'large-scale emigration' – say 10,000 or why not 100,000? Wisliceny then came up with a caveat that should have set off the shrillest of alarms. Years later, Brand testified at the Eichmann trial as follows:

Q. What about the fourth point concerning Aliyah and emigration?
A. His answer in regard to this was very strange: He was opposed to removal by us of small groups of Jews from Hungary, because in that case we would remove the rich, the leadership, and he would be left with the rest. He was opposed to this. However, we should work out a plan for the evacuation of all of Hungarian Jewry. Such a plan had a chance of being accepted by his superiors.
Q. And what about emigration to Palestine?
A. He delivered another lecture to the effect that an agreement between the Mufti [Haj Amin al-Husseini, the Grand Mufti of Jerusalem] and the Nazis existed, and that an exodus to Palestine was out of the question. We should seek out areas like North Africa, North America, Australia, South America, and such places … Of course, if they subsequently went from North Africa to Palestine, then it was no longer any concern of his …
A. Wisliceny demanded a list of names [as candidates for emigration] and again delivered a lecture to us in which he said that *he could not sell Hungarian Jews directly from Hungary. They would have to be brought to German-occupied territory first, become German merchandise, and then they could be delivered* … [my italics]
Q. Did he actually say: 'German merchandise?'
A. Yes, merchandise, German merchandise. It sounded very ominous to us.
Q. Mr Brand, did you pay Wisliceny money as a result of this discussion?
A. Yes, indeed. Although Wisliceny said that he could not accept our terms, that 2 million dollars would certainly be too little, first he would

have to get instructions from his superiors; but initially we would have to pay the first instalment of 200,000 dollars. In this way, he said, the business connections between us would be inaugurated.[8]

There you have it. In order for the lives of Hungarian Jews to be bartered, they would have to be deported from Hungary into Reich territory to 'make the bodies into German goods'. This demand was not merely 'ominous', it showed that the negotiations were utterly bogus. *To stop the deportation of Hungarian Jews, the Va'ada negotiators would have to agree to the deportation of Hungarian Jews.* It was an Alice in Wonderland stipulation that should have ended any further negotiation there and then.

The grotesque charade continued at a second meeting with Wisliceny a few days later.[9] Now that negotiations had begun, the SS offered the Va'ada leaders a number of 'Certificates of Immunity'. These conferred on Brand, Kasztner and the others privileges above and beyond even those enjoyed by the Jewish Council. Unlike members of the Jewish Council, Brand and Kasztner could use their own telephones and cars and were not required to wear the Yellow Star. According to Freudiger's memoir, Stern was upset about this and wanted to protest to Krumey, but Freudiger dissuaded him. Stern pointed out that the thousands of Jews who came daily to the Jewish Council headquarters wearing their Yellow Stars would be distressed if the Council leaders did not have to suffer the same burden. It was Brand who had requested the certificates hoping that he would be able to make contact with the Jewish communities in the provinces. As it turned out, the Germans offered freedom of movement outside Budapest to Kasztner alone. Thanks to the SS, Kasztner would make a number of controversial visits to his home town of Kolozsvár in the next weeks. Why did the SS officers treat Kasztner and Brand so differently? It is impossible to say for certain. Had they noticed that Kasztner was more receptive to the allure of power and hence more malleable? This was certainly Brand's view. In his book *Satan and the Soul*, published in Hebrew in 1960, he spoke of his late friend: 'He loved to be elected president or vice-president of any organisation, he lusted for honour and tribute. To a certain extent he had the character of an English lord. He loved to be in the presence of intellectuals and important persons.'[10]

★★★

At the same meeting, Brand and Kasztner handed over another instalment of funds. Again, the Germans demanded more. This time, Brand remonstrated with Wisliceny that he had not kept his promise: he had information that Jews were now being rounded up. Wisliceny said he would 'find out'. When Brand brought up emigration again, Wisliceny again insisted that any Jews leaving Hungary could not go to Palestine but to 'Africa i.e. west of Tunis and S. America'.

At the third meeting with the SS that took place on or around 12 April, Wisliceny failed to turn up. The former Abwehr agents Schmidt and Winninger were present but this time the money was handed over to SS officers Krumey and Hunsche. Arranging these payments had been very difficult. The money had been begged from the Jewish Council and taken out of the Va'ada's own funds. Brand had poured his own money into the rescue network and now put everything he could spare towards bribing the Germans.

By now news had reached the Jewish Council and the Rescue Committee that large number of Jews were already being rounded up in Subcarpathia and other districts in the north-east of Hungary. This was very troubling. When Brand pressed the SS men at the meeting to explain why this was happening, Krumey was evasive: he would have to discuss the matter with Wisliceny, but he was in Berlin and could not be expected to respond immediately. This was an insolent falsehood. Wisliceny was nowhere near Berlin and, in any case, Krumey was Wisliceny's superior officer; he would not need to confer with his subordinate. The truth is that Eichmann had ordered Wisliceny to travel to Munkács, in north-east Hungary, to prepare for the round-up and internment of Jews.

Krumey was lying. Outrageously. But he must have put on a convincing performance. In his Report, Kasztner wrote that:

Krumey's appearance [he was a senior member of the Eichmann commando] was another indication that the sums we handed over would not be used for bribing individuals. On the German side, the negotiations were undertaken officially. This suited our wishes too. The operation could not be based on individual bribes ...

He was right in one sense but misguided in every other. The negotiations were indeed 'official' and Eichmann knew all about what was taking place, but his intent was not to offer any concessions to the Va'ada but to distract attention from the first phase of deportations.

The Germans used another tactic to focus the Rescue Committee's attention on the process of barter rather than the gathering momentum of persecution. At another meeting with Krumey and Hunsche, Kasztner handed over another instalment of the sum originally agreed with Wisliceny. 'We were still short of a million [pengős],' Kasztner wrote. He went on: 'Hunsche was particularly furious. Krumey threatened to break off negotiations. After great efforts, a new appointment was made'. This was a textbook case of manipulative bullying. The Germans possessed all the power. They expressed anger and disappointment with the behaviour of the weaker side, Kasztner – who came to believe that the worst possible option was that the Germans withdraw from the negotiations. They felt compelled to plead for talks to continue … and the snare tightened.

At the same meeting, Krumey and Hunsche played another card. The deportations, Krumey informed Kasztner, had been organised to please the Hungarian government: 'the appearance of deportation must be maintained' because the Hungarians would be provoked by any sign that the Germans were prepared to compromise by permitting some Jews to emigrate. Kasztner then offered to request permission for emigration from contacts in the Interior Ministry – but the SS men 'protested most energetically'. 'This operation [i.e. the negotiations] is a Reich secret,' insisted Krumey. Here we get a glimpse of a genuine conflict between the German occupiers and the Hungarian government. The SS did not want anyone on the Hungarian side to get wind of the sums of money that were changing hands at meetings with the Va'ada. At the very same time that Krumey and Hunsche were relieving the Va'ada of funds, an SS officer called Kurt Becher, who will become increasingly significant in this story, was hard at work plundering the huge Weiss-Manfréd manufacturing conglomerate on behalf of SS chief Himmler. This brazen case of SS corporate theft had to be pulled off behind the backs of Hungarian ministers.

When Krumey and Hunsche had left the apartment, Schmidt informed Kasztner that the Hungarian State Secretary, Endre, was determined to remove every Jew from Hungarian soil – and that a plan for the deportation of hundreds of thousands was already a 'settled matter'. It is hard to imagine a more egregious example of blackmail. Schmidt went on: German help could be counted on only if sufficient funds were available: 'you can't pay even this insignificant advance, so who's going to believe that you'll be able to pay the two million dollars? And what is two million dollars? Do you know how much more the Weiss-Manfréd company is paying to rescue just a few people?' For Schmidt and Winninger, money, above all, was the allure. But for the SS, blackmail had a less tangible but even more poisonous aim, which was to distract and deceive. For in far-away regions of Hungary, the German plan for the liquidation of the nation's Jews was already in hand.

By mid April, the Jewish Council knew a great deal about the events unfolding in the Hungarian provinces. Freudiger tells us that on 16 April, he was approached by the rabbi and lawyer Dr Imre Reiner, the head of the Judicial Department of the Council, who was 'in great agitation'. He had news from his home town of Nyíregyháza, which is situated in the north-east of Hungary, that during the night the gendarmerie and local officials (Braham points out that the mayor was a 'rabid antisemite') had ordered Jews to leave their homes within a few hours and move to a few streets in the city. They were permitted to take just one suitcase per person and leave behind everything else. Reiner had no doubt that the insidious process of incarcerating Jews in ghettos had begun.

He urged Freudiger to, 'Go to Krumey and try to do something about this'. In the end, both Reiner and Freudiger went to the SS headquarters at the Majestic Hotel. They discovered that Krumey was away from his office – but as they waited in the corridor, Eichmann strutted past. 'What are the handsome ones doing here?' he demanded. They explained that they hoped to meet Krumey – and Reiner blurted out the news he had received from his family in Nyíregyháza. Eichmann led the two men into his office. A map of Hungary took up most of one of the walls. Now a remarkable exchange took place. Eichmann gestured at the map: 'I have ordered the concentration of the Jews in the area of the 8th Army Corps. This is border territory: over these mountains are the Russians and unreliable elements cannot be allowed to move around freely, that is clear. It concerns 310,000 Jews.' Freudiger protested: 'Nyíregyháza is 300 miles from the border!' Eichmann told him to take the matter up with 'your Hungarians' who had assigned the district as a border region. Eichmann pushed the discussion in a different direction: it is up to you, he went on, meaning the Jewish Council, to guard against epidemics: 'The rest will be alright.' Dr Reiner protested that it would be impossible to ensure hygiene because the Jews had been allocated one square metre each in the new houses. 'Shut up with the Greulpropaganda [atrocity propaganda]!'

bellowed Eichmann, 'Where did you get this from?' Reiner replied: 'Because my 90-year-old parents were herded in this manner.' At this moment, Krumey entered the room. Eichmann ordered him to release 'first-degree relatives' of any Jewish Council members in Nyíregyháza. After wrangling about the definition of 'first-degree relatives', Reiner and Freudiger agreed to submit a list of names and addresses. When they returned to Síp Street later that day, the Council debated at length who should be on the list. It was a cruel distraction – as Eichmann had intended. As Freudiger describes, further humiliations followed as the rounding up of Hungarian Jews gathered pace. They begged for a meeting with Endre, the infamous 'Jew eater' – when this request was finally granted, the entire Council turned up at the Ministry. 'We saw Endre coming towards us on the staircase with hat and gloves. In passing, he told us that his secretary would receive us.'[11]

The members of the Jewish Council who were compelled to play their part in the ghettoisation process were horrified by its realities. On 26 April, Stern sent a letter to Jaross that, despite its obsequious tone of address, reveals the terrible despoliation of the Jewish communities in the north-eastern districts. In Ung County, the letter describes Jews:

> placed in a brick factory and in a lumber yard … The number of Jews currently crowded in the brick factory and in the lumber yard is esti-mated at 20,000, who are camped outdoors, exposed to the vicissitudes of the weather. Their daily nourishment is one decilitre of soup. Bringing in food is prohibited. There is a water shortage in the area.

These stark facts reveal experiences of severe deprivation, which Stern emphasises throughout his letter. All over the district, tens of thousands of Jews had been herded into brick factories, pig sties, dilapidated apartments or tiny synagogues with the most parsimonious supplies of water and food.

The letter and other appeals like this one reveal something else. The Council members appear to have concluded that the horrors unfolding far away from Budapest were somehow out of the control of the German and Hungarian authorities. To some degree, this was true. The gendarmerie was in charge; some officers were simply more sadistic than others. The Council members appealed to Jaross and Eichmann and others to make improvements to how Jews were being treated. This is understandable, but Stern and many of the Jewish Council leaders were hoodwinked and outmanoeuvred by an apparatus of mass murder that had developed refined techniques of subterfuge. The perpetrators were, it might be said, the first Holocaust deniers.

Jews in other districts that had yet to be ravaged by ghettoisation were also taken in by sophisticated German ploys. This is revealed in two reports written by Eberhard von Thadden of the German Foreign Office, who visited Budapest in May. He noted that many Hungarian Jews 'remained calm'. The reason was, he suggested, that Jewish Council announcements, which were editorialised by the Germans, emphasised that ghettoisation measures *'applied only to Jews of the eastern areas who had been preserving their Jewish peculiarities.'*

The End of the Beginning

I have devoted quite a few pages to the first phase of the negotiations between the agents of the SS and the Va'ada. So far Eichmann had not been directly involved. This is not to say he was unaware of what was taking place at the meetings in Winninger's apartment. Far from it. It was Eichmann who approved Wisliceny's visit to Bratislava to acquire the legal codex and to secure Rabbi Weissmandel's apparent approval for negotiations. Although there is no paper trail to prove this, Eichmann would have needed to seek the approval of Himmler, Müller and Kaltenbrunner, his masters in Berlin. Himmler may well have informed Hitler. He had no reason to be secretive – playing games with Jews was a moral norm. Deceiving Jewish organisations and extorting money fitted with Nazi war plans. Since the German motivations for the occupation of Hungary embraced plundering its economy and labour recourses for the Reich, Eichmann's schemes chimed with Hitler's broader strategies. For Himmler, the occupation of Hungary offered new opportunities to aggrandise the power and status of the SS through mass murder and financial skulduggery.

The Va'ada rescuers now took an unwitting role in the final liquidation of the Abwehr. Since 1943, the rescuers had been drawn into the convoluted web of agents and couriers tied to the Dogwood network and run by rogue Abwehr officers. At the beginning of 1944, Hitler had lost patience with Admiral Canaris and his intelligence network, which had been ingested by Walter Schellenberg's SD. In the first weeks of the

German occupation of Hungary, Brand and Kasztner continued to meet with former Abwehr agents such as Schmidt and Winninger. It was they who had arranged the first meetings with Wisliceny. Then at the end of April, a new cast emerged from the wings to take the stage. Its leading players were 'Bandi' Grosz and an enigmatic SD officer who we have already encountered called Fritz Laufer.

As Brand recalled at the Eichmann trial:

> On one occasion Bandi [Grosz] arranged for me to be taken by this Laufer … to a small house outside Budapest; [he] lived there. Klausnitzer was also present. There I was treated to a lengthy lecture, during which I got coffee and cake. I was told that only through Eichmann's offer could the Jews be rescued, that Himmler wanted this to happen, that Himmler was really a decent human being; Himmler no longer wants the Jews to be executed, and it was our chance now to rescue the residue of Jewry that still remained.

This was the very same Fritz Laufer who had compromised the Dogwood network. As 'Iris', Laufer had won the blind trust of Alfred Schwarz ('Dogwood') and the Jewish Agency in Istanbul, while at the same time betraying their secrets to German intelligence.[12] When he was interrogated in Cairo in the summer of 1944, Grosz informed the British that Hungarian intelligence had warned him that, 'Laufer was a Czech immigrant, alias Ludwig Meyer and a first-class German agent.' The SD officer Erich Klausnitzer, who had been present at the first meeting with Wisliceny, was his boss. It is also highly significant that in the aftermath of the German occupation Grosz had, for his own reasons, aligned himself with the Gestapo.

In the tranquil setting of the little villa on the outskirts of Budapest, Laufer was, Brand recalled, 'very friendly and a gentleman'. Laufer now spun a shimmering web of lies.[13] He assured Brand that the SS wanted to conduct 'decent, clean business'; the SS could be 'severe and even cruel', 'but they always kept their word'. He acknowledged that Brand had been deceived and swindled by Schmidt, Winninger and the others. His friends in the SS were 'pure and decent'. Brand thanked Laufer for his 'humanity and kindness'. He was rewarded with lurid stories about Schmidt and Winninger's repellent sexual proclivities and fondness for money. He claimed that the suitcases of money Brand had handed over to Schmidt and Winninger had 'slipped into' their own pockets. Laufer's gentlemanly manners and candour seem to have won over Brand.

On the drive back to Budapest, Grosz made a revealing remark. He said that Laufer had once been his 'opponent' and had wanted to 'put a rope round his neck'. Now they 'knew each other quite well and were good friends': he had come to realise that the SS was 'pure and decent'. It need hardly be said that Brand was being drawn ever deeper into the complex web of German intrigue. In the OSS report discussed earlier that referred to the 'Schmidt Group' extorting money from Brand and Kasztner, there is another clue: 'Finally, they [the Schmidt group] were stopped by IRIS (FRIEDRICH [sic] LAUFER) of the S.D., who wanted to make use of BRAND and KASTNER [sic] and who also wanted to prove the S.D.'s authority over Abwehr personnel'.

Following this first encounter, Brand and Kasztner had a number of convivial encounters with Laufer in Budapest. Laufer tapped them for information about their dealings with the 'Schmidt Group'. As Brand and Kasztner's bond with the SS deepened, relations with the former Abwehr agents became acrimonious. Kasztner's Report reveals what happened next. On the evening of 10 May, Gestapo agents turned up at Kasztner's boarding house. He was driven to the office of Gerhard Clages, who was head of the Gestapo intelligence service. He was questioned by SS lawyers about his relations with József Garzoly, the head of Hungarian counter-intelligence. They accused him of informing the Hungarians about the negotiations with the SS. Kasztner suspects Grosz was behind this accusation. Kasztner was held overnight at the SS headquarters. He knew Garzoly well and was, as a consequence, in a troubled state of mind. According to Brand, Laufer now demanded that Kasztner provide a typed list of allegations against the 'Schmidt Group'. He readily complied. The following day, the Gestapo arrested Schmidt, Winninger, Scholz and Dr Sedlaczek. The SD was hard at work digesting its old rivals.[14]

It was at this turbulent moment that Adolf Eichmann sent for Joel Brand.

14

AGENTS OF DECEIT

In mid April 1944, the German occupation of Hungary was a month old. The enormous task of imposing a German solution to resolve Hungary's 'Jewish problem' was about to enter its first crisis – and Adolf Eichmann would adroitly turn an outbreak of ministerial bickering to his advantage.[1]

By then, the concentration of Jews in provincial ghettos was already under way but without agreement on a final objective. There had been bickering between the German Foreign Office and the SS. Veesenmayer and his advisors were reluctant to overturn the agreement struck with Horthy in March to deport 100,000 able-bodied Jews for labour in the Reich. Backed by Himmler, the RSHA head Kaltenbrunner aggressively demanded a more radical solution to the Hungarian problem. On the Hungarian side, radical antisemites in the Ministry of the Interior, László Endre and László Baky, advocated complete removal of all Jews from Hungarian soil. The radicals won. But as conditions in the rural ghettos deteriorated, liberal Hungarians discovered what was happening and launched a barrage of criticism at Andor Jaross, the pro-Nazi Interior Minister. In faraway Máramarossziget, the local gendarmerie commander demanded a meeting with Wisliceny, who was then based in Munkács supervising the ghettoisation in Carpatho-Ruthenia. The Hungarian complained bitterly about the inadequate space and insanitary conditions in the hastily improvised ghettos. His concerns were not in any sense humanitarian: he demanded that the Germans remove the Jews to Western Hungary or to Germany. Wisliceny, accompanied by a cohort of gendarmerie commanders, sped to Budapest to raise the alarm with Eichmann.

Eichmann realised that there was a crisis of responsibility – and it had to be solved. On 14 April, Eichmann, accompanied by the SS elite Otto Hunsche, Franz Novak and Wisliceny, arrived at Baky's office in the Ministry of the Interior to discuss a solution to the crisis. Endre complained that the Hungarian police alone could not 'support' the ghettos, nor could they singlehandedly organise large-scale deportations. This was a cue for Eichmann to take the lead. He offered to assume complete responsibility for all issues and problems arising from the deportation of the Hungarian Jews. Eichmann in effect cut the tangled Gordian knot that had ensnared the SS and the German and Hungarian ministries: a week later, Eberhard von Thadden informed Veesenmayer that, 'Deportation, particularly timetables and the ordering of railway carriages, will be dealt with by … Eichmann …who is receiving all necessary instructions from the Head Office for Reich Security [the RSHA].' This strongly suggests that Kaltenbrunner had quashed the last Foreign Office scruples – thus sealing the fate of the Hungarian Jews. By finally agreeing to a maximalist solution, Veesenmayer was fulfilling his duty both as the Reich plenipotentiary, loyal to Ribbentrop, and as SS-Brigadeführer, answering to Himmler. Von Thaden provided further details. The deportation trains were scheduled to begin operations on 15 May: the aim was to deliver 3,000 Jews every day to Auschwitz. Naturally, care would be taken not to disrupt the war effort. This was the reason, he explained, why a decision had been taken not to immediately deport 50,000 Jews from Budapest, 'since the round-up of the Jews *needs to be total*' [my italics].

To prepare for ghettoisation, Eichmann and his Hungarian collaborators had divided Hungary into operational Zones that comprised one or two gendarmerie districts. This was the plan Eichmann had boasted about when he summoned Freudiger into his office at the SS headquarters and showed off his wall map of Hungary. The Zones would also provide the blueprint for the mass deportations. This was the topography of genocide.

The Zones were demarcated as follows:

Zone I: The Jews in Gendarmerie District VIII (Kassa): Carpatho-Ruthenia and north-eastern Hungary.
Zone II: The Jews in Gendarmerie District IX (Kolozsvá) and X (Marosvásárhely): Northern Transylvania.
Zone III: The Jews in Gendarmerie Districts II (Székesfehévár) and VII (Miskolc): northern Hungary in the area extending from Kassa to the borders of the Reich.

Zone IV: The Jews in Gendarmerie District V (Szeged) and VI (Debrecen): the southern regions of Hungary east of the Danube.

Zone V: the Jews in Gendarmerie District III (Szombathely) and IV (Pécs): the south-western region west of the Danube.

Zone VI: the Jews in Gendarmerie District 1 (Budapest): the capital and its immediate environs.

To begin with, the two State Ministers, Endre and Baky, had strenuously objected to this order of priority. Endre tried to persuade Eichmann that the round-ups should be launched in Budapest. Hungary's capital was, in his mind, the fetid stronghold of the wealthy Hungarian Jews that he despised so deeply. Like many antisemites, Endre referred to the city as 'Judapest'. Eichmann convinced him to change his mind. He pointed out that the Soviet army was fast approaching the Hungarian border through the Carpathians. This meant, he argued, that it was imperative to eliminate Jews from a region that would soon become a military front line. Any Jews who remained alive in an operational area posed a threat to the security of German forces. Eichmann's second argument was even more cunning. Most Christian Hungarians, whether or not they were antisemitic, he had come to understand, regarded the Jews who lived in Zone I, that is Carpatho-Ruthenia and north-eastern Hungary, as manifestly alien. They spoke Yiddish, displayed 'Eastern' manners and had not embraced any significant kind of assimilation to Magyar social norms and culture. These Jewish communities were remote in a geographical sense, and isolated from the main centre of Jewish life in Budapest and other large towns. In short, what happened to these liminal Jews (as they were perceived) would be unlikely to provoke any discomfort among Hungarians and even the more Margaryised Jews. Eichmann's arguments won the day; Jaross and his ministers capitulated. This had significant implications for the way Eichmann would manage the Jewish organisations in the capital – as we will discover shortly. At a meeting at the Interior Ministry on 22 April, Eichmann and the Hungarians resolved most strategic and organisational matters. The fate of Hungarian Jewry was sealed.

Now that German strategy in Hungary had been settled, Eichmann and Wisliceny embarked on a triumphal tour of the ghettos in north-eastern Hungary. The SS men were accompanied by the devoted Endre and Lieutenant Colonel Lászlo Ferenczy, who was Liaison Officer of the Royal Hungarian Gendarmerie to the German Security Police. The German and Hungarian members of the tour group were now all on very good terms. Ferenczy's headquarters were close to Eichmann's office inside the Majestic Hotel: a macabre inscription on the office door described his business as the International Storage and Transportation Company, Inc. When he returned from this tour, Endre informed Jaross, the Minister of the Interior, that he had found 'everything in order. The provincial ghettos have a veritably sanatorium-like character. The Jews are finally getting fresh air and have changed their old lifestyle for a healthier one.' Such propaganda – the report was sent on to Horthy – must have provided callous humour among these devout haters of Jews.

Many local mayors in Zone I had on their own initiative begun to concentrate Jews who resided in their districts. There were many Hungarian administrators who, like Endre, welcomed the chance to strike at the hated strangers who lived in their midst. The round-ups began with a demand to Jewish 'communal organs' to prepare lists of all Jews together with their family members, providing the address and apartment number. Jewish leaders obediently complied. In larger communities, young men who had not been mobilised for the Labour Service worked in pairs, spreading out across their home towns and cities, 'eager not to leave out a single street or building', as Braham tells us. In Budapest, Endre and Baky organised so-called 'dejewification squads' made up of members of the Eichmann Sonderkommando and Hungarian police officers. In his reports to Berlin, Veesenmayer repeatedly commended the close cooperation between German officials, Eichmann's SS men and the Hungarian police and gendarmerie officers.

'Ghettoisation' is an ugly word. It was an ugly, violent and demeaning experience for tens of thousands of Hungarian Jews. A 'Ghetto order' issued by the sub-prefect of Zala county on 4 May shows the full legalistic cruelty of the procedure:

Based on the authorization granted by Articles 8-10 of the Prime Ministers Decree No. 1610/1944 I order that throughout Zala County the Jews relocate ... by the evening of May 16, 1944 ... Jews within the county are allowed to live only within the designated closed areas as well as houses ... The Jewish Council, headed by the Jewish leader, handles all internal affairs of the closed area ... The Jews being resettled are generally allowed to bring luggage with them weighing up to 50 kilograms per person ...

For many Hungarians, ghettoisation was a means of plunder:

> Any valuables that were left behind (gold, silver, jewellery, gemstones)
> must be entered into a separate inventory … [and stored] until such time
> as the Hungarian National Bank arranges for their collection.[2]

A survivor recalled: 'In our home they found the cash hidden by my father
in the bedding. My poor father was terribly beaten and kicked around for
this at the school.' At Soroksár, near Budapest: 'Gendarmerie officers went
through our packages and took objects that took their fancy, papers and
cash, accompanied by blows.' In another town, some of the Jews were taken
to the police station 'where everyone was made to strip to the skin, searched;
any valuable or cash found on the person was taken and its owner beaten.'
Searches carried out by the Hungarians were brutal and cruelly intimate:
'During searches of men and women, cash and other valuables are found
in the most unlikely places.' For the gendarmerie, theft was obligatory:
'before being taken into custody, the Jews are ordered to produce their
cash, jewellery and other valuables. They must be told they would not
be returned here, so if they had hidden anything they should retrieve the
items and hand them over'.[3]

In Kassa, the authorities ordered that 'individuals of the Christian race
[sic] who are living in the ghetto area may not have any contact with individuals of the Jewish race … [who] may not spend time in the streets of
the ghetto, and may only keep the courtyard-side windows of their apartments open'.

Thus, the new ghettos became semi-open prisons. While Hungarians
were forbidden to enter the demarcated streets and buildings, the police
and gendarmerie could enter the ghettos whenever they pleased and
could do whatever they pleased. A survivor recalled that: 'In the ghetto
scandalous beatings were everyday affairs, these left several victims dead'.

Another: 'Police Inspector Dr Csatári [Csatary] beat people with a dog
whip. Whenever he felt like it, he went inside a block [in the ghetto] and
beat everyone he found there with a whip.'

The conditions in the ghettos were meticulously recorded by the
embattled Jewish Councils. In Nagyvárad, we read that 'accommodations
are provided in farm buildings and in the apartments of warrant officers,
in stables and in open sheds. The situation in the small ghetto is desperate
… The food supply is a disaster.' In another town, '10,000 people were

resettled in the brick factory … There is practically no food. Some of them are living outdoors, without a roof.' After the war, H.H. provided this detailed account of his experience:

> About 6000 Jews lived in Huszt; most of them were fairly well-off tradesmen and craftsmen. We had nothing to complain about, but after the Hungarian occupation the trade licenses of the Jews were cancelled, and our situation was gradually deteriorating. They had already arrested a lot of Jews before the German occupation. After that it became even worse and just before Passover they rounded up everybody and closed them up in a ghetto. They boarded up the street gates and nobody was allowed to leave the ghetto. There were two ghettos in Huszt: one for the Jews of the town and another one for the Jews of the environs … Notary József Bíró was a notorious antisemite … At first, they took us into the city hall. Here they undressed all of us and took our jewellery, money and papers. After that they took us into the ghetto. We had a soup kitchen, but raw food was distributed as well, and we could cook for ourselves. The ghetto was guarded by gendarmes and the internal order was maintained by Jewish police … The Germans drafted the men for work. Rumour had it that we were ghettoised because we were unreliable, and we would be taken to work to the Transdanubia region. A few weeks later we were taken into the brickyard ghetto where all of our remaining belongings were taken away, except a few pieces of underwear, clothes and some food. They threatened to shoot down those who were reluctant to hand over their money, jewellery or gold. Hungarian soldiers were beating a tradesman named Winkler with a lath and when he was half dead, they shot him.[4]

Jews were by no means passive victims; leaders of the Jewish Council did not just follow German orders. In Érsekújvár, the Jewish Council established an epidemic hospital, a child care centre and a maternity home, 'all with the most modern equipment which the doctors have provided. A modern, two-storey house may be available for the aged. A Jewish police and fire department has been organised'. When deportations began just a few weeks later, conditions in the ghettos impacted on survival. At the selections that took place on the 'Judenrampe' after the arrival of the trains inside the Birkenau extermination camp, it was the healthier prisoners judged to be fit to work who escaped being herded immediately into the gas chambers. At the end of the same report, the Council leader notes that the Jews from another town 'have been transported via Kassa to Katowice. Several people have sent letters bearing a Waldsee postmark'.

The Germans had perpetrated a ghastly trick. The Jews who had been transported had been taken not to Katowice but Auschwitz. The majority had been killed. The postcards were illusory messages from hell.

15

EICHMANN'S GAMBIT

In late April, the cruellest month, hundreds of miles from Budapest, the SS offensive against the Jews of Hungary gathered momentum at a furious pace. As Hungarian gendarmes forced many thousands of Jewish families to leave their homes and gather inside improvised ghettos in provincial cities and villages, Eichmann summoned Joel Brand to the SS headquarters in Schwabenberg.

Precisely when, on which day, this fateful meeting took place has never been satisfactorily resolved. And, as I will explain, that date matters a great deal. Brand told his British interrogator that he received a message from the former Abwehr agent, Dr Johann Schmidt, on 16 April that 'he would be picked up in the street near a certain café and that Obersturmbannführer Eichmann, chief of the Jewish section of the SD, wished to speak to him'. Brand went on: 'Eichmann was born in Palestine, where his parents are now interned; he speaks fluent Hebrew'.[1] This was nonsense, of course – and Brand was wrong about the date. The final meeting with Krumey and the 'Schmidt Group' took place on 21 April – and it makes no sense for Eichmann to intervene and make a very different proposal any earlier. In mid April, Eichmann was preoccupied with navigating the fractious debate that had erupted between the Hungarians and the German Foreign Office concerning the scale of the planned deportations.

A number of historians, including Bogdanor, conclude that Eichmann's summons came later in the month and that the first encounter took place on or around 25 April. There is an obvious problem with that date. We know that between 24 April and 2 May, Eichmann, accompanied by Wisliceny, Endre and other Hungarian officials, was touring the ghettos in north-east Hungary. That leaves us with one other possible date. In his Report, Kasztner stated unequivocally that the first meeting between Eichmann and Brand took place on 8 May. There are a number of reasons why this is convincing. First, a basic requirement: Eichmann was in Budapest. Secondly, the plan for the ghettoisation and deportation of all Hungarian Jews had been settled and was securely in the hands of Eichmann's staff. Finally, by the beginning of May, the SD, with the unwitting assistance of Kasztner, had finally crushed the 'Schmidt group'. Schmidt and Winninger were excluded from any further negotiations with the Rescue Committee. The stage was clear for Eichmann to step in: he would now take control of negotiations with the Zionist Rescuers.

Dates, chronologies, time lines matter in history. Why does *this* date matter?

Auschwitz Revealed

It is a remarkable fact that in April 1944, no fewer than five Jewish inmates escaped from Auschwitz and reported in detail about what was taking place inside the camp. These escapes took place when Eichmann's comrade, the camp commandant Rudolf Höß, was racing to complete construction of new crematoria and other facilities to deal with the anticipated arrival of hundreds of thousands of Jews who would be brought from Hungary.

On 5 April, Viktor Pestek, a Romanian camp supervisor (he had the rank of SS Rottenführer) of German origin and a Jewish prisoner called Siegfried Lederer, a former Czech army officer who had been transported to Auschwitz from the Theresienstadt (Terezín) ghetto in 1943, calmly bicycled out of the main gates of the camp. It was a brave and daring feat: Pestek had supplied his fellow escapee with an SS uniform, pistol and pay book; he had taught Lederer all the passcodes used by the camp guards. Lederer was a member of the Czech resistance group Plzeňák 28. For him, escape was a sacred political duty. Pestek had more complex motivations. He told another prisoner: 'I hate myself for having to watch women and children be killed. I want to do something to forget the smell of burning human flesh and feel a little cleaner.' And he had another, equally compelling reason to try to escape. He had fallen in love with Renée Neumann, a young Jewish woman who was incarcerated with her mother in the 'Theresienstädter Familienlager' (Family Camp) at Auschwitz.

Pestek discovered that the Germans planned to gas every one of the Czech families sometime in the spring of 1944. The only hope he had of saving Renée and the other families was to escape.[2]

Like Theresienstadt itself, the Auschwitz 'Family Camp' was another SS ploy to deceive any representatives of the International Red Cross should they demand to carry out a tour of inspection. The camp had been constructed inside the BIIb section of Auschwitz II-Birkenau camp and held some 5,000 Jewish families who had been deported from Theresienstadt in September 1943. Other transports had arrived in December. The name of the camp was a misnomer: the SS constructed separate barracks for men and women, who were permitted to meet only at roll calls.

According to eyewitness Walter Rosenberg, who took the name Rudolf Vrba, cited in H.G. Adler's encyclopaedic account of Theresienstadt:

> We could not understand at all why these transports enjoyed an unheard of status. The families were not separated [on arrival], not a single one went to the gassing that was so normal to us; their hair was not even cut … [they] could even keep their luggage … They even had permission to write freely … They were merely bullied by their camp elder, a Reich professional criminal named Arno Böhm …[3]

The practices and rules that seemed so inexplicable to Vrba were, in fact, part of an elaborate deception, hatched up to satisfy any inconvenient observers that Jewish inmates at Auschwitz were being treated humanely.[4]

When they reached the railway station at Auschwitz, Pestek and Lederer boarded a train to Prague, pretending to be luggage inspectors. When they reached the city, they sold some jewellery and bought civilian clothes. Soon afterwards, Lederer boldly sneaked back into the Theresienstadt camp to warn the leaders of the Jewish Council about the fate of the families who had been transported to Auschwitz. It has been suggested that the Council Elders, such as Dr Leo Baeck, the former Chief Rabbi of Germany, were reluctant to take action. Hannah Arendt, in her book about the Eichmann trial, insinuated that Baeck, who survived the war, believed that it was kinder to keep silent about the unavoidable fate of the Jews deported to Auschwitz. Endurance was preferable to resistance.[5]

Pestek and Lederer returned to Auschwitz in June to rescue Renée and her mother – but for reasons that have never been fully explained, the plan went terribly wrong. Lederer fled; Pestek was arrested and tortured. He was shot dead by firing squad on 8 October. His fears about the SS plans for the inmates of the Family Camp were well founded. As night fell on 8 March, the SS marched some 3,800 Jews, including Renée, her mother and many children, to the gas chambers of crematoria II and III. The children walked singing to their deaths.[6]

Bitter and angry, Lederer joined a Slovakian partisan group and fought alongside them until the end of the war. He died forgotten and without commemoration. According to Czech historian Erich Kulka, Lederer planned to smuggle a report about his experience of Auschwitz to the International Red Cross in Switzerland. He seems to have arranged to give the report to a ferry captain on Lake Constance, who promised to deliver it to the ICRC headquarters in Geneva. There is no real certainty that Lederer wrote such a report; there is certainly no record of it reaching Geneva. Lederer's testimony was a silent cry.[7]

Just two days after Lederer and Pestek fled Auschwitz, two more prisoners escaped. This time, the entire world would be forced to listen to what they had to say. The story of the two Slovakian Jews, Walter Rosenberg, who took the name Rudolf Vrba, and Alfréd Wetzler, known as Josef Lanik, has been told many times.[8] Both men had been deported to Auschwitz in the spring of 1942. By 1944, when Vrba turned 19, he was working in the slave labour unit known in camp slang as the 'Kanadakommando' which handled the plundered belongings – food, jewellery, gold and money – of people who had been killed at Auschwitz. The spoils of the 'Kanada' camp were repackaged to be sent to Germany; gold was melted down into ingots and transferred to the Reichsbank. The spoils of Vrba's macabre task meant that he was able to make quite accurate estimates of the numbers of Jews murdered at the camp. With the same forensic insight, he observed that a significant proportion of the deportees seemed to have known little or nothing about what would happen to them at the camp: when 'Kanadakommando' workers tore open the suitcases and packages that had been seized from deportees, they often discovered clothing for all seasons and long-lasting provisions. This implied that they had had fallen for the ruse that they were being 'resettled'. Long after the war, Vrba wrote:

When a series of transports of Jews from the Netherlands arrived, cheese enriched the rations. It was sardines when a series of transports of French

Jews arrived, halva and olives when transports of Jews from Greece reached the camp, and now the SS were talking of 'Hungarian salami'...⁹

Wetzler worked in the mortuary at Birkenau, where he too made meticulous records of the numbers of prisoners who had perished inside the camp as well as the numbers of gold teeth that had been extracted from their corpses. In the spring of 1944, the Slovakian Sonderkommando Filip Müller came to Vrba with disturbing news that the SS had begun to carry out repairs on the crematoria inside the Birkenau camp: 'The Nazis, we estimated, were preparing to kill at least a million people. For a while we wondered in which country they would find so many Jews left; but gradually, as the clues filtered through us, we realised who were destined to break all records. It was the Hungarians'. He continued: 'It was no longer a question of reporting a crime, but of preventing one; of warning the Hungarians.'

Preparations for the removal of hundreds of thousands of Hungarian Jews were indeed in full swing in SS offices in Budapest and Vienna. The transport of hundreds of thousands of Jews across the Hungarian border, through Slovakia and into occupied Poland to Auschwitz, was a formidable logistical challenge. As noted earlier, on 23 April, Veesenmayer had informed the German Foreign Office that: 'Negotiations about transportation have been started ... Auschwitz is designated as receiving station.' One of the most important officers in the Eichmann Sonderkommando was Hauptsturmführer Franz Novak – who was known as the 'Stationmaster of Death'. He was Eichmann's transport specialist. In his Report, Kasztner revealed that he was informed by Rabbi Weissmandel in Bratislava that Slovak and Hungarian officials had begun discussions about the transfer of 150 trains to Hungary. And on 4 May, Novak travelled to Vienna as representative of the Eichmann Sonderkommando to settle the final arrangements.

On Friday, 7 April, the eve of Passover, Vrba and Wetzler hid inside a pile of wooden planks stacked outside the camp perimeter waiting to be used for construction of a new facility. The two men waited in the claustrophobic darkness. The evening roll call always took place at 5.30 p.m. and they expected to hear sirens as soon as their absence was noticed. But no alarm sounded. Then, at 6 p.m., the sirens wailed ominously. SS men cordoned off the camp perimeter and guards, with dogs, began scouring the camp – but the two men remained undetected. They endured three days without food or drink, blind, stiff and motionless inside the wood stack. Then, on the third day, they heard SS guards call off the search – and that night Vrba and Wetzler emerged from their dark, damp hiding place.

They began walking south – towards the Slovakian border, as Vrba put it 'without documents, without a compass, without a map, and without a weapon'. The plan was to cross the Bezkyd Mountains, south of Auschwitz. But they lost their way in the dark and ended up in a small Polish village. In desperation, they knocked at the door of one of the houses. They were taking a huge risk. A woman came to the door: she realised immediately that her visitors were escaped prisoners but invited them inside and fed them boiled potatoes and coffee. Dodging German patrols, Vrba and Wetzler tramped south-east. One evening they were fired on by a German police patrol but escaped into the forest. Soon afterwards, they ran into a Polish partisan, who agreed to take them through the forest to the frontier. One morning, they walked out of Reich territory into Slovakia. In the small village of Skalite, a farmer let the two exhausted men sleep in his barn.

It was 21 April 1944.

Ten days later, the two men, exhausted, still shaven-headed, made contact with the chairman of the Jewish Council, a lawyer called Dr Oskar Neumann. At the Council headquarters in Zilina, Vrba and Wetzler, at Neumann's suggestion, were put in separate rooms to dictate their accounts and answer a battery of questions. On 26 April, Oskar Krasznyansky supervised the typing of a consolidated report, written in Slovak and immediately translated into German, based on the testimonies of the two escapees. It is a remarkable document; one of the most important testimonies about the workings of the Auschwitz-Birkenau death camp. As Neumann explained in his memoir *In the Shadow of Death*, written in 1946 and published in Tel Aviv a decade later: 'the testimony … forty typewritten pages, was one of the most shocking documents the human ear could hear. Our people heard this story and thought they would go mad.' The report described the German methods of mass murder – the tattooing, gassing and cremation – in detail and estimated that about 1.75 million Jews had been murdered at Auschwitz.

That Auschwitz-Birkenau was a site of organised mass murder and not 'just' a concentration camp had been known about for some time. As early as June 1941, the London *Times* carried a short article that referred to the 'dreaded Oswiecim [i.e. Auschwitz] concentration camp'. In the course of the next few years, there was a patchy accumulation of disturbing information from different sources but in the aftermath of the Bermuda Conference in April 1943 the American and British governments were reluctant to publicise 'atrocity stories'. According to Michael Fleming, this reflected an antisemitic strain in government circles and an obsession with marginalising any news of German atrocities to damp down demands to engage in actions that had no strategic or military purpose.[10] As the historian of the German KL system, Nikolaus Wachsman, puts it very succinctly: 'The magnitude of Nazi criminality took a long time to sink in.' The Vrba–Wetzler report and other testimonies about the purpose of the German extermination camps – known as the 'Auschwitz Protocols' – obligated the Allied powers, as well as neutral governments, NGOs and individuals to at last recognise the unprecedented scale of the crime that was being committed in German-occupied Europe. The question that we need to address now has a narrower focus. What was the impact of the report among Hungarian rescuers in the late spring of 1944?

In Slovakia, Gisi Fleischmann and Rabbi Weissmandel and other members of the 'Working Group' did not hesitate to act. Vrba recalled that Krasznyansky and Neumann began sending out copies on 26 April. When Krasznyansky was interviewed in Jerusalem in 1964 he added a crucial detail. He claims that Kasztner was visiting Bratislava at the time and was provided with the German text of the report. When he returned to Budapest, Kasztner took a copy with him and requested a Hungarian translation; this was forwarded to him shortly afterwards. Ten years later, in 1974, Krasznyansky reiterated this claim in conversation with Rudolf Braham.[11] Kasztner himself would never admit to travelling to Bratislava at the end of April – or receiving the report.

Some historians have questioned whether the Vrba–Wetzler *report,* meaning the document compiled at the end of April in Krasina, made any direct reference to the fate of Hungarian Jewry. The notorious reference to 'Hungarian salami', it has been suggested, is apocryphal. It is true that the escapees stated: 'Work is now proceeding on a still larger compound which is to be added later to the already existing camp.' They informed Krasznyansky that they had heard 'that large convoys of Greek Jews were expected.'[12] But these are nit-picks: the two prisoners observed and reported correctly that the SS administrators had begun renovating and expanding facilities at the Birkenau camp in the spring of 1944 to accommodate the arrival of 'large convoys'. As we know, Eichmann had visited Auschwitz in March, shortly before the murder of the Czech Jews, and complained about the dilapidated state of the crematoria and the 'Judenrampe'. His good friend and comrade Rudolf Höß oversaw the renovations and was fully informed about Eichmann's plans.

In his book *The Years of Extermination*, historian Saul Friedländer raises important questions about the significance of the Vrba–Wetzler report. By the end of April, he writes: 'nothing could have been done in any case to stop the masses of Jews in the [Hungarian] provinces from following the deportation orders'. Furthermore, the Jewish leaders in Slovakia and Hungary had 'precise knowledge of what was happening to the Jews all over Europe' before Vrba and Wetzler escaped from Auschwitz.[13] This was perfectly true. It has already been noted that the Brands' rescue network provided a huge amount of information about the mass murder of Polish and Slovak Jews.

All this is to miss the most important revelations of the 'Auschwitz Protocols'. What the Vrba–Wetzler report exposed – and at a critical juncture in the evolution of the Final Solution immediately prior to the deportations from Hungary – was the technologised solution to mass killing that was being developed by the SS managers at Auschwitz – more precisely Auschwitz II–Birkenau. It was by means of these technologies that, as Hannah Arendt wrote, Auschwitz reduced people 'to the lowest common denominator of life itself, plunged into the darkest and deepest abyss of primal equality, like cattle, like matter, like things that had neither body nor soul, nor even a physiognomy upon which death could stamp its seal'.

The Impact of the Protocols

As we will discover in the next chapter, the Vrba–Wetzler report had a shattering impact on many individuals who received and read it – and, in one case, saved the life of George Klein, a young Hungarian Jew who came upon the report by chance when he was working for the Jewish Council. The escape of the two prisoners from Auschwitz and the dissemination of their testimony had significance of a very different kind for the SS men who had been empowered to carry out the destruction of Hungarian Jewry. We know that on 28 April, Kasztner requested a meeting with Eichmann's colleague, Hermann Krumey. The meeting took place on 2 May – the day when Eichmann and Endre returned from their tour of the ghettos in Zone I. It has been suggested by Vrba and others that Kasztner challenged Eichmann by showing him a copy of the Vrba-Wetzler report. This would have been foolhardy to say the least – but certainly implied to Krumey that he now knew a great deal about what happened inside the Auschwitz camp. In any event, the escape of the two prisoners from Auschwitz had provoked a massive manhunt – and a blizzard of reports at every level of the Nazi security services from Himmler down. For Eichmann and his bosses in Budapest and Berlin, the implications were alarming. They would have known that the two Jewish escapees had privileged access to the secrets of the death camp – and the preparations being made to receive the new transports. If Kasztner or anyone else went public with what they now knew, all hell might be let loose. The public order that Eichmann and the other managers of genocide depended on to carry out the planned mass deportations could be under threat.

The ways Eichmann and Krumey reacted to the meeting with Kasztner on Tuesday, 2 May offer evidence to support this hypothesis.

The last weeks of April 1944 were an especially fraught period for the German planners. It was during these weeks that a final agreement to deport all the Hungarian Jews to Auschwitz was reached between the different factions on the German and Hungarian sides. The agreement reflected the schism between pressure to exploit Jewish labour resources in the service of the Reich and wholesale slaughter. It will be recalled that at the Schloss Kleßheim conference with Hitler and Ribbentrop, Horthy had agreed to supply 100,000 Jewish workers to the Reich. The fateful consequence of this contract was a swindle that glued together the pseudo-legal provision of Jewish workers with the deportation of all Jews. The documentary evidence in German Foreign Office records reveals how the radicals on both the German and Hungarian sides closed the gap between their different positions by the end of April. In mid April, Veesenmayer was discussing with the HSSPF Otto Winkelmann where to send 'Jewish workers' made available by the Hungarians. Eichmann's deputy Rolf Günther replied that he was expecting a decision from the RSHA chief Kaltenbrunner in a matter of days. Just a week later, Veesenmayer recommended to the Foreign Office that the deportation of Jews from Sub-Carpathia and Northern Transylvania must now take precedence over sending Jewish workers to Germany. This implied that Veesenmayer had fully accepted the radical SS plan that had been hammered out between Eichmann and the Hungarians. The following day, Günther wrote to Veesenmayer pointing out that, in any event, Jewish workers could not be sent to Germany because 'that would render Germany's "cleansing" of Jews illusory'.[14]

Veesenmayer would persist with the legalistic cover that he was deporting Jews for work. On 27 April, he informed the Foreign Office that a large number of 'able-bodied' Jews aged between 16 and 50 – and thus suitable for work – would soon be deported from internment camps in the vicinity of Budapest, thereby fulfilling the 'first instalment' of Hitler's agreement with Horthy. As it turned out, these Jews would all be despatched to Auschwitz. For Eichmann and his transport manager, Franz Novak, these first transports may simply have been a way of testing the system.

News of the deportations was thoroughly alarming for the Jewish community in Budapest. But many were 'calmed' when they were informed that the Germans had selected only the able bodied. They had no idea that the Jewish workers had ended up in Auschwitz. Few would have understood what deportation to Auschwitz implied. At the very same time that the Slovakian Jewish leaders were making copies of the Vrba–Wetzler report, Hungarian police units drove 3,800 Jews culled from prisons in Budapest and the Kistarcsa and Bácstopolya internment camps into train wagons bound for the Polish border. The following day, Kasztner received a message from the 'Working Group' in Bratislava that a train carrying Hungarian Jews had travelled through Slovakia in the direction of Auschwitz.[15]

On 2 May, the transports from Budapest halted alongside the 'Judenrampe' inside the Birkenau camp. The SS selected 486 men and 616 women for admission into the camp. The remainder, numbering 2,700, were immediately murdered in the newly renovated gas chambers by Rudolf Höß.

On the same day, Kasztner returned to Winninger's apartment to meet Krumey. Why not the SS offices in Schwabenberg? Was it because money would change hands? In any case, Krumey declared 'with a smile' that Berlin had approved the emigration of 600 Jews in two or three weeks.[16] They then discussed bringing at least half of that number from Kasztner's home town Kolozsvár to Budapest, where they would be held in a 'preferred camp'. Kasztner then raised the matter of the Jews recently deported from the Kistarcsa camp. Krumey was prepared for this: 'Have the people in question not written yet?' 'Where are they supposed to have written from?' asked Kasztner. Krumey replied: 'From Waldsee.'

Bad Waldsee is a town in Baden-Württemberg. This was, as noted earlier, one of the Germans' most cynical ploys. The SS forced many of the Jews deported in May and June to write postcards to relatives and friends who remained in Hungary giving 'Waldsee' as a place of origin. Some of those forced to write these cynical 'Postcards from Waldsee' deceived the Germans by writing that they would soon be meeting grandparents – who were known by the recipient to be long dead.

At the Eichmann trial, Freudiger described the way the SS played this trick:

State Attorney Bach: Mr. Freudiger. Can you tell the Court about certain postcards which reached Hungarian Jews from those who were being deported?

Witness Freudiger: Yes ... Two weeks after the first transports were dispatched, possibly by the end of May, we obtained through our liaison officers ... a large quantity of postcards, postcards written by Jews who had been deported. They were dated and marked 'Waldsee'. It said there: We are at work here and send our regards. Things are not bad, we feel well, we are working here, greetings to this one and to that. All the postcards were worded in this style.

Q. And the address was always 'Waldsee'?

A. It was marked 'Waldsee such-and-such a date.' There was no address.

Q. Did you endeavour to ascertain where this 'Waldsee' was?

A. We went to Krumey and asked him where Waldsee was. At first he replied 'in central Germany'; after that he said: 'in Thüringen'. We searched for it on maps, we found it, we did not find it. It may have been a small place. At any rate, the deception about Waldsee lasted for a long time, two weeks, three, four, until they realized it was not worthwhile to lie, that we knew the truth.

Presiding Judge: Was there a post office stamp on these postcards?

Witness Freudiger: There was no postal stamp.

State Attorney Bach: And how were they sent?

Witness Freudiger: They said the cards were brought from the SS command headquarters, the men who brought all the mail. Until a fortnight later, I once came across a postcard with an erasure. The postcards were written in pencil. I noticed that where 'Waldsee' had been written, there had been an erasure. Since I was the owner of a textile factory and I always had a magnifying glass near me, I examined it and I saw that the letters

'ITZ' were still visible on the postcard. Someone had made a mistake and had written 'Auschwitz' instead of 'Waldsee', as they had been told to do.

Afterwards he had erased it and had written 'Waldsee'. I took the post-card and, the next morning, I went to Krumey and said to him: 'Our people are in Auschwitz and not in "Waldsee".' He replied: 'How can you say such a thing? And why are you angry at me?' I took the postcard and the magnifying glass and said to him: 'Please, look.' He looked at it and then said: 'Freudiger, I know you to be a clever man – you do not have to observe everything.' After that no more postcards came from 'Waldsee'. In actual fact, there were no longer any people who could write.[17]

Kasztner was less naïve. Shaken by the revelations in the Vrba–Wetzler report and strongly suspecting that the recent transports had been sent to Auschwitz, he scorned the story of the 'Waldsee postcards'. When Krumey insisted that, 'We only took skilled workers there [to Waldsee]', Kasztner retorted: 'What do mean skilled workers? The deportees were all middle class people.'

Krumey replied: 'They'll soon learn a skill there.'

According to his Report, Kasztner now insisted 'on knowing where we stand … A month ago, Wisliceny declared in this room that you, the German authorities, were not interested in deportation … We have made the first payments on the basis of Wisliceny's declarations.' He now insisted on a meeting with Wisliceny to clarify what the Germans planned.

Krumey's purpose was plainly to run rings around Kasztner. First of all, the 'good news' from Berlin about the emigration of 600 Jews immediately plunged the Rescue Committee into a nerve-wracking exercise in life and death triage. In his diary entry for 2 May, the head of the committee, Ottó Komoly, wrote that:

In the afternoon, Dr Kasztner informs me that the Germans have granted permission for a transport of 600, they demand a list, etc … Constant fatigue; the anxiety and stress of which have got to me terribly; I cannot bear the constant siege of people, the unavoidable injustice that comes with the selection …[18]

Komoly, a war veteran who was exempted from wearing a Yellow Star, refused to have his own name put on the list. This brave, principled man would not survive the occupation.

This frenzy – 'the constant siege of people' – was just what Eichmann and Krumey needed. Even Kasztner acknowledged that 'a list of 600 is impossible to draw up. 600 names – out of 800,000.' Offering such human crumbs from the table of mass murder was a simple and well-tried way to sow distraction. And it would seem that Krumey had another trick up his sleeve. The following day, he informed Kasztner that Wisliceny was busy in Kolozsvár – Kasztner's home town. For an extortionate fee of 'a million pengős' (US$200,000), he would let him travel there to meet with Wisliceny and discuss why he had broken his promise. Krumey told Kasztner that he had arranged for Dr Sedlaczek to drive him to Kolozsvár. It will be recalled that Sedlaczek had some involvement with the 'Schmidt Group' and had been detained for a few days when the SD liquidated its rivals. It would seem that the good dentist was now back in favour.

Kasztner's agreement to travel to Kolozsvár in early May 1944 would blight his moral reputation for the rest of his life.

At about noon, Kasztner and Sedlaczek began the long drive to Transylvania. Ghettoisation had begun two days earlier. Along the country roads, they met groups of Jews everywhere. They travelled on carts crammed with their meagre belongings. Many walked. They dragged themselves along, their faces pale and sad. Gendarme officers with fixed bayonets walked behind. When they reached Kolozsvár, Kasztner found Wisliceny in the office of the Hungarian secret police: he was indeed very busy. In Kolozsvár, the Hungarians had set up the ghetto in the Iris Brickyard on Kajántói Road in the northern part of the city. The ghetto was grossly overcrowded; water and food in short supply. In a building known as the 'Mint' Hungarian gendarmes tortured Jews to reveal where they were assumed to have hidden valuables. Jewish men were beaten on their testicles; girls were intimately searched. Many of the torturers were natural sadists. It was Wisliceny's task to make sure this ghastly process took place without disruption.

Kasztner reports the following exchange. Its naivety is chilling.

Kasztner: I thought that your assignment in Hungary, just as in Slovakia, meant a ray of hope for us. In Budapest you maintained that you had no interest in deportation. What is going on now? At least tell me the truth.

Wisliceny: After the first discussion with you, Eichmann excluded me from the negotiations, perhaps because he saw that my reputation among you was too good. He entrusted me with the dirtiest work and now I'm the person who has to control the transfer of the Jews to the ghettos. Eichmann wants to compromise me through this assignment, cost what it may. I wear a uniform, I have to obey orders. I've alleviated things where I could, but Endre wants to eat all Hungarian Jews alive and Eichmann is certainly not the person to restrain him.[19]

It is hard to believe that Kasztner would still allow Wisliceny the benefit of the doubt; that it was the Hungarians alone not the SS who were driving the incarceration and deportation of Jews. Kasztner claims that he then challenged Wisliceny about the deportations. Were they inevitable? Would it only be limited to the able bodied? Wisliceny lied: 'I don't know … I'm going to [Budapest] next week and will talk to Eichmann.'

In his Report, written immediately after the war, Kasztner chose not to reveal what Wisliceny said next. But a decade later, when Kasztner testified in the libel case brought by the Israeli government on his behalf, he was forced to admit: 'Wisliceny asked me to tell friends in Kolozsvár that they had increased the guard at the Romanian border just 4km away … I had to tell those who wanted to escape to Romania to be more careful and to use other ways.'[20]

According to Bogdanor, the significance of this statement becomes clear when we look at what Kasztner said to Jewish leaders in Kolozsvár, including his father-in-law Dr Fischer, who was the chairman of the Judenrat, before he returned to Budapest. By now, Kasztner knew a great deal about what the Germans planned. He knew, having studied the Vrba–Wetzler report, the real purpose of Auschwitz. He was in a unique position to warn the Jews of Kolozsvár about what the German intended. What he seems to have done is to *misinform*.

At the libel trial in Israel, Avram Feurerman testified that he consulted Kasztner's father-in-law, Dr Fischer, about his plans to try and escape to Romania. Fischer warned him that he would almost certainly be shot by border guards. Fischer advised him instead to enter the ghetto – and await resettlement at a place called Kenyérmező, which means 'field of bread'. The work site here was a fiction, pure and simple hatched up to camouflage the actual destination – Auschwitz.

It seems that Kasztner had other conversations with Jews in Kolozsvár including the former head of the Orthodox community, Zsigmond Léb. According to one eyewitness, after talking to Kasztner, Léb stood on a tree stump and proclaimed that 'we would be taken to work to Kenyérmező'.[21]

Bogdanor argues that many Jews succeeded in escaping to Romania in this period – and that it is plausible that, if they had not been misinformed by Kasztner, many more might have taken the same path to safety. At the Kasztner trial, Arnold Dávid Finkelstein, who had organised a smuggling network in Transylvania, claimed that the Romanian border was still a viable escape route at the time of Kasztner's visit: 'Just as 1,200 crossed the border, I assume that another 2,000 could have followed. Our system wasn't just viable for 2,000 but for 4,000 as well.' Zionist youth activist Hannah Ganz was smuggling Jews across the border throughout April, until she was arrested at the end of May.

What should we make of Kasztner's journey to Kolozsvár? Bogdanor argues that Kasztner was in effect *doing the bidding of the SS* by first deluding the Jewish community about the German plans to deport and murder all Hungarian Jews, and secondly by discouraging escape across the Romanian border. At this critical moment in the German plan to destroy the Hungarian Jews, Kasztner *wittingly* played a part in ensuring that the tragedy unfolded without disruption. The SS offered Kasztner a compelling incentive. When he travelled to Kolozsvár, Kasztner had secured agreement to select 388 Jews from the Kolozsvár ghetto, who were allowed to travel in safety to Budapest. Here they were to be interned in a special camp at the Wechselmann Institute for the Deaf-Mute on Columbus Street. The Jews who were released from the Kolozsvár ghetto had been chosen by a committee of the great and good, which included Kasztner's father-in-law, Dr Fischer. The Columbus Street group would become the nucleus of the much bigger 'Kasztner Group'. Years later, the judge at the Kasztner trial in Israel would denounce Kasztner's agreement with the SS to save a few hundred lives in exchange for silence about the fate of the other tens of thousands of Jews as a 'Faustian Pact'.

There is a problem with Bogdanor's account of Kasztner's journey to Kolozsvár. In a rather obscure memoir, published in 1994, Rabbi Moshe Carmilly-Weinberger, who was the de facto religious leader of the Jews in the city, made plans to take people across the border weeks *before* Wisliceny arrived to begin ghettoisation. Camilly-Weinberger travelled at great risk to Romania, where he met Wilhelm Filderman to discuss a rescue operation of thousands of people. Carmilly-Weinberger reluctantly concluded that the numbers of Romanian guards posted at border crossings made any large-scale rescues impossible. He had some success assisting smaller groups. He also describes how at the beginning of May, Dr Fischer asked him to try and reach out to the Chief Rabbi of Romania, Alexander Safran. At the time, all communications by telephone, telegram or letter were impossible in Northern Transylvania. Carmilly-Weinberger crossed the border at Turda and reached Bucharest shortly afterwards. He met with the Chief Rabbi, who sent a report to Pope Pius XII – which, as it transpired, was completely ignored. The implications of Carmilly-Weinberger's account are very compelling. He shows that Dr Fischer and the Jewish Council in Kolozsvár knew of the German plans – and that the community was imperilled. It would also seem to be true that the Romanian border was indeed heavily guarded. Escape would have been very difficult for all but a handful of very brave individuals.[22]

Carmilly-Weinberger's account does not exonerate Kasztner in any other way. If Dr Fischer and the other members of the Jewish Council knew what the Germans planned and feared for the survival of their community, this implies that during his visit, Kasztner damped down their fears by giving credence to the SS-manufactured fiction that Jews would be deported to a work camp in Kenyérmező.

Kasztner's actions cannot be exonerated, but there are different ways of deciphering his reasoning and intentions. Kasztner was remarkably naïve if he believed that Wisliceny had either the motivation or authority to 'alleviate things'. Yet the fact remains that he and the other Rescue Committee leaders still clung to the battered raft of the avuncular Wisliceny's goodwill. In a coded message sent at the beginning of May to the Jewish Agency in Istanbul, Kasztner claimed that: 'Payments were made to Wisliceny. Negotiations with Wisliceny aim at avoidance of death and deportation. A chance of success exists only if you intervene quickly and positively'. When he wrote this, Kasztner had near certain knowledge about the fate of Jews who had been robbed of everything they possessed and herded into ghettos to await deportation to Auschwitz. Kasztner is duplicitous certainly, but why is he lying? We can see the tragic flaw that led Kasztner into the moral swamp of believing he could negotiate with the agents of genocide. Faced with what he interpreted as the reality of the Final Solution that, like a malign force of nature, it could not be prevented, he faced a predicament that had many different dimensions.

It cannot be doubted that he believed, in good faith, that even as the German plans unfolded relentlessly some lives could be saved and this meant that terrible choices – the triage of genocide – had to be made. To adapt Tomi Komoly's words: he decided badly because it was impossible to decide well. Kasztner did not 'sell his soul to the devil' – the other corrosive phrase used by the judge at the end of the 'Kasztner trial' in 1954. His tragedy was to allow his false and mendacious friends in the SS to become the arbiters of his own sense of worth and personal dignity – the guarantors of his rank. In his home town Kolozsvár, Kasztner had been a prominent figure. He had married well; he was a celebrated journalist with political ambitions. All this had been torn away from him. He had come to Budapest as a supplicant. When he found a role working with the Zionist rescuers, he repossessed his dignity and ambition. As he was drawn into the SS web of deceit ostensibly as a partner in fabricated negotiations, Kasztner became dependent on bolstering his status with the SS and lost his moral compass. Kasztner disregarded the old maxim that if we sup with the devil it is advisable to use a long spoon. Kasztner chose the wrong spoon.

According to Komoly's diary, Kasztner was driven back from Kolozsvár on 5 May. It was soon afterwards that Eichmann sent for Joel Brand. The sinews of the SS trap would become much tighter.

16

EMISSARY OF
THE DECEIVED

Sometime in May 1944, a telegram arrived at the Jewish Agency offices in the Pera Palace Hotel in Istanbul. It was signed by Rezsö Kasztner and advised that 'Engineer Eugen Band and Bandi Grosz' were about to arrive in the city. The letter urgently requested a meeting with 'Chaim' to discuss some important proposals. In his memoir, Ehud Avriel, who was one of the Zionist leaders based in Istanbul and a founder of the Mossad, recalls that the identity of 'Eugen Band' was a mystery. He knew Grosz well as 'a disreputable character who had been jailed for criminal offences before he was of age' – a notorious smuggler of Persian carpets who probably hoped to 'whitewash his soul' by working as a courier for the Zionist underground. A few days later, Avriel went on, the telephone rang in the office of his Agency colleague Chaim Barlas – and he heard the 'squeaky voice' of Bandi Grosz announcing that his aircraft had just landed. He was not happy: 'Here I am with Joel Brand. We have just arrived on the plane that carried the German diplomatic pouch and the courier. We have no visas, and you are not here to meet us properly!'

Some hours later, the two angry and frustrated Hungarians entered the Jewish Agency offices at the Pera Palace. Avriel was struck by Grosz's 'awkward form'. He was a lot more impressed by Joel Brand – who had been travelling with a passport issued by the Germans in the name of 'Eugen Band'. The other Zionists in Istanbul already knew about Brand as a 'dare devil in the Budapest underground'. He was neatly dressed, Avriel remembered, and 'walked with the gait of a sailor, carefully placing one heavy foot after another … His blue eyes were full of sincerity and wonder. He had reddish hair and rosy cheeks.' Grosz immediately drew Avriel to a far corner of the room and launched into a whispered tirade. His 'bad breath mingled with a powerful eau-de-cologne'. 'Don't believe a word of what this fool [Brand] is going to tell you,' Grosz rasped, 'I am the one that put it all on. I was arrested when the Nazis took Hungary. To save myself I invented the greatest stunt of my career. This fool Brand is only the tool of my own salvation. Pay no attention to the fairy tales he will feed you'.[1] It was an inauspicious beginning to Brand's mission to save the lives of 'a million Jews'.

'Trucks, for Example …'

The story of Joel Brand and the mission to save the Jews of Hungary by bartering them for military trucks has been told many times. It has become a kind of myth, or Just So story that tells of a lost opportunity to avert the final spasm of the Nazi genocide. More than seven decades after Brand set off for Istanbul in a German aircraft believing that he could 'save a million lives', historians puzzle over the intent and motivations of the protagonists. There is a profusion of documentary evidence about the German occupation of Hungary but not a single document that reveals definitively the reason why the Germans sent Brand to Istanbul and what they hoped to gain by doing so. There are many who still cling to the notion that the SS offer to trade blood for trucks was made in good faith and that Brand was thwarted by perfidious representatives of the Allied powers. Alternatively, it is argued that the Germans were using the offer as a cover to sow discord by luring the British and Americans into covert negotiations to supply military hardware to be used against the Soviet army on the Eastern Front. Or was the plan to seek back-door contacts with the Allies to end the war? All these questions were raised at the time Brand began his long journey into despair and humiliation. They were the wrong questions then; they are the wrong answers now.

Let us return to May 1944 and trace the events that led to Brand's flight to Istanbul. Remember that for some weeks *before* Eichmann summoned Joel Brand to his headquarters in the Majestic Hotel, the leaders of the Rescue Committee had been negotiating with German agents of the SS and handing over large sums of cash. Some of the Germans involved were former members of the Abwehr who had been associated with the Dogwood network and had been absorbed into the SD – the intelligence wing of the SS. They had been elbowed aside by SS officers in the Eichmann Sonderkommando such as Hermann Krumey, who continued to demand cash payments. Large sums of money had been raised with enormous difficulty by the Hungarian Zionists but in return, the avaricious Germans had offered only to release small numbers of Jews. As the Germans sucked cash out of the Rescue Committee, Eichmann and his collaborators in the Hungarian Ministry of the Interior had reached agreement on the deportation of all Hungarian Jews to Auschwitz. In special Zones, the Hungarian police and gendarmerie, supervised by Dieter Wisliceny, were rounding up Jewish families and incarcerating them in improvised ghettos in preparation for deportation. More than 2,000 Jews, taken from internment camps near Budapest, had already been murdered in Auschwitz. Now in early May, Eichmann took full control of the duplicitous negotiations with the Va'ada committee – with devastating consequences.

In early May, Brand would have four meetings with Eichmann. In his many accounts of these meetings, he is inconsistent about dates – and this confusion about timing is deepened by other accounts, such as the one Kasztner produced after the war. As far as we know, there are no German records at all to cross-reference with these accounts by the members of the Rescue Committee. Brand's versions of what happened and who was present are not entirely reliable: he claimed, for example, that on one occasion Hitler's plenipotentiary in Budapest, Edmund Veesenmayer, was present – which is very unlikely. What we can say for certain is that there was a shifting cast of Germans on the other side of the table – but that Eichmann invariably took the leading role. He was aggressive and arrogant. At the first meeting, Brand was taken to Eichmann's office at the Majestic Hotel. Present too was an 'unknown man', who did not identify himself. This was almost certainly SS-Standartenführer Kurt Becher – who had been despatched to Budapest to negotiate the acquisition of a Hungarian industrial concern on behalf of the SS. We will come back to the significance of Becher's presence shortly.

At the first meeting Eichmann delivered his notorious peroration: 'You know who I am? I solved the Jewish question in Slovakia'.[2] As noted in an earlier chapter, Eichmann needed to establish his role in the proceedings as the key decision-maker on the German side – with power over life and death. Brand and the other members of the Rescue Committee had encountered a bewildering cast of Abwehr agents and SS men – and, not surprisingly, had acquired a confused idea of the hierarchy of authority in the SS. This was the same kind of game of confusion that Krumey had played with Kasztner when he insisted that he would need to 'consult with Wisliceny', who was his subordinate colleague. Eichmann's performance, in other words, rhetorically set in stone the terms of how he would deal with Brand. In that smoke-filled room at the Majestic Hotel, power was concentrated on one side of the table. At no point did the Rescue Committee leaders doubt Eichmann's authority to promise concessions and to barter with lives.

Eichmann: 'I will make a deal with you. We are in the fifth year of the war. We need … and we are not immodest. I am prepared to sell you all the Jews. I am also prepared to have them all annihilated. Anyway what do you want? … Well I want goods for blood.'

Brand did not understand at first and thought Eichmann was demanding money.

Eichmann: 'No, goods for blood. Money comes second.'

Brand: 'What goods?'

Eichmann: 'Go to your international authorities, they will know. For example – lorries. I could imagine one lorry for a hundred Jews, but that is only a suggested figure. Where will you go?'

Brand: 'I must think.'

Was Brand misremembering or was Eichmann really so tentative? 'For example – lorries.' According to the SIME report: 'In reference to the vehicles, Eichmann also said that they would be used on the Eastern Front, and not in the West. Brand took this to be pure propaganda, because they knew Brand would be going to the British and Americans, whom the Germans wished to persuade that the material would be used against the Russians and not against them.'

Brand was then dismissed.

What are we to make of this? At different times during and after the war, Brand offered variants of this bizarre exchange. A decade later, at the Kasztner trial, he testified that Eichmann said: 'I want to do business with you: goods for blood, blood for goods. I'm willing to sell you a million Jews. What [sic] do you want to save?'

In this version, Brand claimed that he refused to make such a choice and said that he must consult his colleagues abroad. Eichmann replied:

'Then go abroad. Go to Switzerland, Turkey, Spain or wherever you want: bring me the goods.'

Brand: 'I asked him which goods.'

'Bring me all sorts of goods,' Eichmann replied. 'Trucks, for example. For 10,000 trucks I am ready to sell you a million Jews: add 1,000 tons of tea, coffee and soap as well, I need all of it.'[3]

What stands out in the many versions of this exchange is the distinctly casual tone of Eichmann's reference to trucks: his words seem to be part of an extemporisation. He seems to have fished the idea of the trucks and the coffee and the soap out of the air. *Trucks, for example ...* Even so, his improvisation was both ingenious and malicious. For Brand and the Rescue Committee leaders would now plunge headlong into a frantic quest to seek out the 'goods' Eichmann demanded in exchange for 'a million lives'.

It is important to stress, without equivocation, before we continue the narrative of the Brand Mission that we can be certain that Eichmann had no intention whatsoever of releasing significant numbers of Hungarian Jews. Some historians have found it difficult to let go of the possibility, the 'glimmer of hope' as Kasztner put it, that Eichmann's makeshift offer to barter a million lives for 10,000 trucks was made in good faith. There can be no doubt at all that Eichmann and his masters in Berlin were fully committed to the destruction of the Hungarian Jews. It was for them both a professional and ideological commitment. We have already shown that during the period following the German occupation of Hungary, Eichmann worked closely with his friend, Rudolf Höß, to ensure that the technologies of selection and mass murder at Auschwitz would be in good order by the time mass deportations were planned to begin in May. Eichmann had to put pressure on Höß to accommodate, under protest, unprecedented numbers of daily transports from Hungary. As we will discover in a later chapter, after the main period of deportation, Eichmann aggressively resisted attempts by Horthy and even his own senior colleagues to halt the deportations.

Even if Eichmann had been serious about bartering lives for goods, SS chieftains Himmler and Kaltenbrunner, to say nothing of his colleagues and friends in the Hungarian Interior Ministry, would not have tolerated a plan to release even a few thousand Jews let alone 'a million'. It has been argued that Heinrich Himmler's faith in the Reich and his devotion to Hitler were wavering. It has even been suggested by the historian Yehuda

Bauer that Himmler knew about the 'Bomb Plot' that was being hatched to assassinate Hitler at his eastern military headquarters and decided not to intervene – hoping to seize power in the aftermath. There is no evidence at all that Himmler knew about the assassination plan – and every indication that both he and Kaltenbrunner, the RSHA chief, were taken completely by surprise when the bomb exploded under Hitler's map table. Himmler was intelligent enough to see by 1944 that the defeat of the Reich was inevitable; he did not, however, possess the courage to stand up to Hitler.

This can be proved beyond a shadow of doubt. During the weeks in May, when Eichmann was hard at work planning the destruction of Hungarian Jewry and hoodwinking the Rescue Committee in Budapest, Himmler made two speeches to Wehrmacht commanders at Sonthofen in the Bavarian Alps. On 5 May, Himmler explained:

> The Jewish question has been solved within Germany itself and in general within the countries occupied by Germany. […] You can understand how difficult it was for me to carry out this military order which I was given and which I implemented out of a sense of obedience and absolute conviction. If you say: 'we can understand as far as the men are concerned but not about the children', then I must remind you of what I said at the beginning. […] In my view, we as Germans, however deeply we may feel in our hearts, are not entitled to allow a generation of avengers filled with hatred to grow up with whom our children and grandchildren will have to deal because we, too weak and cowardly, left it to them.

A few weeks later, on 24 May, he said:

> Another question which was decisive for the inner security of the Reich and Europe, was the Jewish question. It was uncompromisingly solved after orders and rational recognition. I believe, gentleman, that you know me well enough to know that I am not a bloodthirsty person; I am not a man who takes pleasure or joy when something rough must be done. However, on the other hand, I have such good nerves and such a developed sense of duty – I can say that much for myself – that when I recognise something as necessary, I can implement it without compromise … In this circle, I may say it frankly with

a few sentences. It is good that we had the severity to exterminate the Jews in our domain.[4]

There is no equivocation in these pitiless words. Even if Himmler was secretly contemplating releases of Jews in occupied Europe on a mass scale, while preaching about the necessity of annihilation to Wehrmacht generals, he would have had to defy Kaltenbrunner – who was wholly loyal to Hitler and invariably acted to propel forward the Final Solution: and that meant backing Eichmann. There can be little or no doubt that Eichmann's masters in the SS would not have tolerated the scale of the exchange he proposed to Brand.

There was another party that would not have stomached any diminution of the attack on the Jews. I am referring, of course, to Eichmann's Hungarian collaborators in the Ministry of the Interior, the police and gendarmerie. Jaross, the Minister, and his state secretaries Endre and Baky, as well as Ferenczy, the gendarmerie commander, were unswervingly committed to ridding Hungary of Jews and devouring their property and possessions. They jealously protected their right to plunder – and reacted aggressively to any German attempts to siphon off Jewish assets. Eichmann had invested heavily in securing the cooperation of the Hungarians – and his Kommando men depended on many thousands of local police and gendarmes to round up and deport Jews from every occupation Zone in the Hungarian countryside. In May 1944, the sinews of the collaboration were stretched to the limit. Neither Eichmann nor his SS masters would have jeopardised these blood-drenched bonds with their foreign executioners.

After that first encounter, Brand would be summoned to meet Eichmann on three further occasions. At each meeting Eichmann cunningly wove Brand deeper into the web of deceit. During the British interrogations in Cairo, he unintentionally showed how this worked. The Germans, he said, 'must have been serious about the negotiations, because for weeks they spent hours daily listening to his complaints and propositions'. They were, he went on, 'continually complimenting him, saying he was a decent fellow and honest'. He admitted that he was persuaded that 'such people had respect for a man who was fighting for his ideals, and who had the courage to stand up for them'. Eichmann flattered Brand by calling him a 'Jewish idealist': 'You fight for your Jews and I fight for my Germans.'

There has been speculation about why the Germans chose Brand and not Kasztner for the Blood for Trucks mission. It has been implied that Brand was less sophisticated than his friend, who was a former journalist and lawyer and, supposedly, more astute – or even that Kasztner was plotting to seduce Hansi Brand when her husband was sent off to Istanbul. The more convincing argument is that the Germans allocated specific and different roles to the leaders of the Rescue Committee. Kasztner had already shown his unintended worth to the Germans when he travelled to Koloszvár and misled the Jewish leaders about German intentions. Eichmann and Krumey would have seen that Kasztner was becoming increasingly dependent on the status his relationship with the SS conferred. Brand and Kasztner demonstrated equal levels of naivety. With a tragic lack of insight, Kasztner wrote in his Report:

> We have been introduced to new people [i.e. Eichmann and Becher] in the negotiations, whose appearance before us can be treated to some extent as a *deus ex machina*. These new masters seem to have in their hands the comprehensive settlement of the Jewish question. They are not friendly to us in attitude, however they seem to appreciate upright negotiating partners. The negotiations originally started with Wisliceny have thus reached a stage that opens up a glimmer of light in the darkness and an angle for us.

There were other members of the Jewish community who had no difficulty seeing through the mendacity of Eichmann's offer. When Kasztner explained Eichmann's terms at a meeting of the Jewish Council, Fülöp Freudiger was aghast: 'You can't give the enemy trucks! How do you mean to get them? From whom?'

Kasztner replied that: 'In Istanbul there's a rescue committee and there are Jewish Agency representatives: we can fix it.'

This failed to satisfy Freudiger. He insisted the plan couldn't work. Kasztner shot back: 'You're not a Zionist, that's why you think it won't work!'

In other words, Freudiger had no faith in the power of the Jewish Agency. Freudiger shot back: 'True, I'm not a Zionist, but I think it's impossible in any case.'[5]

Like any conman, Eichmann wove a skein of hard facts into his deceit. It was well understood that the German army and the SS desperately needed war materials. In a more sophisticated ploy, Eichmann explained that if Brand's mission to Istanbul succeeded, Jews could not be permitted to travel to Palestine in significant numbers. He explained that this would jeopardise German relations with the Haj Amin al-Husseini, the Grand Mufti of Jerusalem. The Mufti had fled from Palestine in 1936 and had ended up in Berlin. He was lionised by the Nazi elite and, in 1943, travelled to the Balkans to recruit Bosnian Muslims for the Waffen-SS. The Mufti fervently hoped that the Germans would drive the British and the Jews out of Palestine. So, claiming that he was obligated to respect the wishes of the Grand Mufti, Eichmann insisted instead that, if he released Jews, they would have to be sent west into Spain and Portugal.

Eichmann was the master of the well-timed surprise to set the Rescue Committee negotiators on edge. When Brand arrived at the SS headquarters for a third meeting with Eichmann, he was introduced to a Gestapo officer called Gerhard Clages. According to the British report, Eichmann began with, 'I have sent for you because I have something to give you.'

He threw on the table two large envelopes of letters from Switzerland that contained false nationality papers, as well as letters addressed to Brand and other Hungarian Jews. Brand was shocked by this turn of events. Any correspondence between the Rescue Committee and Switzerland was likely to be incriminating. Eichmann had a further surprise. He took a smaller envelope from his pocket. 'Look at this,' he said. Brand opened the envelope and discovered US$32,750.

Eichmann then said: 'This is for your children's relief work. I have nothing against your children's relief activities. Here you have the money and there you have the letters. I have no time to censor them. If they contain anything besides children's relief, report to me about it.'

In future, Brand would receive all foreign correspondence through Clages – and gave him his address: Melinda Utca 24, apartment 1a. Eichmann warned Brand that if he was found to be 'mixing in politics', he would 'take the ground from all his work'.

★★★

It is difficult not to be just a little impressed by the many ways that Eichmann ensnared Brand at this meeting. He distanced himself from the avaricious 'Schmidt Group' by handing back the cash and making clear that he had not taken a cut. He showed that the SS had access to the

Rescue Committee's foreign correspondence and that they would punish any sign of 'political activity'. His threat 'to take the ground away' is a coded way of threatening to end negotiations. By talking to Brand alone, with no other members of the Rescue Committee in the room, he would make him solely responsible for any breakdown in negotiations between the Va'ada and the SS – and the extinguishing of the false 'glimmer of hope' that Kasztner had clutched at.

This is the closest Eichmann came to revealing his real motivation for these sham negotiations. What he meant by 'political activity' was anything that went against the wishes of the SS. From now on, Brand was required to report to the Gestapo officer Clages on any 'political activity'.

Eichmann then turned to details of Brand's mission. He said he had 'confirmation' from Berlin that the 'goods' would only be deployed on the Eastern Front and not on the 'Westwall'. This was a recurrent theme of the negotiations – which has provoked a great deal of confusion. If it is the case, as I have argued, that Eichmann was never serious about exchanging 'good for lives', then the issue of where any of the trucks would be sent is merely 'noise' designed to distract and confuse. When Brand said that 'perhaps he could not get the lorries and other goods', Eichmann retorted: 'the international Jews control the world; they control every British and American official, so that they could lay their hands on anything they wanted.' There's a double bluff here. Eichmann seems to be *parodying* what he assumes that Brand probably believes about Nazi racial mythologies about all powerful Jews. By doing this, he reinforces the sham seriousness of the bartering. The sense that Eichmann is playing a role is deepened by what happened next (according to Brand):

> Eichmann now began stalking up and down the room, saying 'Now I feel absolutely sure of myself. I know you Jews would like to kill me, but now that I am so important for you and do business with you, you will not touch me. But even if the worst comes to the worst, you will never get me, because I will first shoot my wife and child and then myself.'[6]

This is textbook bullying. The aggressor takes on the role of victim to intimidate the powerless. For the rest of the meeting, Eichmann concentrated on practical matters. He asked Brand for two portrait photographs – Krumey, he said, was travelling to Vienna to arrange for passports and to organise the flight to Istanbul. He then asked Brand how long he expected to remain abroad. 'Two or three weeks,' replied Brand. Then: 'Eichmann said he would lay down no definite time limit, but that the quicker the negotiations were concluded the better it would be for the Jews.' If Eichmann used these words, it should have been evident to Brand that the barter deal he was proposing was sham. If Eichmann was bartering 'a million lives' for urgently needed military goods, it would be absurd not to set a 'definite time limit'. Eichmann's transparent bad faith is a grotesque dark comedy.

Brand, however, seems to have been distracted by the vague and contradictory terms of the deal Eichmann proposed. What did the Germans actually want? Blood for Trucks sounds cut and dried. But at different times, Brand reported, Eichmann discussed trucks for the Waffen-SS, railway wagons to transport Jews across Europe, consumer goods, money and even repatriation of interned German citizens to the Reich ... Brand admitted: 'I did not have a clear offer – Eichmann only told me some kinds of goods or money which I should bring.'

At the same time that Brand was wrangling with Eichmann at the SS headquarters, Kasztner was meeting Wisliceny, who had returned to Budapest from Northern Transylvania. His tasks there had been completed. Tens of thousands of Jews were incarcerated in makeshift ghettos. Once again, the wily SS officer took the role of the concerned friend of the Jews who unwillingly followed orders. In his Report, Kasztner remembered that Wisliceny admitted that the Germans had made a final decision to deport all Jews – but that the Brand Mission was a last, fragile chance to *gain time*. From this point on 'gaining time' would run like a slippery thread through all the Zionists' pleas to the Jewish Agency and representatives of the Allied powers. The cruel truth is that *there was no time to be gained*. The timetable of destruction was set.

Eichmann had another surprise to spring on Brand. When he flourished the intercepted mail from Switzerland and the envelopes stuffed with cash, Brand realised that there was only one possible way that the SS could have laid hands on the material. The source must be Bandi Grosz, who had become a trusted envoy of Zionist and Jewish organisations in Switzerland and Turkey. Eichmann confirmed his hunch: 'he [Brand] must give GROSS [*sic*] 10% commission of all monies received. He gave EICHMANN a receipt for the full sum, and later that day handed over to GROSS the required commission, of which GROSS said that he himself would only get 25%.'

There is no evidence that Grosz himself ever met Eichmann. It was the Gestapo officer Gerhard Clages, who was present at one of the meetings at the SS headquarters, who acted as go-between. On the other hand, there is nothing that implies that Eichmann was kept in the dark by Clages – since they had conspired to bamboozle Brand into accepting that the SD would have oversight of any mail and cash sent to the Rescue Committee. As it happened, soon after this meeting at the SS headquarters, Clages himself summoned Brand to his residence at Melinda Utca 24 – and handed him a second batch of mail, unopened, that again must have been passed on to him by Grosz. When Brand peered inside the letters, he was horrified to see a list, written in Hebrew, of some twenty non-Jewish Hungarian politicians who were then in hiding. Thinking quickly, he managed to conceal this incriminating list from Clages – and, after meeting with Kasztner and other committee members, a decision was made to burn the list. The fact that the Rescue Committee members needed to discuss what to do with the list at all implies that they were now very nervous about contravening any promises made to the SS not to engage in politics. There was also money in the post – and Clages, as Eichmann had, demanded a commission on behalf of Grosz.

Bandi Grosz was now deeply involved in the negotiations with the SS. Why?

Grosz Deception

By the middle of May, preparations for Brand's flight to Istanbul had been completed. Krumey had provided him with a fake German passport in the name of 'Eugen Band', an engineer resident in Erfurt, and arranged flights from Vienna to Istanbul. Earlier in the month, the Va'ada committee had sent coded telegrams to Jewish Agency representatives in Istanbul to arrange Turkish visas for Brand and Winninger, the formerly disgraced Abwehr agent who was expected at the time to accompany Brand. The Istanbul office responded immediately: 'Chaim' would be ready to meet the delegate of the Hungarian Jews. This was, of course, Chaim *Barlas*, one of the most important members of the Jewish group in Istanbul. Yet the Rescue Committee immediately assumed they would be meeting Chaim *Weizmann*, the President of the Zionist Congress who lived in London and was an influential member of the British establishment.

This misunderstanding is hard to fathom. The name of Chaim Barlas should have been well known to the Rescue Committee in Budapest, which had communicated with the Jewish Agency in Istanbul for years. Although Weizmann was involved in efforts to aid European Jewry, it would have been an improbable decision on his part to travel to Istanbul to meet an unknown Hungarian. The Rescue Committee did not trouble to enquire any further about the 'Chaim' who promised to meet them in Istanbul – and for their part, no one in Istanbul seems to have bothered to apply for the visas.

It is puzzling that Eichmann had insisted that the former Abwehr officer, Jószef Winninger, accompany Brand on the flight to Istanbul. We know that the 'Schmidt Group', which included Winninger, had fallen out of favour when the SS took over the Abwehr – but this does not completely explain why it was Grosz and not Winninger who flew to Istanbul with Brand. Brand told his British interrogator: 'before he left Budapest, he began to feel that even the S.D. wanted GROSS [sic] to accompany him in order to watch his movements.' He then added this odd detail:

GROSS was always together with LAUFER and KLAGES [Gerhard Clages]. These latter two treated GROSS with scant respect, often sending him for such things as butter and cheese and only paying him the official price. Since the best foods could only be bought on the black market, GROSS forced BRAND to make up the difference in price.[7]

This strongly suggests that Grosz had become a kind of gofer for Laufer and Clages. The question is, to what end?

Brand met Eichmann for the last time in Budapest on 15 May. He would be leaving for Istanbul two days later. These dates are very significant. For some weeks, the Germans had been organising final arrangements for the deportation of the Hungarian Jews. Eichmann's transport expert, Franz Novak, worked closely with Theodor Ganzenmüller, the powerful director of the German railway system, the Deutsche Reichsbahn, to procure the necessary rolling stock demanded by the SS. The schedule of deportations and the complex system of route planning was finalised at an aforementioned conference in Vienna in early May, which was attended by Novak, the German Foreign Office official in charge of Jewish affairs, Eberhard von Thadden, Captain László Lulay of the gendarmerie as well as representatives of the German, Hungarian and Slovak railway systems.

Von Thadden insisted on using a route across eastern Slovakia, passing through Kassa (Košice), the rail hub on the border, Presov, Muszyna, Tarnow and Cracow to Auschwitz. Four trains would be despatched every day – *starting on 15 May*. Deportation from gendarmerie districts VIII, IX and X, which encompassed Carpatho-Ruthenia, north-eastern Hungary and Northern Transylvania, began on schedule on 15 May.

At the end of the war, members of the Hungarian 'National Committee for Attending Deportees' (DEGOB), recorded the testimonies of some 5,000 Hungarian Holocaust survivors. Today, many of these testimonies can now be accessed online and in English: DEGOB is the most extensive Holocaust testimonial online database in the world. These, as well as other eyewitness accounts of the deportations, expose the grotesque brutality of the German perpetrators and their Hungarian collaborators. This was all happening as Brand waited for Eichmann to call him into his office. In the city of Munkács, 12,000 Jews were driven from the ghetto to the railway depot:

> By guards using whips, machine guns and rifle butts. They were then compelled to lay down their baggage and undress – men, women and children alike … women, who were called in specially, together with Gestapo men, policemen and gendarmes went through their baggage and clothing, even opening stitches to discover whether the Jews had hidden anything … The crush of the desperate crowd and the frenzied confusion were terrible. Here, 90 persons were crowded into a freight car … the cars were then chained and padlocked. Each got a bucket full of water and an empty one for excrements …

In Hungary that May, it was hot – and the trains remained standing at the depot platform for a day. 'By that time many became mad, and many more died … The corpses were removed three days later at Csap, where also the mad were clubbed or shot.'

Samu Stern, the head of the Budapest Jewish Council, described how after the Hungarians had beaten and abused a crowd of Jews, 'the SS men of Wisliceny and Zöldi's special unit put in an appearance. They surrounded the ghetto with loaded machine-guns in hand, watching with the eyes of lynxes until the trains rolled in'.

Reports of progress were sent daily to the SS offices and the German Legation in Budapest and were forwarded by Veesenmayer to the Foreign

Office in Berlin. The reports reveal that the numbers deported reached 23,363 within two days. By 18 May, 51,000 people had been crammed into trains and despatched to Auschwitz. The numbers climbed ceaselessly in the days and weeks and months that followed. In just twenty-four days, the SS deported 289,357 Jews from Zones I and II in ninety-two trains. Through June and into early July, the death trains rolled without cease from all the other deportation Zones through Slovakia and into occupied Poland.[8]

Information about the deportations soon reached the Jews in Budapest. When Eichmann summoned Brand into his office on 15 May:

[Brand] had received information that mass deportations had recommenced. EICHMANN and KRUMEY had previously told him that some would be inevitable, but it would be for purposes of work and would be carried out in a humane manner. He now had concrete information that old people and small children were included in the party [sic], and that the deportations had been completed with the same degree of cruelty as previously …

Eichmann, according to the report, 'snapped back that they could not sell him all the Jews, because there was not enough money in all the world for that. Those capable of working would remain in GERMANY; the others would be sold first.' This was nonsense, of course – and another bizarre exchange soon followed. When Brand shouted that he had information that the deported Jews were being taken to Auschwitz: 'EICHMANN laughed – "So AUSSCHWYTZ [sic] has a bad name with you. It doesn't matter. They are only distributing camps'.

Brand's 'complaints' about what was happening were utterly pointless. This macabre exchange suggests that Brand was falling ever deeper into the SS trap. He knew what took place at Auschwitz and yet he seems to have believed Eichmann's cynical deceit that 'they are only distributing camps'. If the SIME report is to be believed, Eichmann then moved the conversation back to Brand's schedule. Brand said he might now be required to travel to Palestine. 'Good,' replied Eichmann. 'But be as quick as possible.'

At this final meeting, Eichmann was joined by Krumey and 'two civilians'. Brand said that Grosz later identified them as the HSSPF Winckelmann, who would surely have been in uniform, and

Veesenmayer. This is impossible to confirm. What we do know from Kasztner's Report is that: 'Kurt Becher, head of the Waffen-SS economic staff in Budapest, also took part in the last discussions between Brand and Eichmann. Brand knew nothing about Becher and in what capacity he was present.'[9]

By now, the Germans had come up with a final list of 'Goods': Eichmann, it would seem, had given up even trying to make the exchange seem credible:

10,000 lorries
800 Zentner [1 Zentner = 50 kilos] coffee
200 Zentner tea
200 Zentner cocoa or chocolate
2 million bars of soap

As Brand left the office, one of the 'civilians' called out, 'Don't forget my lorries – they must be for cold temperature. Some must have trailers, and all must have spare parts.' The SS men were now treating the Brand Mission with open contempt.

When Kurt Becher was questioned after the end of the war, he was asked whether 'this grand "Jews for Goods" deal – a million Jews for 10,000 truck – could succeed?' he replied simply: 'No.' Asked whether Himmler would have released a million Jews: 'No.'[10]

The following day, this bizarre chain of events took another turn. Brand arranged to meet Krumey to discuss at what time they would leave Budapest the following day. They arranged to meet at the Opera House Café at 3 p.m. Shortly afterwards, Fritz Laufer, the former Dogwood network agent who had joined the SD, telephoned Brand and insisted that he come to his office at the same time, 3 p.m. When Brand pointed out he had agreed to meet Krumey then, Laufer said 'he would arrange that'. The next day, Joel and Hansi took a taxi to Laufer's office. She waited outside. When Brand entered the office, he found Laufer in conversation with Clages and 'three or four civilians'. Brand claimed later that Veesenmayer and Winckelmann were also present – but this is highly unlikely. Laufer told him that Grosz 'was expected but had been delayed'. Now Laufer handed Brand an 'open list without an envelope' of the required 'goods'. The list was now absurdly elaborated:

Lorries.
Tea.
Coffee.
Cocoa.
Soap.
Boring machines.
Tool-making machines.
Spare parts for all types of machines.
Lathes.
Hides.
Tanning materials.
Chrome.
Foreign currency, including dollars.
Swiss francs and S. American pesetas.

Not a single figure or quantity was specified. Brand tried to explain to his sceptical British interrogator that 'Swiss Francs had been of particular interest to the Germans'. Did he really take this surreal list seriously? Spare parts of all types of machines? How many hides? Chrome? Echoing Eichmann, Laufer then asked how long Brand would be away. Brand again replied that he might have to go to Palestine. There was no time limit, Laufer replied, but he must be as quick as possible. Eichmann had used much the same words. This was surely collusion in skulduggery.

By this time, Grosz had arrived – and he stayed on to talk to Laufer and Clages after Brand left to meet Krumey at the Opera House Café, taking Hansi with him. Grosz joined them about half an hour later. This was the sting. Brand recalled that 'GROSS [*sic*] drew a letter from his pocket, saying these were his instructions.' Brand went on:

[the instructions] consisted of about 1¼ quarto pages of typing. GROSS said he had to learn them by heart. BRAND was to know nothing about them, and it would be better if he did know nothing. BRAND was too occupied with his own business and was not of a curious nature, so he did not ask any questions …

Brand made no reference to Krumey's part in this encounter. But we can be sure he reported what had been said back to Eichmann. We learn from this that:

Grosz stayed behind at Laufer's office to receive the 'instructions'. The 'instructions' had been composed by Gestapo officers Laufer and Clages. The contents of the document were, at this stage, concealed from Brand. Krumey was present when Grosz revealed the existence of the instructions, which implies that Clages and Laufer were not acting independently of Eichmann.

When Brand testified at the Eichmann trial many years later, he revealed that in the days before his flight, he had argued frequently with Kasztner. At one point Kasztner demanded to know why Grosz was accompanying Brand – and not himself. This is how Brand described these arguments during the Eichmann trial in 1961:

> Q. Who chose you to be sent to Istanbul, Eichmann or the Jews?
> A. Both. Eichmann sent for me and asked where I wanted to go.
> Q. That you would go and no one else …
> A. Eichmann did not say 'no one else.' Eichmann said I should go, whereupon I said I had to have the confirmation of the committee. The committee selected me, and I said that I would see. All the Zionist parties chose me.
> Q. Did the late Dr Kasztner not suggest someone else?
> A. Yes. Dr Kasztner made various proposals; above all, he wanted his father-in-law to go, Dr Jozsi Fischer. The committee was against him, because he was not known in our work, he was a Jewish notable, not a Jewish leader.
> Q. Why did Dr Kasztner not go himself?
> A. Dr Kasztner voiced reproaches to me at the end. At the beginning he never suggested himself as a counter-candidate to myself; at the end he reproached me heatedly: 'Why did you not arrange things,' he would shout at me on the last day or two, 'so that instead of Bandi Grosz I come with you?' I could not have done that. I would rather have gone with Kasztner than with Bandi Grosz.[11]

The answer to the question 'Why Grosz?' was that the *Germans* insisted that he go to Istanbul with Brand – in order *to make sure that Kasztner remained in Budapest*. Brand may well have been happier with this arrangement than he implied during his trial testimony. He did not wish to be outshone in Istanbul by Kasztner. Brand often referred to Grosz with barely disguised contempt, but Hungarian survivor László Devecseri told the historian Szabolcs Szita that Brand and Grosz attended a family gathering together and talked 'as if they were the gods who save the Hungarian Jews'.[12]

At 5 p.m. the following day, Krumey picked up Brand and Grosz in his car and drove across the Chain Bridge into Buda, where they entered the tunnel that ran beneath the Castle. Krumey followed the Danube across the watery flatland of the Szigetköz through Győr and crossed the Austrian border at Hegyeshalom. It was close to midnight when Krumey parked close to the Metropole Hotel on Morzinplatz – the Gestapo headquarters. The next morning, Krumey disappeared to make the final arrangements and returned with tickets for the flight. He insisted that Brand pay for both himself and Grosz. He told the Hungarians that the aircraft was scheduled to take off at 6 a.m. the following morning – but there was a hitch. Another Gestapo officer appeared who informed the two men that the Foreign Office in Berlin had not yet given permission for the flight. He explained that Krumey would take them to the airport in the morning, and 'talk to the pilot'. Brand spent a sleepless night, wondering whether he would ever reach Istanbul.

Krumey, as arranged, picked the two men up at 5 a.m. Just as the twin engines of the Junkers sputtered into life, Krumey took Grosz aside and handed him a briefcase. Grosz, in turn, passed the 'letter of instructions' to Krumey. Presumably he had not learned them by heart. Brand discovered that the mysterious briefcase was empty: Grosz let him store all his cigarettes inside. When Grosz had boarded the aircraft, Krumey took Brand aside and told him 'not to hurry back' but to make sure he had 'settled all the business'. He then asked that Brand make sure that 'in the answer he brought back', he emphasised that Krumey's 'methods' had 'persuaded the Allies that the Germans were serious in their offer'. This a very odd statement. Later, many of the SS men who took part in the Hungarian deportations, including Krumey, would claim that they had helped the Rescue Committee to save Jews. Here, if Brand's recollection is correct, Krumey appeared to be seeking a favourable assessment of his devious activities to be conveyed to Eichmann and his SS colleagues.

The German courier aircraft landed at Sofia to refuel, where Brand noticed that 'Grosz had plenty of friends.' They arrived in Istanbul in the late afternoon. As soon as they landed, Brand was to be badly disappointed. The Jewish Agency had not succeeded – or perhaps even attempted – in acquiring entry visas – and, in any case, Brand was now bearing a passport in a different name that would have been unknown to the Agency. To cap the confusing humiliation of the visas, the 'Chaim' who had come to the airport to meet the two Hungarians turned out to be not the President of the Zionist Congress but Chaim Barlas.

Joel Brand's mission was rapidly falling off the rails.

By the time the German Junkers Ju 52 with Brand and Grosz on board landed in Istanbul, 23,363 Hungarian Jews had been deported to Auschwitz.

17

THE RAMP

At the beginning of June 1944, the atmosphere at the Berghof, Adolf Hitler's Alpine retreat, was relaxed. Every afternoon, Hitler would don his cape and hat, select a walking stick and lead a party of devotees to the Tea House for *Kaffee und Kuchen*. Here he held forth on his favourite obsessions: the Jews, Bolsheviks and architecture. The flow of words was incessant. On 5 June, he invited his Propaganda Minister to accompany him. Goebbels was pleasantly surprised that his idol appeared healthier and in better spirits than he had for many months. For most of the year, he had despaired as Hitler sank into one depression after another and took on the sallow appearance of a crushed old man. Now he listened enthralled as Hitler spoke of his grandiose new plans for Europe and predicted that the Allied invasion would be smashed on the Atlantic Wall. That evening, Goebbels joined Hitler and Eva Braun to view newsreels and discuss, with waspish good humour, the latest film and theatre productions. 'All in all,' he confided to his diary, 'the mood is like the good old times.' As Goebbels left early on the morning of 6 June, lightning flickered, and thunder crashed in the Bavarian Alps. Another hammer blow was about to descend on Hitler's Thousand Year Reich.

Operation Overlord, the Allied invasion of Europe, was planned to start on the morning of 5 June. Weather reports had forced Dwight Eisenhower, the Allied Supreme Commander, to delay. The German navy dismissed the likelihood of an invasion between 5–7 June because of bad weather and cancelled patrols in the English Channel. Generalfeldmarschall Erwin Rommel, who Hitler had made responsible for defending Northern France, decided to leave for Germany to celebrate his wife's birthday.

Then, on the Allied side, new information indicated that the weather might improve on the evening of 5 June and Eisenhower made a decision 'to go'. By the early morning of 6 June, the vast invasion armada had crossed the choppy waters of the Channel and assembled off the coast of Normandy under an overcast sky. As dawn broke, Allied battleships, cruisers and destroyers began a massive bombardment. A German infantry officer reported that it seemed as if the whole horizon was a solid mass of fire. Then thousands of landing craft were released from the Allied ships and began battling choppy seas as they steered towards the beaches.

By the end of that day, British, American and Canadian troops had begun to establish beachheads on the European continent. Six days later, the Allies had forged a single front line backed by the might of their air forces. German optimism that the Allies would be beaten back evaporated in days. When Hitler flew to his old western headquarters at Margival to meet with his military commanders in the west, Field Marshalls Erwin Rommel and Gerd von Rundstedt, he lashed out at the failure to hold the front. The conference became acrimonious. Back at the Berghof, Hitler stepped back into the realm of irrational and fevered optimism. Even as Allied bombers pounded Berlin, destroying the administrative heart of the city, he astonished Goebbels, who was calling for a declaration of 'Total War', that the crisis was not yet sufficiently serious to 'pull out all the stops'.

As the Allied armies pushed, against fierce resistance, from the Normandy coast into France and towards the German borders, there was catastrophic news from the Eastern Front. On 22 June, the third anniversary of the German invasion of the Soviet Union, Stalin's generals launched a new offensive named for one of the Russian generals who pushed Napoleon back from Moscow in 1812, Operation Bagration. A massive force of 2.5 million men, 5,000 tanks and 5,300 aircraft was thrown at the battered centre of the German front line, which was swiftly shattered at Vitebsk. A vast horde of tanks roared through the gap.

Along the German front line clustered a string of fortresses that Hitler insisted should be defended at all costs against the Bolshevik forces. As ever, in the Führer's mind any discussion of strategic retreat was anathema. It was a terrible miscalculation. The immense Soviet attack simply flowed around the fortresses, cutting off the German divisions. A month later, the Soviet Army had smashed a 100-mile gap in the front and pushed 200 miles to the west. The German army lost twenty-eight divisions.

For Stalin's generals, the great barrier of the Vistula and the city of Warsaw now lay within striking distance. Beyond, tantalisingly, was the border of East Prussia.

Let Them Go Through the Chimney

Historians of the Holocaust have been at pains to stress the 'rationality' of the German occupation of Hungary and the deportation of the nation's Jewish citizens. It is true that Nazi leaders and the German industrialists who had grown rich from Hitler's war of annihilation and its monstrous harvest of slave workers calculated that Hungarian Jews would provide a source of labour. On 26 May 1944, Albert Speer, the Minister of Armaments and Production, demanded to be informed precisely when the Hungarian Jews would be available for deployment in his factories. Hans Kammler, the SS construction chief, assured him that the transports were already 'on their way'.

Before hundreds of thousands of Hungarian Jews could be despatched to feed ravenous German factories and work camps, they had to pass through Auschwitz. The SS was interested only in acquiring 'pieces' that could work. This doomed the young, the old and the weak to certain death. The spring and summer of 1944 was the deadliest period for Jews in the history of the Auschwitz camps. This was the period when the Theresienstadt 'family camp' was liquidated. In the aftermath of the mass murder of Hungarian Jews, nearly 3,000 Roma in the 'Gypsy Camp' were killed in early August. When the trucks arrived, some of the Roma realised what the SS intended – and many of them resisted. 'It was not easy to get them inside the gas chambers,' Höß acknowledged. These often disregarded victims of the Auschwitz mass murder machine should never be forgotten. But the majority of losses during this frenzy of killing were Hungarian Jews. As the historian of the SS concentration camp system Nikolaus Wachsmann writes: 'Their murder marked the climax of the Holocaust in Auschwitz, at a time when most European Jews under German control had been killed.'[1]

For nearly two months between mid May and the end of the first week in July, transports from Kassa on the Hungarian border rolled through Slovakia and into occupied Poland. The slowest trains took between four and five days, which was punishing for the people crammed inside the trucks. It was a fiercely hot summer, and many perished or lost their minds. For the SS, thirst was a weapon. It caused severe distress and sapped energy; the thirsty cannot easily resist their fate. It was forbidden to remove the dead from inside the trucks and corpses began to decompose rapidly in the heat. For the deported Jews, the doors of hell opened long before the trains reached their destination alongside the Judenrampe.

For the Auschwitz Sonderkommandos (the Jewish slave workers) such as Filip Müller, who waited near the crematoria inside the camp, the shrill sound of the train whistle, the scream of wheels and the hiss of escaping steam announced the arrival of another laden transport. Locked inside the cattle trucks, survivors of the journey heard, as the clanking and grinding of the locomotive faded, the mellifluous sounds of one of the camp orchestras. Despite the fanatical preparations of Rudolf Höß and his accomplices, the facilities built at Auschwitz II were quickly over-whelmed. On some days, as many as five trains pulled up alongside the 'Judenrampe'. Höß pleaded with his friend, Eichmann, to moderate the tempo but, as Eichmann informed the Dutch Nazi Willem Sassen after the war, he point-blank refused.

The SS deception strategy had worked its malevolent seduction all too well. As the SS guards and prisoners from the 'Kanada' work camp stationed on the ramp hauled back the cattle truck doors, few of the survivors inside had any idea where their journey had ended – and the deadly nature of what was about to take place. Unlike the leaders of the Va'ada Rescue Committee and the Jewish Council in Budapest, few had even heard of Auschwitz. This is the angry leitmotif of Elie Wiesel's liter-ary accounts of the destruction of Hungarian Jewry – and of many other eyewitness narratives that have survived. Some, it is true, knew or feared that deportation meant almost certain death – but preferred to take their chances rather than stay in the ghettos, where they were at the mercy of the cruel and greedy Hungarian gendarmes. When I interviewed Tomi Komoly, in his home near Manchester, he told me of the experience of a Jewish partisan called Asher Arany. One day, during the last weeks of the deportations in early July, Arany stumbled across a line of unguarded cattle wagons that had halted close to the Hungarian border. This is his account, translated by Tomi from an unpublished Hebrew memoir:

> One of the most shocking duties I had to fulfil those days was to drive to the area of the Polish–Hungarian border in the wild Carpathian region

near Hollókő. This was the place where the deportee wagons were handed over from the Hungarians to the SS. I had with me a large packet of documents, arrived at a train which stood about 500 metres away from the station. The Hungarians had already left, and the Germans not yet taken control of it. The guards were at the station, with nothing to worry about, as the wagons were locked awaiting arrival of another consignment, to complete a train. In accordance with the regular habits of the Germans, the initial wagonload could be waiting up to 4 days without food, drink, or the possibility of getting out of the carriages for fresh air or relieving themselves. I approached the furthest wagon, managed to open the door, and talked to the people inside, only resembling humans. I told them 'we are near the Polish border, from here they will take you to a place from which nobody comes back! Follow me, take from me these documents and money, and run into the woods. The guards are momentarily away. I'm approaching you as a free man from the mountains, come with me to the nearby forests, now is your last chance to be saved … Within seconds a great commotion broke out. Those inside started to ask questions and tried to convince me that they are going to a workers' camp, where they are to work in good conditions, even get some spending money. They asked me to shut the door and leave while it was still possible. I went to the next wagon and received the identical response. I then lied to these, saying: 'the deportees of one wagon have already gone to the woods, come with me and follow them' – but in spite of this I was rejected again: 'No! the guards will find us, and we'll be beaten up as a punishment!' I continued to insist, and then they threatened me that unless I closed the door, they would call the guards. One of them shouted at me: 'You Zionist, you adventurer, taking risks at our expense! Go away.' I opened more wagons, but couldn't find anyone who would agree to escape. As the signs of dawn appeared, I had to abandon them, with a sense of total failure.[2]

Hours later, the SS guards turned up and the final consignment of wagons was attached to the train. Soon, it was steaming across Slovakia towards the border of occupied Poland.

Here is one remarkable account of the moment of arrival inside the death camp:

There was a drizzle. Never before or since have I seen such grey skies, such wasteland … As we looked out the window, we saw a terrible sight.

The entire horizon was red, and we thought we would be taken directly into that fire. Older people said the prayer of death and took farewell from each other …[3]

As the trucks were emptied of their human cargo, the SS screamed and bellowed at and shoved the deportees; they ripped packages from their hands and made gruesome comments about their fate. Some of the less brutalised 'Kanadakommando' workers tore children from the arms of young women and handed them over to older men or women. This brutal action saved lives, for any woman with a child would immediately be sent to be gassed. The children and the old could not be saved. The Kommandos whispered warnings, at huge risk to their own lives, that older men and women should claim to be younger, and youths should lie and claim to be older.

There is a photograph of two brothers clad in Hungarian-style coats and hats who in May 1944 were deported from Bilke in Carpatho-Ruthenia to Auschwitz. On 26 May, SS photographers caught their last moments. The two boys stand puzzled and confused on the ramp. We know that their names were Sril (Israel), who is looking straight at the camera, and Zelig Jákob – both were murdered soon after they had been stopped in time by the photographer. So too was their mother. Their older sister, Lili, father, Mordechai, and two older brothers survived the selection on the ramp. The fate of hundreds of thousands was shaped by age and gender. Who was fit for work? Lili tried to stay with her mother as she was led away to the crematoria, but an SS guard shoved her back into the line of prisoners – wounding her with his bayonet. Many weeks later, Lili ended up at the Mittelbau-Dora underground forced labour camp. She was discovered here, close to death, on 9 April 1945 by American soldiers. She was deathly ill with typhus and weighed 90lb. She was, by the end of the war, the only member of her family not to have perished.[4]

A young woman from Munkács testified:

[The selecting doctor] promised that we would meet our relatives again and he tore me from my mother's hand saying I could walk on my own feet. Although the Poles and the Slovaks told us then that my mother and siblings were gassed, we did not want to believe them and learned of the terrible reality only later …

Many of those selected for work could not comprehend the fate of their mothers and siblings: 'the old, the weak, young mothers with children were not sent to the other side to transport them into the camp on trucks, but to be murdered with gas'.

It was the SS medical staff who, like evil deities, were charged with the task of selection. They were the masters of life and death in the abysmal rift of time that followed the arrival of the transports. As Höß had discovered during his visits to Budapest, Hungary's brutal Labour Service decrees had fundamentally altered the demographic of the Hungarian Jewish population by forcibly removing young men to serve, or rather in many cases, be sacrificed on the Eastern Front. The consequences of the Labour Service cull were played out on the ramp. The SS physicians classified as unfit for labour pregnant women, the elderly, young children and their families. At the end of each day, diligent clerks sent reports to the WVHA offices in Berlin to update Himmler's managers on the numbers of slave workers who had become available to the Reich. Höß had calculated that just 25 per cent of the Hungarian Jews would turn out to be suitable for work – and the SS men on the ramp seemed to have picked out just one in four of the new arrivals as 'fit'. The rest would be murdered.[5]

★★★

Müller described the:

> long columns of those who during selections had been chosen for the walk to the gas chambers struggled along the dusty roads, exhausted and in low spirits, mothers pushing prams, taking the older children by the hand. The young helped and supported the old and sick. Some had strayed into this procession because on the ramp they had implored the SS not to separate them from their frail and helpless relatives …[6]

They were all exhausted and thirsty. The SS men promised them tea and soup after a bath. Here at the sham bath house, the Sonderkommando men laboured, 900 of them – herding and pushing Jews into the gas chambers and hauling out their naked bodies for incineration.

We have another remarkable account of the slaughter of the Hungarian Jews. It was written by Dr Miklós Nyiszli, a Jewish pathologist who was deported from the Aknaszlatina ghetto near Nagyvárad – and chosen as a medical assistant by Dr Josef Mengele. Mengele is a notorious figure in many Holocaust narratives – and mythologised as the archetypal evil Nazi doctor. The fact is that Mengele was a respected member of the German medical profession who had been encouraged by his doctoral tutor, Dr Otmar Freiherr von Verschuer, to take a position in a concentration camp where he would have unique access to enslaved bodies available for experiment. The professor and his student corresponded regularly about their shared interest in the genetics of twins. At Auschwitz, Mengele was just one of many doctors who exploited the camp system to carry out unregulated experiments on prisoners. In a series of sterilisation experiments, Dr Carl Clauberg injected various caustic substances into the uteruses and fallopian tubes of Jewish women, without using any kind of anaesthetic, causing severe internal inflammation. Other SS doctors at the camp administered 'vitamin injections' to female prisoners which, unknown to the victims, caused them to become sterile.

After his star student fled into exile, the good Dr Otmar Freiherr von Verschuer enjoyed a lucrative and prestigious career in the new West Germany of Konrad Adenauer – with privileged access to the data harvested from the pain of the experimental victims of Auschwitz.

On 29 July 1945, Dr Nyiszli testified to the National Committee of Hungarian Jews for Attending Deportees (DEGOB). When he arrived on the ramp in Auschwitz, he was first assigned to the Buna work camp as a slave worker, but was soon transferred, thanks to his medical qualifications:[7]

I studied medicine in Germany and practiced as a pathologist for many years. I easily passed the test, as did my colleague who worked in a Medical School in Strasbourg. Within one hour, accompanied by two armed SS guards, we were put in a well-equipped Red Cross ambulance. To my horror, we were driven to the courtyard of Crematorium 1 in Auschwitz where our documents were handed over to the commander of the Crematorium, Oberscharführer Mussfeld. They immediately gave us firm instructions what we may and may not look at. Then we were led into a clean room, and Oberscharführer Mussfeld let us know that it was furnished specifically for us at the orders of Dr Mengele. The Crematorium staff, known as the Sonderkommando and counting some two hundred inmates, lived on the second floor. The Oberscharführer immediately requisitioned for us a full set of clothing and underwear of excellent quality taken from gassed victims.

Dr Mengele arrived after a few hours and put us through another oral examination lasting about one hour ...

Mengele wasted no time putting his new assistants to work:

We took measurements of these people, then Oberscharführer Mussfeld shot them in the head, after which we were ordered to perform an autopsy and prepare a detailed report. Subsequently, we applied chloride of lime to the abnormally developed corpses and sent the thoroughly cleaned and packed bones to the Anthropological Institute in Berlin-Dahlem.

At other times, Dr Nyiszli was able to observe the fate of other Jews deported from Hungary:

We received subjects for our scientific autopsies either from the camp or recently arrived transports. In the months of May, June and July an average of 3–4 Hungarian transports arrived at the Auschwitz Judenrampe. The selections were performed in shifts by Dr Mengele and Dr Thilo. Ability to work was the sole selection criteria and at times it was quite invasive. As part of the selection process, newly arrived transports were divided into two groups one to the right, the other to the left. The right side meant life, the left side the crematorium. In terms of percentage, 78–80% was sent to the left: children, mothers with young children, the elderly, pregnant women, the handicapped and disabled servicemen. In a few minutes, the crowd on the left started to move slowly to the left, carrying their personal belongings. The crematoria were around 200 meters from the Judenrampe, and the crowd of approximately 2000 people passed under the gate to crematoria 1, 2, 3 or 4 as ordered ...[8]

In 1952, a delegation from the Polish ruling party inspected the ruins of Auschwitz and discovered a diary that had been buried close to Crematorium III and signed 'A.Y.R.A'. Researchers eventually identified the diarist as Arye Yehuda Regel Arucha, whom other prisoners called Leyb Langfus: Regel Arucha is Hebrew for 'long foot' (Langfuss). Later, other documents, almost certainly by Langfus, were unearthed in the same area of the camp. Langfus was born in Warsaw and became a rabbi in the town of Makov-Mazovietsk. As a recalcitrant member of the

Judenrat, he always insisted that the Germans should never be believed or trusted and must be opposed. Langfus and his wife and son were deported at the end of 1942: only he survived the ramp. He was forced to work as a Sonderkommando in the crematoria, in which he had the task of disinfecting and preparing huge volumes of women's hair for shipment to Germany. The final entry in his journal (which concludes with the writer's last will and testament) is dated 26 October 1944 – he was another witness to the murder of the Hungarian Jews.

Langfus wrote of two Hungarian Jews who asked him, 'Shall we say the Confession [the Vidui] ... They then pulled out bottles of brandy happily raising their bottles in a toast to life: *L'chaim!*' They were murdered soon afterwards. At the end of May, Langfus recorded, a transport arrived from Kassa. Among the deportees was a Rebbetzin, a female religious teacher:

> already 85 years old ... She said: 'Only now do I see the extinction of the Jews of Hungary ... When the Jews asked the advice of their rabbis, they calmed them. The Rabbi of Belz said that the Jews of Hungary would know nothing worse than fear. Until the bitter day came when the Jews were thrown into hell. Oh yes, the heavenly ones concealed it from them but at the last minute they alone escaped to the land of Israel; they saved their own souls, leaving their flocks to be slaughtered ...'[9]

In his final entry, Langfus wrote that he and the other Sonderkommandos had been put to work dismantling the crematoria ovens, which would soon be sent to Germany. He added that he and another 170 comrades were about to be taken to a shower – and put to death.

The SS officers who presided over the factory of death in the summer of 1944 went about their tasks with a demented haste. They bullied the Sonderkommandos to work ever faster. Filip Müller observed that some victims were still breathing when he pulled open the doors of the gas chamber:

> One after the other the bodies were dragged out by the bearers who placed them side by side on their backs in a long row where their teeth were removed by dental mechanics, their body orifices searched for hidden valuables, and the hair of the women cut off ...

Human hair was a vital raw material for the war industry; it was used to manufacture industrial felts and threads. For the Sonderkommandos, who clung to life by doing the bidding of their SS masters, this was labour intensive work. These crematoria were the factories of the kingdom of death, despatching stolen treasures back to the Reich.

And let us not forget that work in the German camps was itself lethal in the long run and intended to be so. One Hungarian survivor described conditions in the Buna camp:

> 11 people slept on a single bunk. When one of them turned around, all the rest had to turn, because there was simply not enough room … There were 14 of us on a bunk; we slept on top of each other like sardines. We could not climb down from the bed, because we were beaten, and we could not use the lavatories either. This was one of their favourite methods of punishment – refusing to let us go to the toilet. Considering that almost all of us had diarrhoea and at times we had to hold back for 24 hours, we suffered excruciating pain. It happened that some could not hold out any longer and had an accident – the poor soul was severely beaten. There was very little food: a little black water in the morning, turnip soup and a small slice of bread at noon and again half a litre of soup in the evening. We starved a lot and suffered from the cold as well.[10]

That summer, the slaughter at Auschwitz was relentless and the crematoria ovens could not keep pace. In the period before the deportations began, the SS officer in charge, disposal expert Otto Moll, had anticipated the problem of disposal and put crews of Sonderkommandos to work excavating two huge pits behind crematoria V. Here the surplus dead would be burnt. Müller described Moll pacing up and down, clad in a white coat adorned with medals, 'giving instructions for the siting of the pits, a fuel depot, the spot where the ashes were to be crushed, and all the rest of the devices which he had thought up for the extermination and obliteration of human beings'. Moll ordered the excavation of a crude channel 'to catch the fat exuding from the corpses'. Another survivor recorded that:

> He ill-treated and beat Sonderkommando prisoners, treating them like animals. Those who were in his personal service told us that he used a piece of wire to fish out gold objects from the box containing the

jewels taken from new arrivals and took them off in a briefcase. Among the objects left by the people who came to be gassed, he took furs and different types of food, in particular fat. When he took food, he said smilingly to the SS around him, that one had to take advantage before the lean years came.[11]

As the trains rolled in from Kassa, shuddering to a halt alongside the Judenrampe to disgorge tens of thousands more prisoners with cessation, the SS disposal squads resorted to shoving Jews into the burning pits and shooting or beating them to death. The SS had learned valuable lessons from the camouflage methods used in the Reinhardt camps to veil what took place inside the barbed wire. At Auschwitz, Moll planted a thick hedgerow to screen the crematoria and the burning pits. Later, he had an empty barrack block constructed to enclose the reeking pits. The SS could do nothing to hide the plume of dark smoke and the sickening odour that rose into the hot summer air. Historian Debórah Dwork interviewed survivor Alexander Ehrman, who was 18 when he was deported from Királyhelmec (Kráľovský Chlmec). The transport he was taken on arrived at night:

We arrived … in an area of lights, flood lights and stench … The train stopped. Outside we heard all kinds of noises, stench, language, commands we didn't understand … Dogs barked. The doors flung open … It started to get daylight … We walked down an alley … We were prodded to move faster … We were walking, and beyond the barbed wire fences there were piles of rubble and branches, pine tree branches and rubble burning … I heard a baby crying … I knew that things in the fire were moving, there were babies in the fire.[12]

For the managers of mass murder, the sheer numbers of Jews deported from Hungary would become overwhelming. The selection process sometimes buckled under the strain – and the SS were forced to send many thousands of people to transit compounds. The largest was called 'Mexico' and held more than 17,000 prisoners in semi-lethal conditions. There was little food and water, prisoners used huge vats as toilets – and, since they had been robbed of their own clothes, had to wear blankets. These apparently resembled ponchos – hence the macabre humour of the camp nickname. Prisoners slept on the muddy floors of barracks. Many perished in 'Mexico' of disease and starvation – many others were taken away to the gas chambers. A few survived and were deported to satellite camps attached to German factories.

Between 1940 and 1945, some 1.3 million people were transported to the Auschwitz complex: 1.1 million perished. Nine-tenths were murdered because of their Jewish origin; every third victim was a Hungarian citizen. The largest group of victims from any single country killed in this industrial killing centre were Hungarian citizens. Auschwitz is not only the largest cemetery in the world – but the largest Hungarian cemetery.

Hundreds of thousands of Hungarian Jews went to unmarked graves in the sky. Through the spring and summer months of 1944, the air above the Auschwitz archipelago of camps grew ever darker.[13]

As the deportation trains steamed across Slovakia day after day, Joel Brand was about to reveal to the Zionists in Istanbul, and through them the leaders of the western Allies, Eichmann's offer to barter the lives of a 'a million Jews'.

THE FALLACY
OF RANSOM

When I met Joel Brand's son, Daniel, in Tel Aviv in May 2018, he spoke frequently of his father's unforgiving bitterness about the way the Jewish Agency betrayed his mission. Daniel returned again and again to the failure of the Zionists in Istanbul to procure a Turkish entry visa for his father. Their failure, he believes, reflected the muddled attitudes and policies of the Zionist leaders in Jerusalem. The great historian of the Hungarian tragedy, Randolph Braham, concluded that:

> Brand, who conceived of himself as a spokesman for and potential saviour of the doomed Jews of Hungary, was disappointed by his encounter with the Zionist leaders, who, he claimed somewhat unjustly, were not only at odds with each other over policy, but also so preoccupied with Palestine that they did not notice the massacre of their followers in Europe.

Other historians have been less forgiving. The controversial Israeli historian Shabtai Beit-Zvi ('controversial and pioneering' according to his fellow historian, Schlomo Sand) claimed that the 'secret of the annihilation [in 1944] was guarded by the Palestinian [meaning the Yishuv] press just as two years earlier they had not revealed the destruction of Polish Jewry'. Beit-Zvi points out that when David Ben-Gurion, the leader of the Yishuv, made a speech on 11 May, he made no reference at all to the tragedy unfolding in Hungary; nor did another leading Zionist

Moshe Sharrett speaking a few days later. A single, short report about the deportations taking place in Hungary appeared in the left-leaning *Ha'aretz* newspaper – no other Jewish paper in Palestine took up the matter. According to Beit-Zvi, the Yishuv leaders were excessively preoccupied at the time with the task of mending divisions in the Mapai Party. Why was Brand a thorn in the side of both the British government and the Jewish Agency?[1]

What is not in doubt is that Brand's difficulties, which erupted as soon as he and his companion 'Bandi' Grosz landed in Istanbul without an entry visa, would have a calamitous impact on the events that followed.

Trouble on the Bosphorus

Let us now return to Istanbul on 19 May 1944. By then, the first deportation trains despatched from Zone I (Carpatho-Ruthenia and north-eastern Hungary) had begun to arrive inside the Auschwitz-Birkenau extermination camp. It is unclear whether Brand was fully or even partially aware of what was happening in Hungary as he arrived in Turkey; whether he believed that Eichmann had temporarily halted the transports while he sought to find the goods the SS demanded; or whether he was prepared to lie about the ineluctable progress of the Final Solution to make the SS offer appear to be made in good faith. Was he duped or duping himself and others – or both at the same time?

We have a number of contradictory accounts of the calamity that unfolded at the airport. What becomes all too clear, however, is that as soon as he stepped off the German aircraft in Istanbul, Brand was knocked off balance. According to his own version of events, Chaim Barlas had failed to acquire Turkish entry visas, but he had a letter from 'the British authorities asking for Joel BRAND to be allowed to enter the country'.[2] Since Brand was travelling with a German passport under a false name, the letter was in any case useless. Now Grosz sprang a surprise. He informed Brand that *he* had already successfully arranged visas through a travel company in Istanbul. This is plausible since Grosz was a frequent visitor to the city. Later, Grosz would tell his British interrogators a more convoluted story: he and Brand had been met at the airport by Grosz's wife, Madeleine, who had been living in Istanbul, accompanied by an official from the Hungarian consulate: 'Nobody was there to meet Brand.' Grosz revealed that this welcome party had been arranged by a figure already familiar in this narrative, namely Alfred Schwarz, 'Dogwood' himself. The Hungarian official agreed to help Grosz, but not, he insisted, Brand. Frau Grosz even claimed that Schwarz 'ordered G. [Grosz] to have nothing to do with Brand'. Grosz was having none of it: 'A bribe eventually induced the officials to let G. and BRAND through together'. In this version of the story, Grosz makes no mention of Chaim Barlas: he may simply have been unaware of who he was. Nevertheless, many of the details ring true and, most significantly, link Grosz's mission to the Dogwood network. In any event, after waiting for nearly two hours, Brand and Grosz were allowed to leave the airport. Grosz added to the puzzle as they drove into Istanbul by revealing that the second visa was intended for 'a certain JUHASZ of the "IBUS" travel agency' but he had persuaded the Turkish authorities to accept that Brand had come instead.[3]

It was an inauspicious beginning. And for Brand matters rapidly worsened.

From the beginning, Brand's mission provoked scepticism among the Zionists' representatives in Istanbul. The Zionists who were stationed in Turkey such as Venya Pomerantz, Menachem Bader, Avriel Ehud and Teddy Kollek had all been hardened by years of frustration and betrayal. 'A geshenktn ferd kukt men nit in di tseyn! [Don't look a gift horse in the mouth!]' They habitually looked every gift horse in the mouth – and all the way to the end of its tail. Eichmann's ransom offer gave off a bad smell and even Brand admitted sometimes that he was uncertain of Eichmann's good faith. Then there was the roguish Grosz. As Ehud Avriel recalled in his book *Open the Gates*, Grosz warned the Zionists who gathered to meet the visitors from Budapest: 'Don't believe a word of what this fool is going to tell you … Pay no attention to the fairy-tales he will feed you.'[4] But at the same time, 'Blut gegen Waren' (Blood for Goods) took on an insidiously tantalising aura of *opportunity*. Could this outlandish proposal somehow be exploited? Surely, it could not be dismissed out of hand?

As we discovered in an earlier chapter, Brand's précis of the ransom deal that Eichmann was proposing sounded like a perplexing hodgepodge: 2 million cakes of soap, chrome, lathes, 200 tons of cocoa listed alongside 10,000 military trucks to be deployed 'only on the Eastern Front'. In return, the Germans promised, it seemed, to halt the deportation and murder of not just a few thousand but 'a million Jews'. Brand had a brash,

somewhat gauche manner. But even under pressure, he appeared passionate and sincere; he was persuasive. So, after a succession of fiery meetings,
the Zionists in Istanbul were persuaded that however far-fetched the
German ransom offer seemed to be, something could and should be done.

This tormenting paradox shaped all subsequent discussions; a deal that
stretched credulity but should not be ignored. Ehud Avriel's memoir has a
revealing account of a meeting with British intelligence agents that took
place shortly after Brand's arrival. The British and Zionist agencies had
close bonds – and, hoping to extend the terms of Brand's temporary visa,
Avriel visited the office of Major Arthur Whittall, who was an intelligence
agent who used the cover of a passport control officer. Also present was
Colonel Harold Gibson (code-named 'Gafni' by the Zionists). Since
Brand and Grosz had arrived in Istanbul on a German plane, it was natural
that the British would be cautious. Grosz was well known to Gibson as
the slippery Dogwood agent 'Trillium'; he was a dubious sort of fellow
who didn't play with a straight bat. Avriel began by insisting that he was
convinced of Brand's integrity: 'he was not an enemy agent'. But despite his
pleas, '[Gibson and Whittall] regarded both men as equally untrustworthy'.
Avriel was troubled by this because: 'We had not convinced our British
contact that perhaps this was a slight chance to save Jews – provided we
had Allied help in *staging* "negotiations" with Eichmann or his henchmen'
[my italics]. Gibson was 'correct, but cold as ice'. He refused to take the
matter up with 'London' or let the Zionists 'go through the motions of
negotiations'. His argument, Avriel wrote, was 'that the Russians might get
wind of the goings-on and suspect the British – and the Americans – of
negotiating, not the release of "several Jews" [*sic*], but a separate peace.'
From the very moment the Junkers aircraft touched down in Istanbul, the
British had concluded that Brand and Grosz were 'German agents' and
that their missions were intended to sour relations between the Western
Allies and the Soviets. Historians have been fascinated by this notion –
and some still accept that 'splitting the Allies' was the 'real' purpose of
the Brand Mission. I will show in due course that this is precisely what
Eichmann and his 'henchman' *hoped* would be the interpretation put on
both the ransom deal and Grosz's 'peace offer'. Sending two emissaries
with different and contradictory missions was to guarantee failure. In
short, the missions were designed to fail.

The delusion that lives could be saved by 'going through the *motions* of
negotiations' runs through all the panic-stricken debates that Brand's arrival

in Turkey provoked between the Zionists and the Allied governments. Reuben Resnik, who represented the 'Joint Distribution Committee' in Turkey, interviewed Brand and concluded that, while he suspected that the ransom offer might be both an attempt to morally embarrass the Allies if they refused to agree to the terms or a bid to disrupt relations between the Soviets and the Western Allies: 'Everyone with whom I have talked recognizes the impossibility of carrying out the proposals as they have been stated, but everyone believes that *all should be done to continue exploration*' [my italics]. Like the leaders of the Rescue Committee, many of the Jewish and Zionist agencies who received news of the Brand Mission swallowed the same bait.

In Jerusalem, at a meeting on 25 May, the head of the Jewish Agency's rescue committee, Yitzhak Grünbaum, denounced the German offer as a 'satanic provocation' and concluded that 'nothing can possibly come of it'. And yet he still urged the other leaders of the Jewish Agency to do what they could to buy time. This peculiar logic was echoed by some of his colleagues. Moshe Shertok, the head of the Political Department of the Jewish Agency, agreed that the offer was 'fantastic', but 'we should cling to it'. Many lives could be saved. The meeting resolved little. But soon afterwards, Ben-Gurion and Shertok requested a meeting with Sir Harold MacMichael, the British High Commissioner for Palestine, to discuss the Eichmann ransom offer: 'Eight thousand Jews have already been deported to Poland [*sic*]. Plans had been made for the daily deportation of 12,000 Jews as from 22nd May but *presumably this has been deferred pending negotiations*' [my italics]. This outrageous misinformation – there had, of course, been no deferment at all – might have reflected confusion among the Zionists about what was happening on the ground in Hungary but it gave Shertok grounds to argue that the 'seemingly fantastic character of the proposition' should not 'deter the high allied authorities from undertaking a concerted and determined effort to save the greatest possible number'. For his part, MacMichael notified the Foreign Office in London about the message from the Jewish leaders but attached a warning that he believed that the mission was 'a Nazi intrigue based on far other motives than the apparent ones'.[5]

It was not only the Zionists in Istanbul and Palestine who were taken in by the tantalising opportunity to 'buy time'. John Pehle, who was one of the founders and Executive Director of the American War Refugee Board (WRB) based in Washington D.C., believed the story that payments made to SS officers had led to a halt in deportations of Jews from Slovakia. Yet again, Wisliceny's 'Slovak trick' continued to have damaging consequences. When the British forwarded Barlas's report to the WRB, urging that its directors accept that the German ransom offer was a 'sheer case of blackmail or political warfare' and a 'monstrous bargain' that would impose a huge burden of care on the Allies by releasing a 'million Jews', Pehle stood his ground. He told his colleagues at a meeting held just after 6 June that, 'The best thing to do is to keep it alive.'

There is ghastly irony in those words. As Pehle debated how the fledgling WRB should respond to the startling news from Istanbul, every day the deportation trains clanked and hissed across Slovakia. Every day, thousands of Jewish men, women and children judged unfit trudged to their deaths in the crematoria. Every day, flames roared in the huge burning pits. Every day, the Sonderkommandos pulverised human remains and dumped tons of ash in the turbid waters of the Vistula.

In Istanbul, the authorities made it clear that Brand could no longer prolong his stay in Turkey, despite the efforts of the Zionists. When Shertok proposed meeting with Brand in Istanbul, he was frustrated by MacMichael. British intelligence was now keeping a close watch on Brand and Grosz, who they regarded as 'agents of the SS'. The implication of this is that the British and their American colleagues also regarded the two Hungarians as valuable sources of information about the German intelligence services and began planning to find ways to extract that information. The ransom deal was much less important.

In the meantime, Kasztner and Hansi Brand had been arrested by the Hungarian police and were held in prison between 27 May and 1 June. Brand made repeated and frustrated efforts to find out what was happening in Budapest – and became increasingly distressed. He feared returning to Budapest 'empty handed' and, against SS instructions, without Grosz, who now seemed intent on never going back. He was terrified that if he did *not* return, the SS would take revenge on Hungary's Jews and Brand's wife and two small children, who he had left behind as hostages. These conditions were all part and parcel of the German confidence trick but for Brand these consuming fears became all-consuming dread. According to Avriel, the Zionists had begun concealing information sent to Brand from Budapest that made clear the Germans and Hungarians were deporting tens of thousands of Jews without cease.

As Brand's position in Istanbul became ever more tenuous and his own anxieties deepened, Menachem Bader persuaded Brand that he should return to Budapest as the Germans insisted and offered to prepare a 'cover' document that appeared to provide 'evidence of progress'. In other words, Brand would not have to return to Hungary empty handed. This became known as the 'Interim Agreement' or 'Protocol'.[6] It 'empowers Joel Brand in the name of the Jewish Agency to negotiate and enter into binding obligations' and insists that: 'The political and legal difficulties in the way of fulfilment of the other side are very great. A way will be found to overcome them'. This was a clear acknowledgement that acquiring '10,000 trucks' was a daunting task. The 'Protocol' demands: 'The deportations to cease immediately everywhere, in exchange for payment of 10,000 Swiss Francs at the end of every month ... Emigration of people selected by us to Palestine will be allowed and permitted, in return for $400,000 per transport of each 1000 persons'.[7] Although there is a reference to 'emigration through neutral countries' in the next clause, this implies that Brand had not informed the Zionists that Eichmann had forbidden emigration to Palestine because he did not wish to offend the Muslim community. This is not to imply that Eichmann meant what he said, but the all-important proviso seems to have slipped Brand's mind.

At the end of May, Brand sent a number of telegrams to Hansi informing her that he had a 'positive answer to our proposals' and later: 'proposal accepted in principle'. He added that he hoped to return to Budapest on 4 June. There was no reply: Hansi was locked up in a Hungarian police cell. Soon afterwards, Brand's plans were thrown into deeper turmoil. First of all, Grosz vanished on 1 June, evidently pursuing his own interests, and crossed into Syria. Then Shertok sent a telegram from Jerusalem: the Turkish consul there had refused to issue him with a visitor's visa. It would be impossible for him to meet Brand in Istanbul and, to begin with, he urged him to return to Budapest. But then Avriel was again summoned by Major Whittall, who informed him that the British would now permit Brand to meet with Shertok and the other Yishuv leaders in Jerusalem. In his memoir, Avriel tells us that this concession was met with 'deep suspicion'. Was it a plot to ensnare Brand when he arrived in Palestine? Avriel then explains that he proposed to Whittall that Brand should meet Shertok in Aleppo on the Turkish border with Syria: 'Then it could not be claimed that Brand had seen secret British army installations or had learned other secrets, which might serve as an excuse to forbid his return to Budapest'.[8]

This is all rather odd. The British could just as easily seize Brand in Aleppo – and they did. Brand, however, was determined to meet with Shertok, who he hoped would give his mission credibility and, in any case, he now feared he 'would be a dead man' as soon as he crossed the Hungarian border. He was, it seems, not convinced that the faked 'Protocol' would offer much protection against the wrath of Adolf Eichmann.

And so, it was decided. Brand would leave Istanbul and travel to meet Shertok in Aleppo.

The Aleppo Trap

Brand now sent another telegram to Hansi: 'Interim agreement executed. Travelling in accordance with your instructions [sic] first to Palestine for purpose of further negotiations'. On 4 June, he wrote to the Va'ada Rescue Committee in Budapest that 'an interim agreement was concluded on Wednesday, a copy of which I enclose'. He emphasised that Kasztner should be able to make use of the 'Protocol' to impress on Eichmann that actual negotiations had begun.

Brand left for Aleppo with Avriel on the Taurus Express the following day. When Hansi finally responded two days later, it was too late. Brand would never read her replies. In the meantime, the Zionists in Istanbul made a decision to send neither the letter nor a copy of the 'Protocol' to the Rescue Committee in Budapest. That decision has puzzled historians ever since. There is ample evidence that the Germans would not have taken the 'interim agreement' seriously. On 1 June, the SS had Hansi and Kasztner released from prison – and on 6 June, they had in their hands Brand's telegrams from Istanbul. In his Report, Kasztner reveals what happened next:

> Brand informed us that he had concluded an interim agreement, of which the original would be sent by courier … I showed [Eichmann] the telegrams from Istanbul and asked him to suspend the deportations until the arrival of the interim agreement. Eichmann refused and declared. 'That's out of the question. On the contrary, I shall push ahead under full steam.'

He loftily dismissed the telegrams: 'an interim agreement is not a reply and a response to [his] demands. We shall have to wait until the agreement itself arrives'.[9]

And then a sprinkle of poisonous sugar: 'But he saw this as a good token.'

Why did Bader and his colleagues fail to send the 'Protocol' to Budapest?[10] The explanation is not hard to find. In the minds of the Istanbul Zionists, the document was of value only as a protective cover for Brand if and when he returned to Budapest. The value of the document became nugatory at the moment he decided to travel to Syria. That apparently is what they concluded – even if it doesn't make much logical sense. After all, Brand assumed that he *would* return to Hungary after he had met with Shertok in Syria. In any event, none of the Jewish rescuers had any confidence that the 'interim agreement' could be used as a serious negotiating tool: its terms were as fantastical as the original SS ransom proposal. Even Kasztner called it 'fictitious'. Some historians have lamented the failure of the Istanbul Zionists to send on the 'interim agreement' to Budapest as another tragic lost opportunity. This argument is not convincing. Kasztner's description of Eichmann's sneering reaction to the news that an 'interim agreement' had been signed in Istanbul very strongly implies that he would have been just as dismissive of the document itself. When the Istanbul Va'ada finally sent the 'Protocol' to Kasztner at the beginning of July, the document would take on a very different significance for the Jews and the SS. We will come back to that in the next chapter.

For the rest of his life, Brand held to his belief that while the 'Protocol' was 'only a bluff', 'with the help of this provisional agreement I believed the deportations could be halted'. Over the years, his bitterness deepened: 'I do not say that the interim agreement would have accomplished everything, but it should have been executed. The circumstances of actual negotiation would have brought the death machine to a stop.'[11]

To the last, Brand clung to these frail shreds of hope.

By the time Brand and Avriel stepped out of a taxi outside the Haydarpaşa Terminal in Istanbul to board the Taurus Express, Grosz had taken the same route – and was under arrest in Aleppo. According to British documents, he was accompanied by Madeleine, his wife.[12]

When the Express crossed into Syrian territory, Avriel was expecting to be greeted by 'Selim, our man in Aleppo' at the station. There was no sign of him. While Brand waited on the train, Avriel went to look for Selim. It was, it seemed, a false alarm. The train had arrived early and Avriel soon encountered 'our man' rushing to the station. He had good news. Shertok had just arrived in Aleppo and was waiting to meet Brand at the

Hotel Baron. All was well, it seemed. When Avriel returned to the train, Brand had vanished. Selim dashed off to search the platform and the ticket office but there was no sign of Brand: the British had sprung a trap after all. As Avriel found out later, two Englishmen in civilian dress, but with the manner of policemen, had entered the train compartment and ordered Brand in German: 'You come with us.' They led him along the carriage corridor to the door on the opposite side to the main platform. One of the Englishmen bustled Brand onto the track, pushed him aboard another stationary train and then exited on a parallel platform. The two British police officers led Brand away to a taxi waiting outside the station.

Not long before Avriel left Istanbul with Joel Brand on that fateful journey to Aleppo, he had received a telephone call from Bandi Grosz. In a 'creaking voice, audibly greased with liquor', Grosz launched into a long harangue: 'Has my fool companion told you his fairy tales?' he demanded.

Don't believe a word he says. I invented the whole escapade. I was in very hot water after they took Hungary and I had to get out at all costs. So I instilled some of the high-ups with the childish dream of being able to create an alibi for themselves by making an offer to let the Jews go free, late as it is. All they want is to get in touch with Allied officers and make an impression on them. The people Brand quotes, Eichmann included, have as much power to stop the ovens – or the trains – as I have to stop the world. And even if they could stop them, they would never have the courage to propose it to a beast like Himmler. Don't be children! Don't believe a word!

It is one of the tragic ironies of the Brand Mission story that the reviled Bandi Grosz came closest to telling the truth.

19

PLUNDERERS

There is very convincing evidence to suggest that Adolf Eichmann took advantage of the negotiations with the Zionist rescuers in Budapest, which had been initiated by his subordinate, Hauptsturmführer Dieter Wisliceny, to deceive and distract from his task to deport hundreds of thousands of Jews to Auschwitz. His professional *and ideological* commitment was to the successful management of the deportations. Whenever Eichmann was thwarted from achieving this task he reacted with extreme aggression. Eichmann had the unequivocal backing of his masters in Berlin, Himmler and the head of the RSHA Kaltenbrunner – and the SS chieftains remained loyal to Hitler, who never deviated from a fanatical preoccupation with exploiting and liquidating the Hungarian Jews. Woven through these ideological obsessions was avarice. The Holocaust was the most egregious state-organised robbery in human history. The material assets of the millions of victims of the Nazi state were ruthlessly and pitilessly extracted at every stage of the genocide, from the confiscation of property to the extraction of gold teeth, and the harvesting of hair and body fats. Jews deemed fit to work would be enslaved for the benefit of German corporations and 'annihilated through labour'.

Mass murder thus coexisted with rapacity on a monstrous scale. The Nazi state was gluttonous and so were its state actors. Himmler's facile struggle with corruption in the camp system foundered because the ethos of exploitation saturated every level of every Nazi agency and benefitted their most loyal functionaries. The racial ideology of the state that debarred ethnic groups such as Slavs and Jews from almost every social and political norm allowed the agents of genocide to uphold and proclaim values like honour and decency: the exploitation of the excluded was imbued with moral necessity. This was the message of Himmler's infamous 'Posen Speech'.

It was the avarice of the Nazi state that permitted the non-lethal exploitation of relatively small numbers of Jews in special circumstances. On a limited scale, lives could be bartered for hard foreign currency, for example – a practice proposed by Himmler and approved by Hitler. It was this tolerance of barter and ransom that lay behind Himmler's decision to set up Bergen-Belsen as an 'Aufenthaltslager', or 'residence camp' for so-called 'exchange Jews'. As the historian Peter Longerich has shown, Himmler's commitment to exploiting Jews persisted until the end of the war – a matter I will come back to in a later chapter.

Eichmann Thwarted

Seen in this perspective, Eichmann's proposal to barter 'blood for goods' fitted with Himmler's exploitation of 'exchange Jews'. By grossly inflat-ing the terms of ransom – 'a million Jews for 10,000 trucks' – Eichmann thrust the deal into the realms of the absurd and impossible. He would not have done this without permission from his superiors, Himmler and/or Heinrich Müller. Their purpose was simple: to distract. Remember that Brand was dispatched to Istanbul at the moment in mid May 1944 when the SS deportation plan had reached its most critical stages. Attaching 'Bandi' Grosz with another separate 'mission' ingeniously compounded the confusion and guaranteed that the offer to exchange lives for goods would be given short shrift. After all, there was a long and inglorious tradi-tion of German peace initiatives that had invariably ended in disaster.

The impact of the Brand Mission may even have exceeded the expectations of the German side. Eichmann's ransom proposals first of all tied up the Budapest Rescue Committee with a morally compromising battery of demands and a drip feed of petty concessions – and second, very effectively led the Zionist agencies and the Allies into a maze of acrimonious confusion and debate at the very same time that the SS deported and murdered hundreds of thousands of Hungarian Jews. From the summer of 1941 and throughout the years of destruction that followed, the SS exploited many different strategies of secrecy and subterfuge. They deceived victims about their fate and misled any inquisitive observers whose activities might disrupt their plans. Blood for Trucks was one of the most spectacular examples of such subterfuges and only makes sense if we dispense completely with the idea that Eichmann made the offer in good faith. This does not exonerate the Allied governments, who consistently refused to take any effective action to end the German slaughter of European Jewry and other victims of state violence, nor the Zionist leaders in Jerusalem who took the bait of the ransom offer and remained deathly silent about the fate of the Hungarian Jews.

But Eichmann and his masters in the SS and the Nazi state had no means to stem the violent and unpredictable turbulence of Hitler's war. Assaulted on three fronts, Hitler's Reich was fracturing. The steady drumbeat of military reversal was turning into a frenzied percussion of catastrophe. There were many interdependent links in the chain of deportation and mass murder – and it was inevitable that at least one of these links would fail. The watershed moment came at the end of June. The 'Auschwitz Protocols', which had been compiled from the testimonies of a number of Auschwitz escapees including Rudolf Vrba and Alfréd Wetzler, reached Geneva. In Budapest, a copy ended up in the hands of the Regent, Admiral Horthy. The Swiss government, which had a deeply compromised relationship with Nazi Germany, abolished censorship of Nazi atrocity reports – and in the last weeks of June, more than 300 reports and articles were published in newspapers all over the world denouncing the deportations of the Hungarian Jews. Rome had fallen to the Allies on 4 June – and even Pope Pius XII, whose wartime record remains contentious and unresolved, spoke out against the deportations with less than his customary timidity. On 25 June, Pius sent a telegram to Horthy demanding that the Hungarian government stop the deportations. The following day, President Roosevelt issued the Regent with an ultimatum. At the same time, the Swedish Ministry of Foreign Affairs acquired a copy of the 'Auschwitz Protocol' – and King Gustav V sent a rather tepid telegram to Horthy asking him to 'interfere on behalf of those among these unfortunate people who can still be saved' and expressing an 'honest wish that Hungary preserve its good reputation before all nations'.[1] Horthy was mindful of international opprobrium – and, as ever, attuned to the implication that he had effectively compromised the sovereignty of his nation. But Horthy prevaricated. At a meeting with the Swedish ambassador, he heaped blame on the Germans for the deportations and, worse, insisted that he had approved the removal of 'communist elements' from eastern Hungary. What did trouble him, the Ambassador discovered, was the fate of Jews in Budapest. These were his bridge playing partners! Horthy had every reason to be concerned about his 'friends' in Budapest: by the end of June, the main deportations from the Zones in the countryside had nearly been completed. Eichmann was about to turn on the Jews of Budapest: ghettoisation had been launched on 16 June.

What compounded Horthy's problems was turmoil in the Hungarian government. Eichmann's Sonderkommando depended on the coopera-tion of the Minister of the Interior Jaross and his henchmen, Endre and Baky. Now, faced with a gathering tide of international opprobrium, other factions in the Hungarian government began to flex their political muscle. The former Prime Minister, István Bethlen, urged Horthy to curb the 'inhumane, foolish and cruel persecution of the Jews, which was so unfit-ting for the Hungarian character'. On 26 June, Horthy called a Crown Council meeting – the first since the occupation. He proposed a *partial* halt to the deportations – and the sacking of Baky. Endre should no longer have control of Hungary's Jewish affairs. Horthy's demands were deflected: the Council refused to sack the two state ministers and agreed only to permit a few privileged Jews to emigrate.[2]

Then events took an unexpected turn. As Horthy fretted, Eichmann and his Hungarian collaborators, who had become concerned about the turmoil in the government, made a decision to push ahead with their plans to deport Jews from Budapest and came up with a devious strategy. Gendarmerie units would be despatched from the provinces to the capital, ostensibly to take part in a national flag consecration ceremony. It was in fact a subterfuge: the plan was for the gendarmes to close the 'Yellow Star' houses in the city and swiftly herd the occupants into deportation centres in the city.

As the gendarmes marched into Budapest, Horthy was alarmed. He feared that Jaross and Baky, with the connivance of gendarmerie com-mander László Ferenczy, were about to stage a coup. So, he stopped the flag consecration, called on loyalists in the Hungarian army to rally in Budapest and ordered the gendarmerie to withdraw. Yet again, Horthy reacted with some decisiveness to a threat to his own position – even though much of his political power had been drained away by the German occupiers.

On 6 July, the Reich plenipotentiary Edmund Veesenmayer sent a long telegram to Ribbentrop, the German Foreign Minister. He informed him that Horthy was prevaricating about the 'Juden-Aktionen'. Veesenmayer then explained in detail to Ribbentrop the Regent's reasoning.

Assuming that Veesenmayer was truthfully representing Horthy's views, the document is nauseating. Horthy had complained to Veesenmayer that the Romanian government had not been required to carry out any special measures against Jews – and nor had the Slovakians. He went on to point out that he had learnt of the arrival of certain Jewish–Hungarian millionaires in Lisbon – which had raised serious questions about how just and consistent the treatment of the Jewish question was in Hungary. It is only in point three that Horthy brings up the 'barrage of telegrams, appeals, and threats' from the Swedish King and the Pope, the Swiss, the Turkish government as well as 'Spanish dignitaries'. He said that the Papal Nuncio, Angelo Rotta, had taken to calling on the Regent and Sztójay at least twice a day to demand an end to the persecution. Then Veesenmayer reveals that, according to Horthy, the Prime Minister Döme Sztójay had intercepted secret telegrams between the British and American ambassadors in Bern that condemned the extermination of Jews and threatened that Hungarian ministers responsible would be targeted by precision bombing raids. These secret messages had referred to discussions about bombing the 'railroads linking Hungary to this location [Auschwitz]'. Veesenmayer wrote that Sztójay was 'unmoved' by these accounts because 'in the event of our [meaning Axis] victory, the whole issue will become uninteresting'.[3]

It is evident that Horthy's motivations were murky, opportunist and confused. Nevertheless, Veesenmayer's suspicions proved to be well founded. On Horthy's orders, the deportations were halted on 7 July. It would seem, however, that he did not regard his decision as a final one. The arguments with the Interior Minister Jaross and his state secretaries, who were firmly backed by the Germans, raged on … Endre and Baky kept their positions.

The Jews of Budapest were not yet safe. Far from it … In the wings lurked the Arrow Cross militias. Their leader, Ferenc Szálasi, sensed that a historic opportunity was in the making.

When Horthy halted the deportations, Eichmann was angry and disappointed. The Budapest plan had failed; he no longer had the resources to empty the ghettos. But he refused to give up. Now he turned on Jews incarcerated in the internment camps scattered in the vicinity of the capital. On 14 July, SS soldiers ringed the Kistarcsa camp and forced the inmates to march to the deportation centre. Hours later, a train was steaming towards Kassa and the Slovakian border. The Jewish Council Acted quickly. They alerted Horthy, the Swedish embassy and Rotta, the

Papal Nuncio. Horthy ordered the train to return to Kassa. For a few days, Eichmann bided his time. Then on 19 July he stormed the camp for a second time. István Vasdényey, a local police superintendent who was the camp commander, reported what took place. Vasdényey had consistently sought to protect Jews in Kistarcsa. His account exposes the close bond between Eichmann's men and many other Hungarian police commanders. The attack on the camp began when Dr Pal Ubrizsi, who was in charge of another camp and the nephew of Lászlo Baky, turned up at Kistarcsa accompanied by Eichmann's transportation expert Hauptsturmführer Novak – brandishing a document authorising the 'transportation of all the camp's inmates'. Vasdényey refused. Horthy, he insisted to Ubrizsi, had forbidden any more deportations and besides, he had no intention of taking orders from subordinates. At that moment, an elderly prisoner burst in shouting that 'the German SS are setting up a machine gun'. Then three platoons of the Eichmann Sonderkommando launched an attack on the main entrance of the camp, each SS man carrying a sub-machine gun. Vasdényey had just seven men at his command and there was little he could do to hold back the rush of black uniforms. As the SS seized control of the camp, Vasdényey confronted Novak – who insisted that 'he would carry out the deportation on Eichmann's order'. Trucks with canvas awnings now pulled into the camp and the SS men began hurling Jews onto the cargo bed. 'You can't describe the bestial brutality with which they treated eighty-year-old people, people on crutches, and hospital patients'.[4]

Eichmann had not finished yet. On 24 July, the SS seized 1,500 Jews from a second camp in Sárvár. His rage knew no bounds. He was reported to have said: 'Well, it is true, there are some Jews killed in Auschwitz, but there were also some committed for labour service. Because of this order [to halt deportations], now all that is left for me is to pack up and leave. If the Jews are not being killed anymore, I cannot deport any more Jews to Germany.'[5]

The SS officer who reported Eichmann's words of infantile rage now understood that his day had come at last. His name was Kurt Andreas Becher.

The Reichsführer's Most Obedient Becher

Soldier? Businessman? Mass murderer? The White Lamb of the SS? Becher is among the most enigmatic figures in the history of the SS. He has been compared to other morally ambivalent SS officers such as Werner Best and

Kurt Gerstein, who seemed to be driven by loyalty to the German cause and confusion about its consequences: a phenomenon that the American psychologist Robert Jay Lifton called 'Faustian doubling'. Kurt Becher has not received the same kind of attention from historians as Gerstein has, for example, but his activities during the last years of the war are just as enigmatic and equally as revealing of the fractured psychic world of the perpetrators. Saul Friedländer's study of Gerstein is subtitled 'The Ambiguity of Good'; there was nothing 'ambiguous' about Becher.

After the war, Becher was interrogated and interviewed on many occasions. He cunningly distorted the truth or told blatant lies to save his skin and, later, to protect his status and immense wealth in post-war West Germany. He was a highly intelligent liar. His life, however, is so well documented in German and Hungarian sources that much if not all of the patina of mendacity can be stripped away. We can excavate a political life that in many ways challenges tired and well-worn ideas about the character and motivation of men who served in Himmler's elite corps. Becher has been denounced as a mass murderer and feted as 'the greatest rescuer in the history of the holocaust'. He was, in a perplexing way, both – and neither. Becher was, above all, an amoral opportunist.

★★★

Kurt Becher was born in Hamburg on 12 September 1909, and after completing basic schooling found work as a grain and fodder salesman. He seems to have possessed, from early on, a fascination with the equestrian world. This was by no means a trivial passion in the revolutionary new world of the Third Reich; Himmler promoted cavalry brigades as the elite corps of the SS. Hitler preferred automobiles, but he ordered two massive bronze 'Walking Horses' to be placed on either side of the main entrance to the new Reich Chancellery in Berlin. They were designed by Josef Thorak, who was often employed by Albert Speer to create huge works like these to adorn the new architecture of the Reich. The 'Walking Horses' came from the same artistic stable as other monumental works commissioned by Speer and Hitler that included (in historian Richard Overy's description) 'two enormous naked male figures, models of so-called "Aryan" man with bulging muscles and chiselled faces, stand defiantly side-by-side, one clasping the hand of the other in expression of a unique comradely bond between race brothers and soldier-companions'.

Aryan man, it seems, demanded an appropriate mount. It was Becher's expertise in the stable and on the parade ground that would thrust his career into a steady canter through the ranks of the SS.

In 1934, Becher joined the new SS cavalry unit, the Reitersturm. Like many young German men who joined the SS shortly after Hitler's seizure of power, he was enticed by the diligently cultivated charisma of Himmler's 'protection corps'. The SS was the vanguard of a new racial aristocracy. The SS, according to the newspaper *Das Schwarze Korps*, embodied the 'best of all classes, that is the nobility of the Reich'. He joined the NSDAP two years later. This gap does not reflect any deficiency of ideological commitment. It was typical of the ambitious young men who donned the black uniforms of the SS that they initially disdained the 'Brown' party until membership became an obligation. In 1938, Becher began training with one of the SS Death's Head Regiments (SS-Totenkopf Standarte) and was transferred to Oranienburg. In September 1939, the regiment took part in the invasion of Poland – and the brutal liquidation of Polish elites and then Polish Jews. When he was being held by the Americans after the war, Becher denied, naturally, involvement in the atrocities committed by SS units during the Polish campaign; he admitted only to searching houses for weapons. Nevertheless, by the end of the Polish campaign, Becher was a platoon commander of the 1st Cavalry Regiment of the 1st Battalion and, according to reports written by his superior, was 'fully involved in the executions'.[6] At the very least, Becher would have been made aware of the murderous activities of the SS units in Poland. After a period of leave, Becher was sent to Dachau – the headquarters of the Death's Head units. Here he was struck down by some kind of skin disease – which he seems to have been susceptible to – but was released from hospital in early 1940. By the spring, he was back in Warsaw, where he joined the 1st SS Cavalry Regiment. The regiment was headquartered at the Warsaw racecourse and it was here that Becher renewed his acquaintance with an SS officer who would soon have a decisive impact on his career.

SS Hauptsturmführer Waldemar Fegelein was, like his older brother Hermann, a rising star of the SS. The brothers, who were also admirers of horse flesh, became important patrons for Becher, who was still without a commission. Hermann Fegelein sent Becher to the SS military academy in Bad Tölz and on 31 January 1941 – which happened to be the eighth anniversary of the Nazi seizure of power – Becher won the promotion to which he had evidently aspired for so long. He was now Untersturmführer

Becher – and a full commissioned officer. He owed much to his friendship with the Fegelein brothers and would honour his debt by showing a fierce commitment to the brutal ethos of the SS cavalry brigade. Becher's service on the Eastern Front would be the making of him as a *génocidaire*.

In the spring of 1941, as Hitler and his generals prepared plans for the invasion of the Soviet Union, Himmler took personal command of the SS cavalry brigades – bringing them together under his own 'Headquarters Staff', the Kommandostab RFSS, and appointed Hermann Fegelein as commander of the amalgamated SS Cavalry Brigade. Becher's patron was not just a favourite of Himmler's but part of Hitler's personal entourage: he was married to Eva Braun's sister, Gretl. In 1943, Fegelein would celebrate Himmler's birthday with this sycophantic homily: 'in wartime … we have ridden undaunted, even in the most difficult times, assured in our hearts of victory under your command and in obedience to your orders … In my life, you have been the great patron, a strict superior officer and an unfailingly helpful comrade'.[7]

In June 1941, vast German forces rampaged across the borders of the Greater German Reich to smash the hated Soviet Union. Hitler and his courtiers had been preparing for this 'War of Annihilation' since July 1940. Operation Barbarossa was conceived as a ruthless blitzkrieg against an enemy that Hitler and his military staff were convinced would collapse like a mildewed house of cards. The war, Hitler proclaimed, would be done with in a matter of months. But the Soviet Union, the hated realm of 'Jewish Bolsheviks', would not just be annihilated on the battlefield. Its ruling class, its inferior Slavic hordes and the Jewish schemers who, in Nazi mythology, nourished the hated Soviet regime, would have to be destroyed. A vast expanse of the Soviet empire would be violently refashioned as 'Living Space' for the German *Volk*. Himmler, whose career as the 'Policeman of the Reich' was, in early 1941, wallowing in the doldrums, ardently hoped to play a leading role in this 'War of Annihilation'. Divisions of the Waffen-SS would, he proposed to Hitler, fight alongside the German Army – and special SS police units, Sonderkommandos would wage a parallel war against any perceived threats to Reich security. Hitler firmly backed Himmler's plans and on 13 March 1941 the chief of the Wehrmacht High Command issued guidelines that 'at the Führer's request', the Reichsführer would have 'special responsibilities in the zone of army operations … in preparation for the political administration [that] result from the impending final struggle between two opposing political systems'. Himmler and Heydrich developed plans that would allow the SS units to act 'outside the scope of the army units', 'identifying and combating activities hostile to the state and Reich'. Orders and guidelines issued by Hitler and his generals sanctioned the indiscriminate execution of Soviet officials, referred to as 'commissars', and the mass murder of any Jews who were deemed to be security threats.

These were Himmler's 'special tasks' – and it was imperative to muster forces to carry them out effectively. This was the main purpose of the Kommandostab RFSS, which was intended to streamline, from Himmler down, the line of command. As well as the SS Cavalry units commanded by Fegelein, Himmler reorganised the 'Death's Head' units as two motorised SS brigades. Along with the various police units and Einsatzgruppen, these specialised forces would enable Himmler to wage what he hoped would be a decisive war on the Reich's racial and political enemies. On 11 May, Himmler summoned elite SS officers to his 'Order Castle' Wewelsburg, near Paderborn, to inculcate in them the ruthless values of Hitler's 'War of Annihilation'. His special guests that evening included some of the most notorious génocidaires, men such as Friedrich Jeckeln and Erich von dem Bach-Zelewski. According to the post-war testimony of Bach-Zelewski, Himmler spoke of 'decimating' some 30 million 'superfluous mouths' to win power in the East. When Reinhard Heydrich, the head of the RSHA, addressed the leaders of the special police units known as Einsatzgruppen, he introduced a chilling new vocabulary of 'pacification' and 'cleansing' – including 'self-cleansing', by which he meant the supposedly spontaneous actions of eastern European peoples to rid themselves of their Jewish citizens. In a letter to his commanders, Heydrich provided a list of targets ('All these are to be executed') which included Comintern officials and 'Jews in Party and state posts' as well as a catch-all term: 'other radical elements'. These instructions from the top levels of the SS left a gaping space for 'local initiatives' by SS officers, who could decide, in the field, who or what was a security threat that required elimination. As Longerich writes, the guidelines were code for 'kill large numbers of communists and Jewish men'. Hitler's war would be fought not only against Stalin's armies – but against millions of unarmed civilians.[8]

This was the war that SS cavalry officer Becher would take part in under the command of Hermann Fegelein. He admitted to his American captors in 1946 that the SS Cavalry brigade was involved in 'heavy fighting': the truth is that Becher participated in one of most brutal pacification and cleansing campaigns of Hitler's war. This took place in the huge region of the Pripet Marshes that occupy most of the southern part of Belarus and the north-west of Ukraine. In July, Soviet troops retreated into the marshes to try and hold back the German advance behind what was known as the 'Stalin Line'. By August, the Russians had been encircled at the battles of Smolensk and Rostov – and Himmler took personal charge of destroying the survivors. This region of Belarus was also the refuge of very old Jewish communi-ties that, for centuries, had thrived in villages and cities of the marshlands. Himmler made it clear to Bach-Zelewski, who was the SS and police leader of the Pripet district, that the operation must not just break the resistance of Soviet troops but liquidate these local Jewish populations. On 20 July, Himmler issued an order to the SS Cavalry Brigade: 'Jewish men must be executed, while women and children are to be driven into the marshes.'[9] In his campaign diary, Bach-Zelewski described his plans as a 'combing operation' ('Durchkämmung') and diligently listed local demographics: 'Baranowicze: roughly thirty-five thousand people; of these roughly seven-teen thousand Jews, nine thousand Russians and nine thousand Poles'. In the diary, these lists were invariably followed up by a 'killing score': 'Thus the figure [of killings] in my area now exceeds the thirty-five thousand mark.'

This was indeed, to use Becher's phrase, 'heavy fighting'. The SS Cavalry fought its way through the vast marshlands from the end of July to 12 August. According to Becher's mentor, SS-Standartenführer Fegelein, his cavalry men shot or murdered in some other way, 14,000 Jews, 1,000 partisans and 700 Soviet troops in this short period of time. One of the SS officers who served in Becher's unit reported that: 'We drove women and children into the marshes, but this did not yield the desired result, [i.e. drowning to death] as the marshes were not deep enough'. It was high summer and water levels were low. On 1 August, Himmler revised his orders: the SS Cavalry men should start shooting Jewish women as well as men. Fegelein's Brigade moved east through these desolate lands between the Pripet marshes and the River Dnieper through Gomel, Vitebsk – the birthplace of the painter Chagall – Toropetz and Velikie Luki. The mass killings of civilians continued unabated. By December, the SS Cavalry brigade had reached the outskirts of Moscow – and it was here that their murderous progress was halted by elite Soviet units.

At some point during the campaign in the Pripet Marshes, Becher had won a coveted promotion to SS-Untersturmführer and been appointed as liaison officer for the brigade. As a platoon commander he could not have avoided, even if he had wanted to, participation in the mass killings. We cannot say whether or not he murdered Jews with his own weapons or hands – but there is some evidence that he issued orders to kill. He admitted to being present at a number of known killing sites during the campaign – in Smolensk, Vitebsk and Minsk, for example – where the SS men murdered tens of thousands of unarmed Jews, Roma and Soviet POWs. It is also highly significant that at the end of the campaign in Belarus, Becher was awarded a number of prestigious medals, including the Iron Cross First Class, and that Fegelein recommended that he should become a member of the Cavalry brigade Kommandostab as an SS-Obersturmbannführer.

A number of the SS Cavalry brigade officers were brought to trial in Germany in the 1960s – Becher included. The German court concluded that under West Germany's 'Roman Law' it was close to impossible to determine the precise legal responsibility of the accused. Former SS men including Becher, Franz Magill and Gustav Lombard participated in the murder of Jews but it was unclear whether they had done so freely or whether they had acted as tools and assistants of persons unknown. As Mary Fulbrook writes in her important study, *Reckonings*:

> justice [in the Federal Republic] should not be retroactive: that people should not be tried for acts that, at the time they were committed, had not actually been criminal … to prove someone was guilty of murder (*Mord*) or the lesser charge of aiding and abetting murder (*Beihilfe zum Mord*), rather than merely manslaughter (*Totschlag*), meant fulfilling exacting criteria regarding subjective states of mind. The accused must have personally taken the initiative, rather than merely followed orders: acted from 'base motives' (*niedrige Beweggründe*); behaved with particular sadism, cruelty, or ferocity, as an 'excess perpetrator' (*Exzesstäter*); and must have been aware of wrongdoing at the time.[10]

This legal sophistry meant that Becher and the other accused were all acquitted. After the publication of the journalist Karla Müller-Tupath's incriminatory biography of Becher in 1982, lawyers in Becher's home of Bremen launched another investigation – but swiftly abandoned it for lack of evidence. Whenever he was challenged about his activities as an SS officer during the war, Becher claimed amnesia, blamed his old friend Fegelein or insisted that he knew nothing about the mass executions.

In the course of the next few years, Becher cantered through the SS hierarchy, basking in the approval of Fegelein and the Reichsführer himself. He had an important role in the SS Operational Main Office, as Fegelein's adjutant and deputy, in charge of acquiring and training horses for the Waffen-SS. We know that in 1942 he accompanied Fegelein to Lublin in occupied Poland, where they met Odilo Globočnik, who was managing the mass killings in the Reinhardt camps. When he was interrogated by American army officers after the war, Becher denied ever having heard the expression Final Solution – but his closeness to Fegelein and the unwavering support of Himmler, who made no secret among his most favoured acolytes of their sacred mission to 'solve the Jewish problem', demolishes such a fatuous defence. In the winter of 1942, Becher was in action again on the Eastern Front until his battered Kampfgruppe was withdrawn in March 1943. He added a few more medals to his collection – and by the end of 1943 was fighting alongside Fegelein on the Dnieper – the old hunting grounds of the SS Cavalry brigade.

In mid 1942, Becher's career took another turn – which would eventually lead him to Budapest and a fateful bond with Rezső Kasztner. Once again, a new opportunity was all to do with Becher's equestrian expertise. For some time, Himmler had been coveting the famous Schlenderhan stud farm, which had been founded by Baron Waldemar von Oppenheim and his family. The Oppenheims had Jewish origins and Hitler objected to such a prestigious German institution being owned by non-Aryans. Himmler was fascinated by any kind of breeding, whether of humans or animals. Hermann Göring, the Luftwaffe chief, was just as covetous of Baron Oppenheim's spectacular stock – and did what he could to fend off the Reichsführer. The Oppenheims had long dominated German racecourses but in the summer of 1942, Hitler stopped Oppenheim stock competing. The likely next development would have been outright confiscation. Hans Lammers, the Chief of Hitler's Reich Chancellery, advised Baron Oppenheim to seek assistance from the SS – but the plan immediately foundered, and Himmler too began threatening the Baron.

It was at this critical moment that Becher stepped in. As he told the story to his American interrogators, he was, as a person of superior moral sensitivity, appalled by Himmler's heavy-handed approach, and took steps to get a better deal for the Baron and his family. Oppenheim was offered to begin with 4.4 million Marks – but Becher claimed that he was able to get the Baron twice that – and the deal was signed by the

Baron at Hitler's retreat at Berchtesgaden. With the Oppenheim stud in Nazi hands, Hitler granted protection for the Oppenheim family in the form of a 'Schutzbrief'. Becher claimed that to secure the deal for the Oppenheims he and another SS officer called August Frank had stood up to the most powerful members of the SS elite – Kaltenbrunner, the head of the RSHA, Müller, the Gestapo chief and Adolf Eichmann, who was in charge of the Gestapo's Jewish section – and even his good friend Hermann Fegelein. This was all nonsense. Becher later claimed that August Frank was 'decent and honourable' when he dealt with Jews; Frank returned the favour by describing Becher as a 'philanthropist'. The truth is that SS Brigadeführer Frank headed Amtsgruppe A of the SS-WVHA, the economic powerhouse of the SS, which played a leading role plundering Jews: the deportation and mass murder of more than 2.5 million Polish Jews in the Reinhardt camps generated hundreds of millions of Reichsmark – and Frank was responsible for what he called *Verwertung des jüdisches Hehler und Diebesgutes*: the utilisation of wealth stolen by Jews. He was especially preoccupied with recycling underwear. The Nuremberg Military Tribunal dismissed Frank's protestations that he knew nothing of the origins of the extermination camp loot and sentenced him to life imprisonment (reduced later by a West German judge to fifteen years).

It is conceivable that a few crumbs of Becher's story of generous beneficence to a beleaguered Jewish family may not be the stuff of self-serving fantasy. After the war, the Oppenheim bank made a number of generous loans to Becher's company in Bremen and in 1989 invited him to a ceremony celebrating the bank's 200th anniversary. These facts are hardly exoneration. There isn't a huge gulf separating the SS Cavalry officer who plunged into the Pripet Marshes in pursuit of Jews and other unarmed enemies of the Reich and the smiling opportunist who ingratiated himself with a wealthy German dynasty. What is not in doubt is that Becher demonstrated his negotiating skills in fleecing the Oppenheims – and his ruthless charm made a favourable impression on Himmler.

In the aftermath of the Oppenheim deal, Becher's relationship with Fegelein soured. Although Becher explained this as punishment for his efforts to treat the Oppenheims honourably, it is more likely that Fegelein resented Becher's deepening bond with Himmler – just as Eichmann would do when the two SS officers were forced to work together in Hungary. Fegelein did what he could to thwart Becher's rise – and even accused him of having an affair with his wife. This was a serious matter because Gretl Fegelein was the sister of Eva Braun – and Hitler would not have taken kindly to such a transgressive relationship. Fegelein's accusations led to an enquiry – which exonerated Becher and humiliated his former mentor. By now, Becher had a reputation in the SS that was no longer dependent on Fegelein's support.

In January 1944, Becher was promoted SS-Obersturmbannführer. This put him on an equal footing with Adolf Eichmann.

The most lucrative phase of Kurt Becher's career was about to begin.

Himmler's Corporate Raider

By this stage in the war, Himmler's Waffen-SS, the military wing of the SS, had risen to become a serious rival to the German army, the Wehrmacht. Fanatical, hard-bitten 'National Socialist Warriors' fought in its core divisions. The rise of the Waffen-SS reflected Hitler's increasingly argumentative relationship with his generals and his interest in a military force that could balance the Wehrmacht. As Germany's economic and military situation deteriorated in 1944, the SS and the army competed fiercely for supplies. At the end of 1943, Becher became involved with acquiring military supplies for the SS – principally horses. He was referred to as 'the horse dictator'. In March 1943, he was sent to Budapest to search for military supplies. When he was interrogated by the Hungarians after the war he said:

> After March 19, I returned to Budapest as a commissioner for the German armed SS Führungshauptamt [SS-FHA, the operational headquarters of the SS]. My task was partly buying breeding studs for the German SS and partly buying military horses for the German SS and the entire German defence force.

The sequence of events was as follows. On 19 March, Fegelein and Hans Juttner, the head of the SS-FHA, ordered Becher to travel to the Schloss Kleßheim in Austria – at the very moment the Hungarian Regent Admiral Horthy arrived at the Schloss to meet Hitler. It was at this conference that Hitler announced to his Hungarian guests that German troops were about to cross the Austrian border. On evening of the same day, Becher met Himmler, who was staying not far from the Schloss, who ordered him to acquire horses for the SS.

As noted earlier, Hitler's decision to occupy Hungary was driven by a number of interwoven strategic aims and motivations. One was, naturally, to solve Hungary's 'Jewish problem'. But that malevolent ideological intent was bound up with strategic, material and financial priorities. As Soviet armies pushed into the Carpathians, Hitler could not afford to allow Horthy to extract Hungary from its commitment to the Axis powers – or permit so many Jews to remain alive in areas in front-line areas. At the same time, the occupation offered an unprecedented opportunity to carry out a monstrous act of plunder and theft. Theft of bodies to work. Theft of resources to replenish the parlous finances of the Reich. Becher and others would now become agents of this state larceny. But he was one plunderer in an army of robbers. Every German agency that took part in the occupation from the German Foreign Office to the SS deployed many hundreds of expert economists to find the means to squeeze out the wealth of Hungarian enterprises. These agents of the Nazi occupation machine had to work against or behind the backs of Hungarian officials, who struggled to protect their national resources – and competed aggressively with rival German organisations. This polycratic chaos, which defined the entire Nazi state, was even more deeply fractured by Himmler, who was in the habit of skirting the official hierarchies of the Foreign Office and the SS by appointing individuals, often verbally face to face, to take charge of particular matters. Becher was one of those favoured.

So it was that Himmler appointed Becher his 'special envoy' on economic matters to do with the Hungarian Jews. His mission was to milk the Hungarian economy. It is unclear whether Himmler had in mind from the beginning of the occupation the acquisition of the wealthiest industrial conglomerate in Europe that was not yet in German hands, the Weiss-Manfréd works that employed tens of thousands of people in armaments, aviation and many other concerns.[11] The conglomerate would surely have been high on the German agenda. In any event, this single acquisition would turn out to be Becher's greatest success. It would confer on him power and privilege. The head of the SS-WVHA Oswald Pohl testified that:

Himmler had a strange method. He would always use special orders. He would pick someone and give him an order. For instance, [he] appointed Standartenführer [sic] Becher for the purely political task of removing the Weiss Manfréd concern from the Hungarian economy. It was a purely political job which should have been given to me ...[12]

The significance of the form of Becher's appointment is that as special envoy he could go directly to Himmler. He could act independently of the other SS powerbrokers in Budapest – and, in effect, go behind the backs of his superiors Juttner, Winkelmann and Kaltenbrunner. This is why, when Becher turned up in Budapest, Eichmann called Müller, the head of the Gestapo in Berlin, to clarify Becher's status and find out what he was doing there. Eichmann quickly came to resent Becher and sought to undermine his efforts and status. This rivalry explains, as we will discover, some of the puzzles of the Blood for Goods ransom negotiations.

Just days after the German occupation began, Becher and staff set up offices at 114 and 116 Andrássy Boulevard. This is one of the grandest avenues in Budapest – and the mansion is still there today, next to the Russian Embassy. This was the family home of Ferenc Chorin, who was the most influential member of Hungary's economy and the head of the dynasty that owned the Weiss-Manfréd industrial conglomerate. When the SS began arresting hundreds of Hungarian politicians, journalists and prominent Jews, Chorin fled from Budapest: Becher himself and his staff moved into the empty villa. In the meantime, Chorin had been arrested by Hungarian police in the western Hungarian town of Zirc and handed over to the Gestapo. He was interrogated and beaten up – then transferred to an internment camp not far from Vienna at Oberlanzendorf.

By now, Becher was investigating the jewel in the crown of the Hungarian economy – and tracked down Ferenc Keleman, a broker who managed the Chorin family's assets, and Vilmos Billitz, who was director of the Weiss-Manfréd Aviation and Engine factory at Csepel. According to Becher, Billitz impressed on him the importance of finding Chorin: 'if I wanted to be successful here in Budapest I could best do so via Chorin'. So, Becher appealed to the HSSPF Winkelmann to give him permission to travel to Oberlanzendorf, where on 17 April he interviewed Chorin, who was 65, and his wife. Both were now severely underweight and desperately ill with dysentery. In his memoir, which has been published only in Hungarian, Chorin described Becher's arrival at the camp as a 'miracle': '[Becher] and his circles were told that I was the most well informed person on economic affairs in Hungary, and he was asking me if I was willing to help them with information, to which I replied that I was.' Chorin was understandably grateful that Becher was willing to help, but the SS officer had the power to offer rescue. In return for that, Becher demanded money – a lot of it and very quickly. Chorin dutifully wrote a cheque –

but when Becher returned to Budapest, he discovered that the Hungarian government had frozen all Jewish assets. The cheque was worthless. For some days, Becher bided his time. Chorin and his wife slowly and painfully recovered. Becher travelled to Germany, where he met Himmler near Berchtesgaden and discussed how best to exploit Chorin. Evidently some kind of plan was hatched – for on 27 April, Becher arranged for the Chorins to be brought back to the villa in Budapest that now served as Becher's own headquarters.

Chorin, who had not fully recovered from his bout of dysentery, just had time for a bath before he was hustled into the library. Becher awaited him, accompanied by some fifteen other SS officers. Chorin's memoir makes clear that, at this stage, Becher's team was still undecided about how to proceed; there was, he reveals, no clear plan: 'I was interrogated, and they were asking me strange questions. They asked me to give an outline of Hungary's economic situation … They spent a lot of time on the question of which currency was the safest, the US dollar, the Swiss Franc or the English pound sterling'. Becher's team was especially interested in Hungarian banks – which were closely connected with the 'Chorin Group' of big industrial affiliates that held the vast holdings of the Chorin, Weiss, Mauthner and Kornfeld families. It seems likely that by the end of this first interrogation, Becher had grasped that the 'Chorin Group' was the key to unlocking a huge swathe of Hungarian industry. The sick old man whom he had extracted from the internment camp gave him astonishing power over the riches of the Hungarian economy.

Once the exhausted Chorin had given up the secrets of the Hungarian economy, Becher called a doctor to the villa to tend to him and his wife. His ordeal was far from over. The following day, Becher summoned Chorin once more and, very politely, launched a second interrogation session. This time, Vilmos Billitz was also present. It was 28 April, and the discussion now took a remarkable turn. Chorin: 'They got it into their heads that I should go to Switzerland and there give them money which *they could then use to buy army lorries*' [my italics]. This remarkable revelation that Becher was also negotiating with a prominent Hungarian Jew to buy trucks implies that the idea may have come up at his recent meeting with Himmler in Bavaria – and fits with Himmler's interest in motorising SS brigades. However, what happened next is of vital significance. Chorin, who was ill and under threat of being returned to the internment camp, agreed to try and do something – but pointed out that all his funds, including ones held in Swiss banks, remained frozen by the Hungarian government, which meant, of course, that he could not supply the Germans with any funds. Chorin pointed out in his memoir that the Germans soon realised that the new plan was unrealistic. The commander of the Kistarcsa internment camp, István Vasdényey – who would later resist Eichmann's assault on the camp – testified that during this period a number of SS officers including Franz Novak came to visit Jewish industrialists and economic experts on a daily basis: 'They were after the property of these people, and inquired mostly about their deposits in foreign countries, promising to let them go abroad in exchange.' The majority of the Jews who received these visits were deported to Auschwitz.

Relations between Becher and Chorin were close to breakdown. 'So in a matter of 14 days it became clear,' Becher testified, 'that Chorin could not deliver what he had promised.' The old man was frightened. Becher was polite, to be sure – but ruthless. He had his teeth in Chorin's neck and would not let go. He hinted that: 'I no longer had any reason to keep him there and that in fact I would have to send him back [to the internment camp].' Finally, the frail and desperate Chorin came up with an idea that seemed to intrigue Becher. He offered to cede the huge Csepel factories to the SS – on condition that they allowed him and his family to leave Hungary. Becher now saw his chance to close. He demanded from Chorin not only the factories but the *entire* Weiss-Manfréd conglomerate.

Now Becher needed Himmler's approval. But to begin with, Himmler resisted allowing *any* Jews to leave Hungary. We have only Becher's word for this – and it was in his interests after the war to claim that he had to overcome Himmler's resistance to release the Chorin family. But Becher went into some detail about the arguments he made to convince Himmler – and these make his claim somewhat more convincing. He told Himmler that what was in effect ransom to secure the Weiss-Manfréd conglomerate would make it easier to snatch other Hungarian industrial enterprises – and that 'our control of Hungary's largest and most versatile industrial concern would deliver the highest performance figures'. Himmler was finally convinced – but said he wanted to make sure he had Hitler's approval.

There is crucial information here. First of all, Himmler was evidently reluctant to permit the release even of very wealthy Jews. Secondly, he had to seek Hitler's approval. Even though he and Hitler had agreed to accept bartering 'exchange Jews' for foreign currency and the establishment of the 'Residence Camp' at Bergen-Belsen to facilitate these ransom deals, he could not assume that Hitler would agree to each and every proposed deal. Why is this important? Becher was meeting with Himmler in mid May at the same time that Eichmann was negotiating with Joel Brand about 'blood for goods'. If Himmler was loath to agree to release a *handful* of wealthy Jews in exchange for Hungary's most valuable industrial asset, it is inconceivable that he would have approved releasing 'a million Jews for ten thousand trucks'.

Becher was now on the threshold of a remarkable coup. The ripe fruit of the Hungarian economy was about to fall into the lap of the SS. Soon after he had secured Himmler's approval, Becher returned to Budapest and called in special lawyers to hash out the details of the acquisition. By 17 May 1944 the deal was finally completed. As Chorin formally signed over his companies to the SS in exchange for the lives of his family, Joel Brand was arriving in Istanbul and Eichmann's Sonderkommando and the Hungarian gendarmerie had launched their massive plan to deport hundreds of thousands of Hungarian Jews to Auschwitz.

To secure the deal with Chorin, Becher and his lawyers had exploited an arrangement known as a 'Treuhand' or 'Trusteeship' arrangement. Since the Hungarian government forbade foreigners to buy any Hungarian securities without permission from the National Bank, Becher had registered himself at a Budapest address as the representative of an investor group called 'Housing Trade and Maintenance', which now took into trusteeship all assets of the Weiss-Manfréd group of companies. Becher was authorised to dispose of moveable and immoveable property of the group for twenty-five years. The deal gave him the same rights as the original proprietors. Chorin had agreed to the deal – but other directors of the group strenuously objected. Becher and his SS henchman soon forced them all to sign. In return, most members of the Jewish families who owned the conglomerate were permitted to leave Hungary. Becher himself escorted Chorin and his immediate family across the Hungarian border into Austria. He was, no doubt, very polite as he wished his friends farewell.

Becher's deal with Chorin was an astonishing case of a hostile corporate takeover achieved through the most brutal kind of blackmail. The deal signed on 17 May gave the SS control of 51 per cent of the Weiss-Manfréd group of companies and on 17 August, the Hungarian Minister of Finance, who was pro-German, signed a licensing agreement that gave Becher the right to hold general meetings of the concern – thus giving him control of the entire conglomerate. Becher handed the SS a huge weapons and manufacturing base – and held off representatives of Himmler's rival, Herman Göring, who had begun sniffing around the huge Hungarian factories at the same time. With this spectacular coup, Becher won Himmler's unconditional confidence. The success of this clever, smiling SS man with the golden touch angered a powerful colleague. Adolf Eichmann resented Becher's rise to power – and feared that if he continued to have his way, more Jews might be released.

By the time Becher was riding high in Himmler's esteem, Eichmann had his own plan to discredit the very idea of barter. The Final Solution had to be absolute.

Kurt and Adolf

When Joel Brand was summoned to see Adolf Eichmann for the first time, he remembered that another German was present in the room. This was almost certainly Kurt Becher. In his Report, Kasztner confirms that Becher was present at some of the meetings. Becher and Eichmann held the same rank in the SS. Both had served Himmler's elite since the early 1930s. They had little else in common. Eichmann was a single-minded 'desk murderer' who was driven by a fanatical determination to drive Jews from Hungary. When the deportations were halted in July, Eichmann saw himself as superfluous.

In the autumn and winter of 1941, Becher had participated in the mass executions of Jews in Belarus on the Eastern Front. As a protégé of Hermann Fegelein, he would have been informed about German plans to liquidate Jews and other ethnic minorities and we know that he met Odilo Globocnilk in Lublin when Polish Jews were being murdered in the Reinhardt camps. By 1943, Becher had forged a new career within the SS as a ruthless but sophisticated carpetbagger who could play a vital role in the Nazi theft of Jewish assets. He proved his worth seizing the assets of the Oppenheim family – and was a natural choice to plunder the Hungarian economy for the SS. Becher was clever enough to exploit the most ruthless methods while playacting the role of a benevolent new business partner. He was a polite and smiling plunderer. Becher's daring takeover of the Weiss-Manfréd conglomerate won him power and prestige. By acquiring the factories and assets of the Chorin group, he made an enormous contribution to the SS war machine just as hundreds of thousands of Jews were deported to Auschwitz. As part of the same deal, by offering a few score wealthy Hungarians safety outside the Reich, Becher assumed the mask of a different role. He could play the part of a rescuer of Jews. He realised that if he could deepen this role, he could provide himself with moral armour plating. He had few illusions about the fate of Hitler's Reich.

Eichmann feared and resented Becher as a rival. Even though their administrative empires were separated by the Danube, the two SS colonels grated on each other. Both were steeped in blood, but Eichmann was incapable of seeing beyond the fulfilment of his 'great task'. He was, he had been told often enough, 'The Master' – now he had to show mastery. 'You know who I am!' he boasted to Brand. We can imagine him in his office inside the Majestic Hotel in Schwabenburg, smoke from his cigarette rising to the ceiling, his eyes lowered to a desk strewn with maps of deportation zones, railway timetables and lists of the doomed. Still Eichmann envied the suave special envoy.

When Becher's scheme to get Chorin to buy trucks in Switzerland foundered, Eichmann saw an opportunity. His SS colleagues Wisliceny and Krumey had already entangled and compromised Brand and Kasztner with demands for ever increasing sums of money to pay for the release of small numbers of Jews. As the critical period of Eichmann's deportation plan came ever close in April and early May, Eichmann understood that this kind of crude blackmail might not pay dividends for much longer. The collapse of Becher's trucks deal offered him an opportunity. He could take up the role of negotiator just as cleverly as his rival – and secure the acquiescence of the Zionist rescuers by sending one of them on a hare-brained scheme to buy trucks. By escalating Becher's simple idea of getting Chorin to fund the purchase of trucks to an outlandish scale, Eichmann could achieve a number of goals in one fell swoop.

During his trial in Jerusalem, Eichmann was questioned about Becher a number of times:

Attorney General: You have told us here that when you found out about Becher's activities in connection with Jewish emigration, you were furious. You were the person who always wanted to push for emigration [presumably meaning control of emigration], and now suddenly along comes someone else and snatches this out of your hands. That is how I understood you. Correct?

Accused: In principle that is correct. No one snatched it out of my hands, but I flew into a rage because the emigration which had been banned all along was now being carried out by someone who had nothing what-soever to do with the police, but I had to deal with deportations. I did not accept this, no; I became furious, and then I finally resigned myself to such a final solution.

...

Attorney General: ... Now suddenly you ... suddenly you think ... you suddenly have the idea of making a vast proposal to Himmler. Is that what you wanted to say?

Accused: Yes. I must also explain this, because ...

[Eichmann is interrupted ...]

Accused: ... but if it is borne in mind that this man [Becher], who as a result of a special assignment can now deal in emigration, but on the other hand interferes with my field of vision and now presumes con-stantly, without possessing any police status, to set some deadlines for me which anyhow I cannot give instructions and orders about, then natu-rally one would get furious, and that was the reason why I commented on this matter, and that is how it came about.

...

Attorney General: But why did you have to fly into a rage? You had received an order to carry out a transaction. Is that what you got so furi-ous about?

Accused: No, if my superiors gave me orders, I had to carry out these technical transport matters, that is quite clear, I had to obey. But if some-one who is not a member of the police presumes to give me orders about deportation matters, while he deals with emigration ...

Q. That is infuriating, right?

A. Yes, that is infuriating.

Q. And then you have the idea of suggesting not just ten thousand Jews, but a million Jews; that is your idea, or at least that is what you wanted to have us believe, right?

A. Yes, the hundred thousand or the ten per cent, and then the million. This is what happened, and it cannot be dismissed.

Q. That is your idea, you are saying, this is your proposal and your idea, right?

A. At least no one else had it ...[13]

In Budapest in 1944, Eichmann and Becher waged a turf war. More than fifteen years later in the Jerusalem court, Eichmann's anger seems undiminished. Becher wanted to allow some Jews to emigrate in order to achieve the takeover of the Weiss–Manfréd conglomerate. Neither the court nor Eichmann appear to have much knowledge of the fiendish details of Becher's financial machinations, but in any case, Becher intruded on Eichmann's terrain by allowing Jews to emigrate. To counter this, Eichmann hatched up his own 'emigration scheme'. He was not going to admit, fighting for his life in Jerusalem, that this new idea was a sham. But he did say:

> Attorney general: …you will agree that you did not wait at all for the results or outcome of the transaction. And as soon as Joel Brand left Hungary, the deportations started up once again.
> Accused: It was not up to me to halt or order transports to start or run.
> Q. Is that correct or not?
> A. I cannot … yes, it is correct.

During the same session, Eichmann read from a document he had prepared:

> As far as Becher is concerned, I can comment without any sympathy on my part, because by his own ambitious efforts, right from the outset, he acted in a scheming fashion, relying on his power of attorney from the Reichsführer-SS, and now, that is after 1945, he is trying to salve his own conscience by telling such gross lies about myself …

So, for Eichmann and the SS, Blood for Trucks served a number of purposes. The convoluted parleys that took place between the SS Sonderkommando officers and the compliant members of the Rescue Committee generated a dense smokescreen that distracted and confused while the SS and the Hungarians got on with herding Jews into ghettos and then deporting hundreds of thousands to suffer enslavement and death. At the same time, Eichmann exploited the ongoing negotiations with Kasztner and other members of the Rescue Committee to wage a vindictive war with his hated rival for Himmler's favour. What these two men shared was a cynical contempt for the desperate individuals who sought their favours: a disdain that saturated the Nazi state they served. When he was being interrogated by the Americans, Becher revealed:

> When under urging from Dr Billitz I applied for an appointment to see Himmler, which I managed to obtain through the good offices of Winkelmann, I knew from Dr Billitz that a proposal was being discussed about trucks in return for releasing Jewish people. Himmler did not say whether he was aware of this proposal and who had made it. However, as far as I remember, Himmler's words were: 'Get out of the Jews every-thing that can be got out of them. Promise them what they are asking for. As to what we will keep, we'll just have to see!'[14]

For Eichmann the matter was even more stark. When she appeared as a witness at the Eichmann trial, Hansi Brand inadvertently revealed that the SS had acted in the most cynical bad faith:

> Q. When it became clear to you that your husband was not coming back, and that apparently the mission had not succeeded, did you speak about this with Eichmann?
> A. I do not remember whether I spoke first to Eichmann or to Klages [Gerhard Clages]. Obviously, we had to talk about it.
> Q. How did the Accused react to this development?
> A. As far as the fact was concerned that my husband had not returned, he was very angry and upset. But the reason was not that he had not carried out the mission assigned to him, but because yet another Jew had escaped him. He was – I can say quite confidently – that he was very pleased. He was very pleased that this transaction had not come off.
> Presiding Judge: Mrs Brand, that was your understanding of what he said, but can you tell us what he said?
> State Attorney Bach: On what do you base your conclusion?
> Witness Hansi Brand: Very, very pleased that he has a free hand – he does not need to take the transaction into consideration, he can quite happily dispatch them, no one can make any reproaches to him.

This shows beyond any shadow of a doubt that Eichmann had calcu-lated that he was taking a vanishingly small risk that the Allies might take up the offer of exchanging 'blood for goods'. He was reassured when it became evident that this exchange would never happen. He had no wish to be 'hoist by his own petard' and forced to honour his sham bargain. He and his masters in Berlin may have derived an equal satisfaction from the diplomatic and moral quandaries in London and Washington that were unleashed by Joel Brand's arrival in Istanbul.

20

QUANDARY

The perplexing messages brought by Joel Brand and his shady companion 'Bandi' Grosz to the Zionists in Istanbul would send shockwaves through the diplomatic headquarters of the western Allies. The mission was devised by the German side to fail – and yet the way in which the sham offers to ransom Hungarian Jews for goods collapsed would provoke accusations that the Allies cared not a jot about the fate of European Jewry in Nazi-occupied Europe. Until the end of his life, Joel Brand would insist that he had been betrayed both by the Jewish Agency in Jerusalem and by the perfidious Allies. His bitterness has been echoed in many accounts of the Brand Mission and its failure. The Allied governments stand convicted of abandoning the Hungarian Jews as the SS fed them into the maw of Auschwitz. Himmler and his henchmen seeded the morally lopsided idea that the Allied powers and their citizens were complicit in the Nazi genocide. The profound paradox of the Brand Mission is that these accusations, like a moral version of Schrödinger's Cat, are at the same time both true and false.

The public and private memories of the Second World War are profoundly malleable. They are moulded and reshaped by the cumulative efforts of historians and academics and through the appropriation of history in the volatile ecologies of politics and culture. The Second World War in Europe was experienced, in the historian Michael Burleigh's words, as a *moral combat:* struggle of good against evil. No other conflict in human history has been invested with such a pervasive Manichean polarity. The Second World War has been invested by theology. And yet for some time after the end of the war, the public memory of it marginalised the catastrophic experience of European Jews. The other ethnic minorities victimised by the Nazi state, like the Sinti and Roma, were thrust even further to the margins of recollection – just as the systematic liquidation of millions of Soviet prisoners of war leaves minimal traces in popular memory. By the end of the last century, this volatile landscape of public memory had been profoundly transformed. The German genocide was well on the way to being transformed into an historical singularity, and the Holocaust or Shoah dominated the realms of memory. The elevation, after many decades, of the Holocaust to this status as the most significant dimension of a globalised war was, to be sure, resisted by illiberal factions who maliciously sought to question and undermine, thankfully to little effect, the quantifiable facts of historical research.

In Eastern Europe, in the aftermath of the collapse of the Soviet Union, nationalist factions sought to amend the re-evaluation of the German genocide by representing the Holocaust as equivalent to the ravages of the 'double' Soviet occupations that came in the wake of the Nazi–Soviet Pact. The demand for moral equivalence of very different kinds of persecution is tantamount to saying: you western liberals, with your Holocaust preoccupations, *ignore* that *we* Ukrainians, Latvians, Lithuanians ... suffered and died under both Nazism *and* Communism: you are *misremembering*. In the darker corners of this new post-Soviet nationalism is the insinuation that the agents of Soviet oppression were in fact Jews: thus, resurrecting the old 'Jewish–Bolshevik' shibboleth.

This populist revisionism is perverse testimony to the emotive power and status of the German genocide in the memory of the Second World War. It is now conventional to 'remember' the war as if it was fought on behalf of European Jews, or perhaps more precisely, with their terrible fate in mind. The remembered evil of the Nazis is now remembered not just in terms of German military aggression but even more resonantly in the Nazi persecution of European Jewry. The logical inference is that our forebears were fighting to save the Jews.

One of the Blackest Crimes of all History

This contemporary collective memory bears little resemblance to the many conflicted and contradictory experiences of the war as documented in contemporary sources. There was a steadily growing body of intelligence about the German onslaught against the lives and assets of European Jews from as early as 1941, when decryptions of German police radio traffic revealed that very large numbers of Jews were being murdered in Eastern Europe. This led Churchill to denounce 'a crime without a name':

> None has suffered more cruelly than the Jew the unspeakable evils wrought upon the bodies and spirits of men by Hitler and his vile regime. The Jew bore the brunt of the Nazi's first onslaught upon the citadels of freedom and human dignity. He has borne and continued to bear a burden that might have seen beyond endurance. He has not allowed it to break his spirit; he has never lost the will to resist. Assuredly in the day of victory the Jew's suffering and his part in the struggle will not be forgotten.[1]

Fine rhetoric – that had little impact on the conduct of the war. There was little understanding that the mass murders were the enactment of a genocidal plan: the Final Solution.

By the spring of 1944, knowledge among the Allied powers and some of their citizens and soldiers of the 'unspeakable evil' that was being perpetrated in occupied Europe reached a climacteric. The focal point of Allied intelligence was Auschwitz – which had become the main instrument of mass murder. Again, Churchill deployed rhetoric – and promised only retribution after an Allied victory rather than direct action:

> There is no doubt this is the most horrible crime ever committed in the whole history of the world, and it has been done by scientific machinery by nominally civilised men in the name of a great State and one of the leading races of Europe. It is quite clear that all concerned in this crime who may fall into our hands, including the people who only obeyed orders by carrying out the butcheries, should be put to death after their association with the murders has been proved.[2]

At the core of that 'most horrible crime' was the still unfolding tragedy of the Hungarian Jews. The 'Auschwitz Protocols' exposed the unprecedented horror of the 'scientific machinery' that was daily consuming many thousands of lives. What could be done? Pleas from Jewish leaders and others to bomb the railway lines that led into the death camp were debated and rejected as impractical – a decision that remains controversial to this day. Nevertheless, a sustained barrage of threats and protests persuaded Horthy and some of his ministers to call a halt to the deportations, albeit grudgingly. This was a consequence of the exceptional and contingent circumstances on the Hungarian genocide. The Germans had occupied Hungary, but its government retained some limited sovereignty and was split between fanatical pro-Germans led by Sztójay, the Prime Minister, and Andor Jaross, and other ministers who feared the shaming of their nation when the Allies defeated Nazi Germany. Retribution for collaborating in Nazi crimes would surely follow. As Horthy wrote to Sztójay:

> I was aware that the Government in the given forced situation has to take many steps that I do not consider correct, and for which I cannot take responsibility. Among these matters is the handling of the Jewish question in a manner that does not correspond to the Hungarian mentality, Hungarian conditions, and, for the matter, Hungarian interests.

In other words, Horthy had come to understand that collaborating in the mass murder of Jews no longer served the political interests of the Hungarian nation. Horthy's twisted self-justification is very revealing. Historian Timothy Snyder argues that the German genocide of Jews took place in the 'Bloodlands' of Central and Eastern Europe where Soviet occupation had eviscerated national states such as Lithuania and Latvia, rendering their Jewish citizens defenceless. Genocide depended on state destruction. His argument is complicated – if not contradicted – by the case of Hungary. As a member of the Axis, Hungary did not relinquish sovereignty and pursued autochthonous antisemitic policies through its state apparatus. Even after March 1944, the German occupation authorities allowed the Regent and the Hungarians to retain a patina of sovereignty. As emphasised throughout this book, Eichmann's SS Sonderkommando depended on the Hungarian Ministry of the Interior and its state secretaries to help enact every stage in the onslaught on Hungarian Jews. It was only when German-initiated persecution and mass murder threatened to defile the reputation of the Hungarian state that Horthy acted.

In Britain, official responses to the rising flood of intelligence about the 'horrible crime' that Churchill recognised – at least in his rhetoric – were shaped by the opportunist pragmatism acting in concert with the deeply ingrained prejudices of the period. These deeply rooted prejudices straitjacketed the refugee policies of wartime governments on both sides of the Atlantic – and in Moscow. In his seminal work *Auschwitz and the Allies* (1981), Martin Gilbert cited a number of telling documents that lay bare, at all levels of the diplomatic service, an ingrained disdain for Jews and their supposedly habitual lamentations. Just a few examples suffice. Sir Frank Roberts, a consummate Foreign Office mandarin, responded to warnings from a Polish diplomat about the mass murders taking place in Occupied Poland:

> this is not a very suitable moment to breathe fire and fury against the Germans in connexion with their treatment of the Jews … Hitler seems to be in a very difficult mood about prisoners of war. It therefore seems to me inadvisable to irritate him more than is necessary, particularly on a Jewish issue.

Mr J.S. Bennett reacted with the same disdain when he was urged to support plans to rescue Jewish children from Bulgaria: 'What is disturbing is the apparent readiness of the new Colonial Secretary to take Jewish Agency "sob stuff" at its face value. As a political manoeuvre this will establish a good precedent which the [Jewish] Agency will no doubt exploit.'

Just as in our own time, government officials feared the adverse social impact of human migration and the development of a 'refugee problem'. 'Sob stuff' about the German persecution of Jews threatened to compel Britain and the United States to deal with demands to offer rescue and refuge. The consequence, as Michael Fleming has shown in meticulous detail, is that the propaganda agencies of the Allied powers excluded the threat to Jews in German-occupied Europe from the public narrative of the war as it unfolded. This unofficial policy was reflected in the very low number of stories about atrocities committed against Jews – and indeed any ethnic minority – transmitted by the BBC and its European services or published in the mainstream press. Fleming shows that this was a deliberate policy. News was, of course, tightly controlled during the war and the *majority* of atrocity stories that made clear the identity of the victims as Jews were blocked. This choreography of the official news stream – censorship, in short – reflected, Fleming argues, official anxiety that the struggle against Nazi Germany might come to be perceived by British or American citizens as a 'Jews' War'. Propagandists showed Hitler and the Nazis as evil – but stepped back from showing how that evil was being manifested.[3]

There were some who spoke out loudly against the silence of the media. The socialist Archbishop of Canterbury, William Temple, and the British Chief Rabbi, Joseph Hertz, founded the 'Council of Christians and Jews' to combat antisemitism and the moral failure of the government. In March 1943, Temple spoke in the House of Lords:

My chief protest is against procrastination of any kind ... The Jews are being slaughtered at the rate of tens of thousands a day on many days ... The priest and the Levite in the parable were not in the least responsible for the traveller's wounds as he lay there by the roadside and, no doubt, they had many other pressing things to attend to, but they stand as the picture of those who are condemned for neglecting the opportunity of showing mercy. We at this moment have upon us a tremendous responsibility.

Temple emphasised that:

some of the arguments hitherto advanced as justifying the comparative inaction seem quite disproportionate to the scale of the evil confronting us. They are real in themselves, but they are the kind of thing that many of us feel should really be brushed aside if only we have before our minds the situation with which we are trying to deal.[4]

On 29 February 1944, Dr Hertz spoke at a conference at Central Hall in London alongside Temple, using equally powerful words: 'Our great foe,' he said, 'is the ignorance of the rank and file of the people ... If the press throughout the country would but unveil to them the scientific fiendishness displayed by the Nazis in the foul massacring of an entire people, we should have a large and determined body of public opinion behind us ... And be it remembered,' Hertz went on, 'that the Nazis are not confining extermination to one race or people.' Temple reinforced the message of the Chief Rabbi: 'The great mass of English people are passionately urging that we take our full share in rescuing the victims.'

Temple could not have been more wrong.

In 2018, documents released by the British National Archives revealed, in shaming detail, that antisemitism was widespread and pervasive in wartime Britain. The Director of the Ministry of Information, General Cyril Radcliffe, acknowledged that 'from the beginning of the war there had been a considerable increase in antisemitic feeling'. Many of the people he had canvassed for their views had a ready explanation: 'the increase in antisemitism was caused by serious errors of conduct on the part of Jews'. In other words, Jews themselves were the root cause of antisemitism – and Radcliffe was inclined to agree:

> I reminded them that it was part of the tragedy of the Jewish posi-
> tion that their peculiar qualities that one could well admire in easier
> times of peace, such as their commercial initiative and drive and their
> determination to preserve themselves as an independent community
> in the midst of the nations they lived in, were just the things that told
> against them in wartime *when a nation dislikes the struggle for individ-*
> *ual advantages and feels the need for homogeneity above everything else* ...[5]
> [my italics]

Against this background of both official and popular anti-Jewish prejudice, the news of the Brand Mission and the SS offer to barter lives for
goods opened a Pandora's Box of reaction.

Substantial Reasons ...

Adolf Eichmann's Blood for Goods ransom proposal landed on the
desks of British and American politicians and diplomats entangled with
an enigmatic offer to open back door negotiations to end the war. These
confusing messages came at time of heightened tension between the
Allies. From the very moment Hitler's armies roared across the borders
of the Soviet Empire in the summer of 1941, Stalin harboured gnawing
suspicions about the real intentions of his new allies – while, for their part,
his counterparts in London and Washington bickered about the dividends
of victory.

From the moment Britain declared war on Nazi Germany, Roosevelt
exploited every opportunity to cajole Churchill to abandon Britain's
stubborn grip on the vast territories and peoples of the Empire. The
Atlantic Charter that the two leaders signed in August 1941 promised
rights of self-determination to peoples deprived of such rights. For
Roosevelt, the Charter embraced the millions of people living under the
yoke of European colonial rule. But Churchill insisted the promise of the

Charter was made only to peoples enduring German occupation and persecution. Ignoring the brutal colonial history of the United States in continental America and Southeast Asia, when the United States entered the war in December 1941, Roosevelt and his government stepped up moral pressure on the British to free the subjects of Empire while at the same time casting covetous eyes on the material rewards that would come with reshaping the world order and asserting America's own power in the Middle East and Asia.

By 1944, the tension between the two Allies was deepening – most acutely in the Middle East. The experience of fighting a global war on multiple fronts had drilled into the minds of military strategists in Berlin, Moscow, Washington and London the stupendous significance and power of oil to fuel modern warfare. In the Middle East, the Allied powers were intent on exploiting the huge reserves of oil that lay beneath the arid lands of Persia, Iraq and the Arab nations of the Gulf.

Fractious strategic matters stoked tensions between the two powers. Britain jealously held on to Egypt and Palestine so that they dominated the Suez Canal and the sea routes to India and Southeast Asia. The British feared that the sharpening conflict between indigenous Arabs and Zionist Jews, who were contending the narrow strip of land between the Jordan and the Mediterranean, was a dire threat to the security of the Empire. On the other side of the Atlantic, Roosevelt and other ambitious Americans had begun to reflect on the strategic promise of a pliant new state in this volatile neighbourhood.

These tensions began to sharpen at a time when the Western Allies were under pressure to respond to the plight of Jews in occupied Europe. It was no longer enough to sidestep humanitarian action by vowing to defeat Nazi Germany and seek retribution for the crimes of the Nazi state. In early 1944, the founding of the American War Refugee Board (WRB), with the backing of President Roosevelt, sent a clear message that for the American government the murderous persecution of Jews in German-occupied Europe could no longer be pushed to the margins of public attention. No one was quite sure what, if anything, could be done to halt the onslaught on the last surviving Jewish community in Hungary but there was a mounting cacophony of protests from across the Atlantic. When Joel Brand landed in Istanbul bearing a perplexing ransom offer from one of the most notorious agents of Nazi persecution, his message could not be ignored. What to do about it was altogether another matter.

There was no British equivalent to the WRB – a fact that reflected a much deeper ambivalence on the British side about the catastrophe that was overwhelming European Jewry. This is not the same as accepting that the British reaction to the ransom offer was irrational. As we know, the Germans had not sent Brand alone to Istanbul – and his companion was well known to British intelligence as 'Trillium', an unscrupulous smuggler and informer who had served both German and Hungarian intelligence agencies as well as the Zionists in Istanbul. From the British point of view, Brand and Grosz had value *not as emissaries of a ransom offer but as agents of enemy powers.* As to the purpose of the Blood for Trucks deal – that was anybody's guess. It might be a plot to sow seeds of discord between the western Allies and the Soviets or a callous means of making the Allies complicit in the fate of the Jews of Hungary if the offer was refused. In the period between May and June, it was these anxieties rather than the fear that many tens of thousands of Jews might be allowed to emigrate from Hungary that shaped the British response to the Brand Mission. Under pressure from the WRB, the American reaction was more subtle, more attuned to the moral risks of dismissing the German offer out of hand. But neither the British nor the Americans could afford to be perceived and judged as callous and parsimonious about so many hundreds of thousands of human lives. The consequence was an uneasy *pas de deux* between pragmatism and public hand wringing. What is remarkable is not so much that the perfidious German ransom offer was eventually nullified but that it was taken so seriously – and at the highest levels of the Allied governments.

If the ransom offer was a sham then, naturally, so too were its provisos. It is unclear whether Brand conveyed to the Zionists in Istanbul that Eichmann insisted that Jews emigrating from Hungary should not be permitted to enter Palestine. If, as seems to be the case, Brand was evasive, unclear or ambiguous about this stricture, it is unlikely that the ransom offer would have seized the attention of the Zionists, who, naturally, would have welcomed this opportunity to transform the Jewish demographic presence in Palestine. Likewise, Eichmann's insistence that any emigration must take place in a westerly direction, to Spain, Portugal or Switzerland, was equally as problematic for the Allies. It was inconceivable that such large-scale population movements would have been agreed to by the Allied powers – let alone organised and carried out – on the eve of Operation Overlord, the invasion of Europe. Eichmann and his henchman could safely assume that large-scale emigration in *any direction of the compass* would not be welcomed by any one of the Allied powers. In July, Horthy's offer to release some 7,000–8,000 Hungarian Jews set off acute diplomatic anxieties on the British side about having to cope with a 'flood of refugees'. I will come back to the ramifications of the 'Horthy offer' shortly, but the important point here is that in the period immediately after Brand met with the Zionists in Istanbul and *before* the halting of the deportations in early July, the responses to the German offers focused on their political and strategic ramifications. Although any discussion of Jewish emigration set off shrill alarms about Palestine in British ears, this was not from the British point of view the most pressing concern – to begin with.

At the time of the German occupation of Hungary in March, Gerhart Riegner, the representative of the World Jewish Congress in Geneva, who had in August 1942 warned the US State Department and the British Foreign Office that he had evidence that Nazi Germany was planning to murder millions of European Jews, sent a telegram to John Pehle of the WRB that began 'Most concerned about destiny Hungarian Jewry', and warned that the Western powers should insist that 'the attitude of the Hungarian people towards the Jews will be one of the most important tests of behaviour which allied nations will remember in the peace settlement after the war'. Riegner astutely identified national dishonour and fear of retributive justice as a potent means of applying pressure on the Hungarians, and the WRB successfully urged President Roosevelt to follow his lead. On 24 March, the President warned the Regent that in this matter of 'one of the blackest crimes of all history': none who participate in these acts of savagery shall go unpunished.' His Secretary of State, Cordell Hull, went further and insisted that Hungary had to demonstrate 'its right to independence'. Such threats did not address the matter of rescue and refuge, and in London, the Foreign Secretary, Anthony Eden, followed the American threats in the same spirit: he called on nations allied with or subject to Nazi Germany to 'join in preventing further persecution'. These proclamations had no impact at all on the Germans and their Hungarian collaborators.

At the end of May, news of the Brand Mission and the disconcerting SS offer threw the Allies off balance. When Moshe Shertok and Ben-Gurion informed Sir Harold MacMichael about the details, he told the British government that the offer 'was a Nazi intrigue based on far other motives than the apparent ones'. He was perfectly correct. In London, the War Cabinet debated how to respond. A. W.G. Randall, who was the head of the Refugee Department of the Foreign Office, opined that there were substantial reasons for 'not having anything to do with the proposals as they stood'.[6] He warned, presciently, that 'the United States might have a different view'. He feared that Roosevelt might be over-influenced by the WRB, which had committed itself to the 'rescue of Jews'. The implication in Randall's comment is that because Roosevelt was campaigning for a fourth term as President, he would have an interest in securing the votes of American Jews. This has the rather unpleasant odour of antisemitic conspiracy theories, but Randall was merely pointing out the obvious when he went on:

> The evacuation of a million refugees from occupied territories and their maintenance in neutral or allied countries could not be undertaken without a major alteration of the course of military operations.

With a nervous eye on Washington, the British Cabinet did not immediately turn its back on the ransom offer: at least, not overtly. A decision was made to inform Chaim Weizmann about the matter. Weizmann was a friend of the Prime Minister and an influential and respected member of the British establishment, as well as a fervent Zionist. There followed a series of meetings between Weizmann and the highest levels at the Foreign Office, including Eden. The British are frequently portrayed as the villains of the Blood for Goods narrative – so it is important to note here that the Zionists insisted that any response to the German offer should be made with the 'knowledge and approval' of the British government. Weizmann also urged Eden to inform the Soviet government. The British records reveal that Shertok was 'fully convinced of Brand's reliability' and that Brand was convinced that 'the German proposition was a serious one'. The point, of course, was not Brand's credibility but the German *intent*. Had the offer been made in good faith? Even though Ben-Gurion believed that the offer was *likely* to be a trick, it was agreed that there was a chance to save Jewish lives. Shertok arrived in London at the end of June and another meeting was held with the Foreign Office. The Jewish leaders pressured the British to allow Brand to return to Budapest and continue with his rescue work. The British were reluctant to give up Brand, firstly because he and Grosz might provide an unexpected intelligence windfall – and secondly, his return could be construed as an agreement to negotiate. If Brand had been permitted to return to Budapest, his life would have almost certainly been put in grave danger. The British pointed out that 'the Germans were going on with their deportations and killing'.

When Eden discussed the matter with his American counterparts, he urged them not to take the German offer seriously. He was not prepared to offer material concessions to the enemy – and emphasised that he and his staff had concluded that the offer that had come through 'insignificant or suspect channels' was intended to disrupt bonds with the Soviets and, in the event of rejection, to justify extreme measures being taken against Jews. Eden claimed that Shertok agreed with the British view, but on 11 July (after the deportations had been halted) Ben-Gurion made another appeal to the Americans. He now called the German offer a unique and last chance 'of saving the remains of European Jewry'. By this time, the British were holding both Brand and Grosz in custody.

The Hirschmann Ploy

Soon afterwards, there was another twist. When the director of the WRB, John Pehle, had decided to try and 'keep the negotiations alive', he understood that defying the British was fraught with risk and that he could run afoul of the Soviets. But he remained undeterred and turned to a rising star in the WRB, Ira A. Hirschmann. One of the vice presidents of the New York store Bloomingdale's, Hirschmann had a background in the brand new industry of advertising and was an aggressive self-publicist. In 1943, he had become involved with Peter Bergson's Emergency Committee to Save the Jewish People of Europe, but had thrown himself into the work of the WRB. In January 1944, he was sent to Ankara as the board representative. He told a contact on the *New York Times*: 'I may have a ripping story.'[7] He arrived in Ankara on 14 February. He was officially attached to the American diplomatic mission and had a remit to establish links in German-occupied territory and, most significantly, was authorised to disregard the Trading with the Enemy Act. Working with Chaim Barlas, the Jewish Agency representative in Istanbul who controlled legal immigration to Palestine, the determined Hirschmann succeeded in breaking through a dense jungle of red tape to allow small groups of Jewish children to enter Turkey from Bulgaria. It was a remarkable achievement and Hirschmann made sure the world knew about it: 'Palestine Door opens to 5,000 Balkan Children' proclaimed the *New York Post*. Hirschmann was hugely energetic and resourceful as well as hungry for fame. He soon discovered that rescue across borders was dauntingly complex. He returned, chastened, to Bloomingdale's. When the Brand story broke six weeks later, Pehle once again turned to the Jewish rescuer of Ankara, even though other members of the board had warned that 'there are disturbing elements about Hirschmann'. The records of the WRB reveal the astonishing naivety of the WRB board. With the approval of Morgenthau, the United States Secretary of the Treasury, Pehle briefed Steinhardt, the Ambassador in Turkey, that a special representative of the government was on his way to 'convince the Germans that this Government is sufficiently concerned with the problem that it is willing to consider genuine proposals for the rescue and relief of Jews and other victims'.[8] When he arrived in Istanbul, Hirschmann discovered that Resnik had already interviewed Brand and confronted him about 'working a nasty intrigue'. 'He is obviously my enemy.' Hirschmann's petulant tantrum suggests that he had already acquired a jealous preoccupation with Joel Brand. He scented another triumph.

On 21 June, an aircraft with Hirschmann on board took off for Cairo. 'I have the inside track,' he boasted in his diary, 'as *the* government representative'. As the plane bumped and rocked above the Mediterranean, the American Ambassador in Moscow sent an urgent telegram to the WRB: the Soviet government had forbidden 'any conversations whatsoever with the German government'. Pehle sent a telegram to Steinhardt to: 'Please take no, repeat no, further action of any nature with respect to this matter'. But Hirschmann was already in Egypt.

On 22 June, Hirschmann was driven to a small house perched on the edge of the Nile. Waiting for him inside was Joel Brand. He was, Hirschmann noted, fit and healthy – but profoundly anxious about his family in Budapest. The conversation was an edgy one. Brand later described Hirschmann as 'conceited and pompous': 'he promised a great deal'. Hirschmann was, for his part, captivated by Brand's passion and sincerity but judged him 'ill prepared' for the role history had forced upon him. When he reported to Steinhardt, Hirschmann revealed that Brand saw the German offer as 'a great confession of weakness'. He insisted that the proposal was serious and that details could be negotiated. He urged that the British be persuaded to keep the door open.

Closing the Door

Pehle leapt on Hirschmann's report and urged that lines of contact should be kept open to save as many lives as possible. American ambivalence dismayed the British: 'the U.S. government,' Randall wrote, 'particularly in an election year, is desperately anxious to show that nothing, however fantastic, has been neglected that might lead to the rescue of the Jews.' The British need not have been too concerned. In mid June, as the murderous rhythm of deportation and killing at Auschwitz reached fever pitch, the dilemma of what to do about the Brand mission was brutally resolved. On 14 June, the British ambassador in Moscow, Archibald Clark Kerr, met Andrei Vishinsky, the Soviet Commissar for Foreign Affairs, and informed him in detail about the German offer. The reaction in the Kremlin was predictable. The following day, the American Ambassador, Averell Harriman, reiterated the same story without mentioning the trucks – and reported to Washington that the Soviet government did not consider it 'expedient or permissible' to negotiate with the German government.

In early July, there was a surprising development on the German side – and it has led to confusion. On 8 July, Colonel Stiller of the German Consulate in Istanbul approached Bader and offered to fly him immediately to Berlin to meet representatives of the German Foreign Office to continue negotiations. Braham and other historians have interpreted this to mean that the German offer to negotiate was serious. A deeper look into the Stiller proposal soon reveals the hand of 'Direktor Schroeder' – the nefarious SD agent Fritz Laufer. When Bader discussed the offer with the Zionists in Jerusalem, Ben-Gurion wisely ordered him to wait. In this matter, Pehle and the WRB agreed. The idea was turned down.

On 7 July, as relations between the Germans and the Regent deteriorated, Roosevelt ordered Harriman to disclose every detail of the German offer to Vishinsky and to stress that the British and American governments had 'not been deceived' by the 'alleged' German offer, which they concluded was 'part and parcel of the psychological warfare effort of the German government'. The evidence supporting this analysis was 'the alleged German willingness that the trucks would not be used on the

Western Front'.[9] Rather than sowing seeds of discord between the Allies, the German demand for trucks to be used on the Eastern Front exposed the innate perfidy of the offer.

On 19 July, the British Foreign Office leaked the story of the ransom offer and the BBC broadcast the news that same evening. The following morning newspapers were emblazoned with headlines about the 'monstrous offer' to barter the lives of Hungarian Jews for military equipment. On the same day, Pehle was astounded by the headline in the *New York Herald Tribune*: 'Nazis Reported in Bid to "Spare" 400,000 Jews: London Hears of Huge Extortion Demand for Supplies by Allies'. Echoing the language of the British reports, the *Tribune* reporter denounced 'the most monstrous blackmail attempt in history'.

It is a remarkable irony that as the Brand drama played out between Moscow, London and Washington and on the front pages of newspapers, tens of thousands of Jewish lives were about to spared in Hungary for reasons that had nothing to do with Eichmann's sham offer.

HORTHY HESITATES

On 14 July 1944, following days of bitter arguments with his generals, Hitler left the Berghof, his Alpine retreat near Berchtesgaden, for the last time and was flown to his eastern headquarters, the Wolf's Fort at Rastenburg in eastern Prussia. At the first situation conference of the day, many of Hitler's staff were dismayed by his conspicuous stoop and uncontrollable tremors. Since Hitler had eschewed any idea of negotiating an end to the war with the Allied powers, what remained in his armoury was the demonic force of his will. But to display such resolve was hardly a matter of choice: he had incinerated every bridge. The Allies declared Hitler's Reich a criminal regime; there would be no leniency: any negotiations would be punitive.

As well as such pragmatic considerations, waging war for Hitler and his most loyal courtiers was increasingly abstract. He fought his battles inside an airless cavity where the exercise of will could float free from the twisted steel, the sucking mud, torn flesh and saturating blood of the battlefield. Although Hitler had served on the front line during the First World War, he and the Wehrmacht elite refused to imagine the quotidian experience of the battlefields where tens of thousands of human lives were being mangled on a vast scale in the steel maws of modern weaponry. The arena where Hitler exercised his destructive will was buried deep beneath the concrete shroud of the Wolf's Fort and was nourished by two-dimensional maps, charts and abstract icons of military divisions.

Inside this echo chamber, the ghastly realities of war were defanged. But on 20 July, Colonel Claus Schenk Graf von Stauffenberg, a Swabian aristocrat, Catholic and hero of the war in North Africa, entered the wooden barrack house at the Wolf's Fort where Hitler was about to begin his morning situation conference. He carried a leather briefcase, which he placed discreetly beneath the heavy, map-strewn oak table just a few metres away from Hitler. Inside the briefcase was a hastily primed bomb. As arranged with his fellow conspirators, Stauffenberg was called to answer a telephone call and slipped out of the conference room, leaving behind his cap and belt as if he planned to return. His departure went unremarked.

At 12.30 p.m., Hitler began his briefing: a long, wordy, self-justificatory incantation. Minutes later, Colonel Heinz Brandt used his foot to push the briefcase behind one of the thick wooden legs of the conference table. At 12.42 p.m., the bomb inside exploded. The blast demolished the conference room and killed a stenographer. Hitler had been shielded from the blast by the leg of the sturdy oak table.

Just thirty minutes later, Stauffenberg and his aide, Werner von Häften, flew out of the Rastenburg airfield. As the Heinkel He 111 levelled up and turned towards Berlin, Stauffenberg was certain that Hitler could not have survived the blast. He was wrong. At the end of that same day, as the plot and the plotters unravelled, Stauffenberg was marched in front of a firing squad at the army headquarters, the Bendlerblock in Berlin. 'Long live Holy Germany!' he cried, as a fusillade of shots tore away his life.

The botched 'Bomb Plot' and Hitler's survival of the tenth attempt against his life since 1933 had consequences unforeseen by the conspirators. Hitler was convinced that his seemingly miraculous survival had been a gift of providence rather than sheer chance – and this conviction reinforced his perverse conviction that his mission as Führer was semi-divine. If providence bestowed such favours on Germany's leader, then so too could the Reich wrench victory from the catastrophe that was pounding at its borders. The German people, he concluded, must fight on to the bitter end – and responsibility for Germany's national plight could be laid without a shadow of a doubt at the door of disloyal factions that had grown like cancers inside the Wehrmacht. The betrayers would be punished; the loyal rewarded. The events of 14 July and the shockwaves that reverberated across the Reich accelerated the expansion of power by Heinrich Himmler and the SS. Himmler's biographer, Peter Longerich, argues that the failure of the 'Bomb Plot' redefined Himmler's role in the Nazi state as 'the guarantor of internal security and embodiment of executive power in its entirety'.[1]

It has been argued by historian Yehuda Bauer that Himmler had been made aware of the conspiracy to assassinate Hitler at the Wolf's Fort and chose to do nothing to prevent it happening. Himmler knew that the war was lost and hoped that with Hitler eliminated, he could seize power and launch peace negotiations with the western Allies. Bauer believes that Himmler's knowledge of the Bomb Plot and its possible consequences inspired him to approve a plan to send a Hungarian smuggler, namely 'Bandi' Grosz, to Istanbul with an offer to negotiate tucked away in a suitcase. The third and final stage in this argument is that Himmler's prescient awareness that the war was irrevocably lost convinced him that the surviving Jews of Europe could be exploited as hostages to secure a favourable settlement with the Allied powers. It was this insight that living Jews could be of use to him that led Himmler to sanction the plan to send Brand and Grosz on their mysterious mission.

The notion that Himmler took a close interest in the Blood for Goods mission as a means to open a back door to the western Allies has proved tenacious. And yet it is nonsense. It is correct that Himmler would come to see Jews as valuable hostages and that he would seek to use their lives to lever a negotiating position with the Allies. But this change of mind and strategy took place six months after Stauffenberg's bomb exploded at the Wolf's Fort. In the summer of 1944, Himmler had not yet reached that depth of despair and was not yet motivated to pursue the cynical and desperate peace offers that began to obsess him in early 1945. There is no doubt at all, however, that he approved the devious plans hatched by Eichmann and his henchmen to deceive and exploit the Zionist Rescue Committee in Budapest. It is not inconceivable that he hoped to sow mischief among the enemies of the Reich. We are unlikely to know for certain. What we can be certain of is that in the spring and summer of 1944, Himmler would never have contemplated exchanging 'a million lives' for any number of trucks. It is a fundamental mistake to interpret Himmler's motivations in the aftermath of the occupation of Hungary and the destruction of Hungarian Jewry through the lens of his desperate efforts to contact the western Allies in the early months of 1945.

This argument can be further substantiated. When the British and American newspapers splashed the story of the 'monstrous offer' to barter Jews for military supplies on their front pages, the German Foreign Office in Berlin took note. Ribbentrop demanded a full report from Veesenmayer – who swiftly replied that the Brand Mission had been based on a 'secret order of the Reichsführer'.[2] Ribbentrop then called Himmler to seek an explanation – and there the matter ended; he must have been satisfied by Himmler's account. Remember that Ribbentrop would have seized any opportunity to discredit a powerful rival: if Himmler had been caught out plotting to release 'a million Jews' behind Hitler's back, Ribbentrop would have acquired a potent means to bring down the increasingly powerful SS chief: there is no evidence at all that Ribbentrop ever brought up the matter of the mysterious mission with Hitler or anyone else in the Nazi elite. In the aftermath of the 'Bomb Plot', Hitler was obsessed by conspiracies and plots – and would not have tolerated any deviance from his now relentless pursuit of the Final Solution, most of all from his 'loyal Heinrich'.

In the aftermath of Stauffenberg's failed assassination attempt, Himmler exploited the shattering attempt on the life of the Führer to tighten his grip on power – with Hitler's connivance. The organisational ethos of the SS as loyal protectors of the state and its leader would be deepened and rewarded. The plot had been hatched and nourished within the entrails of the German army and although Himmler and his intelligence henchmen in the SD had been clueless about the plot and the identity of the conspirators – he could now bolster the national status and power of the SS by crushing the conspirators and shaming their families. In the days and weeks after 20 July, Himmler launched an orgy of violent purging that came to an end only with the defeat of the Reich. It was in this period of merciless retribution that real and suspected enemies of the regime such as the disgraced former Abwehr head Wilhelm Canaris, his deputy Hans Oster, the theologian Dietrich Bonhoeffer and the long-forgotten Georg Elser, the young carpenter who had tried to kill Hitler at the Munich beer hall in November 1939, were all executed.

As a reward for his exculpating diligence, Hitler rewarded Himmler with command of the Reserve Army, replacing Stauffenberg's immediate superior, Colonel General Friedrich Fromm, who was implicated in the conspiracy, and to spite the Army commanders. Hitler gave Himmler responsibility for the political indoctrination of the Reserve Army recruits, as he was convinced that the Army commanders had succumbed to outright disloyalty and defeatism. The Wehrmacht needed a purgative dose of SS values.

Then on 25 July, Hitler was finally persuaded to declare the 'Total War' that Goebbels had obsessed about since the German defeat at Stalingrad.

In February 1943, the Propaganda Minister had made a speech at the Sportspalast in Berlin: '*Nun, Volk steh auf, und Sturm brich los!*' (Now, people, rise up and let the storm break loose!) Menaced by the spectre of 'Jewish Bolshevism' and its army of 'Jewish liquidators', Goebbels proclaimed, Germany must throw all its human resources – 'soldiers, doctors, scientists, artists, engineers and architects, teachers, white collars' – into the fray:

> Total war is the demand of the hour. We must put an end to the bour-geois attitude that we have also seen in this war: Wash my back, but don't get me wet! The danger facing us is enormous. The efforts we take to meet it must be just as enormous. The time has come to remove the kid gloves and use our fists.[3]

Hitler had for some time resisted Goebbels' demands to wage 'Total War' fearing that the burden thrown on the shoulders of ordinary Germans would further sap morale. By the summer of 1944, his last remaining scru-ples had been liquefied in the acid of defeat and betrayal.

Hitler's declaration of 'Total War' did not mark a sharp break with German combat strategy; the kid gloves had been torn off long before. But it heralded a radical escalation in the extraction of resources both human and material and handed immense power to the 'Gang of Four', Goebbels, Himmler, Bormann and Speer. As the Reich reeled, their stars rose high into a sky contaminated by the ashes of millions. There is an important point to draw out of the evolution to wage 'Total War'. Not one of these four powerbrokers ever challenged Hitler's leadership or authority – nor did they contemplate ways of ending the war that excluded Hitler. These fawning courtiers owed all their immense and still growing power to the Führer and cherished long-held and deep bonds with him personally. They had no great love for each other, far from it, but every one of the 'Gang' demonstrated a deep-rooted and habitual loyalty to their patron and benefactor.

This leads us to an important conclusion. It is nonsense to claim, as a few historians have argued, that in 1944 Himmler was ready to covertly seek peace with the Allies. Nor did he let up his relentless and terroristic persecution of the enemies of the Reich. In what remained of the Greater German Reich, Hitler authorised Himmler to escalate the destruction of any partisan movements. SS men murdered thousands of alleged resisters in Norway, Denmark and the Netherlands. Even harsher savagery fell on the peoples of occupied Poland, the disintegrating Eastern Front and the Balkans. After the Warsaw Uprising in August 1944, Himmler unleashed the brute force of Waffen-SS divisions on the city under the command of the murderous Bach-Zelewski and, when the Polish Home Army had been crushed, demanded that Warsaw be 'razed to the ground'. The desire to completely annihilate the racial enemies of the Reich burned brightly in Himmler's consciousness. In the same month, Slovakian partisans had led an uprising against the puppet government in Bratislava – and German troops, commanded by Gottlob Berger, the head of the SS Main Office, marched across the border to restore order. Accompanying Berger was Hermann Höfle, who it will be recalled had played an important role in 'Action Reinhardt', the mass murder of Polish Jews from 1941–43. Now, as part of a cleansing operation, the SS demanded that the surviving Jews of Slovakia, who had been spared in 1943, and must surely have inspired the uprising, should be deported. The trains began rolling again in September, bearing 8,000 Slovakian Jews to Auschwitz and thousands of others to Sachsenhausen and Theresienstadt. Once more the Hlinka Guards, backed by German troops, scoured the countryside in search of Jews who had fled into hiding or joined the partisans. In Bratislava, Gisi Fleischmann of the Working Group protested against the deportations, but she was arrested and sent to Auschwitz – and murdered. Her cousin, Rabbi Weissmandel, who had fallen for Dieter Wisliceny's scam, was deported with his family. Before he was thrust inside the cattle truck, the rabbi had hidden an emery wire inside a loaf of bread and, as the train rumbled across Slovakia towards the Polish border, used it to prise open the locked wagon door and jump to freedom. The fall broke his leg, but he managed to find refuge in Bratislava. The rest of his family were all murdered.

The Summer of False Hope

That summer, events developed very differently in Hungary. Many thousands of Jews in Budapest *would* be saved – but not because of the Brand Mission nor through the efforts of the Zionists in Jerusalem.

By 24 June 1944, Eichmann and his Hungarian allies had completed the deportation of Jewish communities in the Hungarian provinces. A ghastly whirlwind of destruction had sent hundreds of thousands of men, women and children to the voracious fires of the Auschwitz crematoria. Himmler's special representative Kurt Becher had, with comparable efficiency, plundered the great industrial empire of the Chorin and Weiss families. Now Eichmann and his collaborators turned their attention to the Jews of Budapest.

At the same time, a member of the Va'ada called Moshe Krausz – who was a bitter rival of Kasztner – had managed to send the 'Auschwitz Protocols' to George M. Mantello, the First Secretary of the Consulate General of El Salvador in Geneva. This might seem to be a surprising decision but Mantello had a very impressive record. He was, in fact, a Hungarian Jew from Transylvania called György Mandl. Earlier, he had sent a few hundred 'nationality certificates' to Budapest, circumventing the Salvadoran government with the help of the Consul General, Colonel I. Catellanos. So Krausz knew exactly what he was doing. With impressive despatch, Mantello straightaway began distributing the 'Protocols' to the Swiss government, Jewish organisations and the Papal Nuncio. He also contacted Walter Garrett, the Zürich representative of the British wire service, the Exchange Telegraph. Mantello wrote a hard-hitting press release that boiled down the revelations of the 'Protocols' to four key points – and cabled Roosevelt, Churchill, William Temple, the Archbishop of Canterbury, the exiled Queen of Holland and a handful of writers and intellectuals. Thanks to his efforts and refined communication skills, the news of the German assault on the Hungarian Jews at last went viral, with more than fifty newspaper articles pouring from the presses in less than two weeks deploring the persecution of Hungarian Jews and calling for a halt to the slaughter. As a consequence of the firestorm of protest Krausz and Mandel had set off, the Allied powers began receiving a deluge of pleas for help from governments and Jewish and non-Jewish ecclesiastical leaders. At the end of June, Archbishop Francis J. Spellman – a charismatic American clergyman – warned the Hungarian government that these shocking accounts of what had taken place in Hungary appalled all decent men and women and contradicted 'the doctrines of the Catholic faith professed by the vast majority of the Hungarian people'.

The news from Hungary unleashed a storm of words – and on 2 July, a massive air raid on Budapest, the biggest of the war. Hungarian anti-semites blamed Jews for guiding the bombers to their targets but for Horthy and other members of the Crown Council the message of the raids was unambiguous.

In London, Churchill sent a pusillanimous note to Eden: 'What can be done? What can be said?' and on 5 July, Eden stepped up to the Despatch Box in the House of Commons to reprise the well-worn homily that 'the principal hope of terminating this tragic state of affairs must remain the speedy victory of the Allied nations'. His reply to Churchill's note was – we can say and do not very much. There were other British voices that took a more courageous position: William Temple appealed directly to the Hungarian people to help the Jews. The BBC threw off, albeit briefly, the shackles of wartime censorship and sent messages informing Hungarians about anti-Jewish measures and warning their government about the consequences of their actions. In the United States, the outcry reached a much higher volume.

On 3 July, Sándor Török, a Christian member of the Jewish Council, met with Horthy. According to the Regent's daughter-in-law, Countess Ilona Edelsheim-Gyulai:

> Sándor Török brought all kinds of news with the purpose of informing the Regent. Fortunately, I wrote a diary, in which the memorable day is marked: on July 3rd, 1944, he delivered the 'Auschwitz Notebook' to me. I read this tremendously shocking description of the gas chamber-equipped extermination camp in his presence. One could feel that every word of it is true, as something like this could not be fabricated. I immediately brought this to my father-in-law's chambers …

All this thoroughly rattled the Regent – and he called on Eichmann's collaborators, Endre and Baky, to appear before the Council to explain the brutal treatment of Jews. A number of Councillors seemed to accept their grossly propagandist narrative but Horthy sacked Baky. He refused to go quietly and began conspiring with the gendarmerie commanders to launch a coup. Horthy got wind of Baky's machinations and ordered loyal army units to Budapest: he always reacted decisively to any threat to his own power. He had Baky and Endre arrested – and ordered the gendarmerie to leave the city. On 6 July, Horthy informed Veesenmayer that the deportations must stop. Three days later, the last deportation train passed through Kassa …

This sequence of events might be taken to imply that Horthy agreed to halt the deportations for humanitarian reasons. This was not the case. His decision was pragmatic. It was also tentative, hesitant and opportunist. Hungary had been defamed by the international outcry about the deportations and mass murders – and this shaming was a threat to the limited sovereignty offered by the German occupiers. The crisis on the front lines of the war reinforced Horthy's dilemmas. News from the Western Front made it all too clear that the German army was not about to drive back the Allied armies, and, in the East, Stalin's armies were driving relentlessly towards the Prussian border. Hungary could no longer shelter under the battered wings of the Reich. The American bombing raid on Budapest showed that there could no longer be any doubt about the weakness of the Axis and provided a brutal demonstration that retribution for war crimes was no longer a matter of faraway hand wringing and impotent proclamation. Horthy's actions in early July stymied, to be sure, Eichmann's plans to move against the many thousands of Jews who survived in Budapest – but Horthy's order was, at root, a matter not of morality but of realism.

A report sent by Veesenmayer to the Foreign Office on 11 July reveals another dimension of Horthy's decision:

> The Deputy Foreign Minister today pointed out to me how difficult the situation of the Hungarian Government was as a result of the *discriminatory handling* of the Jewish question by the competent German agencies in Hungary, Rumania, and Slovakia. While we [the Germans] would demand of the government in this country a most ruthless proceeding against the Jews, the Rumanians and Slovakians would be allowed to treat the Jews in a far more indulgent manner [my italics].

In other words, the Hungarian leaders begrudged the way in which other German satellite states such as Romania were no longer obligated to deal with their Jewish citizens as ruthlessly as the Germans demanded the Hungarian government act. In short, the fate of the Hungarian Jews mirrored Hungarian loss of national autonomy. To add insult to injury of national pride, the Romanians and Slovaks were, it was believed, permitting Jewish refugees, including Hungarians, safe passage to Palestine. This claim was a gross exaggeration of the actual generosity of these governments, but for the Hungarians, Veesenmayer pointed out:

> This is obviously done to create a good impression with our enemies. To the outside world the impression is created that the Rumanians and

Slovaks are taking a quite different attitude toward the Jewish question than Hungary, *against whom the whole hatred of the enemy and neutral states will be directed*. This would reflect very unfavourably upon the situation of the Hungarian Government [my italics].[4]

As we have seen, Horthy's order to halt deportations infuriated Eichmann – and frustrated his superior, the HSSPF Otto Winckelmann – who accused Veesenmayer of indulging the Regent. When the Crown Council offered to release 7,800 Jews to the West, German indignation knew no bounds. Hitler was enraged but conscious, as ever, of the fraying bonds with the Hungarians, he made a decision to agree to Horthy's offer – but on condition that he immediately resume the deportations. On 17 July, Ribbentrop informed Veesenmayer that:

The Führer expects that now the measures against the Jews of Budapest be taken without any further delay, with the exceptions granted to the Hungarian government. However, no delay in the implementation of *the general Jewish measures* should occur as a result of these exceptions. Otherwise, the Führer's acceptance of these exceptions will have to be withdrawn [my italics].[5]

Hitler's wishes, conveyed to Horthy by his Foreign Minister, encapsulate an absolutist policy of racial destruction that in special circumstances can tolerate modest exceptions. A few thousands could be exempted from destruction if such spurious generosity ensured the completion of 'the general Jewish measures'. Hitler's insistence on the annihilation of Hungarian Jewry was an expression of racial fanaticism. But his calculated insistence was, at the same time, a political means to enforce German power over a vacillating ally.

It was Eichmann's immoral acceptance of the deadly absolutism of the Nazi elite that emboldened him to flout Horthy's order and launch the attack on the Kistarcsa camp on 14 July. At the Eichmann trial, Dr Sandor Brody provided this detailed account of what happened a few days later:

A. On 19 July, in the morning, SS men, under the command of Novak, appeared with many cars.
Q. Who else was there that you knew, apart from Novak?
A. [Helmut] Lemke.

Q. Were you yourself there personally on that day at Kistarcsa?

A. I was there personally, and I was in Vasdényei's office when Novak and Lemke came in.

Q. Please tell the Court what happened then.

A. Novak told Vasdényei that it was forbidden for anyone to leave the office. He forbade the use of the telephone. And he declared that, on Eichmann's orders, he was going to take those 1,500 persons, who had been placed in the railway coaches on 14 July, since Eichmann – as I heard it said – Eichmann will not tolerate his orders to be counter-manded, not even by the Regent of the state himself.

Q. What happened after that?

A. After that, an order was issued for everyone to go out into the court-yard, and the SS men began throwing them with great brutality into the trucks. Amongst them were people who walked on crutches and, if I remember correctly, there was one invalid chair and there were sick people; but they were told that they could leave all these things behind, for anyhow they would not be needing them anymore.

Q. Who said these things? Who shouted out these words?

A. The SS men who were throwing the people about or who were forci-bly loading them on to the trucks; Lemke told Vasdényei he should also dispatch Brody, since he, too, was to be deported. And Vasdényei ordered his secretary, named Istvan Vass, to accompany me to headquarters.

Q. Did he say anything more about you – any personal accusation against you? Did Lemke add any personal accusation as to why you had to be deported?

A. Yes: 'Brody has already caused us a great amount of unpleasantness.'

Q. Did he also mention a particular unpleasantness?

A. He attributed to me the fact that he was obliged to bring back the transport of 14 July.

…

Q. You were telling us earlier how these people were thrown into the trucks. Where were you standing, and where did you see that?

A. I? Certainly … it was possible from the first floor to observe the courtyard where they were being put on to the trucks.

Q. You told us about cripples. What about elderly people?

A. Yes, I even remember old women, eighty years of age, being thrown in this manner on to the trucks. I also remember, in particular, the widow of Sandor Flussig, who had been a member of the Upper House and chairman of the Stock Exchange, a woman of eighty, who was unable to take care of herself and who was sick.

When the Hungarian Crown Council agreed to the emigration of the 7,800 Jews, Krausz, backed by the Swiss Legation in Budapest and Barlas in Istanbul, began lobbying to organise the emigration of 7,000 *families* – thus widening the 'Horthy offer' to some 40,000 individuals. He claimed, erroneously, that the German government had approved. The consequence was a tidal wave of confusion. On 18 July, the British Foreign Office sent a cable to Washington:

> according to a telegram from the Swiss Legation at Budapest, authorization has been given by the government of Hungary for the departure of all Jews from Hungary who hold entry permits for another country, including Palestine.[6]

Krausz's reports on the Hungarian offer led many Jewish leaders to demand action from the Allies 'to explore and take advantage of the offer'. Inside the British Foreign Office, alarm bells were ringing loudly. Maurice Hankey of the 'Eastern Department' made his displeasure very clear:

> the floodgates of Europe are now going to be opened and that we shall in a very short time have masses of Eastern European Jews on our hands … a serious political situation would arise throughout the Arab world as soon as the Palestine quotas were filled …

Hankey went on: 'It is vital that camps should be established somewhere in the Mediterranean, but not Palestine and preferably not too near to Palestine.'[7]

Krausz had misreported and inflated the 'Horthy Offer' – but from the point of view of the British government it seemed as if there was now a serious cause for concern that their strategic interests would be endangered by 'masses of Eastern European Jews'. Eden feared that Britain would soon confront an impossibly stark choice between appearing callous by refusing the 'Horthy Offer', as it was understood, and supporting it and provoking civil war in Palestine.

On the other side of the Atlantic, the reaction to the offer was very different. Roosevelt insisted that the offer must be 'accepted as quickly as possible in order to save the largest number of lives'. Instructions were issued to American consular officials in neutral countries to begin issuing visas to 'any person to whom an American visa was issued or for whom a visa was authorised on or after July 1, 1941'. American representatives in Portugal, Spain, Sweden, Switzerland and Turkey assured their host governments that the United States would ensure that any refugees would be provided with appropriate support and maintenance. A number of other countries expressed willingness to accept Jewish refugees from Hungary – but the British persisted in opposing any agreement that would, in the view of HM government, threaten the stability of Palestine. British intransigence was vehemently denounced by American senators and congressmen. A deputation was sent to protest at the British Embassy.

The wrangling that erupted between the western Allies reflected British parsimony. In Budapest, Eichmann was equally alarmed by talk of emigration. Veesenmayer reported on Eichmann's views to Ribbentrop. The Jews were 'valuable human material' in Eichmann's view and because many were fanatical Zionists, emigration to Palestine was 'definitely undesirable'. Veesenmayer informed Ribbentrop that Eichmann was planning to speak directly to Himmler and demand a 'renewed decision by the Führer'. This was presumptuous for a mere SS colonel – but Eichmann was not speaking out of turn. He believed with good reason that he had the backing of his superiors in Berlin: Kaltenbrunner and Müller were certain that Hitler would get his way and the deportations would be resumed in due course. Eichmann had the backing too of the radical Hungarian ministers, Endre and Baky, who shared the same fanatical obsession with finishing off the 'cleansing' of the Hungarian nation. It was by no means certain that Horthy would hold his nerve. In early August, Baky informed Eichmann that he should plan to organise deportations again from Budapest by 25 August.

Then the fortunes of war took another turn – and Eichmann would soon be disappointed once again.

22

AFTERMATHS

In July 1944, Budapest was racked by a punishing summer heat. Along the wide avenues of Pest, leaves rattled like parchment on tree branches and Hungarians took refuge under umbrellas and café awnings. A small army of Labour Service men toiled in the broiling sun to repair the damage inflicted by the Allied raids. Many, with time on their hands, flocked across the turbid Danube to the heights of Buda to seek a cool breeze. Some 200,000 Jews remained alive in Budapest. Inside the new ghettos, some dared to hope, but many were worn down by an unrelenting climate of fear.

Eichmann at Bay

At his purloined villa in Rózsadomb, Adolf Eichmann began to fear that he was losing his grip on power. He was confused and angry. News that Hitler had permitted the emigration of thousands of Jews was infuriating. According to Veesenmayer, Eichmann petulantly threatened to go directly to Himmler to insist on quashing any talk of emigration. He continued making plans with his friends in the Ministry – and a date was set to begin deporting all but the most privileged Jews on 25 August. But the day before the plan was to be set in motion, Himmler cabled Veesenmayer to confirm that all deportations of Jews from Budapest would be suspended.

Himmler's decision was not an expression of mercy. By then, the western Allies had more than 2 million soldiers on the European continent. Paris was liberated on 24 August. The Allied advance across Europe would soon run into difficulties but in the East, vast numbers of Soviet troops swept towards East Prussia and into the Carpathians. The number of German allies was dwindling. In the aftermath of the Bomb Plot, Hitler received just a trickle of messages from compliant heads of state or prime ministers congratulating him on his miraculous survival. The Axis web of alliances was threadbare. At the beginning of August, Turkey, already a neutral power, broke off all relations with Germany, threatening vital supplies. This was just the beginning of a catastrophic unravelling. On 20 August, as Soviet troops launched an attack in southern Ukraine, huge numbers of Romanian troops deserted; many threw in their lot with the Russians and turned their guns on former allies. As German troops retreated, towards the Danube, Romanian troops closed off the crossings – and the Soviets fell on the retreating enemy, destroying sixteen divisions. Then a few days later, the Romanian Prime Minister and Conducător, Ion Antonescu, was ousted in a coup and King Michael sued for peace. The new Romanian government declared war on Germany – and its old enemy, Hungary. Now Romanian troops joined the Soviet armies as they pushed towards Budapest.

In his *Journal*, the Jewish Romanian writer and intellectual Mihail Sebastian eloquently expressed the agonising emotional contradictions of this tumultuous time. On Monday, 21 August, he wrote:

The war is coming towards us. It is not the war that has weighed us down for five years like a moral drama; now it is a physical war. Everything is possible – and nothing is easy. Military resistance (however quickly things are over) means destruction, perhaps forced evacuation, perhaps starvation. Capitulation means (who knows!) a repressive German response, in the style of northern Italy. In both cases, moreover, a pogrom once more becomes possible at any time …

On 29 August, we find Sebastian struggling to come to terms with the aftermath of the coup:

It was all quite extraordinary – then horrifying. Last Wednesday evening, we started down an unlikely slope to we knew not where – either to salvation or to disaster … Everywhere there is a terrible (morally) jostling, as people hurry to occupy positions, to assert claims, to establish rights … You can't speak now, only shout … It is true that for years U awaited the moment when I would finally be able to utter a cry of revenge – after so much nausea, after so much disgust.

Two days later, Sebastian watched Soviet heavy tanks rumble into Bucharest: 'these tired, dusty, rather badly dressed men are conquering the world'.[1]

At the beginning of September, Bulgaria too declared war on Germany. From Athens to Belgrade, German power was crumbling, German armies retreating. In the North, Finland signed an armistice with the Soviets on 19 September. It is hardly surprising to learn that Hitler's personal physician, Theodor Morell, reported that his patient suffered from fluctuating blood pressure, 'great agitation', dizziness, throbbing head, and 'return of the tremor' to his legs and hands. By September, Hitler was confined to bed with severe jaundice and appeared 'apathetic'.[2]

Germany could not afford to lose its last eastern ally. Hungary and its capital city were situated in the path of the Soviet advance into south-eastern Europe and were strategically vital. Hungary continued to export a huge tonnage of essential foodstuffs and fuel to the Reich. The restless Horthy needed to be placated – and since the Regent had seized on ending the deportations of Hungarian Jews to Auschwitz to assert his power, Himmler had no choice but to give in and order the SS to halt the planned 'Aktion' in Budapest. Hungary remained a rickety German ally – and the Jews of Budapest were safe, for now. A number of imprisoned Jews were set free and strict curfew regulations were loosened for High Holy Days. Many Budapest Jews started to hope. Perhaps they could avoid the fate of the countryside Jews. After all, Germany could not fight on much longer.

Even though he had the backing of SS chieftains such as Kaltenbrunner, who was equally frustrated, Eichmann now went to Veesenmayer and requested that the Sonderkommando be reassigned: he had, he lamented, become 'superfluous', Veesenmayer reported to Berlin. Eichmann's demand was either ignored or refused, for he stayed put in his villa. According to later testimony by his henchmen, Hermann Krumey and Dieter Wisliceny, Eichmann seemed to have decided to take advantage of the hedonistic pleasures still on offer in Budapest. Inside his villa, he lived the high life, attended by servants – and 'had a very full private life which took up lots of time', according to Krumey. He had little work to keep his stenographers and typists busy. As Cesarani emphasises in his biography, some historians conjured up the image of Eichmann as a perverted psychopath indulging in nightlong orgies while despatching his Jewish victims to their deaths. The truth was more mundane. Eichmann was a great deal less indulgent than his subordinate, Wisliceny, for example, who grew obese on the money he extorted from the Zionist Rescue Committee. To be sure, the married Eichmann had a number of affairs – and devoted a lot of time to riding horses or hurtling around the Hungarian countryside in a Volkswagen-manufactured amphibious vehicle, or 'Schwimmwagen'. He was very popular with his Hungarian colleagues and often enjoyed sampling expensive Tokay wines with his friend, Endre; according to Hansi Brand, Eichmann was frequently the worse for wear: 'you could smell the brandy from a long way off, and then he would be very chatty'.[3]

Cesarani writes that Eichmann was now 'rotten from the inside out' – but his idleness and alleged self-indulgence in the summer of 1944 tell us little more than the fact that Eichmann had difficulties occupying his time when he was no longer required to manage the organisation of mass murder. It is the stuff of cliché to regard Eichmann's pursuit of pleasure as a symptom of evil. For most of his life, he honoured the work ethics of Protestantism: his problem, that summer, was idleness.

When he testified in Jerusalem in 1961, the former German diplomat Wilhelm Höttl provides us with a subtler picture of Eichmann in Budapest. Late one afternoon towards the end of August, Eichmann paid a visit to Höttl's office.[4] He was wearing battledress rather than his customary SS dress uniform and was evidently 'very nervous'. During the course of the meeting Eichmann 'swallowed several glasses of brandy, one after the other'. Eichmann had come to find out more about the 'enemy situation' in the aftermath of Romania's defection to the Allies. He was dismayed by the news. He now had no illusion that German defeat was inevitable, and, for him, this had grim implications: Höttl recalled him lamenting that he 'he stood no chance anymore'. He was aware that, as a consequence of his infamous role in the 'programme to exterminate the Jews', 'he was considered by the Allies to be a top war criminal'. According to his testimony, Höttl then asked Eichmann to provide him with reliable information about 'the number of Jews exterminated'. Höttl was, of course, trying to represent himself to the Israeli court as being unaware of the Final Solution. After the war, he had worked for the United States as an intelligence agent, and by the time Eichmann was kidnapped and brought to trial he was running a school in Bad Aussee in Austria. He was a devious individual with much to lose. It was at this point in his testimony that Höttl stated that Eichmann said that the number of Jews murdered 'was a very great Reich secret' but that the numbers might have exceeded 6 million. 'I presumably reacted in a very shocked fashion,' he disingenuously continued. Some Holocaust deniers have latched onto Höttl's post-war reputation for unreliability to insinuate doubt in this reference to '6 million'. But it is perfectly conceivable that Eichmann did make reference to this figure in the course of this anxious conversation in 1944. German record keeping was meticulous and detailed at every stage of the genocide. In any case, what we learn from Höttl's account is that Eichmann in late August 1944 was in a state of chronic anxiety and fully appraised of his reputation. Although his SS colleagues such as Kurt Becher had blood on their hands, Eichmann seems to have understood that he was ruined by notoriety. By the time Eichmann rose unsteadily to his feet at the end of this strange encounter, he had drunk four or five large brandies. Höttl added to his account that that he solicitously 'asked Eichmann expressly' not to drive. He added that in German police circles, Eichmann's drinking was 'openly talked about'.

Eichmann was wearing battledress that afternoon for a reason. At the end of August, Hans Geschke, appointed by Himmler to serve as the BdS or head of the SD in Budapest, took pity on the under-occupied Eichmann. He ordered him to lead the Kommando on a special mission to rescue thousands of *Volksdeutsche*, ethnic Germans, who were stranded in the path of the advancing Soviet army on the Romanian border. Backed by an SS Cavalry Division, Eichmann charged out of Budapest with fantasies of fighting to the death on the battlefield. His mission ended in farce when the *Volksdeutsche* refused to be evacuated. The frustrated Eichmann returned to Budapest disappointed – and at the end of September, the Eichmannkommando was formally dissolved. Ominously, Kaltenbrunner ordered Eichmann to stay on in Budapest to await developments.

Kasztner's Fall

During this period of frustration, Eichmann was frequently enraged by the machinations of his SS colleague, Kurt Becher. After Joel Brand's departure for Istanbul in May, Eichmann continued to torment Kasztner and the Rescue Committee – but he would soon be outmanoeuvred by Becher. The consequence was that Kasztner and Hansi Brand were drawn ever deeper into a compromising web of illusory negotiations. By now, Kasztner had become Hansi's lover – and they threw themselves into a series of humiliating meetings with the inebriated Eichmann to protest about the treatment of Jews in the new ghettoes and on the deportation trains. Eichmann was confident, of course, that Joel Brand would either come back empty-handed from his mission or not return to Budapest at all. He ruthlessly exploited Brand's silence to blackmail Hansi and Kasztner.

This bullying was integral to the strategy deception. The complex plan to incarcerate hundreds of thousands of Hungarian Jews in ghettoes set up in a number of zones and then deport them zone by zone through Slovakia to Auschwitz depended for its successful implementation on compliance by hoodwinked Jewish organisations and individuals. The process was brutally enforced by the Hungarian security forces at every stage, but Eichmann feared that it might take just one rebellion to spark chaos. To maintain the fiction that Jews were being deported to work camps, it was necessary to impose a limit on the level of coercive violence that could be used against Jews inside Hungarian borders – and before they could be subjected to selection at Auschwitz. It was Kasztner's tragic fate to be seduced into taking a leading part in the SS deception strategy – and become, in effect, an agent of the SS.

There are many incidents that expose Kasztner's descent into immoral compliance. In his controversial book *Kasztner's Crime*, published in 2016, Paul Bogdanor builds a forensically detailed case to argue that Kasztner's actions in 1944 must be judged as crimes. Bogdanor's evidence is powerful, but it is problematic, in my view, to conclude that Kasztner was a 'criminal' – the implication of the title of his book. To begin with, there is no firm evidence that Kasztner ever profited from his actions. He was not motivated by gain. In stark contrast to Kurt Becher, Kasztner was impoverished after the war. Nor is the legal requirement to establish *mens rea* satisfied in judging Kasztner. William Blackstone, an eighteenth-century English jurist, wrote: '[A]n unwarrantable act without a vicious will is no crime at all. So that to constitute a crime against human laws, there must be, first, a vicious will; and, secondly, an unlawful act consequent upon such vicious will.' Or more pithily, Oliver Wendell Holmes Jr noted: 'Even a dog distinguishes between being stumbled over and being kicked'. The American Justice Robert Jackson argued that:

The contention that *an injury can amount to a crime only when inflicted by intention* is no provincial or transient notion. It is as universal and persistent in mature systems of law as belief in freedom of the human will and a consequent ability and duty of the normal individual to choose between good and evil [my italics]. In short, a crime is 'generally constituted only from concurrence of an evil-meaning mind with an evil-doing hand'.[5]

We know from many eyewitness accounts that Kasztner was a strong-willed individual who needed to dominate and control. It was he who persuaded the other members of the Budapest Rescue Committee to embrace negotiation with the Germans rather than resistance – which Joel Brand had advocated. This reflected the fact that he had come to believe that the German plan to liquidate and exploit the Hungarians Jews, as far as he could comprehend the nature of that plan, could not be resisted. He seemed to see the Final Solution as a kind of force of nature. The logical conclusion was it was necessary to perform a kind of triage: a small proportion of Jews might be saved from the German onslaught.[6] The Jewish Councils, bitterly denounced by Hannah Arendt and others, had been performing triage from the moment Nazi persecution plans became apparent after 1933. Only a few could be saved from its unrelenting enactment. Saving the few became a priority, if not an axiom.

Seen in this perspective, Kasztner was merely following a pattern set in 1938, in the aftermath of the 'Kristallnacht', when thousands of Jewish children were allowed to leave Germany and, separated from their families, seek refuge in Britain and elsewhere. Triage took precedence over resisting persecution. The Nazi state was a militarised power that made ruthless and violent use of its political resources to attain its ideological ends. European Jewry was never a singular, let alone armed, entity. Nor were the other ethnic victims of the Nazi state. Resistance was not impossible, as we know from the Warsaw uprising and the rebellions in the Reinhardt camps, but resisters (and there were many) faced formidable obstacles. Nevertheless, the daily practice of triage by Jewish Councils and individuals such as Kasztner had calamitous moral consequences. If only a few could be saved, how was that to be achieved and who was to be selected and by whom? Lives could be saved but at the terrible cost of making unjustifiable decisions about which lives were worthier than others. After the war, Kasztner compared the train that the Germans permitted to leave Budapest on 30 June with some 1,700 Jewish 'notables' on board to 'Noah's Ark', which is, in essence, a myth about triage. The analogy was inadvertently cruel. In the Bible story, God punishes humankind and saves only Noah and his family as well as a selective representation of non-human species. The SS agents of genocide thus forced the victims of persecution to conform to the same barbarous ethics of 'selection' as they did.

For Kasztner to apply triage in the Hungarian situation, he needed to procure status with the SS. We have already seen how he cooperated with German plans when, in early May, he was taken to his home town Kolozsvár (now Cluj-Napoca in Romania). The evidence strongly suggests that, in the course of this visit, Kasztner, despite his knowledge of the Vrba-Wetzler Report about the role of the Auschwitz camp, reinforced the German lie that Jews would be deported to a work camp elsewhere in Hungary. In return, the SS allowed Kasztner to continue to make plans for the emigration of a few hundred Jews.

The story of the 'Kasztner Train' has been told and retold many times; it is celebrated and disputed, memorialised and deplored. There can be no doubt that Kasztner and Hansi Brand courageously seized on the German offer to permit the emigration of a few hundred Hungarian Jews to demand the release of a much larger number of people. Kasztner's Report provides a cumulative account of the torment of meetings with Eichmann and other SS officers to wring out further concessions in exchange for gold, diamonds and cash. A committee comprising Otto Komoly, Hansi Brand and others was formed to make a selection of passengers who would be allowed to leave Hungary. Like the leaders of the Jewish Councils in ghettos all over occupied Europe, Kasztner and his colleagues paid a terrible moral price for making these selections. According to Ladislaus Löb, who has passionately defended Kasztner's actions, the passenger list included Zionists from Kolozsvár and Budapest, some forty rabbis, scholars and artists, journalists, teachers and nurses. One of the passengers was the novelist Béla Zsolt, who later wrote a classic account of the Hungarian tragedy, *Nine Suitcases*. There were many members of Kasztner's family on board: his mother Helen Kasztner, his brother Ernő, his wife Bogyó, who gave birth to their daughter, Zsuzsi, in December, his father-in-law József Fischer, as well as other close relatives. They joined Joel Brand's mother, sister, and niece, Margit, as well as the daughters of Ottó Komoly and Samu Stern.

Kasztner's morally compromised negotiations with the Germans saved 1,700 lives. This is incontrovertible. Survivors of the train such as Ladislaus

Löb and many others have unswervingly defended Kasztner's actions and decisions. It is not appropriate, as I argued earlier in this chapter, to judge his actions as being criminal. Yet even though the term is not appropriate, the moral cost of these negotiations was immeasurable. It is not necessary to employ melodramatic theological metaphors that he 'sold his soul to Satan' – but Kasztner fell headlong into a web of relationships that drew him ever deeper into the world of the perpetrators. His descent began from the moment he persuaded the Rescue Committee to open discussions with Wisliceny. His growing entanglement with a circle of mendacious individuals, who exhibited different shades of ideological fanaticism and opportunism, meant he lost his own grip on appropriate ethical judgement. Kasztner found himself adrift in a world in which truth was turned into ashes.

Every negotiation he undertook with Eichmann and other SS officers tightened the trap. At the beginning of June, the mayor of Vienna, Karl Blaschke, and a consortium of Austrian industrialists sent a request to the head of the RSHA, Ernst Kaltenbrunner, to supply thousands of Jewish slave workers to work in factories and on fortifications. Kaltenbrunner agreed to divert several trainloads of Jews to the Vienna-Strasshof labour camp. In a detailed letter to Blaschke, Kaltenbrunner set out the conditions of his agreement. He would allocate: '4 shipments with approximately 12,000 Jews' to carry out 'these urgent work details of yours'. He warned that only 30 per cent of the transport would 'consist of Jews able to work'. In short, he was despatching a kind of job lot. The issue was what to do about the 'surplus'. He insisted:

It is obvious that only a well-guarded, enclosed place of work … can be utilised and this is an absolute prerequisite for making these Jews available. Women unable to work and children of these Jews who are all kept in readiness for 'Sonderaktion' and therefore one day will be removed again have to stay in the guarded camp also during the day …[7]

In other words, children and women not fit for work would be deported from Strasshof at a later date and murdered at another camp. Eichmann did as Kaltenbrunner ordered and some 20,000 were transferred from the ghettos of Baja, Debrecen, Szeged and Szolnok, to work in industry and agriculture in eastern Austria. Nearly all of the Jews sent to Strasshof, including old people and children, remained alive at the end of the war.

These are the facts. The order came from Kaltenbrunner – and Eichmann complied. When Kasztner wrote about what he called the 'Strasshof Deal' after the war, he disingenuously presented it as a rescue story. Many of his devotees and even some historians have followed the version told in his 'Report' and celebrated the 'rescue' of the Jews despatched to Strasshof. In the 'Report', Kasztner unfolds the story like this. On 13 June he met with Eichmann. He complained that the remorseless progress deportations had shattered the 'moral credit' of the Rescue Committee. What he meant by this was that the Committee's supporters abroad were unlikely to take any German offer to spare Jewish lives seriously. Suppose Brand secured an agreement with the Allies 'to pay for the lives of one hundred thousand Jews'? According to Kasztner, Eichmann lost his temper and insisted that it was impossible to 'feed hundreds of thousands of Hungarian Jews for months' or supply medicine to treat the sick. This was all the purest humbug, but Eichmann seems to have understood the implications of Kasztner's grievance.

We have to read between the lines here. What Kasztner was telling Eichmann was that the fact of the deportations devalued his own usefulness *to the Germans*. If he was to be of further service to the SS, Eichmann had to offer him a means to restore his authority: he needed results. And Eichmann knew that he could indeed perform this service for Kasztner. The following day, Wisliceny called Kasztner and gave him the astonishing news that 30,000 Jews would be diverted to Vienna and 'laid on ice' as a demonstration of goodwill. Eichmann's concession, as it appeared, was Kasztner's moral lifeline – and it came at a price. The SS demanded that the Rescue Committee pay 5 million Swiss Francs for the transfer and that they cover the living costs of the Jews during the time they would spend in the Strasshof camp. Since the deportation of Jews from Carpatho-Ruthenia and Northern Transylvania, referred to as Zone I, had already been completed, only Jews from 'Trianon Hungary' would be considered for inclusions in the transports. According to Braham, Eichmann referred to the Jews in Zone I as 'ethnically and biologically valuable elements' that could not be allowed to remain alive.

In 1954, at the libel trial in Israel, Kasztner spun the story again. He claimed that when he realised that Brand's mission would fail, he made an alternative offer to Eichmann: 'We offered to pay five million Swiss francs to the Germans for the departure of a group of 600 to Spain and for the transfer of 100,000 Jews to Austria instead of Auschwitz, *without undergoing selection.*' His words here clearly show that Kasztner must have known about the selection process that took place on the ramp at the Birkenau extermination camp. He went on to say that *Eichmann* finally agreed to send 30,000 Jews to Austria. This contradicts the documentary evidence of Kaltenbrunner's request for a certain number of Jews to be sent to Austria. What is equally troubling here is that Kasztner seems not to have considered what would happen to the thousands of Jews, including thousands of children, judged to be incapable of work. This perfidious plan went into action immediately. Kasztner informed the Jewish Council about his success and his representatives began making selections of Jews incarcerated in the gendarmerie districts that were already being deported to Auschwitz. As it transpired, some of the transports were sent to occupied Poland in error – and Eichmann 'compensated' Kasztner with a bonus transport from Zone IV. When the Jews arrived at Strasshof, those 'pieces' deemed fit to work were distributed to industrial and agricultural organisations controlled by the Todt Organisation in eastern Austria.

Kaltenbrunner had issued the order to transfer Jews to Strasshof – and Eichmann had, naturally, obeyed. This fitted the pattern of German strategy in Hungary – to exploit, plunder and liquidate individuals deemed incapable of work. The evidence strongly suggests that Eichmann exploited an opportunity to throw Kasztner a deceitful moral lifeline to bolster his value to the SS. Kasztner for his part used what he would call the 'Strasshof Deal' to claim that he had negotiated a spectacular rescue. Few of Kasztner's colleagues in Budapest seem to have been impressed by the Strasshof Deal, but his reports to international Jewish organisations in mid June grossly misrepresented what was happening in Hungary. He informed Nathan Schwalb on 14 June that he was dismayed by 'our friend Joel's' failure to return but went on:

> In spite of this fatal delay [referring to Brand] *I have been able to arrange* that the transports leaving in the next few days will be divided into two parts. A total of 20,000–30,000 Jews is expected to go to Austria instead of Poland … Hopefully these Jews can be rescued later in the framework of Joel's negotiations … [my italics].[8]

From an ethical point of view, it is not necessary to charge Kasztner with criminal intent. This was a *moral catastrophe* – one that followed inescapably from his commitment to negotiation with agents of the Nazi state who were intent on mass murder. The complexity of the SS plans to exploit and liquidate in a matter of weeks an entire community compelled Eichmann to adopt the most complex subterfuges. He was astute enough to recognize that Kasztner's fixation with his own power and prestige made him vulnerable to a spiral of entrapment. Kasztner's tragedy was that, adopting Nietzsche's philosophical terms, he was turned into a slave who believed he was a master.

Catastrophe in Budapest

Even after the Germans were forced to halt the deportation trains in early July, the Jews of Budapest were never safe.

Let us recap briefly. At the beginning of April, Eichmann and his Hungarian collaborators devised a plan to establish a large ghetto in Budapest. For a number of reasons, this plan would never be implemented. The area allocated was also home to large numbers of Christians, whom the Hungarian authorities had no wish to offend. They also feared that the Allies would target other areas of the city if they knew that the Jewish population was confined to a demarcated district. This was a completely irrational anxiety that overestimated both the humanitarian priorities of the Allies as well as the accuracy of their bomber fleets. In any event, Endre compromised by registering Jewish properties and concentrating Jews in so-called 'Yellow Star Houses'. On 16 June, the new city mayor, Ákos Doroghi Farkas, issued a decree that required the 'Yellow Star Houses' to be identified by a canary yellow Star of David attached to the entrance and paid for by the landlord. Soon Jews were being forced to relocate to the 'Yellow Star Houses' – and for the first time the Jews of Budapest experienced the bitter reality of persecution. Many took to sleeping fully clothed, with bags and knapsacks packed, ready to be dragged from their new homes.

Their fears were heightened when, following interventions by Christian Churches, the police began relocating Jews who had converted before 1 August 1941 to separate 'Yellow Star Houses' marked with a cross. This move was aggressively opposed by fanatics such as Zoltán Bosnyák, the editor of *Harc* (Battle), an antisemitic journal, who demanded that all Jews be removed from Budapest just as they had been in the deportations from the rest of Hungary. In the months that followed the halting of the deportations in July, a battery of terrifying events racked up the anxiety. Shock after Eichmann's assault on the Kistarcsa and Sárvár camps reverberated through the community.

In early August, hopes were raised again when Horthy appointed a new Prime Minister General, Géza Lakatos, the former commander of the First Hungarian Army. He transferred responsibility for Jewish Affairs to another ministerial counsellor in the Interior Ministry, Gyula Perlaky, who soon began freeing Jews held at camps near Budapest including Kistarcsa.

It was during this period that the Swedish envoy, Raoul Wallenberg, arrived in Budapest on a mission to assist the Jews of Hungary. As Paul Levine has shown in his definitive account of Wallenberg's work in Budapest, all rescue efforts were by then severely constrained by the unequal political struggle between the German occupiers and different factions of the Hungarian government. As it transpired, the plight of the Jews of Budapest deteriorated in lock step with the collapse of the Reich.

Despite flickers of hope for the future, the foul living conditions of tens of thousands of Jews who were locked up in the 'Yellow Star Houses' for long periods of time persuaded the leaders of the Jewish Council to cooperate with the Hungarian government to requisition thousands of Jews for rubble clearing in the city. The Council became to all intents and purposes an employment exchange for the Ministry of Defence. The Council's compliance was exploited by opportunist Hungarians including Lieutenant Colonel László Ferenczy, who had, as we have seen, played a leading role in the ghettoisation and deportation of Jews from the countryside during the spring and summer. To simultaneously appease the Germans, who continuously ratcheted up their demands for a solution to Budapest's 'Jewish problem', and ingratiate himself with the Jewish leaders, Ferenczy began advocating for the mass concentration of Jews in internment camps close to Budapest, which would, he claimed, be built to 'European standards'. The purpose was to mobilise thousands of Jews, aged between 14 and 70 irrespective of sex, for 'defence work'. Very few exemptions would be permitted. The plan was backed by Lakatos, who informed parliament that 'with regard to the regulation of the Jewish question, we are in the process of implementing a procedure that would ensure the gradual employment for useful work of the most harmful elements and the unemployed'.

The mobilisation plan did little to placate the increasingly impatient Germans. On 15 September, Veesenmayer sent a telegram to Ribbentrop

setting out a long list of complaints that showed that the Hungarian government was dragging its heels. Even as Ferenczy began recruiting 'flying
commissions' to round up and intern Jews, Veesenmayer urged Ribbentrop
to grant him new powers to 'carry out the evacuation of the remaining
Jews from Hungary or Budapest either through German forces themselves
or through pressure on the Hungarian government'.[9] At the same time,
Horthy renewed his efforts to extricate Hungary from the war. Since his
government was riddled with informants, the Regent's clumsy machinations were well known to the Germans.

By the beginning of October, there could no longer be any doubt
in Hitler's mind that Horthy and his allies in the Hungarian government were preparing to defect from the Axis. Although Horthy hated
Bolshevism, he sent a delegation to Moscow to begin negotiations
with the cruel and wily Soviet Minister of Foreign Affairs, Vyacheslav
Molotov. The Hungarians had been forced to accept that the Western
Allies were not planning to invade the Balkans – a strategy that Churchill
had once seriously considered – nor were they likely, as the Hungarians
had hoped, to send special airborne troops to invade Hungary. Roosevelt
and Churchill, the Hungarians suspected, had conceded the fate of
Eastern Europe to Stalin and Horthy had no choice but to bend the
knee in Moscow. Molotov insisted on very tough conditions – that
Hungary immediately declare war on Germany. Under enormous pressure, the Hungarians gave in to his terms on 11 October. In Budapest,
Horthy began planning a coup against the German forces in Hungary.
Molotov again pressed him to act quickly and grew increasingly impatient. Horthy made a decision to act, come what may, on 15 October. He
hoped that he would take the Germans by surprise.

Despite his deteriorating health and a barrage of dangerous medica-
tions, Hitler had already taken steps to thwart the Hungarians. With
Veesenmayer's connivance, he hatched a plan to oust the Regent and
replace him with Ferencz Szálasi, the fanatical leader of the Arrow Cross,
which was also known as the Nyilas. Hitler had hitherto disdained the
thuggish Arrow Cross (just as he did the Romanian Iron Guard) – now he
had a use for the movement. In mid September, the derring-do SS officer
Otto Skorzeny, who had rescued Mussolini, was summoned to the Wolf's
Fort. Hitler ordered him to prepare plans with General Hans Friesner,
the commander of German forces in Budapest, and the HSSPF Otto
Winkelmann to seize the Citadel if, or rather when, the Hungarians made

a move to betray the Reich. Himmler despatched the brutal SS General, Erich von dem Bach-Zelewski, who had, just weeks earlier, smashed the Warsaw Uprising, to take command of all local police and SS units in Budapest. These battle-hardened bullies and mass murderers would not have long to wait.

Under growing pressure from Moscow to act, Horthy requested a meeting with Veesenmayer at the Citadel at noon on Sunday, 15 October. There could be no doubt that the Hungarians were about to make a decisive move against the Reich. Horthy was gambling on surprise, but he had already lost that fragile advantage. With lightning speed, Skorzeny took action. As the Regent met with the Crown Council at 10 a.m., a team of hand-picked SS men fought their way into the Citadel and seized Horthy's son, Miklós – who had been closely involved with his father's efforts to extricate Hungary from Hitler's grasp. The young man was rolled inside a carpet, driven to the airport and flown to Vienna. He was then incarcerated inside the Mauthausen camp. When Veesenmayer arrived for his meeting with Horthy at midday, accompanied by Hitler's envoy Rudolf Rahn, he brusquely informed the Regent that Miklós was in German hands and would be shot if his father committed 'treason' against the Reich. Horthy, shattered, angry, helpless, fell into a state of nervous collapse – but, distraught as he was, refused to back down. Shortly before 1 a.m., he was driven to a studio at the State Radio. In his proclamation to the nation, Horthy lashed out at Germany for dragging Hungary into the war. 'The Gestapo,' he protested, 'took the handling of the Jewish question into its hands'. Horthy called on all Hungarian soldiers to remain loyal – but he had made a fatal strategic error. There was no one to guard his back. Divisional commanders most devoted to the Regent had been stationed outside the capital. Many of the Jewish Labour Servicemen in the city would have fought for Horthy, but none were armed. The Hungarian resistance was feeble and cowed. Horthy had no pieces left to play. Soon after Horthy's broadcast, the Hungarian General Staff issued new instructions to troops that they should ignore the Regent's proclamation.

In the aftermath of Horthy's broadcast, many Jews tore off their Yellow Stars and rushed into the streets to rejoice. Likewise, many Labour Servicemen downed their picks and shovels. The years of persecution were over! By late afternoon, these fragile moments of euphoria had been brutally quashed. Now antisemitic terror would overwhelm the Jews of Budapest.

Moments after the broadcast, Szálasi ordered armed Arrow Cross militia men to surround the radio station. Later that afternoon, he made a counter radio proclamation that he was taking power and pledged to support Germany's struggle against Bolshevism. On the evening of that bewildering day, it was Veesenmayer who delivered the final blow. He promised Horthy that, once he had formally recognised the new government, Miklós would be released, unharmed, from Mauthausen. The kidnapping had been Skorzeny's master stroke: he had struck at the heart of the Regent's family and now Horthy, to secure his son's life, bowed low to his German masters. As Skorzeny led a spluttering line of 'Panther' and 'Goliath' tanks into the Citadel, Horthy and his family boarded a train bound for the Austrian border. He would spend the rest of the war interned in the Schloss Hirschberg in Bavaria.

On 21 October, an ebullient Hitler welcomed Skorzeny to the Wolf's Fort. He promoted him to Obersturmbannführer – and gleefully began telling him about a secret new plan to turn back the Allied advance in Western Europe. Germany, he proclaimed, would soon launch 'a great offensive' – and Skorzeny, the hero of Budapest, would 'have a great part to play'.[10]

The fate of the Jews of Budapest rested in the hands of Ferencz Szálasi and his Arrow Cross fanatics. From 16 October until 28 March 1945, Szálasi served as Prime Minister of Hungary and its plenipotentiary head of state as 'Leader of the Nation' (Nemzetvezető).

For the Jews of Budapest, the time of their final torment had come.

The Terror

According to Hungarian historian Krisztián Ungváry: 'the battle for Budapest was one of the longest and bloodiest city battles of the Second World War'.[11] The siege began in November 1944; by Christmas Day, Budapest was completely encircled. In February 1945, the titanic struggle ended only when the last Hungarian and German troops were slaughtered in a failed attempt to break out of the city. The battle was intimately lethal. Forty thousand civilians died as soldiers fought at close quarters in streets and houses, in kitchens, bedrooms and bathrooms. Historian Isztvan Deak has written:

> No one but those who were there can recall the naked bodies floating down the Danube while elegant waiters at the Hotel Ritz on the river

shore served plain rice and ersatz coffee to similarly elegant guests. Or the crazed Arrow Cross hoodlums beating old Jewish women in the rain and snow on the forced march from Budapest towards Austria. Or the deaf-mute squad of militiamen who ordered all passing men into a courtyard, there to drop their pants and submit to a quick 'racial test' …

During the last chaotic months of Hitler's Reich, a whirlwind of violence fell on the civilian population of Budapest. Stubborn German insistence on purging the last surviving Hungarian Jews inflamed the fanatical rage of Arrow Cross militias in a frenzied orgy of killing. When the Arrow Cross Foreign Minister, Gábor Kemény, dared question whether Hungary was 'rich enough to lose four million working hours a day', callously referring to the killings of Jews who might be fit for work, he was shouted down by his fellow ministers. From Berlin, Ribbentrop kept up the pressure. On 21 November, he sent a telegram to Veesenmayer urging him to ensure that Szálasi understood that the defence of the Hungarian capital depended on the final purging of all Jews from the city. This was in no sense a new development in German military strategy. From the beginning of the war in 1939, Wehrmacht commanders had feared the presence of Jewish civilians in front-line areas as a threat to security. This is why Eichmann had insisted to his Hungarian collaborators that deportations begin in the regions of Hungary that lay in the path of the advancing Soviet armies. Now Budapest was on the front line.

The day after Skorzeny's troops had marched into the Citadel, General Ivan Tscherniakowski led the 3rd White Russian Front as it burst across the border of East Prussia and began pushing towards the city of Königsberg. Huge numbers of panic-stricken German refugees fled to the west. Although the Wehrmacht clawed back some territory, the first breaching of the old German border was calamitous. In towns such as Gumbinnen, Russian soldiers showed little restraint, plundering, raping and murdering in terrible acts of revenge. On the cold, dark afternoon of 20 November, Hitler and his staff left the Wolf's Fort and boarded his special train, bound for Berlin, for the last time. He would never return to the Fort. In Berlin, Hitler began planning the new offensive in the Ardennes, code-named Autumn Mist. In his diary, Goebbels noted that Hitler was 'back to his old form' – like a man revived. On 10 December, Hitler moved to a new headquarters on the Western Front. It was called, with perverse grandiosity, the Eagle's Eyrie. It was an extraordinary performance. Invoking the triumph of Prussia against the odds in the Seven Years' War, Hitler insisted that German forces must go on the offensive to 'make plain to the enemy that whatever he does he can never reckon with capitulation, never, never. That is the decisive point.' Striking a 'really heavy blow' at the Alliance might be enough to fracture 'this artificially sustained common front'.[12] The immiserating of Europe would not be diminished, and new paroxysms of violence would erupt.

By the time Szálasi and the Nyilas seized power, between 150,000 and 160,000 Jews remained alive in Budapest. A near equal number had survived the Labour Service. Many others were in hiding with Christian families. Among them were Joel and Hansi Brand's two sons. Now the last surviving Jews of Hungary fell prey to the Nyilas terror. On the night that Szálasi ousted Horthy and seized power, gangs of boisterous young Arrow Cross fanatics rampaged through the Jewish areas of Budapest armed with rifles, knives and grenades. They had no difficulty, of course, identifying the Yellow Cross Houses and began dragging terrified, screaming Jews into the street. Hundreds were driven to the banks of the Danube, to be shot and hurled into the river. These Nyilas gangs often targeted Labour Servicemen who were known to have resisted the Arrow Cross coup. Many of these units were stationed outside Budapest and the Nyilas gangs extended their murderous campaign to the countryside, where terrible slaughters soon took place.

Nyilas terror and the Germans' insistence that Jews be purged from the besieged city became inextricably entangled. On 17 October, the Germans ordered Jews in District VIII to assemble in courtyards. Arrow Cross thugs forced their way into Yellow Star Houses and dragged Jews into the street. They beat up or killed anyone who failed to move fast enough. In Teleki Square, an old man was dragged by his feet from the fifth floor. His skull was fractured, and he was left to die in the street. Arrow Cross killers began executing Jews on the Danube Embankment, shoving bodies into the freezing waters of the river. Some were recovered downstream. A police report made on 25 November notes that: 'Labour service man András Pitschoff was recovered by police officers (numbers 2017 and 2048) from the Danube with a gunshot wound. Jews were shot at Széchenyi Quay … and several got stuck in the canal'[13]

The Arrow Cross gangs targeted other enemies of the state as well as Jews. An officer in the Hungarian Army described seeing a line of victims lined up along the track of the Number 2 tram:

> Those close to the Danube were already naked, the others were slowly walking down [towards the embankment] and undressing. It all happened in total silence … In the afternoon, when there was nobody about, we took another look. The dead were lying in their blood on the ice slabs or floating in the Danube. Among them were women, children, Jews, gentiles, soldiers and officers …

When they dragged their victims to the Danube, the enraged Arrow Cross men often shot wildly. Some of their captives escaped by leaping into the freezing and ice-flecked waters of the river. Many drowned or froze to death. Early one morning a police officer reported stopping '5 Jewish looking men, running and soaked to the skin, who were so confused that they were unable to say who they were or how they had fallen into the Danube'. What happened to these five men is unknown. Hungarian police and civilians often watched the Arrow Cross thugs in action, apparently unmoved. Reports made at the time expose widespread indifference:

> The officer told us that the Jews had been stripped to their shirts, shot at the Danube Embankment and thrown into the water. 'The trouble is not that this is done,' he said, 'but that some were left alive, because so long as they aren't completely exterminated, they'll all turn into vindictive swine.'

Fear of revenge is a *leitmotif* winding through these eyewitness accounts:

> Two deaconesses are having a conversation. One says: 'It's certain that the Arrow Cross are preparing something dreadful against the Jews.' The other: 'I'm sorry for the poor people, but maybe it's just as well, because then they won't get a chance to take revenge.'

More prosaically, but no less callously, a farmer was reported worrying: 'I've got two acres of Jewish land. Do you think I'll be allowed to keep it?'

Terror like this could not be hidden away and reports of the Nyilas terror soon led to international protest. Unnerved, Szálasi and his new Interior Minister, Gábor Vajna, issued a warning to the gang leaders on the streets that they could not act as 'self-appointed judges of the Jews'. It was a matter of proper procedure and control. This is a recurrent theme in genocides; there are always leadership cadres who want to tidy up the slaughtering. A minister in the Szálasi government urged that 'something must also be done to stop the death rattle going on in the ditches all day, and the population must not be allowed to see the masses dying … the deaths should not be recorded in the Hungarian death register.'

A police commissioner echoed these words: 'The problem is not that the Jews are being murdered, the only trouble is the method. The bodies must be made to disappear, not put out in the streets.' This may explain why the killers despatched so many victims on the Danube Embankment. Its freezing waters would flush away the inconvenient dead:

> In one of the streets leading to the Danube … I saw men and women in shirts, underpants and petticoats, with the snow and broken glass crunching under their bare feet. Appalled, I stopped in my tracks … and asked one of the Arrow Cross men who they were. I shall never forget his cynical reply: 'The holy family.' I stood petrified for a long time, until the sound of submachine gun salvos from the Danube Embankment made me realise that it had been these people's last journey.

Another witness reported seeing a teenage Arrow Cross thug beating an old woman with a rifle butt. 'Haven't you got a mother, son?' 'She's only a Jew, uncle …'

For the young men who joined the Arrow Cross, murder was a rite of passage, a test of loyalty to the cause. In 1966, the Hungarian government began investigating former activists. One of those investigated was a former officer in the post-war Hungarian Air Force. In 1944, he was 15 – and had joined the Arrow Cross. He told the tribunal that he and his companions had willingly taken part in savage torture and executions. He confessed that on Christmas Day, his unit had murdered more than fifty people. Altogether, he suspected that they had killed some 1,200 individuals – on the Embankment, in Városliget Park, where bodies were piled up for days, or in the backs of lorries that drove around the Jewish areas. By late December, an acutely observant eyewitness observed:

> In narrow Kazinczy Street enfeebled men, dropping their heads, were pushing a wheelbarrow. On the rattling contraption naked human bodies as yellow as wax were jolted along … They stopped in front of the Kazinczy Baths and awkwardly turned into the lattice gate … bodies were piled up, frozen stiff like pieces of wood. I crossed Klauzál Street.

> In the middle people were squatting or kneeling round a dead horse and
> hacking the meat of it with knives …

On some occasions, German soldiers disobeyed orders and joined in the
slaughter. Among Jews, there was an epidemic of suicides; some mothers knocked their daughters unconscious with rolling pins and held them
under open gas taps.

Some cohorts of Arrow Cross killers became especially notorious.
One of the most vicious killers was a rogue Catholic monk called 'Father'
András Kun. He had joined the Arrow Cross that year but had swiftly risen
in the party hierarchy. He possessed charisma and was fond of tirades. He
was addicted to violence. The top Arrow Cross leaders and party intellectuals were rarely involved directly in atrocities. Instead, they exploited
charismatics such as Father Kun. One of the leading party ideologues was
an internationally renowned botanist, Professor Vilmos Kőfaragó-Gyelik.
He employed Kun at the party headquarters at Pasaréti Road 10 and
involved him in propaganda work. In the Hungarian Film Archives, there
is a remarkable pseudo-documentary that shows Kun, clad in immaculate priestly regalia, directing militia operations in Budapest. We see this
strikingly handsome killer meeting with other Arrow Cross men and
exchanging vigorous 'Hitler Salutes' before driving off to wreak havoc.[14]
In January, Kun led a gang into the Jewish Hospital on Maros Street,
where they murdered more than 170 patients. A few days later, Kun and
his gang broke into the Jewish Almshouse on Alma Street and killed at
least ninety elderly Jews – then the following day, he and his followers
rampaged through the Jewish Hospital on Városmajor Street and hacked
149 patients and staff to death. Kun was an obsessive antisemite. In the
Hungarian National Archives, there is a transcript of a speech he made to
his followers, which reveals the depth of his hatred. Radical nationalism
had bred the most pernicious bigotry:

> Brothers! The Jews and the other plutocrats who swished their bundle of
> money and pale gold and subjugate the workpeople while they exploit
> them and aim for their fate. When workpeople will understand who the
> real enemies are and would want to throw off the yoke and harness, and
> will break into their thick carpet covered rooms, they will cry out revo-
> lution and flee abroad, and from there they make war with their money
> and produce weapons. Brothers, this is how this present war broke out,

in which the Hungarian motherland is bleeding, and our brothers, our children, and our fathers are bleeding. That is why now, when the traitorous Horthy-clique laid down arms to surrender to the enemy, they have lost the nation, because the enemy will subjugate us, and woe to those who will come under the enemy's trampling boots. Brothers, I summon you up, let's join forces, let's protect the homeland until our last drop of blood, and learn who our true enemies are, fight them, break them without compromising. Do not be weak brothers, take up arms, because the Arrow Cross will bring us victory.[15]

The Arrow Cross leaders and their German masters had no intention of relenting in their persecution of the last Jews of Hungary. Vajna promised that all Jews would be treated without mercy. The German Waffen-SS Commander, Karl Pfeffer-Wildenbruch, ordered his men not to take part in attacks on Jews – but it suited the Germans that the Arrow Cross were doing the dirty work on the streets. Ribbentrop instructed Veesenmayer to assist the Arrow Cross government 'in every way' because 'it is in our interest that the Hungarians should now proceed against the Jews in the harshest possible manner'.

The task of recording the terrible experiences of Hungarian Jews began soon after the end of the war. This went hand in hand with the trial and punishment of leading perpetrators. As a consequence of this frenzy of record making, we have many accounts of the atrocities that took place in Budapest during that dreadful winter. Here is one:

On Sunday the 14th of January … The Arrow Cross appeared in the Dániel Bíró [Jewish] hospital at 11 o'clock in the forenoon. Their leader was a red-haired marauder with a wicked face, and two German soldiers were with them too. I ran to the window, I looked out and staggered back in horror. One of us fainted from the terrible sight. Four–five nurses in white veil were standing in a row, facing the coal chamber in the yard of the hospital. Behind them some Arrow Cross in uniforms, one of whom shot, and the nurses screamingly collapsed … The Arrow Cross previously sorted out those, who had Christian papers and sent them to the basement. Then they gave the order that anyone who can walk should get out of bed and get dressed. These people were sent in smaller groups down to the hospital's courtyard, where they were ordered an about-face and they were shot with submachine guns in the back of their head and their back ... When the ambulant patients and the Jewish employees have all been lying in the courtyard, the Arrow Cross comrades continued to work in the wards. They were walking from room to room and were done away with everybody. Old people, seriously ill people, and small children were equally shot dead. The dead bodies of two little boys were found later on their mother, embracing her ... On the next day Arrow Cross guards stood in front of the house and would not let anyone in. On Tuesday morning, the dead bodies, lying in the courtyard and covered with a red carpet, were spilled with petroleum and then they were set on fire along with the building. The building was burning for two days and the corpses partially burned completely down, some were only charred. The dead bodies were later transported by the Russian authorities, but some limbs and human bones are still visible in the ashes. There is for example a woman's shoe with a charred leg in it. Here and there some bones. This is all what left behind from the residents of Dániel Bíró hospital ... [At the Old People's Home] the green-shirted comrades appeared between 7 and 8 o'clock in the evening. They declared that the patients should be transported off. They separated the men and women. They lead down the women into the Városmajor [park], and they made them stand in triple rows on the Szamos street side. They took down those who could not walk in sedan chair and put them down in lines onto the ground. Then the submachine guns rang out ... On the Maros street ... the Arrow Cross chased 170 undressed Jewish men and women to the street, way back in the first days of January. They shot all of them down as well.[16]

There is an important caveat to make here. The Arrow Cross has been called the 'Alibi of a Nation'. In Budapest today, the 'House of Terror' museum explicitly impugns the Arrow Cross and the Soviets together for the catastrophe that overwhelmed Hungary in the last years of the Second World War. Instead of confronting the willing involvement of Hungarians at every level of society in the German onslaught on Hungarian Jews, the new regime and then generations of Hungarian historians loaded the blame for the horrors of the winter of 1944–45 on Szálasi and his government. The truth is that the Arrow Cross militias were responsible for fewer than 10 per cent of the victims of the Hungarian Holocaust. The murders were brutal, ruthless and chaotic: acts of barbarism. But the majority of Hungarian Jews were deported by Eichmann's men and their Hungarian collaborators – and murdered in the orderly world of the Auschwitz-Birkenau camp

In the decades that followed, historians argued that Arrow Cross perpetrators were mainly uneducated working-class men, common criminals and teenagers who fell prey to propaganda. In other words, lesser kinds of Hungarian. More systematic studies carried out by the European Holocaust Research Infrastructure (EHRI) reveals a different picture. This research has shown that the core Arrow Cross 'foot soldiers' were family men in their thirties and forties who often coerced other family members to join the militias. None had a criminal record. They usually lived close to the 'Yellow Star Houses' and other Jewish institutions that became their targets. The records show that the Arrow Cross killers were workers, craftsmen and blue-collar employees – including for example, a hairdresser, a shoemaker, a baker, a painter, a janitor, a mechanic and an electrician. More than a third belonged to the lower middle class – and had jobs as clerks and state employees. More than 40 per cent had had a secondary education. When they were questioned about their motivations, many claimed that the anti-Jewish campaign was legal: a means to recover the jobs, positions and wealth that was rightfully theirs. In the bedlam of the siege, social frustration and greed had exploded in an orgy of torture, rape and murder. The Arrow Cross killers were average, law-abiding citizens who followed their basest instincts in extreme conditions.

It was in this time of terror and violence that a familiar SS officer returned, eagerly, to Budapest.

Well, As You Can See, I Am Back Again ...

Adolf Eichmann returned to Budapest on 18 October. The SD and Gestapo cohort took up residence in the Royal Hotel on the Great Boulevard – and the former SS haunts on Svábhegy Hill, like the Majestic Hotel. Eichmann smelled blood and was eager to get back to work.

Under the diktat of 'Total War', there was insatiable need for slave workers in the massive underground aircraft and armaments factories that fed the German war effort – and Eichmann had, once more, been ordered to satisfy demand. On 18 October, he met Szálasi and requested that the new government supply 50,000 Jews for labour in the Reich. The Arrow Cross leader, for reasons of his own, was reluctant to permit the deployment of

Hungarian Jews in the factories of the Reich. But Eichmann brooked no argument. Providence had granted him an opportunity to complete his task: as Veesenmayer made clear to Ribbentrop, Eichmann planned to persist with repeated demands for Jewish labour until there were no Jews left in Hungary. As before, German demands came with a patina of sugar coating: a few thousand Jews, who had acquired valid foreign provisional passports, safe-conduct passes, or other protective certificates issued by the Vatican and neutral states, would be offered protection or permitted to emigrate. The bulk of surviving Jews would be deported to the factories of the Reich. It did not take for Eichmann long to secure agreement with the new government. Szálasi was not without guile. He would rid Hungary of Jews, while at the same time mollifying the Churches and neutrals.

By then, Allied bombing raids and the shrinking of the front line had severely damaged German transportation links. So, Eichmann proposed despatching the tens of thousands of Jewish slave workers to Germany – on foot. His alcohol-fuelled resolve to fulfil his new orders and complete unfinished business would have ghastly and tragic consequences. A few days later, Eichmann summoned Kasztner to his office. In his Report, Kasztner describes the chilling experience. 'Well, as you can see, I'm back again …' Eichmann gloated. Kasztner was appalled by the new plan to force march Jews to the Reich, but his old foe 'seemed to be the happiest man on earth. He was in his element again. Besides, as usual in that period, he was drunk.'[17]

The drive against the Jews began a few days later. Early on the morning of 20 October, Nyilas militias and police units entered the Yellow Star Houses and ordered Jewish men aged between 16 and 60 to assemble in the block courtyards. They had an hour to make preparations to depart. Soon afterwards, the Nyilas squads marched the Jews to the race-track at Kerepes or the KISOK sports field. And so it went on. By 26 October, more than 35,000 Jews, including 10,000 women, had been organised into companies and forced to repair trenches and dig fortifications for long hours with little or no food. At the end of the month, the Hungarians began rounding up more Jews and transferring the labour battalions to the Óbuda brickyards and other assembly points – and from there to the Hegyeshalom checkpoint on the road to Vienna. The long, hot summer had given way to a bitterly cold and wet autumn. The Nyilas squads mercilessly harried the exhausted marchers, shooting any stragglers. At the checkpoint, the Hungarians transferred the starving and exhausted Jews into the hands of a German commission commanded by Dieter Wisliceny. The Jews who arrived at the checkpoint had been profoundly dehumanised.

At the Eichmann trial, one of the prosecution witnesses, Arye Zvi Breszlauer, who was a Swiss Embassy official in 1944, managed to enter the camp at Hegyeshalom. In the filmed record of his testimony, the excruciating pain of remembrance is etched on his face:

> There was a barn. These people were locked in there by the thousands. I saw the faces of these people who had made their way for over two hundred kilometres without food. The fear of death was in their faces. They were in a horrible state, without any hygienic conditions. They had to relieve themselves inside the barn. There were women and men there. I could only hear shouts of 'Help!'. They thought that people had come from the embassy to save them all, and they began shouting. I saw they were in an awful state … I am not capable of describing the situation in which I saw these people. There were thousands. The next day they were handed to the Germans across the border …[18]

Later, when Hungarian gendarmes discovered that that Breszlauer was observing the horrors at Hegyeshalom, they threatened him with bayonets – and he was forced to flee. He noticed many German SS and SD men at the checkpoint who appeared to be busy organising matters with the Hungarian police.

Saving Skins

Since the period of deportations to Auschwitz, Kasztner and Kurt Becher had grown ever closer. The polite attention of the suave SS Lieutenant Colonel flattered Kasztner and bolstered his conviction that he was doing something important. For Becher, the relationship with this ambitious Jew was all about reputational investment. The SS Cavalry man who had ridden into the Pripyat Swamp in 1941 to liquidate the Jews of Belarus had no doubt that the downfall of the Reich would unleash a torrent of retribution by the Allies. In place of rescue or respite, threats of retribution had come to define Allied responses to reports of Nazi persecution. Power-hungry perpetrators such as Himmler and even Eichmann would reap the

392 DECEPTION: HOW THE NAZIS DECEIVED THE LAST JEWS OF EUROPE

harvest of ambition and notoriety. The Allies had published incriminating lists of top war criminals. Despite his glittering career as Himmler's protégé, Becher was not yet on any such list. In the summer of 1944, he had a narrow window of opportunity to clean up and polish his reputation and, he fervently hoped, escape punishment. The instrument of his salvation would be his good friend Rezső Kasztner.

It is crucial to understand that at no point did Becher act against orders from Himmler or indeed the fanatical ethos of the SS. He was clever enough to pursue SS objectives while exploiting his bond with Kasztner to prepare the way for rehabilitation. He had been deeply involved with Eichmann in the negotiations that led to the release of Jews on the 'Kasztner Train'. While Eichmann had demanded $500 per head, Becher had greedily insisted on $2,000. Himmler had been forced to step in to resolve the argument. The price was set at $1,000. The Rescue Committee was compelled to hand over $1,684,000 in money and valuables. The train was another opportunity for avaricious plunder. From Eichmann's point of view, the grudging release of this tiny fraction of the Hungarian Jewish population, for a price, had a profoundly cynical intent. The prominent Jews who clambered aboard the train in Budapest were *hostages*. The Jewish VIPs unknowingly acted as guarantors that Kasztner and other Jewish leaders would do nothing to disrupt the destruction of Hungarian Jewry. As the Rescue Committee negotiated with the Germans, the deportations and mass killings at Auschwitz were reaching a fiery climax.

That the release of the 'Kasztner Train' was an exercise in hostage taking is proven beyond any serious doubt by Eichmann's manipulative tactics following the departure of the train. These were evidently designed to ratchet up the pressure on Kasztner and the Jewish Council. To begin with, he sent orders for the train to be stopped at Auspitz in the Sudetenland. The unexplained stop provoked panic among the passengers, who concluded that the train would be diverted to Auschwitz. When he got wind of what had happened, Kasztner protested to Eichmann, who ordered the train to proceed to Linz, in Austria. But he was not finished playing games. At Linz, German guards boarded the train and ordered passengers to take showers. There was more consternation. Were they about to be gassed? Finally, Eichmann despatched the VIP train to Bergen-Belsen. Here the Hungarians were dumped in Himmler's 'Residence Camp'. They would be held there for months. Bogdanor discovered a revealing exchange between Kasztner and Becher – that was inexplicably removed from the

English translation of the 'Kasztner Report'. Kasztner says to Becher: 'I've wondered many times whether, instead of the negotiations, it wouldn't have been better to call on the Zionist youth and rally the people to active resistance to entering the brickyards and the wagons.'

Becher replies: You wouldn't have achieved anything this way.'

Kasztner replies: 'Maybe, but at least we would have kept our honour. Our people went into the wagons like cattle because we trusted in the success of the negotiations and failed to tell them the terrible fate awaiting them.'

Kasztner's activities in the aftermath of the departure of the 'Hostage Train' have caused led to a great deal of confusion. When the Allies released details of the Blood for Trucks proposal in mid July, crushing the last deluded hopes of the Zionists, Kasztner renewed his efforts to seek help from Saly Mayer of the JDC, the 'Joint' that had its headquarters in Switzerland. Naturally, he turned to Becher to represent the German side in any negotiations. It took many weeks for Kasztner to get a result. Kasztner urged Becher to seek the release of some of the 'Prominents' who remained incarcerated in the 'Hungarian Camp' at Bergen-Belsen. When Himmler agreed to permit a few hundred 'Prominents' to travel to Switzerland – in other words, expending a portion of their value as hostages – Mayer agreed, reluctantly, to a meeting with the SS emissaries.

On 21 August, Kasztner and Becher arrived at the St Margrethen Bridge on the Austrian border with Switzerland border to meet Mayer. The 'Joint' had not been able to obtain Swiss visas for Becher and his party – and he felt humiliated by the ignominy of being forced to meet halfway across a bridge. In any event, Becher repeated the essence of the Blood for Trucks proposal: goods for lives. When Daniel Brand showed me Becher's correspondence with Himmler on the matter of the negotiations, he argued that the revival of the terms of the original proposal was evidence that the Germans had been serious about offering to exchange lives for goods. The problem with this argument is that Eichmann's strategy in May was very different from Becher's ploy at the end of August. By then Eichmann had been sidelined and the deportations halted, at least temporarily. Circumstances had changed fundamentally – and would again. Becher had won tremendous prestige for himself with his ruthless takeover of the Manfréd-Weiss industrial conglomerate in exchange for the lives of a handful of wealthy Hungarian Jews. When Becher discussed the Blood for Trucks offer with Himmler, the record of their conversation shows that any negotiations with Jews would never be carried out by these men in good faith. 'See what you can get,' as Himmler put it. Becher was motivated by greed. He had extracted more than a million dollars from the Rescue Committee to permit the release of the 'Hostage Train'. Now, as he walked across the St Margrethen Bridge to meet Mayer, he was still intent on plunder. He made this very clear when Mayer made an appeal to spare the lives of the Hungarian Jews for humanitarian reasons: 'I cannot negotiate on this basis,' Becher replied.

A few historians have been misled by the timing of Becher's negotiations with Mayer. Four days after the meeting on the St Margrethen Bridge, Himmler ordered Winkelmann to cancel the plan devised by Eichmann and Endre to deport the Jews of Budapest. In his book *Jews for Sale*, Yehuda Bauer suggests that the negotiations with Mayer influenced Himmler's decision. He refers to a statement made by Becher after the war claiming that following the meeting with Mayer, he rushed to Berlin and convinced Himmler to stop deporting Jews. Becher was lying: after the meeting, he and Kasztner returned immediately to Budapest. Bauer's efforts to justify these negotiations as a rescue strategy do not bear scrutiny. As described earlier, Himmler was scrambling to deal with Romania's defection from the Axis on 23 August. Renewing the deportations risked provoking the Hungarian government. To be sure, Becher did get in touch with Himmler: he sent a cable to Himmler's office in Berlin requesting permission to 'continue [talking to Mayer] in the spirit described'.[19]

The talks with Mayer went nowhere, slowly.

The corruption of Kasztner reached its lowest depths at the end of December. At the beginning of the month, Kasztner was still in Geneva. Arrow Cross gangs rampaged through Budapest – but instead of returning there, Kasztner chose to travel to Vienna. Here he stayed at the Grand Hotel as a guest of the SS. He was warned not to reveal he was a Jew – but in every other respect was treated very well. He spent time with old friends such as Wisliceny, Krumey and of course Becher. In the spring of 1945, Himmler arrived in Vienna. Years later, at his trial in Jerusalem, Kasztner described the occasion in the most troubling way:

> Himmler came to Vienna to take military measures for the defence of the city. They took me to the building … where the meeting had convened, with Himmler presiding. I stood there in the corridor with Krumey and Becher. When Himmler came out, Becher approached him and pointed to me …[20]

The Last of Himmler

There is no convincing evidence that in the spring of 1944 Himmler seriously considered the Blood for Trucks ransom offer as a means to secure military supplies or to open the door to secret negotiations with the Allies. Historians have confused his *knowledge* of the negotiations with his intent. Himmler would have completely understood the necessity of deceiving and confusing the leading figures in the Hungarian Jewish community. If this meant releasing a few hundred Jews in return for material or strategic gain, then it was a bargain worth making. We should never forget that the Final Solution was a monstrous act of plunder. Jews were commodities, or 'pieces' in Nazi terminology, to be exploited, exchanged and finally sacrificed if they were bereft of value. After the summer of 1945, Himmler began to regard surviving Jews as bargaining chips in a new game. With spectacular naivety, he hoped to exploit surviving Jews as human capital in a quest for power.

For this reason, Himmler needed to hoard this human capital. As the Soviet armies pushed the Wehrmacht back towards the borders of the Reich in the autumn of 1944, Himmler's strategy faced a severe crisis. He could not afford to leave the many thousands of Jews and other prisoners who remained alive in the camps in occupied Poland to the rapidly advancing Russians. They not only knew too much about the Final Solution but were expensive human capital. In the late summer, Himmler ordered the SS commanders to begin clearing and evacuating the camps. Prisoners would be marched westwards towards the camps inside the old German borders. This final act in the German genocide would lead to a new wave of suffering and death. Many of the prisoners would be forced to march on foot – and no mercy was shown to those too ill or weak. As winter descended across Europe, the movement of tens of thousands of prisoners turned into death marches. Many of the prisoners were shot en route if they failed to keep up. Some were murdered as they passed through German towns and villages. Later, Himmler would present himself as a humanitarian when he met with representatives of the Allies and neutral powers, who held in his gift the lives of thousands. The truth is that he and his henchmen showed no regard at all for the lives of the camp prisoners. They needed only a fraction to survive.

In the late summer, Hitler began favouring Himmler with new military commands. He was grateful to the Reichsführer for his prompt and decisive crushing of the attempted coup in July. He was in no doubt that Himmler remained his 'true Heinrich'. The more military power Hitler conferred on Himmler, the most disastrous was his performance. According to his young Chief of Staff, Colonel Hans-Georg Eismann, Himmler's feeble attempt to pass himself off as a military strategist resembled 'a blind man discoursing on colour'. Eismann's memoirs reveal not just Himmler's utter incompetence but also his abject and unabated terror of Hitler: 'The dreaded Reichsführer was completely at the mercy of his own fear of Hitler ... This fundamentally subaltern attitude did much damage and cost a great deal of unnecessary bloodshed.'[21]

This was not a man who would go behind Hitler's back and make an offer to release the Jews of Hungary.

By the time the German offensive in the Ardennes had collapsed, Hitler began to lose all hope. The grotesque paradox of the endgame was that Hitler's charismatic authority remained unassailable until the very end. Few doubted his right to absolute authority. Arguably, Hitler's hubristic ambition to conquer a new empire in the East had been weakened in the winter of 1941 – and fatally damaged a year later at Stalingrad. The Wehrmacht lost the initiative for good. By the end of 1944, Hitler had shed all illusions but had not released his grasp on power. Since the war could only end with his own destruction and since he was the embodiment of the Reich, Germany too would have to be consumed by the inferno of defeat. Consumed by an obsession with treachery and betrayal, he lashed out at his generals and the German people. They lacked his ruthless faith in the force of the will and thus deserved annihilation in the flames of downfall. The *Volk* had proved unworthy of its leader. Captain Nicolaus von Below recalled an encounter with an angry and depressed Hitler: 'I know the war is lost,' he lamented. 'The superior power is too great. I've been betrayed ... We'll not capitulate. Never. We can go down. But we'll take the world with us.' He was true to his word.

On the evening of 15 January 1945, Hitler and his entourage left his western headquarters, the Eagle's Eyrie in Ziegenberg, and steamed east towards Berlin. On every front, German divisions fell back in disarray. That night, Hitler's special train arrived at the Lehrter Stadtbahnhof in the ruined capital of the Reich. Hitler had ordered the blinds drawn for most of the journey. He was driven through rubble-strewn streets to the Reich Chancellery. Few Berliners knew that Hitler had returned to their city. Now he retreated inside Speer's Chancellery and the concrete bunker that had been constructed beneath its grandiose façade. Hitler made his last radio speech on 30 January. He described the 'most serious crisis for Europe in many centuries' brought on by 'Kremlin Jews' who were already 'eradicating people in their tens and hundreds of thousands' – and must now be 'fought off and mastered'. It would be the last time that Germans heard Hitler's voice – and the speech did little to restore his credibility.

Four days earlier, an SS unit had set off explosives in the last remaining crematoria in the Birkenau camp at Auschwitz. The next day, the Soviet Army's 322nd Rifle Division entered the grounds of the camp, mounted on shaggy ponies. On the seventieth anniversary of the liberation, Ivan Martynushkin recalled what he had seen that day. Inside the huge camp was a desolation. The SS had marched 60,000 inmates out of the camp ten days earlier. He could see hundreds of mouldering corpses – and 'some people behind barbed wire'. Some 7,000 of the weakest and most infirm inmates remained, clinging to life, in the camp. 'We saw emaciated, tortured, impoverished people,' Martynushkin remembered. 'We had the feeling of doing a good deed – liberating people from this hell.' By then more than a million people had been killed in the camp. The Germans had tried to erase evidence of what had happened inside the camp but Martynushkin and his unit discovered some 370,000 men's suits, 837,000 women's garments and 7.7 tons of human hair. These were the relics of the Final Solution.

Himmler's disastrous experiences as a military commander had psychological consequences. He was disabused of any remaining hope that Germany had any chance of avoiding a humiliating catastrophe if Hitler refused to seek terms with his enemies. Even in this he was deluded, for neither the Western Allies nor the Soviets had any interest in contemplating negotiations with the Nazi leadership. Hitler had a more realistic view. As he confided to Goebbels, the only hope was a split in the Allied coalition – but he understood that while tensions between the Western Allies and the Soviets had undoubtedly deepened, the destruction of the Reich held the Alliance in an iron grip. In March 1945, Himmler suffered a severe attack of angina and had himself admitted to the sanitorium at Hohenlychen. This fashionable establishment north of Berlin was the domain of Hitler's personal physician, SS-Gruppenführer Professor Dr Karl Gebhardt. An orthopaedic surgeon who specialised in knee injuries, Gebhardt was much disliked. Otto Ohlendorf dismissed him as 'a corrupt, self-seeking schemer with a keen eye for the main chance'. Speer was treated at Hohenlychen for severe depression and the treatment very nearly killed him. It has been conjectured that Himmler was using Speer's breakdown to have him sidelined or even murdered. In any event, Himmler admired the dubious Professor Dr Gebhardt unreservedly. On his sickbed, Himmler conferred with Goebbels, who reported in his diary:

> Himmler sums up the situation correctly in what he says. His reason tells him that we have little hope of winning the war by military means, but his instinct tells him that in the long run a political route will open up so that we will turn the war in our favour. Himmler sees the possibility more in the west than in the east. He believes that England [*sic*] will come to its senses, though I am somewhat doubtful about that …

Both were deluded. Goebbels entertained variant fantasies that Stalin was 'more realistic than the English–American maniacs'.[22] In any case, Himmler now embarked on a Sisyphean round of meetings and soundings to seek a way to end the war on his terms – and so cash in the human capital of the Jews he still held alive in Germany. His chosen intermediary was his personal physician and masseur, Felix Kersten, who had moved to Sweden. He now returned to his estate in Germany. Through Kersten, Himmler offered to order camp commandants not to kill any more Jews and to improve conditions in the camps. Kersten informed Hillel Storch of the World Jewish Congress that Himmler was also prepared to release 10,000 Jews to Sweden or Switzerland. These offers from Himmler were not new. In February he had meetings with the Vice President of the Swedish Red Cross, Count Folke Bernadotte, and offered to release prisoners. These negotiations had come to nothing – but now Bernadotte was once again summoned to meet Himmler. Bernadotte – who would be assassinated by the Stern Gang in Israel – gave us an eerie portrait of Himmler: he was, he recalled, 'strikingly, astoundingly obliging, showed his sense of humour, even a touch of gallows humour, a number of times, and liked to make a joke to lighten the tone a little'. Later Himmler wrote a letter to Bernadotte claiming that he had always struggled for the same end – a solution to the 'Jewish Problem' through emigration.

When Bernadotte communicated Himmler's offers to the British Ambassador in Stockholm, Victor Mallet, who passed the message on to Eden and Churchill, he was given very short shrift: 'No link with Himmler.'

And that was effectively that. By then Himmler was either confused or obtusely persisted in believing that he would be considered by the Allies as an appropriate successor to Hitler. The implications of being at the top of the Allied list of war criminals seemed opaque to his mind. He had entered, it seems, a flickering, twilight world of fantastical possibilities. Encouraged by the SD intelligence chief, Walter Schellenberg, he began to speculate about the implications of Hitler being killed or being removed from power. Hoping to prevent a final and vindictive massacre of prisoners held in Germany, Bernadotte and other negotiators kept Himmler talking. And talking … and talking. On the night of 23 April, Himmler made his last and most desperate bid for salvation. He had fled Hohenlychen for Lübeck on the Baltic Coast – and it was here that Bernadotte met him for the last time. Himmler asked Bernadotte to inform the Swedish government that he wished to meet Eisenhower, the Supreme Commander of the Allied Expeditionary Forces, to discuss the terms of a grand military alliance. He proposed that German troops would hold the Eastern Front as long as they could. Bernadotte politely conveyed Himmler's terms to the Allied ambassadors in Sweden. The answer from the Allies could never have been in doubt: there could be no negotiations with Heinrich Himmler.

On 28 April, sealed inside the fetid atmosphere of the Führer Bunker beneath the Reich Chancellery, Hitler learned of Himmler's machinations from the international press. He exploded in anger. Russian forces were a mere 1,000 yards from the Chancellery, but Hitler still hoped that General Walther Wenck's 12th Army could break through. Towards midnight, Hitler summoned Gertrud Junge, his 25-year-old secretary, to his rooms: 'Come along I want to dictate something.' He reflected for a few moments then began: 'My political testament …' In this macabre document, Hitler vituperatively blamed European Jewry for the downfall of the Reich – and denounced both Himmler and Göring, who had both defied his authority: 'through secret negotiations with the enemy, which they held without my knowledge and against my will, and through their attempt in defiance of the law to seize power in the state' these traitors 'had done untold damage to the country and to the whole nation, quite apart from their treachery towards me personally'. Himmler had good reason to believe that Hitler had to all intents and purpose abdicated from power. He had declared at what turned out to be his final briefing that he was no longer in a position to give orders. Himmler seems not to have realised that Hitler was distancing himself from the possibility of an ignominious surrender. Himmler was shattered when he heard that Hitler had expelled him as a traitor.

Himmler failed to keep his word to Kersten. With the exception of Bergen-Belsen – where an epidemic of typhus had broken out – the camps in Germany were not handed over to the Allies. He ordered the clearance of Mittelbau-Dora and Buchenwald at the beginning of April, with fatal consequences for thousands of inmates. He issued orders to the commandants of Dachau and Flossenbürg that not a single inmate should fall into enemy hands. As his hopes of trading lives for power faded, the prisoners became expendable. Prisoners were forced to march hither and thither across Germany. Huge numbers were shot by their guards. At the beginning of 1945, some 714,000 prisoners remained alive in the camp system. It is estimated that between 240,000 and 360,000 perished before the war ended.[23]

The Jewish leaders who had been compelled to collaborate with the Germans suffered different fates. Otto Komoly, the decorated war veteran who had led the Rescue Committee, survived the Arrow Cross slaughters through the winter of 1944. He devoted his time to rescuing Jewish children. In January, he was seized by an Arrow Cross gang – and was never seen again. Komoly, as his nephew Tomi relates, had a tense relationship with the Orthodox member of the Jewish Council, Fülöp Freudiger:

> [In October] Komoly decided to become a member of the Jewish Council, to try to influence their activities. The threat made some Jewish leaders work closer together, while in other cases, antagonisms deepened ... The relationship with Fülöp Freudiger, the Orthodox member of the Jewish Council, had its ups and downs. As for Miklós Krausz, secretary of the Palestine Office, his talks with Komoly and Kasztner were always tense.[24]

It will be recalled that Freudiger had diligently cultivated Dieter Wisliceny – even satisfying his ravenously sweet tooth with presents of chocolates. Freudiger and his family had been selected 'as Jewish public functionaries' to leave Budapest on the 'Kasztner Train' but at the last minute Eichmann insisted that Freudiger remain in Budapest. 'He would not allow a member of the Judenrat to leave his post.' Then in the middle of August, Freudiger met with Wisliceny: '[He] said to me, suddenly, without any preamble (we had been talking about other matters) "Freudiger, go away now!'" He did not hesitate:

> We left Hungary and escaped to Romania as Romanian Jews ... The genuine Romanian Jews simply had the right to return to Romania ... On 11 August we went by the ordinary train from Budapest to Romania ... We remained in Romania for 14 months and from there we came to Palestine.[25]

In this chaotic period, fate was capricious.

Even at the very end of the war, Himmler continued to regard the Jews and other persecuted minorities who survived in the camps as objects or 'pieces' of barter and exchange who were ultimately expendable. It is simply not plausible that more than a year *before* the collapse of the Reich, Himmler would have taken seriously a plan to exchange 'a million Jews for 10,000 trucks'. It is equally incredible that he hoped to use the ransom offer to open negotiations with representatives of the Allies through the offices of a shady Hungarian smuggler.

For the Germans, Brand's mission to Istanbul served altogether different purposes. The story of the Rescue Committee's negotiations with the SS is a tragic one. Eichmann and his colleagues exploited the Hungarian Zionists to expedite the destruction of Europe's last Jews. The tens of thousands of Jews who survived the onslaught of 1944 owed their lives not to the Rescue Committee – but the brute force of circumstance.

EPILOGUE: ENDGAME IN ISRAEL

Three years after the downfall of the Third Reich, Zionist Jews went to war to build a new state in the former British mandate of Palestine. In the cauldron of a globalised war, German state violence sought the physical annihilation of European Jewry and other ethnic outsiders. This genocide intimately tied together the exploitation of bodies for labour and their destruction as racial types. And yet in the aftermath of this unprecedented paroxysm of racialised state violence that consumed the lives of between 5 and 6 million Jews, a Zionist state was forged in another tremor of violence in a strategic corner of the post-war world.

Joel Brand and Rezső Kasztner would both live the rest of their lives as citizens of the State of Israel. As the Arrow Cross gangs rampaged through Budapest, the British had released Brand from his comfortable house arrest in Cairo and he had drifted to Palestine. Here he had joined the terrorist 'Stern Gang'. He was angry with the British, who had denounced him as a German agent and prevented his return to Hungary. He was angry with the Zionist establishment in Jerusalem, who had betrayed him. He was eventually joined by Hansi and his two sons – and the family settled down to a precarious life in the new state. Few knew of Joel Brand and his mysterious mission – until he entered the courtroom in Israel in 1961 to once again confront Adolf Eichmann.

Even before he settled in Israel in December 1947, Kasztner was tormented by whispers and innuendoes about his bonds with German SS officers. In the autumn of 1945, his father-in-law, József Fischer, sent troubling news from his new home in Palestine. It will be recalled that Fischer was head of the Jewish Council in Kolozsvár and had left Hungary on the 'Kasztner Train'. He informed Kasztner that many of the Hungarian survivors arriving in Palestine were hostile to the 'Kasztner Group'. There were rumours that the wealthy 'Prominents' had conspired to accelerate the deportations of the less-favoured Jews in the ghetto so that they could escape. It was whispered that Kasztner was not the saviour of Jews, as he claimed, but a collaborator. Fischer had heard that the matter was under investigation by a Tribunal in Cluj. The rumours became so widespread that David Ben-Gurion, who had other very pressing matters on his mind, commented that 'Kasztner was afraid to come to Palestine'.[1]

There can be no doubt that Kasztner was extremely anxious.

Kasztner was right to be afraid. He would not live to see Eichmann brought to Jerusalem to stand trial. His shocking fate reflected the turbulent politics of the new state and his own psychic contradictions. Both he and Brand had been spared the harsh realities of the German onslaught on the Hungarian Jews. They had never observed the brutality of the ghettos and the gassing and incineration of the Jews deported to Auschwitz. The fate of many of the Jews of Budapest, murdered by Arrow Cross fanatics, was not one they shared.

In the aftermath of the war, Kasztner sought ways to burnish his reputation: he became an important witness for the International Military Tribunal in Nuremberg to judge and punish the crimes of the Nazi regime. He submitted affidavits and was called on to testify against Ernst Kaltenbrunner, the head of the RSHA, and Edmund Veesenmayer, the German plenipotentiary in Hungary. Once again seduced by the attention of the powerful, Kasztner made a fatal mistake. From an ethical point of view, he was not obligated to offer mitigating evidence on behalf of the SS officers he had negotiated with during the occupation to rescue Jews. But in April 1945, Becher pleaded with Kasztner to enlighten the Allies about the efforts he *and Himmler* had made to 'save Jewish lives'. The fact is that as well as money, moral alibis were all Kasztner could offer. He had been urged, more than once, by Jewish Agency officials to 'convince your clients [*sic*] … We will never forget those who have helped us'. Kasztner described a chilling conversation with Dieter Wisliceny, who unashamedly confessed that 'by keeping me alive and by making some concessions in the campaign against the Jews he might have a defence witness when he and his organisation would have to account for their atrocities'.[2]

Alibis provided an expedient currency; Kasztner should have treated Becher's plea with the contempt it deserved. The record shows that he did nothing of the kind. During the Nuremberg trial process, Kasztner *went beyond* honouring any pledges he had made to Becher. Himmler was, of course, dead – and Eichmann had vanished. In September 1945, Kasztner wrote that:

> I escaped the fate of the other Jewish leaders because the complete liquidation of the Hungarian Jews was a failure [*sic*] and also because SS Standartenführer Becher took me under his wings in order to establish an eventual alibi for himself. He was anxious to demonstrate after the fall of 1944 that he disapproved of the deportations and exterminations and endeavoured consistently to furnish me with evidence that he tried to save the Jews.[3]

In other words, he realised that Becher's change of heart was opportunistic. In the course of the next two years, Kasztner appeared to change his mind.

It is disquieting to read Kasztner's affidavits submitted on behalf of members of the Eichmann Sonderkommando. He devoted most of his mitigatory efforts to Becher, but wrote to Krumey's wife that: 'I will take this opportunity to testify in your husband's case … I shall not fail to point to the mitigating circumstances'. Later he wrote to Krumey of the 'steps taken' that would 'make it easier for you to regain your freedom'. When Kasztner discovered that Dieter Wisliceny was on trial in Bratislava and likely to be put to death, he sent a handwritten memorandum dated 22 July 1947 arguing that members of the Eichmann Commando should be arraigned in a separate trial to elicit information about the 'extermination process'. It is hard to prove that he made this proposal in good faith. It has to be said, however, that Kasztner's memorandum made it clear that Wisliceny had taken part in 'one of the greatest crimes ever committed'.

At first sight, Kasztner's strenuous efforts on behalf of Becher are damning. In 1947, he wrote that Becher 'belongs to the very few SS leaders having the courage to oppose the programme of annihilation'. He then listed Becher's achievements – the release of the 'Hostage Train', and, he claimed, persuading Himmler to order the cessation of mass killing at the end of 1944. Becher had *profited* from the release of the 'Prominents': he was never motivated to save lives. Kasztner's other claims are a tissue of distortions and outright lies. He even credited Becher with saving no fewer than 233,760 lives. His language is often obsequiously mendacious:

> Becher did everything … to save innocent human lives from the blind fury of killing of the Nazi leaders … In my opinion, he is deserving … of the fullest possible consideration.[4]

The following year, Kasztner wrote yet more affidavits testifying to Becher's impressive humanitarian achievements. He praised the Waffen-SS General, Hans Jüttner, who had objected to the brutal treatment of Jews on the march to Austria; and redoubled his efforts on behalf of Krumey and Wisliceny. He was unaware that the latter had just been executed in Bratislava. According to Joel and Hansi Brand's book *Ha'Satan veha'nefesh* (The Devil and the Soul) published in Tel Aviv in 1960, at least one of the Nuremberg prosecutors became increasingly uneasy about Kasztner's pleas on behalf of the SS prisoners. Robert Kempner described him as 'roaming the detention centre … looking for those he could help'. He was 'very glad when [Kasztner] left Nuremberg'.

Why did Kasztner choose to debase himself? It has been argued that he was hoping to persuade Becher to return some of the funds, valuables and property that the Rescue Committee had been compelled to hand over to him to secure the release of the passengers on the 'Kasztner Train'. In 1948, Kasztner corresponded with the new Israeli Finance Minister Eliezer Kaplan about the 'Becher Deposit'. Although it is unclear whether these discussions led to anything concrete, Kasztner may well have had a good reason to coddle Becher in the hope that he might disgorge some of the plunder. Kasztner's memorandum seeking to intervene in the trial of Wisliceny in Bratislava might imply another motivation. He proposed using Wisliceny's connections with former Sonderkommando officers to build a case against Eichmann – who had vanished. He writes:

> It is therefore important that such members of staff as may be available be put on trial and the facts [of the Final Solution] be made public. In the IMT judgement (pages 265–266), the crimes committed by Eichmann's office were specifically enumerated, thus indicating its importance and perhaps the necessity for a separate trial … Furthermore, the proof presented in such a trial can be used at a later date against Eichmann, whose whereabouts are now unknown, as well as for other members of his

staff who are not yet in custody. It is particularly fitting that the United States conduct such a prosecution because politically German satellites are implicated too in the anti-Jewish programme and may not be able to conduct the trial with all its ramifications in an impartial manner.[5]

Kasztner was surely right to press for a thorough investigation of the perpetrators of the Final Solution. Vengeful execution is not the most effective way to understand the minds and motivations of perpetrators.

The problem with these justifications is that they do not completely explain why Kasztner worked so hard on behalf of Kurt Becher. Bogdanor argues that the explanation can be found in Kasztner's alarmed reaction to the letters from Dr Fischer, his father-in-law, which warned him that Hungarian survivors were openly accusing him of being a collaborator. By making a case for Becher as a decent Nazi who genuinely hoped to rescue Jews, Bogdanor claims, Kasztner retrospectively justified forging bonds with the SS officer. He was hoping to prove that he had a chance of saving lives because he had genuine allies on the German side: he was compelled to morally validate his negotiating partners who now stood accused of war crimes. This argument is not entirely convincing. If Kasztner was anxious about the damaging accusations that were being slung at him in Israel, it was unwise to deepen his bonds with former SS officers. To counter claims of collaborating, he would surely have washed his hands of any contact with Himmler's henchmen. Incontrovertibly, he chose a different course.

There is a much simpler explanation. Kasztner intervened in the judgement of his former negotiating partners *because he relished the power conferred on him at Nuremberg.* Since the spring of 1944, he had been debased, humiliated and threatened by the Germans. He was intelligent enough to realise that for all Becher's charm and Wisliceny's macabre bonhomie, he, Kasztner, was still a Jew. In the eyes of the SS, he could never be fully human. Now the downfall of Nazi Germany and the incarceration of the SS had turned the tables. The SS officers who had slaughtered the Jews of Hungary and exploited the Rescue Committee for their own ends had been forced to their knees. After the destruction of the Reich, it was Kasztner who wielded power over life and death.

We will never understand completely why Kasztner made the decision to defend criminals such as Becher, Wisliceny and Krumey. It is very unlikely that he had a single motivation – and there is no reason to completely dismiss the possibility that he was seeking to restore Jewish assets and committed to gathering evidence against Eichmann. Nor can we attribute the fate of these individuals to Kasztner's interventions alone. As Mary Fulbrook has shown in her book *Reckonings*, there was a systemic failure to bring the perpetrators of the Holocaust to account in the decades after the end of the war. As she writes: 'In none of the Third Reich successor states, was it easy to undertake a legal reckoning with the Nazi persecution.'[6]

The different fates of Eichmann's men after the end of the war were not in any sense consistent. Despite Kasztner's intervention, Wisliceny was executed by the Czechs in 1948. Hermann Krumey was released in 1948, but two decades later was sentenced to life imprisonment by a court in Frankfurt. At the same trial, the prosecutor demanded a fifteen-year sentence for Otto Hunsche, another Eichmann aide in Budapest. They had both been acquitted at a previous trial.[7] Even the wealthy Kurt Becher was never entirely secure. He had been called only as a witness in Nuremberg and released in 1947. In 1961, Becher submitted evidence to the Eichmann trial *in absentia*, fearing that he might be arrested if he travelled to Israel. By the time Karla Müller-Tupath published a damning account of Becher's life in 1999, he was one of the wealthiest men in Germany. The revelations in her book provoked a flurry of interest in his wartime activities on the Eastern Front and in Hungary – but while his reputation was tainted, Becher was never brought to account. He long outlived his rival, Adolf Eichmann, and his negotiating partner, Rezső Kasztner.

Kasztner did not see himself as a Nazi agent, but this is how the Germans perceived *him*. When the Hungarian survivor and author Elie Wiesel interviewed Himmler's quack, Felix Kersten, in September 1959, the following exchange took place:

Kersten: … General Walter Schellenberg and General Rudolf Brandt. The first was head of Himmler's SD counterintelligence and the second was the Reichsführer's secretary and adjutant.
Wiesel: What did they say about him?
Kersten: Schellenberg said to me that Kasztner was one of his agents and that he did a good job in Budapest. He also told me that Kasztner asked him to release a few hundred Jews from the camp because he wanted to prepare an alibi for himself. In the espionage services it's common practice to provide assistance to agents, because often one might require their services after the deluge.

Wiesel: Are you sure that Schellenberg told you about Dr Kasztner? Rudolf Kasztner?

Kersten: Yes, I'm absolutely sure.

Wiesel: And what did Rudolf Brandt tell you?

Kersten: Once he told me, laughing, that in Budapest there's a Jewish agent in the service of Nazi intelligence who has a name like mine: Kasztner – Kersten.

Wiesel: Did Himmler ever mention Kasztner?

Kersten: I can't remember. I assume that he didn't. But when I complained about the brutal Nazi methods used against Jews, he told me that he had Jews working for him, for money, in Switzerland and other countries.[8]

These accusations would haunt Kasztner for the rest of his life. A life-long Zionist, Kasztner was uncertain about travelling to Israel. He spent a few years in Switzerland, obsessively defending his reputation. At the end of 1947, he finally judged it was safe to take his family to Tel Aviv, but life in the new Jewish state was a struggle. His arrival immediately provoked outrage from Hungarian survivors. At a public reception to honour Kasztner's work, a former slave worker called Levi Blum leapt to his feet and shouted: 'You were a Quisling, you were a murderer'. The past bit and gnawed at his heels, but Kasztner slowly clawed his way to respectability. By the early 1950s, he was serving the socialist Mapai government as an assistant to the government minister, Dov Yoseph, and spokesman for the Ministry of Supply and Allocation. He had returned to his old profession as a journalist. He worked for the Hungarian language newspaper Új Kelet, issued by the ruling Mapai Party, and broadcast regularly on Kol Yisrael (Voice of Israel) radio in Hungarian. Kasztner was at last back within striking distance of the realms of power.

Then Malkiel Grünwald entered his life.

My Dear Friends, the Smell of a Corpse Fills My Nostrils

From its troubled birth, Israel was a divided and quarrelsome society. The Jews who gathered and began making new lives in this disputed sliver of land had their origins in many different regions of the world and brought with them singular traditions, experiences and expectations. As the Israeli historian Schlomo Sand has shown, Jews had never been a single people, but a tangled web of divergent identities bound together by a shared faith. European Ashkenazim, bearing the terrible wounds of genocide, now lived uneasily alongside Sephardic Jews from the Middle East and North Africa. The shadow of the German genocide fell unevenly across this human landscape and the new nation's struggle for survival barely disguised the fiercely antagonistic currents that lurked close to the surface of this bristling and prickly new world. Israel was a cauldron of political animosity and one of the most clamorous denizens of this bubbling ferment was Malkiel Grünwald.

Grünwald had Hungarian roots but, before the war, had spent most of his life in Vienna.[9] He had been caught out in an antisemitic riot in 1937 and fled to Palestine with his family the following year. He bought a modest hotel in Zion Square in Jerusalem, which he ran with his wife. His son and daughter became deeply involved with the paramilitary organisation, the Irgun. For the American screenwriter and polemicist Ben Hecht, who became a committed Zionist during the Second World War, Grünwald was a hero who took on the perfidy of the establishment. But new information released by the Israeli Home Intelligence in the 1980s exposed a murkier story. It seems that Grünwald had a long criminal career in Hungary and Austria – and that even before he emigrated to Palestine, he had engaged in skirmishes with left-wing Zionists – and had often denounced his enemies to the right-wing Austrian government. It is also alleged that Grünwald misled Jews travelling to Palestine and pocketed their money. The Home Intelligence files revealed that when Grünwald arrived in Palestine he began working with the British CID and used any opportunity to denounce Zionists as 'Nazi spies' – often with calamitous consequences. Most of his own family perished in the Holocaust.[10]

By the early 1950s, Grünwald had become a thorn in the side of the ruling Labour (Mapai) Party. In these early years of the new state, Menachem Begin's opposition party, the Herut, waged an aggressive political war on Mapai that was focused on the contentious matter of reparation payments to Israel from the Federal Republic of Germany. Begin denounced David Ben-Gurion's acceptance of the reparations agreement with West Germany as a 'pact with the devil' – an ongoing collaboration with the heirs of Hitler. There were some angry voices on the right wing of the Israeli government who implied that during the war,

Ben-Gurion and the Jewish Agency had collaborated with the 'Nazo–British' authorities and squandered the chance to rescue Hungarian Jewry. These attacks spilled over into rancorous arguments about the ambivalent roles played by the Nazi-appointed Jewish Councils. Begin's side denounced Ben-Gurion for 'Palestinocentrism' – meaning, focusing all their efforts on maintaining the Yishuv and neglecting the fate of Jews in German-occupied Europe. Begin and his 'Sternist' followers claimed that if their own revolt against the British had been successful and 'the gates of Palestine been forced open', the rescue of the many rather than the few would have been feasible. Since it was the Germans who closed the door to emigration, Begin's attack was founded, as Schlomo Aronson put it, on a 'string of libels and falsehoods'.[11]

After 1948, Grünwald aligned himself with the Orthodox party, the HaMizrachi – the ancestor of today's reactionary Jewish Home Party – which had been founded in Lithuania by ultra-religious Zionists. For some time, Grünwald had struggled to pursue a career as a journalist but was handicapped by his inept grasp of Hebrew. He was no doubt jealous of Kasztner's now thriving career in print and on radio. The frustrated Grünwald, who would have relished Twitter and Facebook, turned to self-publishing a 'bulletin' he called *Letters to My Friends in the Mizrachi*. He used this scurrilous and shabby rag to fire venomous tirades at supposedly corrupt politicians, greedy public officials and unworthy religious leaders. In Issue No. 17 Grünwald turned his ire on Kasztner.

'The smell of a corpse fills my nostrils!' ranted Grünwald. 'This will be the finest funeral yet. Dr Rudolf Kasztner must be eliminated.' He unleashed a torrent of defamation accusing Kasztner of saving his own relatives and 'rich Jews'. Kasztner, he accused, was a Nazi collaborator and profiteer who had 'indirectly' prepared the way for the destruction of Hungarian Jewry. Instead of rescuing his fellow Zionists, he had become the saviour of a war criminal.

To begin with, the Israeli government hoped that this torrent of invective directed at a member of the Mapai government would offer a chance to crush this foul-mouthed nuisance. The Attorney General, Haim Cohn, who was also the Justice Minister, decided to file criminal defamation charges against Grünwald – and forced a reluctant Kasztner to go along with the plan by threatening to sack him from his government post. Cohen rationalised his decision: 'In our new, pure, ideal State … a man cannot officiate in a senior position … when there is a stain on him, or even only a grave suspicion of collaboration with the Nazis.' There were other members of the government who shared Kasztner's disinclination to turn on Grünwald. But now the die was cast. The Attorney General would put Grünwald on trial. By defaming Kasztner, he had in effect defamed the Mapai government – and its wartime record.

Facing the full weight of the government of Israel, Grünwald searched for a lawyer to get him out of trouble. He found Shmuel Tamir. Tamir was not just a gifted lawyer with a talent for showboating tactics, he was a former commander in the Irgun and a passionate supporter of Herut. He was obsessed with exposing the betrayals of the leftist Zionist leadership during the war – and, like his new client, was preoccupied with Kasztner's bond with the SS. Tamir agreed to take on the case on condition that the trial would be turned into a 'trial of the Jewish leadership during the period of the Holocaust'. He demanded 'absolute power of attorney', meaning that he would shape legal strategy in court. In the words of Shalom Rosenfeld:

> As soon as he took upon himself the defence of the accused ... Tamir's political intuition told him that here for the first time was an opportunity to raise before a Court in Israel – and through it, before the entire public – the whole web of political and ethical problems involved in the Holocaust and rescue ... problems ... How did the Nazis succeed in implementing their satanic programs without meeting organized resistance on the part of the Jewish masses? What was the function of the Jewish bodies, and, first and foremost, of the Jewish Councils appointed by the German occupying authorities...? To what extent, if at all, was contact permitted with the enemy in the desperate effort to save life and property? And what are the limits of such contacts? In particular: what did the Jewish Community and the Yishuv – [in Palestine] do or not do to save their brothers in Europe?[12]

Tamir's ruthless legal strategy had astonishing and, for Kasztner, deadly consequences. This was a trial in which the prosecutor became the defender, the defender the prosecutor, and the witnesses turned into the accused.

It is not necessary here to follow every twist and turn in what became known as the 'Kasztner Trial'. That this is how '*The Attorney-General of the Government of Israel v. Malchiel Gruenwald*' is remembered reveals how effectively Tamir turned the legal tables on the Attorney General and the unfortunate Kasztner. The case was heard before Judge Benjamin Halevi in the Jerusalem District Court. For a long period during the proceedings, the prosecution case promised to be what American lawyers call a 'slam dunk'.

Then on 18 February 1954, the prosecutor, Amnon Tel, called on Kasztner to testify. This was Kasztner's moment to crush his accusers, or so he believed. To begin with he put on a compelling performance recounting his struggles with Eichmann and how he had persuaded the Nazis to release more than 1,000 Jews. He replayed the Strasshof myth, claiming to have persuaded Eichmann to send 15,000 Jews to a work camp instead of to their certain deaths in Auschwitz … and, crucially, how he had exploited a working relationship with Kurt Becher to save Jews in the last months of the war. That day on the stand was a triumph for Kasztner. Judge Halevi even asked Grünwald if he would now consider pleading guilty.

But Tamir had a powerful card to play.

During his time on the stand, Kasztner had been cross-examined about his relationship with Becher. Had he provided mitigating testimony on behalf of this SS officer? Kasztner vehemently denied that he had. This was Tamir's chance to strike – and his attack would prove to be Kasztner's undoing.

On 25 February, Tamir bluntly stated: 'I tell you now that Kurt Becher was released at Nuremberg thanks to your personal intervention.'

Kasztner: 'That's a dirty lie.'

Now Tamir, relishing the high drama of the proceedings, delivered his master stroke. He walked slowly towards Kasztner and showed him a letter that had been submitted to the court *by the prosecution*. In July 1948, Kasztner had written to the Israel Finance Minister, Eliezer Kaplan, boasting that Becher had been released 'thanks to my personal intervention'. Kasztner was appalled, but there was no way to deny he had made this boast. He had been well and truly hoisted by his own petard.

From this moment on, Tamir battered away without respite or mercy at Kasztner's actions during the war and the claims he had made about saving Jews – and on behalf of Becher. So relentless was Tamir's attack that Kasztner collapsed – and Judge Halevi was forced to postpone the trial for a month. Kasztner was shattered but there was no way he and his supporters could halt the destruction of character and reputation wreaked by Tamir. Appalled by the turn of events, the Attorney General himself took over the prosecution – but to no avail. When Kasztner was well enough to return to court, Tamir thrust at him a copy of the damning affidavit he had written in August 1947 in the name of the Jewish Agency and the World Jewish Congress claiming that Becher deserved mercy. Kasztner now stood before the court and the world exposed as a liar – and as a defender of Nazis.

Now it was Tamir's turn to make a case for the defence. He would need to show that Grünwald's attack on Kasztner was justified. It was not a libel because it was true. To make his case he called witnesses who had survived the Holocaust and in a rising chorus of testimony, their eyewitness accounts eviscerated the prosecution case and shredded Kasztner's tottering moral reputation.

Nine months later, on 22 June 1955, Judge Halevi returned to the court. It would take him fourteen hours to read through the verdict. It was a judgement, in short, not of the defendant Grünwald but of Kasztner. And it was damning. Halevi concluded that Kasztner had failed to understand the Classical axiom: *Timeo Danaos et dona ferentes:* 'I fear Greeks even when they bring gifts.' Using another powerfully corrosive phrase, Halevi concluded that Kasztner had 'sold his soul to the devil'. He argued that Kasztner had knowingly collaborated with the Nazis and assisted them. The defining aspect of his collaboration was expressed in the fact that he had deliberately concealed the truth about the destination of the deportation trains. He had 'oiled the destruction machine as a whole, prevented possible interference with its operation and made an important contribution to its overall efficiency'. He had, Halevi argued, acted thus in return for an opportunity to save a few people, among them his own relatives and friends. The rescue of the few 'Prominents' was integral to the German plan:

> The Nazi partner, unfathomably stronger than Kasztner, swept its dependent 'partner' into a whirlpool of blood. For the Nazis – and they controlled the unequal partnership – the extermination and the 'rescue' were a single project … the plan for the extermination of 800,000 people.

The Prime Minister, Moshe Sharett, who will be more familiar to the reader under his former name, Moshe Shertok, described the verdict as 'strangulation for the Mapai Party … it was a nightmare, horrible'. And so, it proved. When, in the aftermath of the trial, the Mapai government refused to prosecute Kasztner under the Nazis and Nazi Collaborators (Punishment) Law (1950), it lost a no confidence motion in the Knesset – and was forced to call a general election. The Herut Party subsequently doubled its representation in parliament and the Mapai government collapsed. In the margins of the new state, extremists clamoured for Kasztner to be punished – by death.

Kasztner was compelled to take refuge in a place of shame and fear. He lost his government job and eked out a living as a journalist. He and his family were treated as outcasts. On the morning of 4 March 1957, Kasztner was returning from the offices of *Uj Kelet*, where he was the night editor, to his home at 6 Emanuel HaRomi Street in Tel Aviv. He parked his battered 'Henry J' car and reached across to switch off the engine. As he did so, a young man called Ze'ev Eckstein stepped out of the shadows and called out 'Are you Dr Kasztner?' When Kasztner replied, Eckstein pulled out a revolver, aimed it at Kasztner's head and pulled the trigger. But the gun misfired. Kasztner, in shock, hauled himself out of the car and ran towards the main door of the apartment building. Eckstein fired again. Kasztner fell to the pavement, blood pooling around his body. Eckstein fled into the night.

Eight days later, Kasztner died in the Hadassah Hospital. A few days earlier, a telegram was handed to the dying man. 'Shocked by the inhuman act,' it read. 'Wishing you a complete recovery ...' It was signed – Malkiel Grünwald.

Kasztner's ghost has never rested quietly. There is no reason to believe that it ever will.

A NOTE ON NUMBERS

In 1946, Jenö Lévai wrote in *The Black Book About the Martyrdom of Hungarian Jewry* that 'the losses which befell Hungarian Jewry cannot be definitely established'. Unfortunately, his conclusion still stands today. The matter of numbers is contentious in Holocaust studies – and deniers exploit any opportunity to question claims made by historians. This does not mean that uncertainty should not be acknowledged. In the case of Hungary, one of the most intractable problems that researchers confront is that Hungarian borders were redrawn after 1945 – making comparisons of Hungarian Jewish populations before and after the Second World War to calculate losses an almost impossible task. Different studies carried out immediately after the war put the number of Hungarian Jews murdered as a consequence of persecution between 200,000 and 123,000. Later studies, which were used by Randolph Braham, concluded that 564,507 Jews were murdered on Hungarian lands during the Second World War. More recently, the historian Tamás Stark has applied a more rigorous analysis in 'Hungary's Human Losses in World War II', published by Uppsala University in 1995.

Stark points out that before the German occupation that began in March 1944 some 15–16,000 Hungarian Jews were murdered by Einsatzgruppe C at Kamenets-Podolsk in Galicia in the autumn of 1941. In January 1942, over a thousand Jews were murdered in the Újvidék massacre, a military operation carried out by the Honvédség, the armed forces of Hungary. As the Germans pressed ahead with the 'Final Solution' in 1942, the Hungarian Prime Minister Miklós Kallay fended off Hitler's insistent demands for action against Hungarian Jews. In the aftermath of the occupation, Hungarian Jews were subjected to a tide of anti-Jewish legislation and the Eichmann group met with Hungarian Interior Ministry officials to plan a programme of deportations.

According to the German plenipotentiary Edmund Veesenmayer, 437,402 persons were deported from the Hungarian provinces between May 15 and July 8. This figure was roughly confirmed by the Hungarian gendarmerie commander László Ferenczy who calculated that 434,351 persons were handed over. Evidence submitted in the course of trials of surviving members of the Eichmann group in the 1960s refer to the same figures. We can say with certainty that some 400,000 Jews were deported on 120 trains to the German camps.

The deportations ended at the beginning of July. But persecution of Jews persisted – and was intensified when the Arrow Cross leader Szálasi seized power in October. Approximately 50,000 Jews were handed over to the Germans and deported on forced marches – and 15,000 were murdered by Arrow Cross militias. By the end of the war, some 25,000 Hungarians had perished after conscription into the Labour Service.

Of the approximately half a million Hungarian Jews deported during the war, Stark estimates that 370,000 did not return to Hungary. What happened to these individuals? Contemporary records suggest that between 34,000 and 37,000 remained alive in Austria and Germany. A few thousand had fled to Switzerland, Sweden and Italy. That strongly suggests that of the hundreds of thousands of Jews deported from Hungary in 1944/45, a minimum of 320,000 individuals perished in the German camps.

IMPORTANT ORGANISATIONS AND TERMS

Abwehr   German military intelligence, absorbed by the SD at the beginning of 1944.

American Jewish Joint Distribution Committee, AJJDC   or 'The Joint', the main financial benefactor assisting Jewish emigration from Europe and rescue attempts of Jews from German-occupied territories.

Arrow Cross   Hungarian fascist party founded by Ferenc Szálasi that took power in October 1944.

Der Bericht   referred to as the 'Kasztner Report' or 'Report', was written in 1946 by Rezső Kasztner for the 22nd Zionist Congress. The original German title was *Der Bericht des jüdischen Rettungskomitees aus Budapest 1942–1945* (The Report of the Jewish Rescue Committee of Budapest, 1942–1945), 1946. For the English version see the bibliography.

Columbus Camp   SS camp established for 'preferred' Jews selected by Kasztner.

Eichmann–Kommando or Judenkommando   Special SS unit led by Adolf Eichmann.

Europa Plan   Scheme to barter the lives of European Jews for US$2 million proposed by the 'Working Group' in Bratislava to the SS.

Final Solution   The Nazi plan to liquidate European Jewry.

Gestapo   The German secret police in the Third Reich.

Irgun   Right-wing Jewish underground organisation.

Jewish Agency   Jewish representative organisation based in Jerusalem during the period of the British Mandate.

Mapai   Labour Party of Israel.

Neolog   The reformist manifestation of Judaism in Hungary.

Palestine Office   Department of the Jewish Agency assisting Jews making Aliyah, i.e. emigrating to Palestine.

RSHA (Reichssicherheitshauptamt)   The Reich Security Main Office, founded by Reinhard Heydrich as the SS institution with responsibility for combating domestic and foreign enemies of the Reich. The main agent of the Final Solution.

Va'ada   The Budapest Aid and Rescue Committee, Va'adat Ha-Ezrah ve-ha-Hatzalah be-Budapest, referred to as the Rescue Committee.

Waldsee   The SS forced Jews deported to Auschwitz to write fictional 'postcards from Waldsee' to relatives to disguise their fate.

War Refugee Board (WRB)   US agency established by President Roosevelt in January 1944 to assist in the rescue of persecuted civilians in German-occupied Europe.

Working Group   The Jewish rescue committee established in Bratislava, Slovakia, by Rabbi Michael Weissmandel and his cousin, the secular Zionist Gisi Fleischmann.

Yellow Star House   Jews in Budapest were concentrated in allocated residences, marked by a Yellow Star.

Yishuv   The Jewish community – including the pre-Zionist **Old Yishuv** – that lived in mandate Palestine before the proclamation of the State of Israel in 1948.

SS Ranks

SS	British	United States
Reichsführer-SS (Heinrich Himmler)	None	None
SS-Oberstgruppenführer	General	General
SS-Obergruppenführer	Lieutenant General	Lieutenant General
SS-Gruppenführer	Major General	Major General
SS-Brigadeführer	Brigadier	Brigadier General
SS-Oberführer	None	None
SS-Standartenführer	Colonel	Colonel
SS-Obersturmbannführer	Lieutenant Colonel	Lieutenant Colonel
SS-Sturmbannführer	Major	Major
SS-Hauptsturmführer	Captain	Captain
SS-Obersturmführer	1st Lieutenant	1st Lieutenant
SS-Untersturmführer	2nd Lieutenant	2nd Lieutenant
SS-Sturmscharführer	Regimental Sergeant Major	Sergeant Major
SS-Hauptscharführer	Battalion Sergeant Major	Master Sergeant
SS-Oberscharführer	Company Sergeant Major	Sergeant 1st Class
SS-Scharführer	Platoon Sergeant Major	Staff Sergeant
SS-Unterscharführer	Sergeant	Sergeant
SS-Rottenführer	Corporal	Corporal
SS-Sturmmann	Lance Corporal	None
SS-Oberschütze	None	Private 1st Class
SS-Schütze	Private	Private

NOTES

Prelude: Cairo, June 1944

1 babel.hathitrust.org/cgi/pt?id=mdp.39015028745217;view=1up;seq=8
2 Lewis, David Levering. *The Improbable Wendell Willkie: The Businessman Who Saved the Republican Party and His Country and Conceived a New World Order* (2018).
3 Roger Arditti (2016) Security Intelligence in the Middle East (SIME): Joint Security Intelligence Operations in the Middle East, c. 1939–58, Intelligence and National Security, 31:3, 369-396, DOI: 10.1080/02684527.2015.1034471.
4 See Weissberg, Alex. *Desperate Mission: Joel Brand's Story* (1958, 2017).
5 www.timesofisrael.com/yitzhak-shamir-why-we-killed-lord-moyne

Chapter 2

1 This account is based on Weitz, Y. *The Man who was Murdered Twice: The Life, Trial and Death of Israel Kasztner* (2011). Jerusalem, Yad Vashem. p. 31 *ff*.
2 The English edition of *The Black Book* was published in 1948. See bibliography for details.
3 'At the end of World War I, tens of thousands of Jews were living in Palestine. They constituted a heterogeneous community in a remote part of a declining empire, having neither institutional infrastructure nor recognized leadership. Within 30 years, however, this community, known as the Yishuv, evolved into an autonomous society; "a state in the making," ready for independence.' www.jewishvirtuallibrary.org/israel-studies-an-anthology-the-yishuv
4 Weissberg, Alex. *Desperate Mission* (1958, 2017).
5. Quoted in Black, Ian. *Enemies and Neighbours* (2017).

Chapter 3

1 Bullock, Alan. *Hitler: A Study in Tyranny* (1952).
2 Burgwyn, H. *Mussolini and the Salò Republic, 1943–1945: The Failure of a Puppet Regime* (2018).

3   der-fuehrer.org/reden/english/43-11-08.htm
4   See Stone, Norman, *Hungary: A Short History* (2019).
5   www.terrorhaza.hu/en/museum
6   For Veesenmayer's reports see *The Holocaust in Hungary* (2013) and 'Edmund Veesenmayer on Horthy and Hungary: An American Intelligence Report' by N.F. Dreisziger, *Hungarian Studies Review*, Vol. XXIII, No. 1 (Spring, 1996).

Chapter 4

1   www.spiegel.de/international/germany/nazi-death-marches-book-details-german-citizens-role-in-end-of-war-killings-a-739518.html
2   Sakmyster, T. *Hungary's Admiral on Horseback: Miklós Horthy, 1918–1944* (1994).
3   There is a detailed discussion of the Balkan campaign as a prelude to the mass killings on the Eastern Front in my book, *Hitler's Foreign Executioners* (The History Press, 2011).
4   Gerlach, C. 'The Wannsee Conference, the Fate of German Jews, and Hitler's Decision in Principle to Exterminate all European Jews.' *The Journal of Modern History*, Vol. 70, No. 4 (December 1998).
5   *Ibid.*
6   Snyder, Timothy. *Bloodlands. Europe Between Hitler and Stalin* (2010), p. 411.
7   Brayard, F. (2008). 'À exterminer en tant que partisans »: Sur une note de Himmler.' Politix, No. 82, (2), 9-37. doi:10.3917/pox.082.0009.
8   Cox, J. *Circles of Resistance: Jewish, Leftist and Youth Dissidence in Nazi Germany* (2009).
9   Quoted in Cesarani (London, 2016).
10 Fulbrook, Mary. *Reckonings* (2018), p.112.
11 www.yadvashem.org/odot_pdf/Microsoft%20Word%20-%20607.pdf. Despite the existence of the report, Katzmann was never brought to justice for his crimes. He died in 1957.
12 Witte, Peter; Tyas, Stephen (Winter, 2001), 'A New Document on the Deportation and Murder of Jews during "Einsatz Reinhardt" 1942' in *Holocaust and Genocide Studies*. Oxford University Press. 15 (3): 472. doi:10.1093/hgs/15.3.468. Retrieved 5 May 2015.
13 Smith, Peterson. *Heinrich Himmler Geheimreden*, Speech index, pp. 68–277.
14 Sereny, Gitta. *Into That Darkness: An Examination of Conscience* (2003).
15 www.orwell.ru/library/articles/antisemitism/english/e_antib

Chapter 5

1   hungarianspectrum.org/2019/01/15/the-genesis-of-orbans-anti-soros-campaign; www.buzzfeednews.com/article/hnsgrassegger/george-soros-conspiracy-finkelstein-birnbaum-orban-netanyahu; author's personal correspondence with Hannes Grassegger.
2   Hungarian nationalists have egregiously smeared Soros by misrepresenting his experience during the German occupation and insinuating he was a collaborator. The facts are as follows: 'As a 14-year-old child in Budapest, [Soros] was hidden by a Ministry of Agriculture official who had a Jewish wife. Soros's father, Tivadar Soros, helped protect her, and in return the official agreed to let George pretend

to be his Christian godson. On one occasion, rather than be left alone in Budapest for three days, the young teen accompanied the official, who was sent to inventory the estate of a Jewish family that had fled the country.' www.thenation.com/article/soros-slander-reveals-anti-semitism-at-the-heart-of-the-far-right

3   For Hungarian sources used in this book, see *The Holocaust in Hungary: Evolution of a Genocide* (2013).

4   These confessions were tape recorded in 1957 by Willem Sassen, who was a Dutch Nazi who served in the 'Viking' division of the Waffen-SS. At the end of the war, Sassen escaped to Argentina, where he met a number of other fugitive Nazis including Eichmann. Because Sassen was sympathetic to the 'cause', Eichmann was recklessly frank about his wartime role in the Holocaust. He would come to regret being so candid at his trial.

5   www.cultures-of-history.uni-jena.de/debates/hungary/goodbye-historikerstreit-hello-budapest-city-of-angels-the-debate-about-the-monument-to-the-german-occupation/#fn-text5

6   Avraham Gordon Testimony, Eichmann Trial – Session 54, Jerusalem, 26 May 1961.

7   After the Compromise in 1867, the Habsburg Monarchy became a constitutional monarchy, divided into Austrian and Hungarian parts: the Austrian part of the monarchy included Upper Austria, Lower Austria, Styria, Carinthia, Tyrol, Voralberg, Salzburg, Carniola, Dalmatia, Bohemia, Moravia, Silesia, Galicia and Bukovina. The Hungarian part included the Kingdom of Hungary (including Transylvania), Croatia–Slavonia, and the city of Fiume.

8   The territories of the Russian Empire in which Jews were permitted permanent settlement. Although large in size (approximately 472,590 square miles or 1,224,008 sq. km), and containing areas of dynamic economic growth, the Pale (known in Russian as *cherta postoiannogo zhitel'stva evreev*; the English word pale was borrowed from the term applied to the area of English settlement in Northern Ireland, where the lands of the 'wild Irish' were considered 'beyond the pale') was considered the greatest legal restriction imposed on the Jews of the empire. www.yivoencyclopedia.org/article.aspx/Pale_of_Settlement

9   www.yivoencyclopedia.org/article.aspx/Kiss_Jozsef

10 A fascinating account of life inside the Orczy House can be found in Frojimovics, K., Komoróczy, G., Pusztai, V., & Strrbik, A. *Jewish Budapest, Monuments, Rites, History* (1999).

11 As recently as 2012, a right-wing Jobbik MP, Zsolt Baráth, delivered an inflammatory speech that brought up, in a grotesque parody of historical truth, notorious events that took place 130 years ago in a provincial village called Tiszaeszlár in eastern Hungary. Several days before Passover in 1882, a servant girl called Eszter Solymosi was sent on an errand and did not return. As it happened, poor Eszter had drowned accidentally in the Tisza River – but grossly malicious rumours began to be spread that local Jews had murdered and decapitated her and used her blood in ritual preparations for Passover. Her mother accused the Jews of murder and the 5-year-old son of the Jewish sexton was tricked into confessing that he witnessed the murder. When Eszter's body was recovered from the Tisza, her mother denied it was her daughter's. Eszter had, she claimed, been murdered by Jews, not drowned. Agitators began to call for the expulsion of all Jews from Hungary and in Budapest a Jewish student was attacked and killed. The accused were eventually acquitted, unanimously, after a long and acrimonious

trial. Although the acquittal provoked ugly anti-Jewish riots as far away as Poszony and Budapest, the Hungarian establishment firmly supported the accused Jews. The Prime Minister declared that Hungary needed *more* Jews. In the aftermath of the acquittal of the accused Jews, a small antisemitic party won a few seats in parliament, but by 1900 it had vanished. But in modern Hungary, the unfortunate Esztner Solymosi has been transformed into a martyr for the Hungarian nationalist right. In Tiszaeszlár today, her death is commemorated by a memorial that has become a pilgrimage spot for Jobbik thugs and other far-right activists. In his 2012 speech, Baráth alleged that 'there is one point common to the known variants [of the story]: The Jewry and the leadership of the country were severely implicated in the case.' Antisemitism thrives on the lies perpetrated by authoritarian states in the twenty-first century.

Chapter 6

1   Andrej Angrick, Christoph Dieckmann, Christian Gerlach, Peter Klein, Dieter Pohl, Martina Voigt, Michael Wildt, and Peter Witte. *Der Dienstkalender Heinrich Himmlers 1941/42* (1999).

2   Vági, Z., Csósz, L., & Kádár, G. *The Holocaust in Hungary: Evolution of a Genocide* (2013). p. 44.

3   This account of the career of László Endre is based on *Self-Financing Genocide*, (2004). See bibliography for details.

4   projects.iq.harvard.edu/expose/pavuluri

5   In the *London Review of Books*, Wolfgang Streek noted that: 'Henry Ford was a global icon who counted Hitler among his admirers. As soon as he took power, Hitler had tried hard but in vain to make German car manufacturers abandon their small-scale production methods in favour of mass production of a simple car "for the people" – a Volkswagen. Ford's example inspired Hitler to set up a car plant on his model in a place that would later be named Wolfsburg (there were already two much smaller Ford and General Motors plants in Germany, at Cologne and Rüsselsheim), allegedly with second-hand machinery imported from Dearborn, Michigan. In 1938 Hitler awarded Ford the Nazi regime's highest decoration reserved for foreigners, the Great Cross of the German Order of the Eagle.' www.lrb.co.uk/v41/n03/contents

6   Centropa, www.centropa.hu

7   Testimonies accessed on degob.org/index.php?showarticle=2019

8   Alternative spelling, Kamianets-Podilskyi.

9   UKNA HW 16/6 and HW 1/35.

10 www.yadvashem.org/untoldstories/database/chgkSovietReports.asp?cid=278&site_id=288

11 degob.org/index.php?showjk=447

12 degob.org/index.php?showjk=1532

13 degob.org/index.php?showarticle=2032

14 Braham, R. 'Hungarian Labour Service System'.

15 degob.org/index.php?showjk=3395

Chapter 7

1   See Terry, Nicholas. 'Conflicting Signals: British Intelligence on the 'Final Solution' through Radio Intercepts and Other Sources, 1941–1942', *Yad Vashem Studies*, XXXII, 2004, pp. 351–396. There is an invaluable compilation of files and reports held by the UK National Archives here: www.nationalarchives.gov.uk/education/resources/holocaust

2   I am using the term with some degree of imaginative license. In fact, Hitler issued the 'Nacht und Nebel' ('Night and Fog') decree on 7 December 1941 to allow the German army to circumvent normal military procedures and conventions governing the treatment of prisoners. The decree and others undermining the security of the Reich. Anyone suspected of undermining the security of the Reich could be sent 'by night and fog' to special courts in Germany in which their fate would be decided. It was in essence a process of punitive abduction. In the Special Courts, suspects were sentenced to death or to long prison sentences to be served in concentration camps. Prisoners wore uniform jackets bearing the letters 'N.N.'.

3   An English version of Freudiger's memoirs can be found in Braham, Randolph L. (ed.). *Hungarian Jewish Studies,* Vol. 3 (New York: World Federation of Hungarian Jews, 1973). pp. 75–146.

4   Quoted in MacMillan, M. *Peacemakers: the Paris Peace Conference of 1919 and its Attempt to End War* (2001). p. 252.

5   Friedländer, S. *The Years of Extermination: Nazi Germany and the Jews 1939–1945* (2007). p. 374.

Chapter 8

1   See Longerich, P. *Goebbels* (2015). pp. 624–6.

2   Horthy, A.N.M. *Memoirs* (1957). pp. 123–35.

3   Black, P. (1984), pp. 123 *ff.*

4   See Longerich, P. *Holocaust* (2010). pp. 405 *ff.*

5   Quoted in Braham (2000), pp. 378 *ff.*

6   Gerlach, C., Aly, G. *Das Letze Kapitel: Der Mord an den ungarischen Juden* (2002).

Chapter 9

1   Fulbrook, Mary. *Reckonings* (2018), p. 282 *ff.*

2   See Klaus Wiegrefe's report for *Spiegel,* April 2011, 'The Holocaust in the Dock'.

3   Braham, R.L. *Eichmann and the Destruction of Hungarian Jewry* (1961). p. 14.

4   Hitler's order: *'Zivile deutsche Stellen irgendwelcher Art, die in Ungarn tätig werden sollen, sind nur im Einvernehmen mit dem Reichsbevollmächtigten einZürichten, sind ihm unterstellt und üben ihre Tätigkeit nach seinen Weisungen aus. Für die mit deutschen Kräften in Ungarn durchzuführenden Aufgaben der SS und Polizei, insbesondere für die polizeilichen Aufgaben auf dem Gebiet der Judenfrage, tritt zu dem Stab des Reichsbevollmächtigten ein Höherer SS- und Polizeiführer, der nach seinen politischen Weisungen handelt.'*
(Civilian German authorities of any kind who are scheduled to work in Hungary shall be appointed only in agreement with the Reich plenipotentiary, shall report to him and shall exercise their duties in accordance with his instructions. For

the tasks of the SS and police to be carried out with German forces in Hungary, in particular for the police tasks in the field of the Jewish question, a Higher SS and Police Leader, acting on his political instructions, joins the staff of the Reich plenipotentiary.)

5   My summary of Eichmann's career is based on accounts in Cesarani, D. *Eichmann: His Life and Crimes* (2005) and Stangneth, B. *Eichmann before Jerusalem: The Unexamined Life of a Mass Murder* (2014).

6   Quoted in Leni Yahil, Ina Friedman, Ḥayah Galai. *The Holocaust: The fate of European Jewry, 1932–1945* (Oxford University Press US, 1991). pp. 160–1, 204.

7   When he was interviewed by the 'Sassen Group' in Argentina in the mid 1950s, Eichmann complained that the name of the Referat was frequently confused: "'IV A 4 – just a moment. What?? Can I see that please? Look at this, you can see this jackass of an author, you know. These authors believe they sucked wisdom at the teat. And if you ever see a collection of Roman numerals and upper and lower case letters, these morons will have mixed them up. That's IV A. IV A is a completely different group!" And then Eichmann gives a long-winded, self-assured, overbearing, and ultimately convincing explanation of why this departmental designation could not have existed. But the fact of the matter is that from March 1944, Eichmann's department really was IV A 4. His office over the years: IV R; IV D 4; IV B 4; and finally IV A 4.' Stangneth (2014).

8   Quoted in Roseman, M. *The Villa, the Lake, the Meeting. Wannsee and the 'Final Solution'* (2002).

Chapter 10

1   Stangneth (2015). p. 49.
2   Stangneth, *op. cit.*; Sassen interviews 34:4.
3   Every one of Eichmann's men had taken part in the organisation of deportations across Europe. After the assassination of Heydrich in 1942, Hitler had ordered the destruction of the village of Lidice among other punitive measures. Krumey had a direct involvement in the deportation of eighty-two children to the Łódź ghetto. The majority of the children were murdered.
4   Documents supplied to author by Dr Detlef Siebert.
5   www.holocaustresearchproject.org/ghettos/orderpolice.html
6   Moczarski, Kazimierz. *Conversations with an Executioner* (1984).
7   It is a myth that King Christian defied a German order that Jews wear a yellow star by wearing one himself. No such order was ever issued.
8   www.nytimes.com/1997/01/26/weekinreview/the-not-so-neutrals-of-world-war-ii.html
9   www.facinghistory.org/rescuers/georg-duckwitz
10 Quoted in Vági et al. (2013). p. lvi.

Chapter 11

1   See, for example, the discussion in Paehler, K. *The Third Reich's Intelligence Services: The Career of Walter Schellenberg* (2017).
2   cryptome.org/0003/cia-dogwood.pdf
3   Quoted in Paehler (2017). p. 167.

4   CIA Archive, www.cia.gov/library/readingroom/document/0000493983
5   Rubin, B. *Istanbul Intrigues* (1989). Introduction.
6   The following account is based on Aronson, S. *Hitler, the Allies and the Jews* (2006) and Friling, T. *Arrows in the Dark: David Ben Gurion, the Yishuv Leadership and Rescue Attempts during the Holocaust* (2005).
7   German security agencies are frequently referred to in contemporary documents as the 'Gestapo'. The 'Geheime Staatspolizei' was the Nazi regime's secret police. The Gestapo was not the same as the SD – the Sicherheitsdienst, which was the SS security service, part of the SS-RSHA, the Reich Security Main Office. Himmler presided over the entire German security empire. In 1936, Himmler centralised the various criminal police departments in Germany into the Reich Criminal Police Office (Reichskriminalpolizeiamt). He appointed Reinhard Heydrich as chief of the Security Police Main Office (Hauptamt Sicherheitspolizei) which included both the Gestapo and the Criminal Police. Then in 1939, Himmler fused the Security Police and the SD into the Reich Security Main Office (Reichssicherheits hauptamt-RSHA).
8   UK National Archives, KV 2/130: SIME report: Andre GYORGY, alias GROSS, alias GRAINER: a Hungarian Jew, operating mainly from Budapest. Bauer (1994) calls Grosz a 'petty criminal and an unsavoury character'. He describes him as an 'ugly, small, red haired man with protruding teeth'.
9   According to the UK National Archives: Richard KAUDER, alias Klatt: Austrian. An Abwehr officer operating first from Vienna, then Sofia and later Budapest under the title Dienstelle Klatt, KAUDER reported mainly on the Soviet order of battle (under code name Max) and his information was highly regarded. His reporting on the British Middle East (under code name Moritz) was less reliable. One of the Klatt bureau's principal sub sources on the USSR was a White Russian, Ira Longin, based in Sofia with wide access in White Russian circles and what were claimed to be wireless agents in the Soviet Union itself. Another contact was a leading White Russian in Rome, General Turkul. After the war it was concluded that Ira Longin and possibly Turkul had LL long been under Soviet control.
10 References to the OSS/X-2 Report on Dogwood: Records of the Office of Strategic Services (Record Group 226) 1940–1947 Entry 210. Boxes 1-538. Location: 250 64/21/1. CIA Accession: 79-00332A.
11 Quoted in Paehler, K. (2017).

Chapter 12

1   See Biss, A. (1973) and Cesarani (2005). p.175.
2   Bogdanor, P. *Kasztner's Crime* (2016). p. 5.
3   My sources here are Bogdanor (2016), Weitz (1995, 2011), Kasztner (1946, 2013).
4   'Eichmann Tells His Own Damning Story', *Life*, 49, No. 22 (28 November 1960).
5   Bauer (2000). p.134.
6   Sources for this account, Braham. *The Politics of Genocide* (2000); Vági et al. (2013).
7   Quoted in Braham (2000). p. 464.
8   Wachsmann, N. (2016). p. 203.
9   Höß, R. (1959). p. 213 *ff*.

10 Document UK-81 COPY OF AFFIDAVIT C: Affidavit of Dieter Wisliceny, Nazi Conspiracy and Aggression. Volume VIII. USGPO, Washington, 1946. pp. 606–19.

11 remember.org/witness/wit-sur-mul; www.auschwitz-prozess-frankfurt.de/index. php?id=63; Müller, Filip (1999, 1979); *Eyewitness Auschwitz – Three Years in the Gas Chambers*. Ivan R. Dee in association with the United States Holocaust Memorial Museum.

12 Müller, op. cit. (1979). pp. 124 *ff.*

13 Braham, R. (2000). p. 216.

14 *Ibid.* and Vági et al. (2013).

Chapter 13

1 For more details see the SIME interrogation of Brand UKNA KV 2/132 and of Samu Springmann, UKNA KV 2/129.

2 Both Cesarani (2005) and Stangneth (2014) cite extracts from the Sassen interviews. The transcripts are held by the Bundesarchiv, Koblenz, the 'Eichmann Estate' N/1497.

3 See *The Holocaust in Hungary* (2013), following p. 71 for the texts of the anti-Jewish decrees.

4 A second public decree was issued later in the month to tidy up some legal issues and to define more clearly what was meant by 'Jews'. The Minister of the Interior, Andor Jaross, justified the new decree as a way to improve housing conditions for Christians through the justified confiscation of Jewish apartments.

5 Quoted in footnote 75, Kasztner Report (2013). p. 111.

6 www.truetorahjews.org/images/guardian3-2.pdf.

7 See earlier note regarding the Gestapo and SD. Although these were distinct organisations, both the SD and Gestapo were part of the RSHA – which was headed by Kaltenbrunner, who answered to Himmler. It is evident that the Gestapo and the SD were cooperating in Hungary during the occupation.

8 Brand testimony at Eichmann trial: collections.ushmm.org/search/catalog/ irn1001688

9 The reports of the meetings with the SS officers in the period before Eichmann became involved made by Brand, Kasztner and Freudiger contain contradictory information about the sequence of meetings and who was present at each encounter. Wisliceny's role must have been to facilitate the meetings on behalf of his superiors. As the ghettoisation gathered pace, and Wisliceny's tasks outside Budapest became more demanding, he began to play a less prominent role.

10 Quoted in Weitz (2011). p. 19.

11 Braham, R. *Five Days* (1986). pp. 251–2.

12 According to Braham, Laufer was also known as 'Direktor Schröder', Ludwig Meyer and Karl Heinz. For more details of this duplicitous double agent see Breitmann, et al. *US Intelligence and the Nazis*. Chapter 4.

13 The account here is based on Brand's interrogation report, SIME, UKNA KV 2/132.

14 According to most accounts, Scholz and Dr Sedlaczek played a minor role in the negotiations with the Rescue Committee. They were released a few days later.

Chapter 14

1 The main sources for this chapter are Braham, *The Politics of Genocide* (2000) and Vági et al. (2013).
2 Cited in Braham (2016). p.90 *ff.* See also the survivor testimonies in DEGOB: degob.org/index.php?showjk=5
3 DEGOB survivor testimonies.
4 Cited on the DEGOB web site, degob.org/index.php?showjk=696

Chapter 15

1 I have made extensive use of the Brand interrogation records in the UK National Archives. See Archive Sources for details.
2 This should not be confused with the Gypsy/Roma family camp that the SS also constructed at Auschwitz. See Wachsmann, N. (2015), p. 358.
3 Adler, H.G. *Theresienstadt 1941–1945: The Face of a Coerced Community* (2017).
4 See also Linn, R. 'Naked Victims, Dressed-up Memory: The Escape from Auschwitz and the Israeli Historiography', *Israel Studies Bulletin*, Vol. 16, No. 2 (Spring 2001). pp. 21–5.
5 Arendt, H. (1963). pp. 118–19.
6 Anna Hájková writing in *Tablet* magazine, October 2014, notes that: 'Several dozens of the Family Camp prisoners survived the selection: These included medical doctors and the prisoners in the infections barrack, as well as the twin children on whom Mengele was experimenting … In July 1944, the Nazis closed the Family Camp; their plans of using the camp for a propaganda visit by the Red Cross had not been put to action, and they needed the manpower for forced labour.'
7 Kulka, Erich. *Escape from Auschwitz* (1989).
8 See Linn, R. *Escaping Auschwitz* (2004) and her essay in Braham, R., & Heuvel, W.J.V. (eds.). *The Auschwitz Reports and the Holocaust in Hungary* (2011). p. 153 *ff.*
9 Vrba & Bestic (1964).
10 Michael Fleming offers a definitive account of how the Allies responded to intelligence about the Final Solution and the mass murder of Jews and other minorities, Fleming (2014).
11 Braham, R. (2000). p. 845.
12 See the essay by Zoltán Tibori Szabó in Braham & Heuvel (2011). p. 99.
13 Friedländer (2007). p. 615.
14 Braham (1993). p. 664.
15 Kasztner Report. p. 122.
16 Ibid, p. 123 *ff.*
17 www.nizkor.org/hweb/people/e/eichmann-adolf/transcripts/Sessions/Session-052-04.html
18 Quoted in Braham (2000). p.268.
19 Kasztner (1946, 2013). p.124–125.
20 Quoted in Bogdanor, P. *Kasztner's Crime* (2016). p.47.
21 Ibid. p. 50 *ff.*
22 *The Road to Life: The Rescue Operation of Jewish Refugees on the Hungarian–Romanian Border in Transylvania, 1936–1944* (Bibliotheca Judaica (Cluj-Napoca, Romania)).

Chapter 16

1   Avriel, Ehud (1975). p. 174 *ff.*
2   Brand-SIME 1-4, UKNA KV 2/132.
3   Brand's testimony at the Kasztner trial, quoted by Bogdanor (2016). p. 34.
4   Sonthofen speeches: Bundesarchiv, Berlin NS 19/401.
5   Freudiger, 'Five Months' in Braham, *The Tragedy of Hungarian Jewry* (1986).
6   Extracts from Brand interrogation, UKNA, FO 371/42807.
7   UKNA, KV 2/132-3, p.2 6.
8   Braham, R. (2000). pp. 671–3.
9   Kasztner report. p. 131.
10 Quoted in Bogdanor (2016). p. 35.
11 The trial of Adolf Eichmann, session 59: www.nizkor.org/hweb/people/e/
    eichmann-adolf/transcripts/Sessions/Session-059-04.html
12 Szita, S. *Trading in Lives? Operations of the Relief and Rescue Committee in Budapest,*
    1944–1945 (2005). p. 79.

Chapter 17

1   Wachsmann, N. (2015). p. 458.
2   Testimony in Tomi Komoly's personal collection.
3   degob.org/index.php?showarticle=2023
4   As she was recovering, Lili stumbled on a remarkable discovery: an album of
    photographs taken in Auschwitz in the spring of 1944 by two SS officers, Ernst
    Hofmann and Bernhard Walter. Many showed Jews on the ramp – and Lili was
    shocked to find pictures of her brothers and other family members and friends. As
    Lili Jacob-Zelmanovic Meier, she donated the photograph album to Yad Vashem:
    www.yadvashem.org/yv/en/exhibitions/album_auschwitz/index.asp
5   According to the authors of the DEGOB website: 'The SS physicians selecting the
    arriving transports on the Birkenau ramp tried to avoid conflicts that would have
    slowed down the annihilation process. Therefore it was a general principle to send
    the mother to the gas chamber with her children. Accordingly, a majority of the
    young and the middle-aged mothers – those belonging to the 26–35 and 36–45
    age groups – were killed on the day of arrival, while women without children had
    a greater chance to survive.'
6   Müller, P. (1979). pp. 126–32.
7   The Nazis sent thousands of prisoners from various countries, the majority of them
    Jewish, to Buna (the largest Auschwitz sub-camp: there were approximately 10,000
    prisoners in this camp in 1944). For more information visit the Jewish Virtual
    Library: www.jewishvirtuallibrary.org/buna-subcamp
8   DEGOB, protocol No. 3632.
9   Quoted in Vági et al. (2013). pp. 221–3. See also Avrech, Isiah (ed.). *The Scrolls of*
    Auschwitz (1985).
10 Adapted from degob.org/index.php?showarticle=2023
11 Quoted in Pressac, Jean-Claude. *Auschwitz: Technique and Operation of the Gas*
    Chambers (1989). p. 496.
12 Dwork & van Pelt (1996). pp.341–2.

13 The SS destroyed unknown numbers of documents when they fled the Auschwitz camp. But summarising the analysis of Gador Kádár and Zoltán Vági in their book *Self Financing Genocide* (2001, 2004), it is possible to say that 80 per cent of the deportees, or some 340,000 people, were judged to be unfit for work and murdered within hours of selection on the ramp. Brutal forced labour, illness, unremittingly cruel treatment and further selections carried out inside the camp ended the lives of many thousands of other Jews deported from Hungary.

Chapter 18

1 For a discussion of these issues see Schlomo Sand, *The Invention of the Land of Israel: from Holy Land to Homeland* (2012) p. 196 *ff*, and Beit-Zvi's *Post Ugandan Zionism on Trial: A Study of the Factors that Caused the Mistakes Made by the Zionist Movement During the Holocaust* (1991).
2 For Brand's account, see UKNA KV 2/132.
3 UKNA KV 2/130 p. 43–4.
4 Avriel, Ehud (1975). p. 176.
5 UKNA, FO 371/42810.
6 According to Braham (2000), p. 1084, it was Brand who persuaded the Istanbul Va'ada to come up with evidence of an 'interim agreement'.
7 Quoted in Weissberg, A. (1958). pp. 131 *ff.*
8 Avriel, Ehud (1975). p. 182.
9 Kasztner, R. (1946, 2013). p. 213.
10 Avriel claims the Protocol *was* sent: 'a Swiss courier took the document to Budapest and delivered it safely into the hands of Rejô [*sic*] Kastner [*sic*].' Avriel, *op. cit.* p.183.
11 Quoted in Rose, Paul Lawrence, *The Historical Journal*, Vol. 34, No. 4 (December 1991). For the full transcript of Brand's comments, Yad Vashem Archives No. 15 15/44.
12 UKNA: KV 2/130.

Chapter 19

1 Quoted in Braham (2016). p. 135.
2 Historian Judit Molnar writes: 'While collection camps were being organized, and then freight trains crowded with humans were being sent off to Auschwitz, the humane Deputy Foreign Minister, Mihály Jungerth-Arnóthy more than once addressed the meetings of the council of ministers, informing the members of the government on the mistreatment of the Jews. In addition to the fact that "the deportation of the Hungarian Jews was often carried out within forms that were cruel and objectionable with respect to humanitarian considerations", Jungerth-Arnóthy argued, foreign newspapers carried news about "Jews being gassed and burnt in Poland." To Jungerth-Arnóthy's complaints Under-secretary of the Interior László Endre replied, among other things, that "the atmosphere and order of the ghettos was usually calm and satisfactory. There were hardly any suicides, and those occurred mostly in the pre-deportation camps." Interior Minister Jaross also held unambiguous views on the Jewish question: "We are not really interested in where the Jews are going. The welfare of the country demands that the Jews be removed fast." And indeed, in the spirit of this comment, orders, instructions and

decrees kept arriving to the heads of local and municipal administration.' www.jewishvirtuallibrary.org/behavior-of-hungarian-authorities-during-the-holocaust

3 Braham (2016). p. 140–142.
4 *Ibid*. p.140–141.
5 Becher testimony, in Mendelsohn, J., *The Holocaust* (1982), p. 206.
6 Cited in Müller-Tupath, K. (1999). p. 16.
7 Quoted in Longerich, *Heinrich Himmler* (2012). p. 306.
8 *Ibid*. p. 523.
9 There is a detailed account of SS actions in the Pripet marshes in my book *Hitler's Foreign Executioners*.
10 Fulbrook, M. (2018). pp. 245–246.
11 In this chapter, I have drawn extensively on Kadar and Vagi's *Self-Financing Genocide* (2001).
12 MILITARY TRIBUNAL NO. II CASE 4 THE UNITED STATES OF AMERICA against OSWALD POHL, AUGUST FRANK, GEORG LOERNER, HEINZ KARL FANSLAU, HANS LOERNER, JOSEF VOGT, ERWIN TSCHENTSCHER, RUDOLF SCHEIDE, MAX KIEFER, FRANZ EIRENSCHMALZ, KARL SOMMER, HERMANN POOK, HANS HEINRICH BRIER, HANS HOHBERG, LEO VOLK, KARL MUMMENTHEY, HANS BOBERMIN, and HORST KLEIN, Defendants.
13 www.nizkor.org/hweb/people/e/eichmann-adolf/transcripts/Sessions/Session-104-01.html
14 Becher, testimony provided to the Eichmann trial, 1961 www.nizkor.org/ftp.cgi/people/e/eichmann.adolf/transcripts/Testimony-Abroad

Chapter 20

1 www.jta.org/1941/11/14/archive/jews-will-not-be-forgotten-in-day-of-victory-churchill-assures-in-special-message
2 Quoted by Sir Martin Gilbert, www.bbc.co.uk/history/worldwars/genocide/churchill_holocaust_01.shtml
3 For a detailed account of wartime censorship of the holocaust see Fleming (2014).
4 api.parliament.uk/historic-hansard/lords/1943/mar/23/german-atrocities-aid-for-refugees
5 Quoted in www.haaretz.com/world-news/europe/u-k-authorities-ignored-anti-semitism-in-wwii-documents-show-1.6429829
6 Quotations from the UK NA file FO 371/42810, 371/42807 and CAB 95/15.
7 See Erbelding, R., *Rescue Board* (2018), Chapter 8.
8 *Op. cit.*, pp. 134 *ff.*
9 See Foreign Relations of the United States. Diplomatic Papers, 1944. Vol. 1 pp. 1089–1091.

Chapter 21

1 Longerich, *Himmler* (2012). p. 697.
2 Correspondence between Ribbentrop and Veesenmayer between 6 and 10 July: ADAP E V111, 101.

3   research.calvin.edu/german-propaganda-archive/goeb36.htm
4   IMT Document NG-5586, Prosecution Exhibit 3715.
5   Quoted in Friedländer (2007). p. 624.
6   *Summary Report of the War Refugee Board*, p. 17.
7   UKNA: FO 371/42810.

Chapter 22

1   Sebastian, M. (2000). pp. 608–10.
2   Kershaw, I. *Hitler 1936–1945 Nemesis* (2000). p. 869.
3   www.nizkor.org/hweb/people/e/eichmann-adolf/transcripts/Sessions/
    Session-058-02.html
4   www.nizkor.org/hweb/people/e/eichmann-adolf/transcripts/Testimony-Abroad/
    Wilhelm_Hoettl-07.html
5   Source www.mackinac.org/19578. Morissette v. United States, US 342 at 251 n.8.
6   The use of the concept adapts a medical term: triage, a word once used by the
    French in reference to the sorting of coffee beans and applied to the battlefield
    by Napoleon's chief surgeon, Baron Dominique-Jean Larrey. Today triage is used
    in accidents and disasters when the number of injured exceeds available resources.
    Surprisingly, perhaps, there is no consensus on how best to do this. Typically,
    medical workers try to divvy up care to achieve the greatest good for the greatest
    number of people. There is an ongoing debate about how to do this and what
    the 'greatest good' means. Is it the number of lives saved? Years of life saved? Best
    'quality' years of life saved? Or something else? www.nytimes.com/2009/08/30/
    magazine/30doctors.html
7   See Kaltenbrunner documents www.loc.gov/rr/frd/Military_Law/pdf/NT_Nazi_
    Vol-I.pdf
8   Letters quoted in Bogdanor (2016), p. 134, sourced from the Haganah Archive
    Division 80/p187/32.
9   Quoted in Braham, *The Politics of Genocide* (2000). p. 178.
10 Kershaw, I. (2000). pp. 736–7.
11 Ungváry (2003). Preface.
12 Quoted in Kershaw (2000). p. 742.
13 My source for these accounts is Ungváry (2003), part VI, Chapter 3.
14 filmhiradokonline.hu/watch.php?id=5883
15 Historical Archives of the Hungarian State Security (ÁBTL) Records of State
    Security Investigations of Hungarian War Criminals, 3.1.9.V-119575. English
    translation: blog.ehri-project.eu/2017/07/05/murdered-on-the-verge-of-survival-
    massacres-in-the-last-days-of-the-siege-of-budapest-1945-part-ii
16 Emil Böszörményi Nagy, blog.ehri-project.eu/2017/07/05/murdered-on-the-
    verge-of-survival-massacres-in-the-last-days-of-the-siege-of-budapest-1945-part-ii
17 Kasztner, R. (1946, 2013). p. 323 *ff*.
18 Eichmann Trial: Sessions 61 and 62, Testimonies of A. Breslauer, A. Fleischmann, L.
    Gordon Accession Number: 1999.A.0087 | RG Number: RG-60.2100.074 | Film
    ID: 2073.
19 See Becher's statements (in German) in Mendelsohn (1982).
20 Kasztner trial testimony, 22 February 1954, quoted in Bogdanor (2016), p. 234.

21 Eismann, Hans-Georg. *Under Himmler's Command: The Personal Recollections of Oberst Hans-Georg Eismann, Operations Officer, Army Group Vistula, Eastern Front 1945* (2006). Helion. Warwick, UK.

22 Quoted in Longerich, *Heinrich Himmler* (2012). pp. 721–2.

23 *Ibid.* p. 731.

24 Tomi Komoly, interview with the author and www.tabletmag.com/jewish-news-and-politics/257386/distorting-the-holocaust-in-hungary

25 See Freudiger's testimony at the Eichmann Trial, Session 52: www.nikkor.org

Epilogue: Endgame in Israel

1   Weitz (2011). p. 66.

2   *Ibid.* p. 60 *ff.*

3   Trial of the Major War Criminals, document 2605-PS affidavit of Dr Rezso (Rudolph) Kastner, 13 September 1945: details of the persecution and massacre of Jews in Hungary 1941 to 1944; historical and statistical summary of actions against the Jews in several European countries (exhibit usa-242).

4   www.kasztnerscrime.com/documents/index.html

5   Cited, *op. cit.*, Trial of the Major War Criminals, document 2605-PS.

6   Fulbrook, M. (2018), p. 265. [title and first name needed]

7   www.jta.org/1969/08/27/archive/ex-gestapo-chief-sentenced-to-life-imprisonment-for-slaying-jews-aides-are-freed

8   www.kasztnerscrime.com/documents/index.html

9   See Asher Maoz, 'Historical Adjudication: Courts of Law, Commissions of Inquiry, and "Historical Truth"', *Law and History Review*, University of Illinois, (2000).

10 See Aronson (2006), p. 334; Weitz (2011), pp. 101–4; Harel, Isser (1985).

11 Aronson, S. 'The Holocaust and Israel's Domestic, Foreign and Security Policy', December 2009. www.jewishvirtuallibrary.org/jsource/isdf/text/aronson.pdf

12 Rosenfeld, Shalom, Tik Plili 124: Mishpat Grunwald-Kastner [Criminal Case 124], Tel Aviv Karni, 1955. Extract quoted in Moaz, op.cit.

SELECT BIBLIOGRAPHY

Main Archival Sources

The National Archives UK (UKNA)
Brand-SIME 1, KV 2/132, SIME Report No. 1: Brand, Joel Jeno (2 July 1944).
Brand-SIME 2, KV 2/132, SIME Report No. 2: Brand, Joel Jeno (21 July 1944).
Brand-SIME 4 KV 2/132 SIME Report No. 4: Interrogation of Brand (21 July 1944).
Brand-WRB: FO371/42807, Interrogation of Joel Brand by Ira Hirschmann of the US
    War Refugee Board (22 June 1944).
Grosz-SIME 1: KV 2/130, SIME Report No. 1; Andor Gross (24 June 1944).
Grosz-SIME 2, FO 371/42810, Sime Report No. 2: Andor Gross (23 June 1944).
Grosz-SIME 3: KV2/130, SIME Report No. 3: Andor Gross (4 July 1944).
Springmann-SIME 1: KV 2/129, SIME Report No. 1: Samuel Springmann (21 May 1944).
Springmann-SIME 2: KV 2/129, SIME Report No. 2: Samuel Springmann (21 May 1944).
SIME-Springmann 3: KV 2/129, SIME Report No. 3: Samuel Springmann (21 May 1944).

DEGOB, National Committee for Attending Deportees
www.degob.org

State of Israel, Ministry of Justice
The Trial of Adolf Eichmann: Record of Proceedings in the District of Jerusalem, six
    volumes (English translation).

United States Holocaust Memorial Museum
Video recordings of Eichmann trial sessions:
collections.ushmm.org/search/catalog/irn1001739

Bundesarchiv Ludwigsburg/Zentralle Stelle
Eichmann Trial Files, B162.

Bundesarchiv, Koblenz
Transcripts of Sassen interviews, Eichmann Estate n/1497.

United States National Archives
T175: Records of the Personal Staff of the Reich Leader of the SS and Chief of the
   German Police, Heinrich Himmler.
T976: Records of the Economic Enterprises of the SS (Econombetriebe, SS
Wirtschafts-Verwaltungshauptamt), 1936–1945.
RG 319, Dossier XE 004471, Adolf Eichmann.

*Yad Vashem Archives, The International Institute for Holocaust Research,
Jerusalem*
Record Group: P 52: Yehuda Bauer Collection.
Record Group: P 13: Benjamin Sagalowitz Archive.
Record Group: P 54: Kasztner family archive.
Tr. 3: Documents from the Eichmann Trial.
P31/44: Ottó Komoly Diary.

Books and Journal articles

Arendt, Hannah. *Eichmann in Jerusalem: a Report on the Banality of Evil.* (1963). Viking
   Press, New York.
Aronson, S., Breitmann, R. 'The End of the 'Final Solution?': Nazi Plans to Ransom
   Jews in 1944', *Central European History*, Summer 1992.
Aronson, S. *Hitler, the Allies and the Jews.* (2006). New York, Cambridge University Press.
Avriel, Ehud. *Open the Gates: the Dramatic Personal Story of 'Illegal' Immigration to Israel.*
   (1975). New York, Atheneum.
Bankier, D. (Ed.) *Secret Intelligence and the Holocaust.* (2006). New York, Enigma Books.
Bauer, Y. *Jews for Sale: Nazi–Jewish Negotiations 1933–1944.* (1994). New Haven, Yale
   University Press.
Bilsky, L. *Transformative Justice: Israeli Identity on Trial.* (2004). Ann Arbor, The University
   of Michigan Press.
Biss, Andreas. *Der Stopp des Endlösung: Kampf gegen Himmler und Eichmann in Budapest.*
   (1966). Seewald.
Black, Peter R. *Ernst Kaltenbrunner: Ideological Soldier of the Third Reich.* (1984). Princeton
   University Press, Princeton.
Bloxham, D. *The Final Solution: A Genocide.* (2009). Oxford, Oxford University Press.
Bogdanor, P. *Kasztner's Crime.* (2016). London, New Brunswick, Transaction Publishers.
Braham, R. (Ed.) *The Treatment of the Holocaust in Hungary and Romania during the
   Post-Communist Era.* (2004). New York, NY, Columbia University Press.
Braham, R., & Heuvel, W.J.V. (Eds) *The Auschwitz Reports and the Holocaust in Hungary.*
   (2011). New York, NY, Columbia University Press.
Braham, R., & Kovács, A. (Eds.) *The Holocaust in Hungary: Seventy Years Later* (2016).
   Budapest: CEU.

Braham, R.L. *Eichmann and the Destruction of Hungarian Jewry.* (1961). New York, World Federation of Hungarian Jews.

Braham, R.L. *The Politics of Genocide: The Holocaust in Hungary.* (2000). Wayne State University Press.

Braham, R.L. *The Holocaust in Hungary: Seventy Years Later.* (2016). Central European University Press.

Braham, R.L. *The Tragedy of Hungarian Jewry: Essays, Documents, Depositions.* (1986). Columbia University Press.

Braham, R.L., & Miller, S. *The Nazi's Last Victims: The Holocaust in Hungary.* (2002). Wayne State University Press.

Breitman, R., & Lichtman, A.J. *FDR and the Jews.* (2013). Cambridge, Ms., The Belknap Press of Harvard University Press.

Cesarani, D. *Eichmann: His Life and Crimes.* (2005). London, Vintage.

Cesarani, D. *Final Solution: The Fate of the Jews 1933–1945.* (2016). London, St Martin's Press.

Cesarani, D. (Ed.) *After Eichmann: Collective Memory and the Holocaust Since 1961.* (2005). New York, Routledge.

Cooper, A. *Cairo in the War: 1939–1945.* (1989). London, Hamish Hamilton.

Cornelius, D.S. *Hungary in World War II: Caught in the Cauldron.* (2011). New York, Fordham University Press.

Erbelding, R. *Rescue Board: the Untold Story of America's Efforts to Save the Jews of Europe.* (2018). Doubleday, New York.

Feingold, H.L. *The Politics of Rescue: the Roosevelt Administration and the Holocaust 1938–1945.* (1970). New Brunswick, NJ, Rutgers University Press.

Fleming, M. *Auschwitz, the Allies and the Censorship of the Holocaust.* (2014). Cambridge, Cambridge University Press.

Friedländer, S. *The Years of Extermination: Nazi Germany and the Jews 1939–1945.* (2007). New York, NY, Harper Collins.

Friling, T. *Arrows in the Dark: David Ben Gurion, the Yishuv Leadership and Rescue Attempts during the Holocaust* (2 volumes). (2005). Madison, Wisconsin, The University of Wisconsin Press.

Frojimovics, K., Komoróczy, G., Pusztai, V., & Strrbik, A. *Jewish Budapest: Monuments, Rites, History.* (1999). Budapest, CEU Press.

Fulbrook, Mary. *Reckonings: Legacies of Nazi Persecution and the Quest for Justice.* (2018). Oxford University Press.

Goda, N.J.W. *The Diplomacy of the Axis, 1940–1945 (The Cambridge History of the Second World War).* (2015). Cambridge, Cambridge University Press.

Harel, Isser. *The Truth about the Kastner Murder: Jewish Terror in the State of Israel.* (1985). Edanim, Jerusalem.

Hausner, Gideon. *Justice in Jerusalem.* (1977). Jerusalem.

Horthy, A.N.M. *Memoirs.* (1957). Robert Speller & Sons.

Höß, Rudolf. *Commandant of Auschwitz: the Autobiography of Rudolf Höß.* (1959). Phoenix Press, London.

Kadar, Gabor & Vagi, Zoltan. *Self-Financing Genocide: The Gold Train, the Becher Case and the Wealth of Hungarian Jews.* (2000). CEU Press, Budapest.

Kállay, N. *Hungarian Premier: A Personal Account of a Nation's Struggle in the Second World War.* (1954). New York, Columbia University Press.

Kasztner, Rezső, eds Lászlo Karsai, Judit Molnár. *The Kasztner Report: the Report of the Budapest Jewish Rescue Committee, 1942–1945*, (Originally published in German 1946, English translation 2013). Yad Vashem, Jerusalem.

Kershaw, I. *Hitler 1936–1945 Nemesis*. (2000). London, Allen Lane.

Kershaw, I. *The End: Hitler's Germany 1944–1945*. (2011). London, Allen Lane.

Klein, George. *Piéta*. (1989). MIT Press, Cambridge, Massachusetts.

Kramer, T.D. *From Emancipation to Catastrophe: The Rise and Holocaust of Hungarian Jewry*. (2000). Lanham, Maryland, University Press of America.

Levai, E. *Black Book on the Martyrdom of Hungarian Jewry*. (1948). Zurich, The Central European Times Publishing Co., Ltd.

Lévai, J. *Eichmann in Hungary: Documents*. (1987). Howard Fertig.

Levene, M. *Annihilation: the European Rimlands 1939–1953*. (2013). Oxford, Oxford University Press.

Levine, P. *Raoul Wallenberg in Budapest: Myth, History and the Holocaust*. (2010). London, Portland, Or, Vallentine Mitchell.

Longerich, P. *Goebbels*. (2015). London, Vintage Penguin.

Longerich, P. *Heinrich Himmler*. (2012). Oxford, Oxford University Press.

Lozowick, Y., H. Watzman (Trans.). *Hitler's Bureaucrats: the Nazi Security Police and the Banality of Evil*. (). (2002). London, New York. Continuum.

Lukacs, J. *Budapest 1900: A Historical Portrait of a City and its Culture*. (1988). New York, Grove Press.

MacMillan, M. *Peacemakers: the Paris Peace Conference of 1919 and its Attempt to End War*. (2001). London, John Murray.

Mendelsohn, J., *The Holocaust: Selected Documents in 18 Volumes, 15. Relief in Hungary and the Failure of the Joel Brand Mission*. (2010). New York, London, Garland Publishing.

Müller, Filip, *Auschwitz Inferno: The Testimony of a Sonderkommando*. (1979). Routledge, London.

Müller-Tupath, Karla. *Reichsführers gehorsamter Becher*. (1999). Aufbau Verlag, Bremen.

Musmanno, Michael A. *The Eichmann Kommandos*. (1961). Philadelphia.

Paehler, K. *The Third Reich's Intelligence Services: The Career of Walter Schellenberg*. (2017). Cambridge, Cambridge University Press.

Radnoti, M. *The Complete Poetry in Hungarian and English*. (2014). Mcfarland & Co Inc.

Rich, I. *Holocaust Perpetrators of the German Police Battalions: The Mass Murder of Jewish Civilians, 1940–1942*. (2018). London, Bloomsbury Academic.

Roseman, M. *The Villa, the Lake, the Meeting. Wannsee and the 'Final Solution'*. (2002). London, Penguin.

Sakmyster, T. *Hungary's Admiral on Horseback: Miklós Horthy, 1918–1944*. (1994). New York. Columbia University Press, East European Monographs.

Sebastian, Mihail. *Journal 1935-1944: The Fascist Years: with an Introduction and Notes by Radi Ioanid*. Ivan R. Dee in association with the USHMM, Chicago.

Smith, B.F. *The Shadow Warriors: OSS and the Origins of the CIA*. (1983). New York, Basic Books Inc.

Stangneth, B. *Eichmann before Jerusalem: the Unexamined Life of a Mass Murder*. (2014). New York, Alfred A. Knopf.

Steiner, Z. *The Lights that Failed; European International History 1913–1933*. (2005). Oxford, Oxford University Press.

Szita, S. *Trading in Lives? Operations of the Relief and Rescue Committee in Budapest, 1944–1945*. (2005). Budapest, CEU Press.

Ungváry, Krisztián. *Battle for Budapest: 100 Days in World War Two.* (2003). I.B. Tauris, London-New York.

Vági, Z., Csósz, L., & Kádár, G. *The Holocaust in Hungary: Evolution of a Genocide.* (2013). Alta Mira Press.

Vrba, R. & Bestic, A. *I Cannot Forgive.* (1964). New York, Grove Press.

Wachsmann, N., *KL: A History of the Nazi Concentration Camps.* (2016). Abacus, London.

Weissberg, A. *Advocate for the Dead: the Story of Joel Brand.* (1958). London.

Weitz, Y. *The Man who was Murdered Twice: the Life, Trial and Death of Israel Kasztner.* (2011). Jerusalem, Yad Vashem.

Yahil, L. *The Rescue of Danish Jewry: Test of a Democracy.* (1969). Philadelphia, The Jewish Publication Society of America.

Zweig, R. *The Gold Train: The Destruction of the Jews and the Second World War's Most Terrible Robbery.* (2003). London, Penguin Books.

ACKNOWLEDGEMENTS

What I hope independent researchers can offer is a passionate commitment to disentangling an obsession; a readiness to look outside the canon; and a preoccupation with problems that have eluded solutions. Hence the book now on your screen or in your hands. My reading of the voluminous literature on the Brand Mission and the Blood for Trucks ransom offer always left in its wake a back flow of tantalising riddles whose solution appeared to be just out of reach. Why did Adolf Eichmann make this fantastical offer to barter a million lives for 10,000 trucks? The Blood for Trucks story is a mystery of *intention*. On the German side, we have only fragmentary evidence. Because Brand stirred up such a furore in Jerusalem, London, Moscow and Washington there is a great deal more evidence in American and British archives. The interrogations of Joel Brand, 'Bandi' Grosz and Samu Springmann by British SIME agents based in Cairo is an archival trove that has never been examined properly. At first sight, the records are intimidating; they are crammed with obscure German and Hungarian names and references. Time lines and dates are confused. But it was during these marathon interrogation sessions that these key dramatis personae of the Blood for Trucks affair spoke for the first time about their experiences and the events that had led to the desperate mission to barter for Jewish lives. This is the raw material of history unmediated by retrospection and self-justification. It becomes evident, in my view, that the German plan to solve Hungary's 'Jewish problem' and plunder the resources of Hungarian Jews could never have been prevented or ameliorated by the Zionist rescue committee. If we accept that brute reality, the pieces of the puzzle fall at last into place.

I owe a debt to the librarians working behind the scenes of the Staatsbibliotek in Berlin, the British Library in London as well as the dedicated archivists of the UK National Archives in Kew and Yad Vashem in Jerusalem. By serendipitous chance, I completed this book at the Qatar National Library in Doha, which turned out to possess a valuable collection of books about German history. When I was working on the manuscript, I had a number of indispensable books always to hand. I am indebted to the authors. The first, of course, is Randolph Braham's two-volume account of the Hungarian holocaust, *The Politics of Genocide*. This is a monumental history that despite being unwieldy and in some of its details out of date will always remain an essential source. I have made very frequent use of an invaluable documentary history, *The Holocaust in Hungary: Evolution of a Genocide*, edited by Hungarian historians Zoltán Vági, László Csösz and Gábor Kádar. *Self-Financing Genocide: The Gold Train, the Becher Case and the Wealth of Hungarian Jews*, by Gábor Kádar and Zoltán Vági, is an important contribution to genocide studies that stresses – perhaps to breaking point – that plunder of Jewish assets was a crucial part of the Final Solution. I must thank Daniel Brand and Tomi Komoly, who offered their profound insights into the tragedy of Hungarian Jewry. Ron Lustig of the very moving 'Memorial Museum of Hungarian Speaking Jewry' in Safed spent time showing me his collections. In Budapest, I thank László Csösz at the Hungarian National Archives and Zoltán Tóth at Holocaust Memorial Centre. My colleague, Jonathan Schütz, introduced me to Klara Májaros, who generously gave up an afternoon to talk about her family's history and the ideological traumas in contemporary Hungary. Thanks to a recommendation from Dr Peter Carrier, Ben Niran took on the task of interpreting some problematic documentary sources. The veteran British producer Rex Bloomstein kindly sent me a copy of his superb documentary *Auschwitz and the Allies*, which was based on ground-breaking research by Sir Martin Gilbert. I was privileged to meet and discuss the Jewish rescue efforts with Dr Paul Levine, who is the world's leading scholar on Raoul Wallenberg. Professor Bill Niven asked challenging questions whenever we met in Berlin. It was my good friend Dr Laurence Peters of the Johns Hopkins University who first inspired me to think about the puzzling story of Joel Brand back in 2013 – and he has been a constant source of ideas and committed encouragement ever since. I am not sure if he will agree with my conclusions. I thank Mark Beynon at the History Press for backing the project – and his committed team Jezz Palmer, Martin Latham, Paul Middleton and Dan Coxon. It goes without saying that none of the above-mentioned authors and scholars is responsible for any factual and interpretive mistakes or errors of judgement. I would welcome comments and corrections at this website: www.deception44.education

INDEX